The Second Twelve Months Of Life

A Kaleidoscope of Growth

The Second Twelve Months Of Life.

A Kaleidoscope of Growth

The Princeton Center for Infancy and Early Childhood

Frank and **Theresa Caplan,** authors

Includes a Mini-Course
in Infant and Toddler Development

With monthly charts and over 150 photographs

A GD/PERIGEE BOOK

PERIGEE BOOKS
are published by
The Putnam Publishing Group
200 Madison Avenue
New York, New York 10016

Library of Congress catalog card number: 77-78748
ISBN 0-399-50776-0

First Perigee printing, 1982
Five previous Grosset & Dunlap printings
Printed in the United States of America

This book is dedicated to Caroline Pratt, Margaret S. Mahler, Hiag Akmakjian, Erik H. Erikson, Benjamin Spock, T. Berry Brazelton, Richard I. Feinbloom, Selma H. Fraiberg, and other professionals who have shared their meaningful insights with parents on how to raise and enjoy healthy and happy individuals.

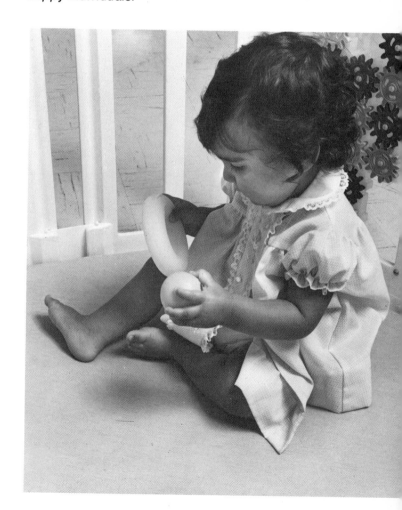

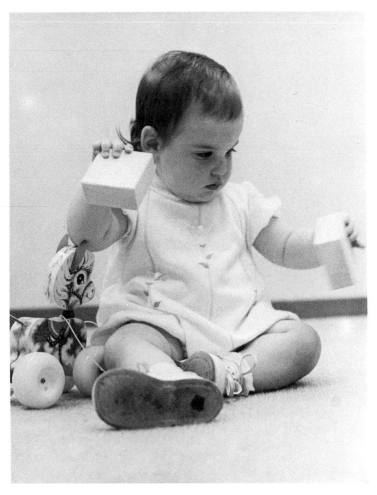

There was a child went forth every day,
And the first object he looked upon and received
with wonder, pity, love, or dread, that object he
became,
And that object became part of him for the day, or
a certain part of the day, or for many years, or
stretching cycles of years . . .
His own parents . . .
The family usages, the language, the company, the
furniture . . .
Men and women crowding fast in the streets . . .
These became part of that child who went forth
every day, and who now goes, and will always
go forth every day.

—adapted from "There was a child went forth"
Leaves of Grass, Walt Whitman

Acknowledgments

This book exists only because parents asked for it. When *The First Twelve Months of Life* appeared in the fall of 1973, it was introduced as a "sleeper." You can finish the balance of the script for this success story. Parents spontaneously wrote to tell our publisher how much our book helped them to understand their babies' behaviors in the critical first year of life and asked for a sequel. *American Baby Magazine* published three-page digests of each of our monthly analyses. Little did the editors of the magazine realize that despite the fact that their publication caters to the needs of the parents of newborns and infants up to the sixth month of life, parental demand for additional material beyond their cutoff month would cause them to continue it as a permanent feature.

The Committee on Public Information of the American Academy of Pediatrics officially approved *The First Twelve Months of Life,* one of the few books it has ever endorsed.

Today some 500,000 copies have been sold by word-of-mouth recommendation. In 1976, the Princeton Center for Infancy and Early Childhood was authorized to write *The Second Twelve Months of Life.*

Our pioneering efforts in 1973 to describe growth in infancy, month by month, also stimulated federal government agencies to finance university and other early childhood research groups to record the behavior of toddlers. One of the better baby-watching projects was conducted by the Nova University "Play and Learn Program" in Fort Lauderdale, Florida, under the leadership of Marilyn M. Segal, Ph.D.

Throughout this book, we have quoted or paraphrased numerous portions of the book *From One to Two Years,* by Drs. Marilyn M. Segal and Don Adcock, of Nova University. (Their project was financed by a grant from the Children's Bureau, Office of Child Development, of the U.S. Department of Health, Education, and Welfare.) Rather than digest their material inadequately, we received their permission to quote from their student case studies and their book, which we have indicated by quotation marks wherever feasible. We are grateful for their generosity in sharing their findings and writing with us, and thereby with you. We also thank Nova University and Bill Sarchet for the use of some one hundred photos taken by Bill Sarchet of the children and their parents who were the subjects screened in *From One to Two Years.*

We owe a debt of thanks to Dr. James L. Hymes, Jr., retired professor of early childhood education at the University of Maryland, for his lifelong campaign to interpret and preserve the dynamics of play and self-learning during the early years of childhood. His book, *Teaching the Child Under Six,* is respected by all professionals in the field.

We want to take this opportunity to thank most sincerely Grace Bechtold, vice president of Bantam Books, for her ongoing interest in our efforts.

The research data, case records, and new books by experts in the field could not have been collected and analyzed without the help of our devoted staff members and other professionals. Our project was slowed because most researchers' data and writings examine the second year of life in three-month periods rather than month by month. We believe that three-month summaries rather than monthly observations during this time span miss those sensitive behavior clues that need definition for concerned new parents. The whole project underscored for us the need to do baby-watching month by month, and only parents are best equipped to do this during the first two years of their children's lives.

Writing *The Second Twelve Months of Life* has sharpened our appreciation of the difficulties that infants and toddlers and their parents face in this critical year—and the deep joys and satisfactions they share.

Finally, we wish to thank Dorothy J. Naylor for her steadfast, enthusiastic typing of our manuscript and Mary Linda Copeland for helping us to collect the material that is the core of this book.

Frank and Theresa Caplan
The Princeton Center for Infancy and
Early Childhood

Contents

Biological and psychological birth; "hatching" period; early practice
periods; practicing locomotor skills; slowing down of physical growth;
fine-motor development; interest in movement; walking creates
problems; "ages and stages"; sensori-motor years; "shadowing" and
darting patterns; drive for independence; role of father; diminishing of
rapprochement phase; discovery of sex differences; independence
vs. dependence; self-identity; emergence of language; progressions
in language acquisition; theories of language development; from
sounds to language; anatomy of speech; organization of speech
sounds; grammar and language structure; intellectual development in
the second year; how and what an infant learns; "ages and stages"
of sensori-motor learning; social development; beginning of
interpersonal relations; toddler behaves egotistically; infant-toddler
play groups; growth of emotions; earliest emotional development;
second year is emotional milestone; emotions and performance;
positive and negative emotions; anger and aggression; temper
tantrums; fears; jealousy; the family and emotional development;
personality problems of short duration; more on "ages and stages" of
psychological development; stages of autonomy; self-help; coping
and autonomy; feeding; implications of walking for feeding; sleep
behavior; undressing; growth of autonomy and learning through play;
play and playthings; a responsive environment; rationale for early
intervention and stimulation; animal and human research; modifying
and enriching the environment; parent education.

---

powers/learning; listening; tactile discrimination; phonograph records; concept of time; cognitive accomplishments; social development; quality parenting; social skills; sense of trust; negativism; sibling rivalry and fighting; personality/psychological development; expressing feelings via language; dependence/independence; fears; sharing; sketch of twenty-four-month-old; self-help routines; eating; "Do it myself!"; play and playthings; creative activities; play activities; equipping the playroom

Introduction

Those parents who have used and loved our book, *The First Twelve Months of Life,* in their child-rearing efforts are semiprofessionals by now. Most could probably teach a child development course in their local high school, or lead a community parenting study group. What would distinguish them from university professors of early childhood education is that they have probably not been sufficiently exposed to the complex "ages and stages" growing-and-learning progressions during infancy that emerge from the maturation of physical skills. Crawling, walking, climbing, talking, emotional stability, coping and competency, learning and concept building, and the growth of trust in parents and the world take time and encouragement.

In the late sixties and early seventies, "professional" child rearing was in its infancy. The writings of a few *medical* experts (Gesell and Spock, to name two of the outstanding ones) and early infancy researchers did not provide parents with complete enough data on early human development. Since then, however, publishers have discovered the great interest in scientific child rearing practices and have published some fifteen hundred books written by all kinds of child specialists: *psychoanalysts* (Mahler, Anthony, Erikson, Akmakjian, Bettelheim, Anna Freud, Wolf); *psychologists* (Lipsitt, Piaget, White, McV. Hunt); *animal researchers* (the Harlows, Rosensweig); *infant education researchers* (Caldwell, Kagan, Bruner, Bereiter); and a new breed of *pediatricians* (Brazelton, Feinbloom) who use interdisciplinary approaches; as well as *knowledgeable parents* (the Boston Women's Health Collective, Marzollo and Lloyd, Kelly and Parsons, and so on). All these authors have provided the Princeton Center for Infancy with a considerable storehouse of opinions, ideas, and research data that has enabled us to offer parents many more child-rearing alternatives and to present the "ages and stages" insights of top professionals.

To present these theories (some of which start with the newborn and go beyond the third year) adequately, we have written an extra-long "overview" chapter. At the same time, we have not discarded the month-by-month baby watching and growth analysis that proved so successful in *The First Twelve Months of Life.* The same approach has been applied to toddlers in *The Second Twelve Months of Life.*

In the second year of life, motor and language development and the acquisition of social skills cannot always be set forth in precise chronological sequence. Every toddler has his or her own timetable. There are many reasons why one child begins to walk at ten months and another at sixteen months. Some children are born with a slower growth rate. Of course, they can be just as smart as other children even though their teeth erupt more slowly and they walk and begin to talk a little later than their peers. Some children are heavier than others and their extra weight may slow their walking and their immediate need for talking.

Some toddlers internalize the words and sentences they hear in the active verbal environment of older siblings, sometimes for as long as six months before their first words are spoken. Then, at twenty-two to twenty-four months, words and sentences are spewed out without letup. If your child is doing a lot of crawling, do not fret if other agemates have skipped this stage and are walking. "In all children, at all times," James L. Hymes, Jr., Ph.D., points out, "something takes a backseat. Let it. Enjoy each stage as it comes."

A KALEIDOSCOPE OF GROWTH IN THE SECOND TWELVE MONTHS OF LIFE

A Minicourse in Infant and Toddler Development

We seek to acquaint parents with the typical patterns of behavior that are growth related; the actions and reactions that are most characteristic of each month of development during the second twelve months of life. Included are the "ages and stages" in motor development, language acquisition, the onset and practice of sensory and learning powers, social interaction, personality traits, feeding and self-help accomplishments, and play life. Parents need to be aware of the "critical periods" of growth and development when appropriate intervention can result in the toddler's making great strides forward, when newly-emerging skills are in need of challenge and ample opportunities to use them.

We wish to show parents how self-image and ego evolve in this important year of life and how conflict and lack of understanding between parent and child can bring about unnecessary disciplinary problems, negative behavior, fears, and even odd antics.

Although there are similarities in the behavior of all toddlers, there also are differences. Each child is a unique individual. It is not our intention to tell you what your specific child should be doing at any given month. Rather, we wish to share with you insights, information, and experiences that will help you to be a proficient parent who enjoys child rearing.

"Biological and Psychological Birth of the Human Infant"

Of course, there is a stunning difference between the first and second years of life of an infant. Throughout the first four months of the first year (what Dr. Margaret S. Mahler, a psychoanalyst, calls the "biological birth" of the human infant), uppermost are the onset, practice, and maturing of physical and sensory powers (sucking, listening, seeing, fingering, manipulating). This is a dramatic period when the infant's inborn unresponsiveness to outside stimuli is readily noticed. The infant spends most of the day in a half-asleep, half-awake state. She awakens only when hunger and other needs cause her to cry. When these are satisfied, she falls asleep again. Physiological rather than psychological processes are functioning at this time. The infant is protected from extremes of heat and cold and any undue stimulation by a cocoon-like home environment (resembling the prenatal state) to make physiological growth easier. The newborn brings with him certain reflexive powers and equipment (sucking, rooting, grasping, clinging, and so on) that facilitate feeding and the growth of organs.

In the first few weeks, there is a lack of awareness on the part of the baby of the

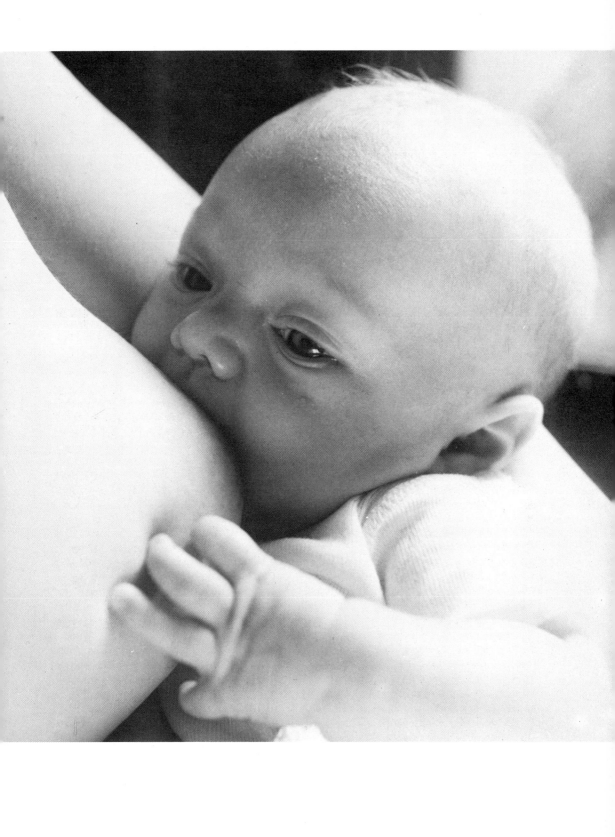

mothering or feeding source. This period is followed by a new stage of dim consciousness that hunger and other needs cannot be provided by oneself; rather, they come from somewhere outside the "self."

Dr. Sigmund Freud called attention to other remarkable inborn reflexive aptitudes at birth: the ability "to turn one's head towards the breast or nipple in order to achieve wished-for pleasure" (a derivative of the rooting reflex). Also present is the ability to track visually. The abilities indicated above show progress in development, while the reflexes of sucking, rooting, and grasping steadily decline and then disappear.

Mothering stimulates the young infant to increased sensory awareness and contact with the environment. The infant is not yet able to distinguish the mother's reducing of the pangs of hunger from his own tension-reducing attempts, such as urinating, defecating, regurgitating, and other ways of getting rid of unpleasurable feelings. The gratification provided by mother care and the infant's own biological actions help him in time to differentiate agreeable from painful experiences and to establish a pleasurable memory bank.

The infant behaves as if he and his are an omnipotent system. Although the infant is completely dependent on the mother, the mother's need of the infant is relative. Beginning ego development impinges upon the emotional support of the mother's nursing care and responsiveness to the baby's whole body (the pressure the holding mother provides, the hugging, and so on). This special contact merges at the end of the second month with the infant's first visual image of the mother's face. The "love affair" between infant and mother (symbiosis) is at its highest point whenever eye-to-eye contact occurs (especially at breast- or bottle-feeding time).

Soon the eye-to-eye contact activates the infant's social smile, a perfect communication/response device for indicating pleasure. This marks the onset of need-satisfying object relationship; the infant begins to comprehend that need satisfaction comes from some object (the mother). From these experiences come the baby's first representation of "body image," with inner and outer perceptions. These inner sensations are what psychologists and psychoanalysts call "the care of the self." This is what Dr. Mahler calls the "psychological birth of the human infant."

At the fourth or fifth month, at the peak of the "love affair" between mother and child, the infant indicates recognition of the mothering half by his social smile whenever she is near him. He goes through a series of explorations with his mother—molding to her body, feeling his own and her body, and so forth. These experiences result in an optimal inner and outer state out of which differentiation and going beyond the mother-and-child circle can take place.

The "Hatching" Period

At five and six months, there is more sensorial purpose during the infant's alert waking times. No longer does she appear to drift in and out of alertness, but has a permanent goal-seeking look. Dr. Mahler calls this a "hatching" period. At six months, experimentation with separation and self-identity takes place. "The infant pulls mother's hair, ears, nose, putting food in mother's mouth." The baby is beginning to be aware of the external environment.

Seven months is the high point of the infant's visual exploration of the mother's face, as well as her body. There are weeks of enchantment with mother's eyeglasses and necklaces. By sight and by touch, the infant puts together a sensory body image and awareness of self from nonself. During these early months, all normal infants take a first step toward breaking away in a bodily sense from the passive period of babyhood. As their motor ability matures, they like to slide down from mother's lap, stay just a little distance away from her arms, and then crawl back or play as close to mother's feet as possible.

Says Dr. Mahler, "From about seven to eight months we see the visual pattern of 'checking back to Mother' as the beginning of the differentiation process, the beginning of an emotional process." The baby begins a comparative scanning of mother with others, feature by feature, and by objects that belong to her. Now he is able to discriminate between mother and the "he, she, or it" that looks, feels, and moves differently from or similarly to mother.

At eight and nine months, the visual and tactile experimentation is far enough along for infants to differentiate strangers from mother. From this conduct comes recognition of what many psychologists call *stranger anxiety.* For some infants, this reaction heralds a prolonged visual and tactile exploration of faces and the gestalt of others. Where basic trust between infant and mother is not fully established, a period of anxiety about strangers results in the baby's crying, hiding, and withdrawing—all of which interferes with the initial pleasurable inspection behavior.

At the end of the first year and the beginning of the second year, one can clearly see the process of separation and individuation intertwined, but not necessarily on the same development track. One is the evolution of autonomy, perception, memory, and reality testing; the other runs along the track of differentiation, distancing boundary formation, and disengagement from mother. In due course, these tracks of development converge.

Early Practice Periods

There are two early practice periods: (1) ushered in by the infant's ability to move away physically from the mother by crawling, paddling on; and (2) a practice period characterized by free, upright locomotion—walking. With expanding locomotor ability, body differentiation and distancing from mother come more rapidly; so does the establishment of a special, specific bond with her.

Most exciting to watch are the growth and functioning of the autonomous ego apparatus in close proximity to the mother (or constant caretaker). In the first early practice period,

infants are not ready to give up closeness and interest in mother. This interest spills over onto inanimate objects that are provided by the mother: a blanket, a diaper, a toy. The infant explores these objects with all her sensory powers: visually with her eyes; taste and texture with her perceptual organs, and so on. However, interest in mother still takes precedence over objects. Expanding locomotor capacity widens the infant's world. She now takes a more active role in deciding distance and closeness to mother, which often results in ambivalent behavior. Because there now is more for the toddler to see and touch and learn about, she becomes absorbed in her own activities for longer periods of time. Nonetheless her feelings of uncertainty impel her during this temporary period of *separation anxiety* to return often to her mother for physical contact and emotional reassurance.

Practicing Locomotor Skills

With the spurt in upright locomotion and physically active learning, a "love affair with the world" begins. The toddler's plane of vision from a new vantage point brings new perspectives, new pleasures, and frustrations. During the period from ten to eighteen months, the world is the child's oyster. He invests his full energy and his growing ego and its functions in practicing motor skills, in exploring his expanding environment and reality. He is less impervious to knocks, falls, and other frustrations. He seems intoxicated with the greatness of his own world and his ego takes forward strides.

Slowing Down of Physical Growth in the Second Year of Life

During the second year, there is a deceleration of the rate of physical growth. The average child gains about five to six pounds in weight and about five inches in height. After the tenth month, there often is a loss of appetite that extends well into the second year. The plump infant begins to change gradually into a lean, muscular child. The abnormal forward curvature of the spine and the protruding abdomen appear and are evident throughout the second and third years.

The growth of the brain also eases off during the second year. Head circumference, which increased approximately four inches (twelve centimeters) during the first year, will increase only two centimeters during the second year. By the end of the first year, the brain has reached about two-thirds its adult size, and at the end of the second year, four-fifths its adult size.

During the second year, eight more teeth erupt, making a total of fourteen to sixteen teeth, including the deciduous molars and cuspids. The order of their eruption may be irregular, with the cuspids appearing after the first molars have erupted.

The infant moves from an awkward, upright standing position by walking with support by her first birthday (in most instances). Several months later, she may even run, albeit rather stiffly. During this period, she can seat herself on a chair if the height is right (ten inches from the floor to the top of the seat). At eighteen months, the child can climb stairs, one step at a time. By twenty months, she can walk downstairs with one hand held. By twenty-four months, she can run well and falls less often. Between eighteen and twenty-four months, the toddler enters the "runabout" age and moves quickly from a safe, protected environment to a dangerous one; therefore she requires constant surveillance.

By fifteen months, the child is able to put a one-inch cube on top of another one; by eighteen months, he can make a tower of three cubes; and by twenty-four months, a tower of six or more cubes. Imitative behavior continues to evolve with spontaneous scribbling of vertical lines at eighteen months and circular ones at twenty-four months.

At the onset of the second year, parents feel their child has left infancy behind and is now a "big" boy or girl. Unfortunately, nature does not inform the child of this. He just keeps on doing what he has been doing, only more of it and more proficiently. Although nothing startling occurs right after a first birthday, the child's behavior takes on a distinctive quality. Many things that used to be done awkwardly and with effort now are accomplished smoothly and easily. There is zestfulness in his performance and he is capable of a surprising variety of activities.

Fine-Motor Development

The way she handles objects that go together is a good illustration of the halfway state the baby has reached. She puts her doll's sock next to its foot, for example, but cannot carry the operation further. She does the same thing with her own shoe, indicating that she knows where it belongs by holding it against her foot. She recognizes that her action is incomplete, gestures to any nearby adult for help, and gives a grunt of satisfaction when the task is performed for her. Her intentions clearly outrace her abilities at this point, a most frustrating state of affairs.

From the baby's point of view, unfamiliar objects are expressly made to be investigated, usually by being pulled apart. Doors that open and shut and drawers that pull out are much more interesting than his own small toys. If he can reach nothing else, his clothing will do. A period of silence in the playpen can often mean that he is busily pulling his garments off. Mothers who do not look on this particular activity with favor may come to tolerate it more easily if they regard it as an important prelude to their child's learning to dress himself.

Movement, a New Focus of Interest

Shortly after discovering the delights of opening and closing and taking things apart the toddler notices that parts of objects move in other ways. Knobs that turn now take her attention. No radio or television program is safe from her during this period, which may start anytime between her first birthday and halfway to her second. Larger moving objects also fascinate her; she may sit happily in her carriage or at a window watching cars, bicycles, and people. She is becoming increasingly aware of events that are taking place at some distance from her.

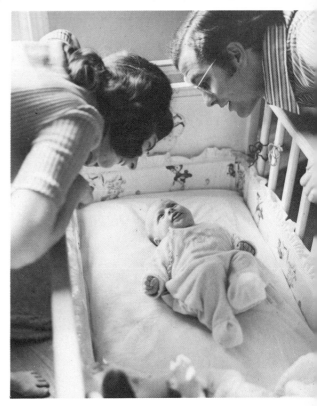

The growing sense of self-identity that appears to make possible the toddler's ability to function at a greater distance and without mother's physical presence includes (1) the development of language in terms of naming objects and expressing desires with specific words. The ability to name objects seems to provide the toddler with a greater sense of ability to control his environment. Use of the personal pronoun *I* also often appears at this time, as well as the ability to recognize and name familiar people and oneself in photographs. (2) The internalization process—identifying with the providing mother *and* father, and the acceptance of rules and demands (beginnings of the superego). (3) Progress in the ability to express wishes and fantasies through symbolic play, as well as the use of play for mastery.

Discovery of Anatomical Sex Differences

There seems to develop at this time a rather significant difference in the development of boys as compared with girls. Boys, if given a reasonable chance, show a tendency to disengage themselves from mother and to enjoy their functioning in the widening world. Girls, on the other hand, appear to become more engrossed with mother in her presence. They demand greater closeness and are more persistently enmeshed in the ambivalent aspects of the mother-daughter relationship.

Whatever sexual differences may have preexisted in the area of innate ego apparatuses, they generally are compounded by the effects of the child's discovery of the anatomical sex difference. This takes place sometimes during the sixteenth- to seventeenth-month period or even earlier, but more often in the twentieth or twenty-first month. The boy's discovery of his own penis usually takes place much earlier. The sensory-tactile component of this discovery may even date back to the first year of life. Around the twelfth to fourteenth month, the walking position facilitates the boy's visual and sensori-motor exploration of his penis.

The girl's discovery of the penis confronts her with something that she is lacking. This can bring on behaviors that clearly demonstrate her anxiety.

Independence or Dependence?

As the toddler begins to learn that he himself can control his actions and actually make things happen, he has an overwhelming urge to try out everything, to find out just how far his independence will extend. Concomitantly, his lack of experience makes him uncertain and sometimes even fearful of things and events that are new or different. The manner in which he copes with the situation is to compromise. He will go ahead and explore as long as he knows that you or another familiar adult is within sight or easy reach.

Give your toddler as much freedom as she can manage comfortably. Do not push her or force her into situations for which she is not prepared. Let her set her own pace. She may be afraid of the big dog next door or terrified of the noise of the vacuum cleaner. All the while, however, she is working on ways to handle her fears. If you leave her alone, eventually she will have the courage to pet the neighbor's dog or to push the button that makes the vacuum cleaner roar.

The toddler has learned to recognize his family, close relatives, and friends. Nonetheless, when visitors come, let your child take his own time about becoming friendly. Do not be embarrassed if he ignores their greetings or even cries and hides his face. After he has become used to their presence and has decided for himself that they are to be trusted, *he* will make the friendly overtures, possibly by presenting them with one (or many) of his toys. Not permanently, of course—he will soon take them back—but this is his equivalent of shaking hands. Also do not worry if he is timid about meeting other children at this age. It is a natural stage he is going through. Never push him into relating to others because that will only frighten him and make him more timid.

Most parents feel something of the toddler's struggle for autonomy without knowing just what it means. On the one hand, they see that the child is constantly testing them out in order to see just how much they will permit. On the other, they find that their child is also clinging to them, needing them quite desperately at times. Small wonder, therefore, that parents also have conflicting feelings in responding to the dramatic shifts in their child's desires and needs. Some of these reactions are experienced by almost every parent, prompted in the main by the child's own state of disequilibrium at this time. When parents are able to recognize the complex drives and ambivalent feelings with which their child is struggling, their own negative reactions often drop away, permitting them to respond positively to the various, changing needs of the child as they appear.

Despite what parents may feel at a given moment, they know that their toddler has made great forward strides. Their child probably has begun to speak, albeit not very well; she is learning to use and enjoy toys; she makes use of tools, too, though in a very crude way; and she has learned to avoid obstacles. The toddler knows only vaguely that the relationship to other people is a reciprocal one; that one has to give in order to get. She even is able at times to part with something. The child has learned that people are important to her in different ways and that each person is different.

Helping Your Child Know Who He Is

You can reinforce your child's developing sense of identity by supplying him with information, stimuli, and encouragement that emphasize his uniqueness. If the normal events and emotional climate of a home enable a healthy child to develop self-identity, then what factors can work against such growth? The mother-child relationship is the most important element. Dr. Erik H. Erikson, a leading figure in the field of psychoanalysis and human development, points out that when an infant first is willing to let his mother out of his sight without alarm or anger, he has begun to develop a sense of basic trust and rudimentary ego-identity.

Dr. Erikson writes, "The firm establishment of enduring patterns for the solution of the nu-

clear conflict of basic trust versus basic mistrust in mere existence is the first task of the ego, and thus first of all a task for maternal care . . . the amount of trust derived from earliest infantile experience does not seem to depend on absolute quantities of food or demonstrations of love, but rather on the quality of the maternal relationship."

Ego development can be stunted by a defective or inconsistent relationship between the infant and his mother (or mother substitute).

The Emergence of Language at Eighteen Months (or Thereabouts)

The middle of the second year is a milestone in child development. It is at about this point—sometimes sooner, often later—that the toddler begins to acquire language and language ushers in the beginning of a new era. With language, the toddler is able to move from a primitive system of thought ("picture thinking") to a higher mode of thought in which word symbols predominate. It is this second system that is used later for the complicated mental acrobatics of logical or ordered thinking.

Language is a developmental skill that commences at birth and grows with the child. It is not a matter of saying words only; rather, language acquisition involves the child's *senses* (particularly seeing and hearing), the development of many *muscles* (especially of the mouth and tongue), and all his *experiences* with people and things, feelings, sights, and sounds. It entails a *wish to communicate;* the child must need and want speech. If making sounds brings a reward (if crying brings him food, his babbling brings smiles and imitation, his accidental *dada* brings an excited response, and the first attempts at *cookie* bring a cookie), the child soon learns that language is a means to control his environment.

The language the child learns is the language he sees (gestures) and hears (speech) about him. The child's environment, his experiences in it, and his reaction to those experiences determine his language achievement. Language growth begins with listening, rec-

ognizing, sorting, and remembering information seen and heard. Language production begins with crying and babbling, followed by repeating sounds, and, finally, by the use of words and groups of words or sentences.

Progressions in Language Acquisition

Children's ability to discriminate the sounds and meaning of the language spoken around them improves, as does their ability to imitate and produce speech sounds themselves. Because of their preoccupation with motor learning (creeping and walking, for example), toddlers may make very slow progress in language development in the first part of the second year. Toward the latter half of the year, however, they will make fast gains in vocabulary (from an average of ten to twenty words at eighteen months to over two hundred at two years, in some instances), and will begin speaking in short phrases by their second birthday. During this period, most children go from a few words mixed in with a lot of jargon to mostly all real words.

In the second year of their lives, children's memories increase—for things, people, places, and ideas. Not only do they recognize the familiar, they now begin to demonstrate the ability to recall and reproduce recent memories of words, actions, and events. In solving new problems, children rely on their old experiences. They try out different known modes of action in the new situation and begin, toward the end of the year, to develop new procedures through combining and changing old ones. They commence to have representations of real things in their heads (memories of pictures, sounds, feelings, and so on) that help them to think about something without its being physically present—an important milestone.

A child is not likely to acquire language unless it is rewarding to do so. The child whose wants are anticipated may be denied the need and opportunity to develop the skills necessary to make his wants and needs known. For example, if a parent always anticipates the child's thirst or responds to his gestures and hands him a cup of water, the child does not have the need or opportunity to learn to ask for a drink. However, the reason a child is delayed in language development may be more complicated than that of having all needs anticipated. In the event of any problem, it would be advisable to seek help from a pediatrician, psychologist, and/or speech and language therapist.

Some Theories of Language Development

There are considerable differences among educators and psychologists about how language is learned. Noam Chomsky (of Harvard University) and the late Eric H. Lenneberg maintain that the child should not be taught language; rather, the parents' role is simply to provide their child with the opportunity to teach herself, so to speak. If the child is talked to, if she is surrounded with language, if she hears people talking to one another, she will naturally (and without any teaching) go from one stage to another in her own language acquisition.

However, most educators believe that today's families neglect talking to their infants. In disadvantaged homes, especially, both parents may go to work and leave their children with teenage sitters who do not talk to the infants in their care. Bringing such children up to proper development requires structured programs of vocabulary learning.

Morris M. Lewis of England, in a scholarly book, *Language, Thought and Personality in Infancy and Childhood,* presents the following steps in language mastery:

1. *The spontaneous sounds of the newborn: Discomfort cries* are earliest vowel-like sounds that are augmented by two successive groups of consonant sounds (sounds made by partial closure of the vocal apparatus).
   Comfort sounds usually are gurgling noises of open vowels; throaty sounds to express security.
2. *Babbling* (after six weeks) is a repetitive string of sounds, a kind of playing with sounds as if it were an art. Babbling represents the beginnings of the highly complex skills that go into the production of the sounds of speech.
3. *Imitation* is so characteristic of child behavior that it might be regarded as an inborn power. The infant imitates the mother's or father's voice or inflections, which brings reinforcement in the form of a parent's smile, being cuddled, and so on.
4. *Conceptualization* covers the ability to generalize in terms of universals; the infant abstracts the word *mama* from a whole set of different circumstances.
5. Through language and undertones *(no! no!* or *yes!),* the child comes to understand patterns of *approved behavior.*
6. The increased need to *communicate* with people other than the parents (at around eighteen months) forces the toddler to adopt conventional words.

7. Soon the child is able to generalize *quality* words (opposites) such as good/naughty, clean/dirty, pretty/ugly, and so on.
8. *Directed speech:* expressions of assertion and self-awareness. Inhibiting through speech the act of another person toward the child. Insistence on personal prowess, assertion of ownership; as in naming himself and using such words as *I* and *mine.*

From Sounds to Language

Babies everywhere approach their first birthday with an average "vocabulary" of three to ten words; actually a stream of sounds that are largely unintelligible to all but the mother or father. Yet this seemingly unimpressive performance actually signals one of man's most incredible feats, according to Dr. Lenneberg (formerly a psychologist at Cornell University). A baby, nothing short of a linguistic genius, has solidly begun to learn language!

The Importance of Walking

The importance of upright locomotion for the emotional development of a child cannot be overestimated. Walking gives the toddler an enormous increase in reality discovery and testing of the world at his own control. With the attainment of toddlerhood, a first great step toward identity formation takes place.

Walking Brings Problems

You will be thrilled by your child's walking, but some headaches will come along with it, too. Once your child can get around by himself, the world is his to conquer. Nothing is safe: the bottle of perfume on your dresser, the detergent in the kitchen cupboard, the butter on the table, and so on. Headaches, yes, but something wonderful is going on that you would not want to stifle. Your child is finding

out what he can reach and master and control—and this is how ideas grow. Ash trays, dirt in the flowerpot, wires, fluff under the bed—it is hard to believe that world-shaking ideas grow from the likes of these, but they do! You want your child to feel free to explore, to discover, to grab hold of life with both hands. This is the beginning. Your child has to know what his world is like—its textures, shapes, and other properties. These are what a young child thinks with.

"Ages and Stages" In Physical Growth

There are sequences in each child's physical action system that he has to pass through by himself. Right from the start, he sucks, tastes, sees, moves his hands and arms, grasps, fingers, hears, supports his head, moves his feet. Control of the eyes antecedes that of the fingers; head balance that of body balance; grasping with the palm of the hand that of digital retention; willful grasp that of voluntary release; banging that of poking; vertical and horizontal hand movements that of the circular and oblique; crawling usually that of creeping; pulling oneself up that of standing; and creeping usually that of upright walking. Large body movements develop first. More refined physical control comes later; for instance, the shoulder, hip, and knee move before the wrist and ankle.

The Sensori-Motor Years

Dr. Jean Piaget, professor of child psychology at the University of Geneva, describes the span from birth to two years as the "sensorimotor period." The infant moves from being a "reflexive organism" who responds in an undifferentiated way to his environment to a "relatively coherent organization of sensorimotor actions" who can master and affect his immediate environment. He uses external stimulation—parents and play—and his inherent reflexes in an unreflective manner. An infant's movements lack precision. His ac-

tivities and his attention are dominated by external stimuli.

John H. Flavell, professor of psychology at the University of Rochester, has also studied these earliest years. He points out that a child goes through six distinct maturation stages. The first lasts about a month, and during it, the baby shows little but reflexive behavior. During the second stage, from one to four months, varied reflex activities are modified by touch, taste, and auditory experiences that coordinate with one another. Infants at about three months look at objects from which sounds are coming—human beings and their voices, for example—and seem to realize that they belong together. In the third stage, at four to eight months, the baby begins to act toward objects and events outside his body as though they had permanency. He begins to engage in purposive activity.

Writes M. D. Vernon, professor of psychology at the University of Reading, in his book, *The Psychology of Perception,* "During the fifth month, the infant flings out his hands towards an object dangling in front of him and if it touches one of his hands, the hand may close on it. Presently, he deliberately reaches out and grasps it, and if he can, pulls it towards him and puts it in his mouth. These actions indicate that the baby is beginning to realize that if he sees something, he can also reach out and touch it; that he can move it about and try to taste it. He is learning that certain visual and touch impressions may belong together; and that by his own actions he can investigate how this happens—how something with a particular visual appearance will feel when he touches, handles, and mouths it. This is the real beginning of all the experimentation and observation which children carry out to find out what the world and the objects in it are like." The foregoing is the beginning of investigative play that needs full encouragement with a suitable environment and the proper tools.

In stage four, between eight and twelve months, the child tends to use what he has already learned in searching for objects and repeating patterns of behavior. Stage five, twelve to eighteen months, marks the onset of experimentation. The child seeks new ways to solve problems. He begins deliberately to invent actions he has never tried before and to explore the unique features of objects. He tries to find out what will happen if he uses objects in new ways and combines them with other objects to create new ways of doing things. He uses trial and error to discover new solutions to problems.

In stage six, at eighteen months to about two years, the toddler demonstrates the ability to grasp primitive symbol relations. He is commencing to invent solutions mentally rather than by trial and error only. The sensori-motor period ends with the beginning of mental pictures of objects, actions, and places in the external world. The child starts to "figure things out in his head" in very crude ways. Although he still needs the objects present, he is starting to build thought symbols for them and these symbols help him to create "new ideas"; namely, actions that he has not seen or practiced before.

Space is becoming "filled in" for the child. For instance, even though part of the pathway of a ball that has rolled under a sofa is invisible, the child can now make a mental map of the ball's path and trot around behind the sofa to find his ball. He now begins to play "pretend" games. Most of his intellectual development comes because he has learned to coordinate physically, which enables him to respond actively to his environment. Each child is dominated by the physical attributes of his environment. If parents provide propitious physical challenges and opportunities at each stage of development, they help augment their child's physical growth. Dr. Piaget calls these major learnings "schemata," each schema being an organization of interrelated actions.

"Shadowing" and Darting-Away Patterns

Two characteristic patterns of the toddler's behavior, the "shadowing" of mother and the darting away from her, with the expectation of being chased and swept into her arms, indicate both the child's wish for reunion with the love object (mother) and fear of reengulfment by her. (By "shadowing" we mean the child's incessant watching of and following every move of the mother.) One can continually observe in the toddler a "warding-off" pattern directed against any impingement upon his recently achieved autonomy. On the other hand, his fear of loss of love represents an element of the conflict that interferes with his ability to "internalize mental schemata" in his learning power. Some toddlers appear to be rather sensitive to disapproval; nonetheless, autonomy is defended by *no!* and increased aggression and negativism on their part.

In brief, by the time the beginning toddler of twelve to fifteen months has grown into the toddler of over fifteen to twenty-four months, a landmark emotional turning point has been reached. Now the child begins to experience, more or less gradually and more or less keenly, the obstacles that lie in the way of what he evidently anticipated would be his "conquest of the world." At the very height of mastery, toward the end of the "practicing" period, it already begins to dawn on the "older" toddler that the world is in fact *not* his oyster; that he must cope with it very often as a relatively helpless individual, unable to command relief merely by feeling the need for it or just by giving voice to particular needs.

During what Dr. Mahler calls the "rapprochement crisis," misunderstandings can be observed even between a normal mother and her normal toddler. The child's demand for the mother's constant involvement appears to be contradictory to the mother. Although the child is as dependent as he was a half-year before, he now appears eager to become less and less so. Nevertheless, the toddler even more insistently indicates that he expects his mother to share every aspect of his life. Some mothers are unable to accept their child's demands; others cannot face their child's push toward increasing independence.

Somewhere around fifteen months, the mother ceases to be just "home base"—she becomes the person with whom the toddler wishes to share his ever-widening discoveries of the world. The most outstanding behavioral sign of this new relating is the child's perpetual bringing of things to the mother, filling her lap with objects he has found in his expanding world. They all fascinate him, but the main emotional investment is in the child's need to share them with her. The toddler indicates to the mother by sounds, gestures, or words that he wishes her to be interested in his findings and to enjoy them with him.

Along with the toddler's rudimentary awareness of separateness comes the realization that her mother's wishes do not seem to be always identical with her own and that her own wishes do not always coincide with her mother's. This appears greatly to inflate the child's feeling of omnipotence. At the same time, the toddler's preoccupation with locomotion and exploration is beginning to wane. The source of the toddler's greatest delight shifts from independent walking and exploration of her expanding inanimate world to *social interaction.* Peek-a-boo games and games of imitation become favorite pastimes. Recognition of mother as a separate person in the large world parallels awareness of other children's separateness. The toddler now indicates a greater desire to have or to do what another child has or does; that is, a desire to imitate and identify to an extent with the other child.

Social Expansion and the Importance of the Father Relationship

The toddler's desire for expanded autonomy not only finds expression in negativism toward the mother and others, it also leads to an active extension of the mother-child relationship, primarily to include the father. Father, as a love object, from the very beginning belongs to an entirely different category of love objects from mother. Although the child is not fully outside the mother-father union, neither is he ever fully part of it. It is probable that very early he perceives the special relationship between the father and the mother.

The Drive for Independence

The eighteen-month-old appears eager to exercise her rapidly growing autonomy to the hilt *(I do it myself!)*. Increasingly the child chooses not to be reminded that at times she could not manage on her own. Conflicts ensue that appear to hinge upon the desire to be separate and omnipotent on the one hand and to have mother fulfill all her wishes on the other (without having to recognize that help actually is coming from the outside). In most cases, there is a tendency during this period to rapid swings of mood and even to temper tantrums. This developmental phase is best characterized by the toddler's rapidly alternating desire to push mother away and to cling to her, the typical ambivalent behavior of most eighteen- to twenty-four-month-olds.

It is characteristic of children this age to use mother as an extension of themselves, a process whereby they somehow deny the painful awareness of separateness. Typical behavior includes pulling mother's hand as a tool to get a desired object or expecting that mother, summoned by some magical gesture alone rather than with words, will guess and fulfill the child's momentary wish.

Diminishing of the Rapprochement Phase

By twenty-one months, a general lessening of the rapprochement struggle can be observed. The clamoring for virtually unlimited control, the extreme periods of separation anxiety, the alternation of demands for closeness and for separateness subside, at least for a while, as each child once again seems to find the optimal distance from mother, the distance at which he can function best.

The Nature of Language

People the world over have ideas about language and its role in child development. The Mohave and Tlingit Indians of North America believed that newborns could understand adult speech. The Ottawa thought infant vocalizing to be intelligible. Today's North Americans believe parents must *do something* to make their infants learn language.

All languages do certain things. They have units, called words, that label objects, living things, people, feelings, and ideas. These units stand in a limited number of relationships to one another; for example, verb and object or subject and verb. These relationships are called grammar. Words and strings of words are uttered with a limited number of sounds, partly because humans are anatomically limited in their production of sounds.

All babies learn language similarly, and whether they are English, Nigerian, Vietnamese, or Navaho, they acquire language within a couple of years. Grammatical speech does not begin before about the twenty-second month, yet the most salient features usually are acquired by age three and a half. Also interesting is that a baby learns language in spurts: a spurt of syllables around six months; a dramatic increase in number and clarity of sounds between eighteen and twenty-four months; a burst of naming ability at eighteen months. From a few words at twelve months, the child quickly gains (by about the end of the third year) a speaking vocabulary of more than a thousand words and an understanding of another two to three thousand.

The baby quickly moves from a blurred understanding of what is said to a grasp of clearly defined relationships between sounds and words. By age two, about 70 percent of her speech sounds are fairly clear and half of what she says is understandable. From primitive grammatical constructions, she differentiates increasingly grammatical classes and multiplies their possible combinations. From overgeneralized name words, the child evolves precise adult meanings. The *bye-bye* that meant all exits and accompanying feelings and behaviors becomes *goodbye* for separations more permanent than mother's leaving for the next room.

All language development progresses along a universal outline, very much as an infant's physical growth follows the broad course taken by babies all over the world. Language begins when the brain's measurements are about two-thirds their mature values. As with motor milestones (sitting, crawling, standing upright, and walking), linguistic development is influenced by genetically-determined changes in the maturing child. The remarkable correlation of language progress with physical development, even in adverse circumstances, prompted Dr. Lenneberg (who was a biologically-oriented researcher) to suggest that internal physical factors rather than training determine major changes in language ability during the earliest years.

The sounds of the one-month-old consist of just different kinds of crying. There is very little distinction between crying and noncrying sounds. At about four weeks, entirely different sounds begin to emerge. These new sounds are sometimes called *cooing.* They are vowel-like and usually uninterrupted by consonants. If a mother has ever wondered why her infant's sounds are so difficult for her to reproduce, it is because the baby's vocal tract is quite different from that of an older child. Sound spectrograms (electronic printouts of sound patterns) clearly show the difference between infant vocalizations before six months and more mature sounds. Unlike the sounds of a mature, healthy voice, the baby's babbling and cooing appear to a practiced ear to be unsteady and fluttering. Hardly any of these sounds come from the repertoire that normally occurs in English.

An Anatomy of Beginning Speech

The shape of a baby's sound-making organs change. For example, the vocal chords grow and the distance from the glottis to the lips lengthens; the roof of the mouth arches differently. Lack of teeth and tongue control probably impedes the articulation of certain sounds; for instance, *t* and *s.* The infant's neck also lengthens. The jaws widen and lengthen. Gradually the maturing of the vocal apparatus permits the production of recognizable vowel and consonant sounds.

Besides having rather awkward individual articulation, a baby's speech organs also are a bit uncoordinated. The production of every speech sound requires an appropriate signal from the brain to each of more than a hundred muscles in the tongue, lips, cheeks, palate, jaws, larynx, diaphragm, and thoracic and abdominal walls. During the first three months, the brain stem, which monitors the coordination of speech organs (the lips, tongue, palate, and larynx), is not completely functioning. The brain's cell sizes and shapes are different; the coating around nerves (called myelin sheaths) is incomplete. With speech organs growing at different rates and the brain itself slowly changing, small wonder that the smooth meshing of speech mechanics takes a while. Only by about the twelfth month does the baby begin to produce some sounds acoustically close to those in more mature speech.

About the end of the third month, babbling, the next major speech event, appears. When the baby produces a chain of rhythmic, syllablelike sounds, *mamama, dadada, bababa,* many parents and doting grandparents are led to believe that the baby is tagging them. More likely, the infant is merely playing with her vocal organs much the same way that she plays with her fingers. For the next two months, babbling increases. Its sounds become more and more controlled. Often a baby will spontaneously launch into her repertoire with or without the benefit of an audience.

By the end of the eighth month, the baby is already superimposing on her babble adult intonations, such as those heard in questions and exclamations. Intonation contours are one of the first facets of language to normalize. At this point, the babbling and vocalization begin to be influenced by the baby's language community.

Occasionally the baby also imitates the two-syllable utterances, *mama, dada, bye-bye,* spoken so often by his parents. During the next several months, he may seem to imitate unconsciously more of their words. Even more exciting, just after walking and before more social skills are attained, he actually begins to use a few words with understanding.

Of course, the most important developments of the first year of language learning are mental. The baby's word production generally lags behind his capacity to understand language by two to four months. As any experienced parent knows, a ten-month-old understands *No!* before he can say it. He can point to a ball, when asked, long before he can put its component sounds together and articulate its name.

Organizing Speech Sounds Into Classes and Groups

Just as the infant begins to categorize and pattern her world of sight and sound into classes and groups, so she starts to organize the world of speech sounds into classes (for example, *p, b, t, d, k, g* are a subgroup of English consonants called *stops; p, t, k* also belong, with such sounds as *f* and *s*, to a group of "soft" or voiceless consonants). The baby also must learn to attend to those sounds that are important in English and to ignore others that are not meaningful. For instance, in English, a puff of air accompanies such sounds as *p, t, k* when they begin words, although its presence or absence is not distinctive. Linguists say it is *not phonemic.* On the other hand, the presence or absence of voicing does make a difference, as in *pin* and *bin.*

By eighteen to twenty-four months, the contours of a language-specific sound system have emerged. A North American baby reproduces English sounds that are part of an overall sound system—its phonemes—not just individual English sounds independent of one another. Even more important, the baby has learned a processing technique valuable for later language learning. To "understand" what she hears, she learns to use information about which language units may or may not go together. Phonemes overlap acoustically so that the baby cannot rely on auditory cues alone. For example, rapid speech vowels, such as *ah* and *ow* are often neutralized to a sound like the vowel in *but*. Linguists use this symbol for the sound: *e.* As speakers of English, we know that *e* does not really occur in the word *ivory,* even though we often say it that way, just as we know that the second vowel in *ovary* is really *ah,* even though we "neutralize" it to *e*.

Grammar and Language Structure

Mothers and fathers everywhere assist their children by showing them through their own speech the relationship between the internal, unconscious language system that every child has and the particular language their child must learn in order to get along in his environment. As in the development of his sound system, every baby learns grammar in much the same way his peers do the world over. After the first year, the need to differentiate and express his rapidly growing vocabulary and grammar spurs his language development. From about twelve to eighteen or twenty-four months, the toddler tries to represent everything with single words. At first, words may be used as other events within an undifferentiated behavior pattern. *Truck* labels a whole play sequence with toys, for example. Often words are embedded in streams of what we adults take to be meaningless jabbering. This jargon peaks at eighteen months and usually disappears by the end of the second year. It has the cadence and fluency of adult conversation. Its sounds are highly varied and often occur in conjunction with some activity. It is almost as if the toddler were verbally expressing his imprecise understanding of behavior sequences.

Then words begin to assist in further classification. They may stand for groups of objects. One day the baby says *pei* on seeing an airplane and then repeats *pei* on seeing a kite. Truck may mean vehicles, toy-sized or otherwise. *Papa* is all men. Eventually *papa* labels only the most significant man in the toddler's life. Single words also can stand for whole sentences. Mothers know that depending on the intonation, *Mama* can be a declarative: *Here's Mama;* a demand, *I want Mama;* a question, *Is that Mama?* In fact, control of his language's intonation patterns at twelve to sixteen months is one of the baby's first bits of language mastery. Soon the toddler discovers that the single unit does not work too well. Functionally overloaded, each entry has too many interpretations.

Grammar reflects internal developments. It seems to appear with the ultimate step in mental development, logical thinking. According to Dr. Piaget, the renowned developmental psychologist, toddlers around eighteen months of age begin to combine and manipulate mental images of real objects so that they can figure out sequences of behavior without seeing or acting them out. Now they begin to combine words, symbols par excellence, into sequences. Mentally a *coup d'état,* these first attempts are terribly ungrammatical. Articles, prepositions, "helping" verbs, and verb inflections are all candidates for omission, possibly because they are grammatically unstressed in adult speech and, therefore, harder for the child to discriminate. A toddler will say *Adam go,* regardless of when the event occurs.

Most child development scientists agree that human interaction is essential for a child's ability to produce language. As long ago as 1948, it was proved that at six months, infants in families vocalized more and had more vowel and consonant sounds than did those in institutions (who usually were ignored by their caretakers). Infants as young as four months babble most to talking faces and more to smiling faces than to unsmiling ones or to geometric objects. Lots of babbling appears to relate statistically to lots of later verbalization (and to high I.Q.).

Most linguists believe that adults are better models than children for language learning. First-born children have better articulation and more words in their vocabularies than latter-borns, whose speech models are brothers and sisters. Many child education specialists are recognizing, on the one hand, the inborn biological aspects of language and, on the other, the specific areas of language acquisition where adults are especially useful. However, they differ significantly about the *how* of adult interaction. One group says that

parent speech arbitrates choice at every point in acquisition and, therefore, training is critical. Another group maintains that parents need only talk a lot to and around their babies.

Intellectual Development in the Second Year of Life

Being able to "adapt" and "make it" requires competencies that are highly valued by our society; i.e., the ability to make independent decisions and a feeling of self-confidence and self-worth. There is general unanimity among educators about what factors contribute to a child's success in these times: verbal competence, problem-solving ability, a sense of independence, sociability, and control over anxiety and one's emotions. Burton L. White, Ph.D., of the Harvard School of Education, would add to the foregoing the development of curiosity and nurturing the foundations of intelligence.

Today more and more early childhood educators believe that the *first weeks* of life are vital to intellectual development and that parents must be educated in the best way to establish immediate, positive mother-child relations. Children without a sense of basic trust, personal security, and a close parent-child relationship prove not to be good learners. Numerous researches have proved that the newborn learns. How a baby goes about learning from the moment of birth (and perhaps even before) is a question that is far from being answered. What is known is that an infant's learning is almost completely interwoven with his physical development and his emotional state.

How and What an Infant Learns

Human learning is a process that is more intricate than the workings of the most sophisticated computer. A baby comes into the world with the ability and drive to learn. Her brain is not completely finished at birth; it continues to develop as she grows. Each interaction with the environment—people and things—imprints a pathway in her brain. Every bit of information is stored and further expands her brain power. Her mind and the information it receives continually interact, creating new connections that are capable of interpreting and using new information. Early childhood learning authorities consider the first two years of life, when the brain is not yet completed, a most sensitive and critical period for "learning to learn." They believe that the more environmental stimulation of the right kind at the right time, the stronger and more agile the child's mind will become.

Cognitive development (growth in the ability to learn) has two phases: accumulating information and learning to learn. It is important that the baby's first learning experiences be rewarding ones because they tell him that the world is worth finding out about. Experiences can either encourage or discourage further exploration. From all his early successful encounters, the child learns that he *can learn,* which gives him a sense of mastery over his environment.

"Ages and Stages" of Sensori-Motor Learning

The stages of cognitive development, as summarized on page 28, are variations on Dr. Jean Piaget's "ages and stages" of sensori-motor learning. He determined these by undertaking intensive month-by-month observations of his three children:

Stage 1 (Birth to One Month). The infant uses the innate reflexes with which she enters the world. She sucks, tastes, smells, sees, hears, cries, and grasps. As each of these reflexes matures, the baby has a strong urge to practice them and use them to explore her world.

Stage 2 (One to Four Months). The onset of a life based on learning now appears. The infant begins to change his reflex behavior because of the experiences he has had in the new world in which he finds himself. He

changes hearing to listening, passive seeing to active looking, and he begins to try to comfort himself (by thumb-sucking, for example) and to communicate (by different kinds of crying).

Stage 3 (Four to Eight Months). The baby begins to "feel" her effect on other things. She becomes interested in cause-and-effect actions. Her striking, rubbing, shaking, and kicking seem to begin to have the purpose of making interesting or pleasurable events happen again and again.

Stage 4 (Eight to Twelve Months). The baby shows unquestioned intention. He pulls a string in order to bring closer to himself an attractive toy attached to the string. He uses a stick as a tool to rake in objects out of his reach. The baby now begins to understand when his mother is leaving; i.e., he will cry when she puts on her hat. He begins to see objects clearly as having stable functions and properties of their own and not dependent upon him for existence. For instance, an object hidden by a cover is no longer forgotten as soon as it is out of sight. The baby will remove covers to find the disappeared object. In imitating the actions of others, the baby performs actions, such as tongue waggling, that he has already done on his own, but which he has never seen himself do.

Stage 5 (Twelve to Eighteen Months). This stage marks the onset of experimentation. The child begins deliberately to invent new actions she has never tried before and to explore the novel and unique features of objects. She tries to find what will happen if she uses objects in new ways. She combines objects with other objects to create new ways of doing things and uses trial-and-error approaches to discover new solutions to problems.

Stage 6 (Eighteen to Twenty-four Months). The sensori-motor period ends with the beginning of mental pictures of objects, actions, and places in the external world. The toddler

Learning to learn skills comes easily to the toddler who is given a chance to explore the world, as well as encouragement and sometimes needed assistance by adults or siblings. During the second twelve months of life, children are not yet able to build finished constructions (with their blocks, puzzles, and so on), but they are learning the prerequisite skills for later erection of block towers, community layouts, and so forth.

The retrieval skills that eighteen-month-olds learn when they roll or throw a ball and retrieve it are part and parcel of the more creative play activities that will come a year or so later.

It is up to parents to help their toddler achieve optimal levels of ability in the fundamental disciplines of language, curiosity, social development, and intelligence.

Social Development

A child's growth and learning progress more smoothly when he is engaged in interactions with other people, in mutually fulfilling relationships. By the time he is twenty-four months old, the child's social style seems to become well established. He has acquired most of the social skills he will exhibit at the age of six. These skills include getting the attention of adults and holding onto it, using the adult as a resource to help deal with problems, being able to express affection or hostility toward adults in a variety of ways, and being capable of exhibiting fantasy behavior on an interpersonal level.

The child is autonomous and socially related from her earliest days. As she grows, her autonomy (sense of separateness) takes new forms and enables her to be socially active in more sophisticated ways. The child's autonomy begins with her constitutional preferences, which must be taken into account in her social encounters if she is to blossom. This separateness goes through various stages, reaching a high point by three years of age, at which time her basic ways of self-regulation are established. If her experiences during her first three years are not happy and

starts to "figure things out in his head" in primitive ways. He still needs the objects present, but is beginning to build thought symbols (concepts and percepts) for them. These symbols help him to create "new ideas"; namely, actions that he has not seen or practiced before. Imitations of some actions of a model are now possible after the model has left. Now the toddler is able to begin to play "pretend" games.

After the age of two years, the child can tell the difference between words and ideas and those happenings or objects to which words and ideas refer. She can work with words and ideas and manipulate them. She begins to identify a past, present, and future. She can differentiate between an action and a plan of action. She can form an image (a "picture in her head") about activities, a generalized group of facts or ideas; i.e., a concept. She now can make a judgment on the properties of objects and can conserve quantity, weight, and numbers. She is able to *categorize* (put similar things into related groups), *seriate* (arrange objects in sequence and special order; the longest and shortest, and so on).

fruitful, she will have established means for avoiding intrusions by the world and the novelty in it. As a result, she may resist help, even when needed, including help in her cognitive and emotional development.

Children learn the ways of social relatedness from the social experiences they have. They also learn through imitation, which is partly repetition of what is observed and partly by experimentation with self.

The Beginning of Building Interpersonal Relations

At eighteen months, when locomotion and some language enable a child to begin to shape her relations with others besides close relatives, she can approach or avoid individuals and actually influence them. Maturing and learning cause most of the changes that take place during a child's development. Often these changes are stages in the dynamic growth of each child. Walking changes the supportive emotional and communicative relations between the child and the meaningful people in her life. Her mobility permits her contact with ever-expanding varieties of people, things, and places; no longer is she wholly dependent upon her parents.

The Normal Toddler Behaves Egotistically

He still is not experienced enough to have awareness of the feelings of others. He is interested in other children or adults chiefly as objects to touch, explore, hug, and sometimes to hit or bite. If another child is in the way of a toddler pushing a carriage, the toddler moves forward as if the other child were an inanimate object. Should the other child fall over or cry, the toddler continues along in his self-centered way. At this stage, a teddy bear or other stuffed toy is a perfect playmate because the toddler can do anything he wishes to it.

The eighteen-month-old may cry if a companion leaves or may tag along after him. The toddler's quick changes in attention are reflected in her gross-motor shifts. She moves with lightning speed from place to place and gets into everything. She is completely egocentric because she does not yet see other persons as beings like herself.

Although the happy toddler (from eighteen to twenty-four months) does not yet see other persons as beings like himself, he will gravitate to his agemates. However, he is not yet prepared for steady play with other children, no matter what their age. He has to learn how, and social development takes much time and experimentation. The two-year-old likes to be with other children even before he is ready for cooperative play. Normally he is affectionate and happy and laughs wholeheartedly and infectiously. He will mimic the emotional expressions of all the people in his social sphere. Two-year-old boys and girls act out the mother-baby relationship through play with their stuffed animals and dolls. They respond especially to playthings they can hug, pat, or pound. Their interest in stuffed animals and dolls will continue for many years.

The child who has been treated with affection and consideration will develop his own spirit of generosity in the course of maturing. However, his unselfishness and feelings for others are limited during his first three years of life. It takes a long time for a child to learn to share and to control his negative behavior when he is frustrated.

Much frustration among two-year-olds stems from their inability to control the adult world. Things are too big to manage, to push around, or to make do what the toddler wishes. The toddler seeks to be in the driver's seat of every car, to push every carriage herself, and throw herself into every doll bed. The two-year-old feels she must play the dominant role in every situation, and perhaps that is her temporary right at this stage because ego building is a necessary first step to developing social competence.

To assuage the inevitable frustrations all two-year-olds face, it is important to provide them with a planned environment of toys, equipment, and furnishings that are scaled to their size and capabilities. Everything should

be neither too small for their inexperienced hands nor too large for their not yet fully developed bodies to handle.

Infant-Toddler Play Groups

Some mothers form infant-toddler play groups that usually include five or six little ones who meet regularly in one another's homes to play, with mothers taking turns supervising the activities. Such play groups are not babysitting arrangements; rather, they are cooperative undertakings. The participating mothers plan the play sessions and provide suitable play materials and activities. Even though the children do not play together, it may be that their play takes on more meaning when they are in a group. Each play session usually lasts about two hours.

Even if babies do not need or benefit from a play group, some psychologists say their mothers may. Most young mothers, especially of first-borns, learn a great deal from watching the behavior and play of all the children in the play group and many grow more relaxed. In addition, the organized play setting permits the little ones to choose from a broader variety of well-chosen playthings and activities than they may have available to them in their own homes.

The Growth of Emotions

Parent-child relationships determine to a large measure the early patterning of a child's personality. Competent parents provide their children with a home atmosphere of "relaxed concern." They communicate their feelings and standards directly and clearly and what they impart is appropriate to each situation, to the child's stage of maturation, and to his particular temperament. Effective parents are consistent in their demands and responses. They express displeasure when poor behavior or disobedience is intentional, but they never humiliate their children. They react with approval to their children's efforts to learn and

show appreciation for accomplishment and consideration. Parents who enjoy their children can be sure their children are thriving.

Nonetheless, storms of open defiance are common toward the end of the second year of life and for a year or two later, even in children who have been placid babies. These seem largely to be an early form of self-assertion that passes as the child attains greater skill and social ease. Although very trying at the time, a calm home atmosphere of steady affection and firm patience will help disperse most of the tensions of toddlerhood.

A child's emotional development is as vital as his physical and intellectual growth. It is, in fact, an integral part of both. The emotions are the important force governing human behavior, the nucleus of personality. Changes or growth spurts in emotional development are associated with the growing child's altered expectations and demands. They are related to each child's capacity to handle, know, understand, and manipulate his environment. For example, an eighteen-month-old may become totally frustrated by his inability to verbalize a certain need. Therefore, he will stamp his feet, lash out with both hands, and even cry in anger. A few months later, his language skills greatly improved, this same child has learned to deal with his environment to such a degree that he now can *say* what he is feeling. Exit his need for a tantrum!

According to a textbook definition, "Emotions are the process by which behavior or the potentiality for behavior is modified as a result of experience." According to human observation, the emotions are a shrug of the shoulder, a sigh of love, a consuming jealous rage, and so on. Basically, the emotions reflect both love and hate. The shades and nuances in between are culture-learned and often defy definition. To put it another way, the emotions are strong physical or social feelings that indicate such internal sensibilities as fear, anger, disgust, joy, grief, surprise, tenderness, yearning, and so forth. Inasmuch as emotions are introspective, they often are difficult to pinpoint and almost impossible to evaluate. This is especially the case with very young children who are unable to verbalize their feelings.

Earliest Emotional Development

A baby is born with her basic emotions dovetailed with her survival. Her physiological drives or needs must be satisfied if she is to grow. All but two of these needs are taken care of in a self-regulatory way. The newborn breathes oxygen, voids waste, and sleeps without any other person's participation. However, hunger and thirst are not gratified automatically; their satisfaction depends upon another's help. When an infant's hunger and thirst are not administered to, tension mounts. If left totally unattended, the tension becomes severe; the baby produces a great deal of bodily activity and cries in angry sounds. An emotion is born.

Of course, even when the basic needs are taken care of, it still is not the whole story. It has been shown that babies left in institutions for long periods of time, who are kept dry and fed but have no other interaction with caretakers, grow up severely retarded. Not only are they emotionally starved, but intellectually as well. The mother does more than take care of her baby's obvious needs. When she feeds or changes her baby, she also talks to him, touches him, fondles him, and responds to his sounds. When he is frightened by a sudden loud noise, she comforts him; she smiles at him and, sometime around the third month, he returns her smile. The deep pleasure each derives from the other is manifest; emotional communication is taking place.

The Second Year Is an Emotional Milestone

During the second twelve months of life, the human being progresses from the status of helpless infant (responsive to stimuli, but dependent upon others for the gratification of most of her wants) to that of toddler with some measure of independence. The psycho-social world of the child changes dramatically. Of course, the most remarkable development of this period, the one with far-reaching emotional implications, is the toddler's enormous progress in language. Greater understanding, learning, and sociality emerge with verbalization. The child begins to express her emotions. Now when she cries she can tell you what is troubling her—a pin unstuck, hunger, a wet diaper, and so on.

Emotions Are Associated With Performance in the Second Year

The toddler's burgeoning language skill, together with an expanding understanding of his world and his improved capacity to cope with it, permits him to take a much more active role in his relationship to the various elements in his environment. Dr. Erikson sees this period as the critical one for a child's development of autonomy, self-reliance, and competence.

Actually this age is a mixed bag emotionally. The child really is being buffeted by conflicting feelings about himself and his world. While it is true that he is beginning to taste the sweet sense of independence, he remains strongly attached to and dependent upon his parents for sustenance, guidance, and emotional support. This is the time when socialization begins in earnest, with parents helping their child to acquire the rules of the social unit to which he belongs, be it the family, the community, or the play group.

Positive and Negative Emotions

Positive feelings (happiness, pleasure, excitement, and so on) are love-based and elicit a sense of well-being in all concerned. Security and competence produce positive emotions. Negative emotions (anger, fear, anxiety, jealousy, and so on) are hard for the child and the parents to deal with. Parents need to understand that while negative emotions are

just as "natural" as positive feelings, the former are self-defeating, and it is up to them to help their child resolve the reasons for his big and little problems.

Anger and Aggression

Parents are appalled when their child shows anger or hate. They feel that their child is being "bad" and doing something that is "wrong." The strong impulse to destroy things (which almost every child has to some degree) is very upsetting to adults. This is especially true when the destructive tendencies are directed toward another child or the new baby. Anxiously, parents try to *squelch* such negative actions, and if they succeed, they conclude that all is well. But is it? All they may have accomplished is to channel surfacing emotions underground. Instead of helping their child give vent to his feelings and redirect them (get them out and over with), they have persuaded him to turn his hostility inward.

Aggression in childhood seems to be universal and learning to control it is an important aspect of socialization. A young child's anger and aggression are expressed in many ways: kicking, holding his breath, screaming to get his own way, and so forth. (Peevishness, whining, and sulking usually are expressions of the older child.) Actually all negative behaviors are tests to see how the parents will react and how far the child will be permitted to go.

The important thing is for parents to find appropriate ways to help their child in each instance of negative behavior. For the very young child, water play, pounding clay, showing him how to hammer, running, jumping, and so on are creative approaches to handling aggressive and hostile impulses. Another important aspect is allowing your child his anger (if he is not being physically destructive) and showing him that it is all right to be angry at times—everyone is. One of the best ways to show him how to deal with his hostility is by the manner in which you deal with your own anger. Children pattern themselves on what they see.

Temper Tantrums

The penultimate of anger, frustration, and aggression is the temper tantrum. When a child has a tantrum she simply is going to pieces emotionally for a while. Now all stops are out; all systems are out of control. This is not a time for parents to use restraint; this will only drive her screams higher and her kicking wilder. If the child is not harming herself bodily, the most effective means of control is to let the tantrum spin itself out. Do not give in to any demands, however. Temper tantrums are to be understood, not rewarded.

When relative calm returns, examine the events that led up to the hysterical outburst. Frustration is the most common cause of a temper tantrum. Often parents do not realize that they are being unreasonable by preventing their child from doing something. It always appears to be easier for parents to say *No!* However, there are times when a reasonable *Yes* can head off a temper tantrum.

Fears

In spite of everything that parents do or say, some fears are certain to appear in their child. One fear can and often does lead to another. Often it is hard to tell which fears are natural to a child and which he has learned from his surroundings. What is known is that infants are afraid of sudden loud noises and of falling; toddlers usually fear the unfamiliar, including large or barking dogs, and so on.

Fear is a form of self-preservation. It is normal for a child to be afraid on occasion, but if a child fears too intensely or for too long a time, it can be detrimental to his emotional well-being. Most children worry that their parents will cease to love them or will leave them. The fear of abandonment can be devastating and manifest itself in many ways: overreacting when the child is separated even momentarily from the mother in a crowded store, being unable to go to sleep at night without countless requests, a night light, and constant assurance that the parents will remain close by, and so forth.

In the changing world of childhood, children can feel secure and less fearful if they feel sure that even if they make mistakes and are clumsy, their parents will still love and value them. An abiding sense of security fosters self-worth and self-reliance, reduces fearful attitudes, and bolsters curiosity and courage.

Jealousy

Jealousy in a young child can be so bitter that it can warp her outlook on life temporarily or sometimes even permanently. Jealousy is a negative emotion that should be dealt with at once, avoided when possible, and minimized at all cost. Nothing so greedily consumes a child's inner emotional reserves than feelings of jealousy. Of course, the most jealousy-provoking situation is the arrival of a new baby in the family. All children, especially those under six, find it hard to accept a new baby.

The Family's Role in Emotional Development

During her first two years of life, the child's world is her mother. All her major learning experiences, satisfactions, and frustrations occur in relation to this basic bond. Also important is the child's interaction with her father and her siblings (if any). Because of the strong emotional ties and identifications between all the family members, the early emotional imprinting that takes place in the home is likely to be much more significant and resistant to change than that which occurs elsewhere later on.

Personality/Behavior Problems of Short Duration

All toddlers display minor, transient behavior problems at one time or another, but these usually disappear without the need for special treatment. These problems include masturbation, thumb-sucking, fear of the dark, temper tantrums, disobedience, willful destruction, and so forth. Parents of toddlers find most distressing their child's seemingly compulsive need to suck his thumb, to masturbate, or to destroy. If the parents are not successful in helping their child work through his unacceptable modes of behavior or if they persist too long or too intensely, the child will require outside professional help.

Very early the toddler senses his parents' attitudes of approbation or disapproval. Even in the second year, a child may rebel against the adult who limits him and structures the world too rigidly for him. The toddler wants to make plans for himself now and again and feels strongly about carrying them out in his own way. If parents interfere, the child gets angry and rebellious. Most parents find the above behaviors difficult to bear and usually react by punishing their child. Thus, the child has his first inkling that his parents' anger and punishment represent loss of their love and he becomes frightened and even less sure of himself. It is in such circumstances that the conflict between the child's need for parental acceptance and care and his drive toward independence collide.

There is no one pat way to help the child and his parents through the unacceptable behaviors of toddlerhood. Parents need to find their own ways of helping their child overcome his problems, employing approaches that are dictated by undiluted affection, understanding, and patience.

When a toddler finally begins to show some control of his behavior, it is because gaining parental approval and love is more important to him than his unacceptable behavior. If a child's negative behavior gets out of control and both sides (toddler and parents) resort to stronger and stronger methods of retaliation, the parents need to make sure that they do not permit their relationship with their child to deteriorate into a state of war. In the event of such a battle of wills, all teaching will be blocked. Instead of resorting to self-des-

tructing "blocking" techniques, parents need to try "substitution" techniques; that is, redirecting unacceptable behaviors by offering substitute satisfactions.

More on "Ages and Stages" In Child Development

We have attempted to present the varying types of developmental behavior that result from physical growth at each "age and stage" of a toddler's life. With every advance in bodily growth, there is a corresponding change in behavior. Developmental behavior can be broken down into (1) motor behavior, (2) adaptive behavior, (3) language behavior, and (4) personal-social behavior. The growing child manifests his increasing capacities in various patterns of typical behaviors, and with each mode of behavior, there is a whole series of functioning abilities that, in turn, trigger other behaviors.

The three-month-old's ability to push his chest up and rest on his arms is a motor skill that indicates improved bodily control, just as the maturing of his eye muscles allows him to focus on and recognize distant objects and familiar faces. Now it can be said that the infant is able to "adapt" to an environmental factor—his crib—and is learning to overcome its limitations by pushing and peering out. Once he has met this challenge, he may make cooing sounds about his success (language behavior) with nearby persons (social contact).

The eighteen-month-old's maturing locomotor ability puts her in direct contact with persons other than her parents (social) and brings about verbal efforts to communicate her needs and desires. Her personal-social development is closely interrelated with the cultural patterns of the family group in which she is reared. In some families and cultures, self-reliance is encouraged at an early age, whereas in others it may be postponed.

Toilet learning reflects this situation very well. The toddler's ability to control his bowel movements is a motor skill that is maturing at about twelve to eighteen months. However, in many families the learning is delaying until twenty to twenty-four months, when the child's *adaptive behavior* (his ability to understand language to verbalize his toilet needs) has developed sufficiently.

Psychological Development of Infants and Toddlers

Doctors Margaret Mahler and Hiag Akmakjian include psychological development as another very important pattern of behavior. Says Dr. Mahler, "It is the developmental task of infancy and early childhood to lead to *psychological independence* and autonomy by the end of thirty-six months. Birth was merely a physical separation from mother. By three years, if all goes well, the child will have achieved psychological birth and become an individual."

The many forces that mold a child's development are indeed complex. Her burgeoning abilities, specific needs and drives, innate perceptions, and bodily skills are tested constantly against a "panorama" of the people, places, and things that make up her environment. The normal, optimally developing child is able to achieve a balance between internal and external forces and to progress toward maturity and autonomy with self-confidence.

Developmental Stages of Autonomy

With the maturation of each physical/motor power, there is corresponding growth in the child's feeling of independence and autonomy. From about the third month onward, autonomy is revealed in the child's management and control of his own body. At about the same time, there is the beginning differentiation of the self from the environment. Between three and six months, the child experiences pleasure in being able to "cause" an action; getting the attention of his parents; relating differently to his regular caretaker and to other persons; and so on.

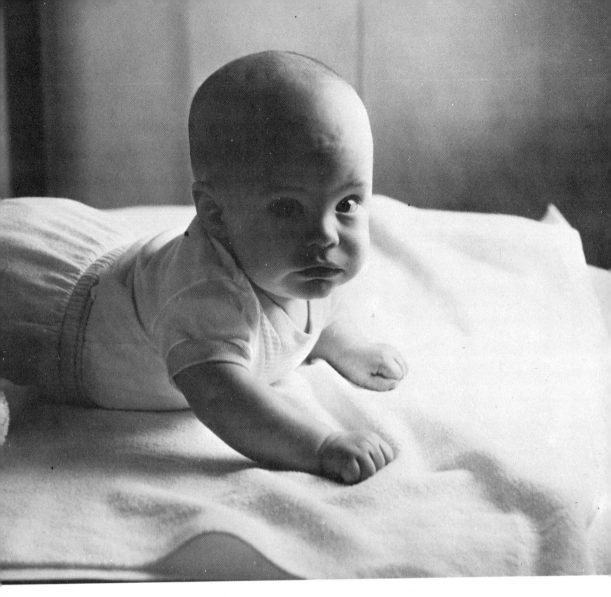

By the early part of the second year, the toddler's ability to walk enables her to move further away from her caretaker, thus giving her a greater sense of independence. With the onset of verbal language in the second year, toddlers develop highly individualized patterns of behavior that include defense mechanisms and coping styles. Psychologists have concluded that the individual differences (personality) of children in the management of new and strange circumstances are clear-cut; that autonomy is well established by the third year. The child can make his wants known, has the capacity to set limits on demands and pressures from the environment, can delay and/or avoid difficult situations, and has de-termination, persistence, and the ability to succeed by himself.

One to two years is an important age for trying to manage by oneself. During this period, the child begins to develop a sense of herself through her name, to claim posses-sions as "mine," and to recognize her mirror-image. The skills she is mastering enable her to become increasingly self-reliant. The tod-dler is learning to feed herself; help undress and dress herself; control her bowels and bladder; eat solid foods; and, of course, get around well on her own two feet. In addition, she is learning the power of words with regard to her own and others' behavior.

Self-Help, Practice in Coping, and Autonomy

Self-help is concerned with those behaviors that enable the child to care for himself in the areas of feeding, dressing, bathing, and toilet training. The child's ability to care for many of his basic everyday needs is considered most important by parents. It also is vital to the child because it relates to his being able to see himself as an independent, competent, individual member of his family and community.

Behaviors in the self-help sphere, as in the other developmental areas, follow a sequential developmental pattern that usually is determined by the child's motor growth. Sequences have been developed in terms of what have been found to be the most usual steps for accomplishing a particular skill. They reflect, too, the child's capacity to handle a particular task in the light of his motor skills and general level of understanding. For example, the child should be able to use his thumb and fingers in varying play activities before being required to button the buttons on his coat.

Feeding: A Self-Help Routine For Toddlers

Toddlers not only begin to develop a sense of themselves as persons, they also learn the skills that permit them to become increasingly more self-reliant (in sharp contrast to their helplessness during much of their first year of life). The drive to be independent is self-evident in the feeding process. Your toddler will not be satisfied with just feeding himself. Long before he can do an efficient job, he will want adult eating tools and desire to be part of the family in good standing. Despite his beginning clumsiness and sloppiness, the baby should be encouraged in his wish to feed himself. His urge first shows itself when he tries to hold a cup or spoon—with your help, of course, at first. Soon he will want to do it all by himself and almost push you away. This can be a mess—with milk, water, or juice spills;

food falling off the spoon before it gets into his mouth; the highchair and floor getting splattered, to say nothing of grubby hands and face.

There are things you can do to make the physical setting amenable to your toddler. The right spoon will help, one with a straight, broad handle that is as long as your child's fist. Eating time should be pleasant and relaxed. Although mealtime often is a battle, it need not be. There are many things you can do to make it a time of good feelings. Allow for plenty of time and do not worry about dawdling. Let your toddler play with the food a little. Let her spill it, if she must. Let her use her fingers, if she wishes. Keep in mind that you want her to *like* to eat; that you want her to learn to do things for herself. An attractive setting helps, too. Appealing color in food and good consistency also are important.

Walking Has Far-reaching Implications for Feeding

The toddler's fervor and single-minded dedication to walking will interfere with his eating (and sleeping). In addition, his ceaseless activity will slow down his weight gain even if he remains a good eater and enjoys every mouthful. Weight gain slackens for most babies at about ten months, the period of intense crawling and creeping. His deceleration of weight gain at this time is good. Despite the once popular belief that healthy babies are fat babies, being overweight is not healthy for anyone. Your baby should begin laying down muscle instead of fat tissue. Recent research suggests that heart disease may be caused by overfeeding babies with fats and sugars.

The independence that walking inspires may further complicate mealtime and vex parents. Some toddlers use food as a means of punishing parents for restricting them. At the same time, obstreperous behavior at mealtime may reflect the child's self-differentiation and assertion over her environment. So forget your dreams of three meals a day and a well-balanced diet for your toddler. Do not be surprised if she eats one good meal, one so-so meal, and rejects the third altogether. She may have very definite likes and dislikes, refuse to try new foods, and stick to only three or four staples. Trying to convert her to a well-rounded diet would be more trouble than it is worth at this time. Babies and toddlers who comply with their mothers' notions of "a proper diet" are rarities.

Many parents are so intent upon getting food into their child that they miss the importance of his exploratory behavior with it. Handling, smelling, and testing food are extensions of the investigatory behavior that began earlier with inedibles. One indication of this learning would be the child's avoidance of fingering slippery foods (bananas, for example) in contrast to crumbling cookies and breads beyond recognition. Too, when the child is allowed to enjoy his food and permitted some of his early sloppy eating habits, he learns that the world is to be trusted; that it is not a forbidding place where signaling his own feelings and earnest desires only brings trouble.

Parents who pressure their toddler to eat can trigger real feeding problems. Teasing or tricking a child into accepting the food you offer or startling her so that you can shove food in when she drops her jaw in astonishment are two of the worst things you can do. At about thirteen to fourteen months, or earlier, the toddler will demonstrate her determination to eat what and when she chooses. She will win the battle or be completely beaten into uneasy submission. Of course, no child should be allowed to use food to provoke or heighten tension in the family.

Another not so subtle form of pressure is feeding the toddler between meals because he "eats so little." This will only get you more trouble: a child who fusses and picks at his food. Do not let him get into the habit of consuming between-meal carbonated beverages, cookies, and sweets that will curb his appetite for more nourishing foods.

During the second twelve months of life, your child should be on table foods completely. Although it may be a while before she has good table manners, do let your child feed herself.

Sleep Behavior of the Toddler

The desire for independence and autonomy that emerges with regard to feeding and toileting also shows up strongly in the toddler's sleep behavior and routines. The resistance to nighttime sleeping, according to Doctors Naomi Ragins and Joseph Schachter (who researched sleep behavior in two-year-olds), appears to be related to the child's incomplete separation from his primary caretaker. As the toddler relinquishes his daytime involvements for sleep, he is asking his parents to confirm that they will be available if needed. If your child makes the adjustment from waking to sleep, it may mean either that he is adjusting adequately to caretaker separation or that he has not yet confronted the transitional phase of separation from his parents. Most parents, recognizing this insecurity on the part of their child, develop a whole series of activities (reading bedtime stories, singing lullabies, playing the guitar, turning on a night lamp, and so on) to provide the needed reassurance. Some parents set definite rules about preparing for sleep: no stimulation before bedtime, no roughhousing, minimal playing in a warm bath, a glass of water on the night table, and so forth to smooth the way to their child's dropping off to sleep.

There is a psychological rationale for the practice of singing or reading to a child at bedtime. Giving the child her teddy bear, favorite blanket, and so on provides reassurance and makes the child more at ease. Somehow the child deduces that "the world of beloved things and people which she surrenders with much difficulty will be there tomorrow," which affords her a sense of continuing reality.

Undressing

Between twelve and eighteen months, the toddler tests her primitive sense of independence by beginning to undress herself. By two she can do a fair job and will demonstrate this by running around the house or even outside quite naked. The same spirit of *I do it myself!*

shows up in her wanting to wash herself, brush her teeth, brush her hair, and so on. If a child feels that she can cope with a problem, she will try her hand at it. If she is not quite sure of her ability, trials and errors can lead to frustration and negative parent-child encounters. This period requires especially sensitive approaches and understanding on the part of the parents to win their toddler's cooperation.

Growth of Autonomy and Learning Through Play

Play is the natural way for a child to live and learn. It is his way to concentrate, exercise his imagination, try out new ideas, imitate, practice grown-up behavior, and gain a feeling of control over his world. Young children at play combine a seriousness of purpose and wholehearted enjoyment that adults often envy.

Children, toddlers especially, are blessed with insatiable curiosity. They are open to all kinds of learning. In the first year of life, they want to touch, taste, see, smell, and hear everything—and the more they learn, the more they want to learn. In the second year, they want to talk, to imitate adults, explore the whole blooming world. Because of these strong urges, they are susceptible to environmental influences. In a home in which

play and discovery are encouraged, the minds and personalities of children expand and grow.

Play and Playthings for the Active Toddler

Some psychologists say that missing any physical developmental stage (creeping and crawling, for instance) may lead to deficiencies in spatial perception, left-right relationships, and even to difficulties in picture and word understanding. It is necessary to make special play provisions for the crawling, standing, and walking stages of physical maturation. Parents need to provide equipment that can enhance beginning walking. For example, a stable walker with colorful, resounding rollers is a welcome device. A sturdy push truck with heavy hollow blocks also can give a toddler confidence and walking pleasure.

Walking opens up fresh vistas to the toddler, who is into everything and always on the go. He savors to the full his ever-increasing sense of self-determination. To the toddler, everything is physical. Perpetually in motion, he lugs, tugs, pulls, pushes, dumps, drags, and pounds. He tries to maneuver anything and everything within his reach—a chair, table, lamp—even if his strength is not up to it. He will try to carry a package, open a door, turn on a faucet, and button up his coat.

The insatiable, indefatigable "walker-runner" needs playthings and equipment that are engineered to her size and current capabilities so that instead of feeling helpless, she will get to be more and more self-reliant. Small wonder the toys the toddler most enjoys are those that add to her feelings of bigness and power. Playthings that make big noises (drums, pounding benches, and so on) rank high because noisemaking is one way for little children to feel omnipotent. Hammering also is a test of strength and getting the wooden pegs banged down is a real accomplishment.

Dr. James L. Hymes, Jr., retired professor of childhood education at the University of Maryland, puts it this way: "Often we buy toys to show love. This doesn't work. But toys that are right for one-to-two-year-olds stand a chance of giving a child a sense of power. The youngster learning to walk is the world's most eager 'pusher.' A baby carriage, a toy lawn mower, anything on wheels that he can hold onto for support means both good walking and good feeling. A little later the slightly more skilled walker is the world's most eager 'puller.' He toddles along pulling his wagon . . . feeling as big as all-get-out."

A Responsive Environment for the Toddler

Important factors in your toddler's development are you, her parents, and her environment—the space, toys, and stimulation available to her. If a child has a physical handicap, her space has to be arranged so that she can still do as much as she possibly can. If she has a sensory problem, all her other faculties must be exercised. If her patterns of development are slow, she will need more stimulation and encouragement. If she is hyperactive, her environment must be controlled so that she does not have excessive excitement. In short, every child requires an environment that is *responsive* to her particular needs and abilities.

Children learn by *acting on their environments*. What we mean by a responsive environment is one that is properly planned and supportive. The toddler requires an amplitude of experiences with all elements of her environment—physical, mental, social, and so forth—that permit her to try and to succeed.

Parents need to be careful not to push their child into attempting the impossible—anything that the child is not convinced she is ready for. However, when your toddler does attempt something new, you need to be quick with your praise for each effort and remember not to be unduly critical of clumsiness or incompletion. The attention span of the toddler is still very limited. Maturation will extend the duration of concentration and effort.

Unless the environment is sensitive to the child's maturation level and his play activities are suitably challenging and satisfying, he will not invest his energy. He will stop trying because he sees no reason for reaching out to dull or frustrating experiences, and in so doing, will limit the optimal realization of his intellectual, emotional, and physical potentials.

Rationale for Early Intervention and Stimulation

Early in the Johnson administration, intervention programs for culturally disadvantaged preschoolers (Headstart and Follow Through, for example) were introduced, and more recently (in 1970) funds were allocated by the Federal Bureau of Education for curriculum research demonstration projects for exceptional children from birth to three years of age (the retarded, brain-damaged, and so on). Most of the efforts catered to an age level (two to eight years) when attentiveness, word labeling, language, and so forth were either already being mastered or neglected because of a responsive or deprived home environment. When independent researchers evaluated what the Headstart project had accomplished for the child entering first grade, there was great disappointment because the Headstart group did not do better than the control group (without Headstart).

When former Secretary Robert Finch of the U.S. Department of Health, Education, and Welfare called a nationwide meeting of experts to assess this apparent failure, the specialists were unanimous in their conviction that the skills of learning (learning to learn) are preset in the earliest periods of life. Dr. Burton L. White, of the Harvard School of Education, has defined the critical period as eight months to three years, when parents stimulate infants with visual learning experiences (at eight to fourteen months), labeling their infants' sensory experiences with words (at eighteen to twenty-four months), and then putting words into sentences (at twenty-four to thirty-six months).

Dr. W. Reagan Callaway, Jr., of the University of California at Los Angeles, points out that the human brain at birth has a built-in preference and capacity to deal with form and pattern and that visual stimulation at three to eight months facilitates perceptual-cognitive development. Dr. Callaway asks, "Would we prevent many instances of reading problems involving perceptual inadequacies if we began the child's exposure to letters and words much earlier than six years so that he can profit more from nature's gift of a *sensitive period* for form perception which apparently begins at birth?"

Coupled with this perceptual-sensitive period is the innate ability at eighteen to twenty-four months to perceive speech and the elementary grammar of language without too much external teaching. In brief, in the second twelve months of life, except for such conceptual operations as sequencing from left to right and correlating auditory and visual stimuli, the only skills a child needs for reading are perceptual, not cognitive.

Animal and Human Research

The rationale for early intervention at *sensitive periods* is based on a review of the literature on the effects of early experience on the behavior of animals that showed that such experience had a marked effect on adult behavior. For example, Gene P. Sackett, of the Regional Primate Research Center, University of Wisconsin, found that infant monkeys reared under conditions of social isolation and visual impoverishment became inactive and displayed a minimal amount of exploratory behavior in adulthood ("Exploratory Behavior of Rhesus Monkeys as a Function of Rearing Experiences and Sex." *Developmental Psychology*, 1972 [*6, 2,* 260–270]). The Harlows found that infant monkeys raised under conditions of deprivation became socially unresponsive adults and the females often became brutal toward their offspring (Harlow, H. F., Dodsworth, R. O., and Harlow, M. K. "Total Social Isolation in Monkeys." *Proceedings* of the National Academy of Science, 1965 [*54*, 90–97] and Harlow, H. F., Schlitz, K. A., and Harlow, M. K. "Effects of Social Isolation on the Learning Performance of Rhesus Monkeys." In C. R. Carpenter, ed. *Proceedings of the 2nd International Congress of Primatology,* 1969 (Vol. 1)).

In a number of studies (from 1953 to 1963) by leading researchers, depriving chimps, dogs, and kittens of visual stimulation resulted in difficulty in all the subjects' later ability to function. R. Held and Joseph A. Bauer, Jr. found that infant monkeys deprived of practice in eye-hand coordination encountered difficulty with visually-directed reaching ("Visually-Guided Reaching in Infant Monkeys Following Restricted Rearing." *Science,* 1967 [*155*, 718–720]).

On the other hand, studies of enrichment of the environment of very young animals showed positive results (Forgays, D. G., and Read, J. M. "Crucial Periods for Free-environmental Experience in the Rat." *Journal of Comparative Physiology and Psychology,* 1962 [55, 816–818]). Krech, D., Rosenzweig, M. R., and Bennett, E. L. "Relations Between Brain Chemistry and Problem-Solving Among Rats Raised in Enriched and Impoverished Environments." *Journal of Comparative Physiology and Psychology,* 1962 [55, 801–807]). These and other researchers found that stimulating early experiences carried over to positive adult learning and behavior and to their offspring as well (Denenberg, V. H. A. "A Consideration of the Usefulness of the Critical Period Hypothesis as Applied to the Stimulation of Rodents in Infancy." In *Early Experience and Behavior,* Newton, G., and Levine, S., eds. Springfield, IL: Charles Thomas, 1968). They revealed, too, that there is a time factor involved; i.e., critical periods exist for humans and animals when neglect, isolation, or lack of stimulation—usually in the earliest periods (the first twenty-one to twenty-four days of rats, the first seven weeks of life of Scotch terriers, the first ten weeks of birds, and so on)—can adversely affect adult behavior.

Recent research strongly suggests that there are *critical* or *sensitive* periods during which certain important physical and psychological developments are advancing most rapidly. Disturbances during these periods may alter the process of these developments in important ways. For example, if chimpanzees are raised in darkness during the first year of life, certain cells in the retina will fail to

develop and vision will be permanently impaired.

Another rationale for early intervention (during the first three years) is provided by studies of children reared in deprived institutional or unstimulating home environments. Today there is proof that very early, properly timed intervention and encouragement are closely related to later academic achievement. (See Callaway, W. Ragan, Jr., Ph.D. "Modes of Biological Adaptation and Their Role in Intellectual Development." *Perceptual-Cognitive Development Monograph Series,* 1970 [Vol. 1, No. 1]).

Dr. Myrtle B. McGraw, one of the pioneer developmental child psychologists, has stressed the optimal periods for the physical growth of infants. Her experiments have included teaching a twelve-month-old to roller skate (at the time of greatest readiness when an infant stands on his tiptoes) and to climb a steep slide unaided. Dr. McGraw believes that "parents must learn to recognize a child's developmental signals and provide the kind of environment that will challenge the baby to develop a particular function at the most opportune time." (Article by Dr. Myrtle McGraw in *The Fourth Month of Life,* illustrated pamphlet issued by Princeton Center for Infancy, 1971.)

Changing Unacceptable Behavior by Modifying the Environment

Dr. Thomas Gordon, in his popular book, *P.E.T.* (Parent Effectiveness Training), bemoans the fact that "not enough parents change the behavior of their children by changing the children's surroundings." He believes that environmental modification is used more with infants than with toddlers and older children. Most parents use verbal methods to discourage unacceptable modes of behavior. This is unfortunate since environmental modification is often very simple and more effective with children of all ages.

An increasing number of parents are beginning to use his approach, which includes the following:

1. *Enriching the environment.* Some parents set up special areas in the garage or a corner of the backyard where the child is free to dig, paint, mess, and create. They enrich their child's environment by putting into it a playroom, an easel for painting, a puppet theater, a dollhouse, and so on. Equipping the playroom as a home version of the preschool makes sense because two-to-six-year-olds generally use the same materials (large building blocks, play people, puzzles, clay, rhythm instruments, and so forth).

2. *Simplifying the environment.* Often children produce "unacceptable behavior" because of the confusion and complexity of their environment. To avoid frustration, the breakage of toys, and so on, many parents simplify the environment by bringing it down to the child's size. They put closet hooks at a low level, use washable wall coverings on playroom walls, purchase child-sized homemaking play equipment (tea table and chairs, for example), and install easy-to-get-at low open shelves.

3. *Child-proofing the environment.* Parents remove expensive breakable items and dangerous chemicals; keep the basement door locked; pick up slippery rugs; repair frayed electric cords; build a handrail on the staircase; and so on.

4. *Preparing the child for changes in the environment.* Unacceptable behavior can be circumvented by preparing the child ahead of time for spending the family vacation at the beach, moving to another location, sleeping in a strange bed, going to the doctor for shots, proper behavior in a boat, and so on.

The more parents use environmental modification, the more enjoyable living with their children will be.

Parent Education

Child psychologists Burton White, Myrtle McGraw, and others would mount a national parent-child education campaign to consist of the following:

1. Exposing parents to major child development concepts in the Western world and their effects on child rearing.
2. Providing observational experience with one's own infant, using a development log to record progress and/or lags.
3. Conducting child-rearing workshops for high school and college students.

Dr. White suggests that the eighth to twenty-fourth months of life are a critical stage for the development of competence. He believes that if parents are to play a vital role in this fundamental stage, society will have to prepare and assist families to rear their children. He would make every family aware of the steps in language acquisition, which begins at eight months and culminates in the mastery of a basic vocabulary and common grammatical constructs by age three. He also would include the foundations of intelligence and the social attachment process in training for child rearing. Although complete information is not yet available and much more research needs to be done, there are enough new data to justify changing some current child-rearing practices.

As serious and difficult as the process of development is in the second twelve months of life, the remarkable achievements of children during this period are especially rewarding to parents. Older toddlers hold "real" conversations with family members and strangers. Their personalities are becoming more defined and individualistic. All the phases of growth and development, including the fantastic spurts in walking, running, and more precise bodily control make the second twelve months of life one of the most exciting, "magical " times of childhood.

THE THIRTEENTH MONTH
Beginning of the Second Year

Gross-Motor Development

"An infant's first birthday is a chronological milestone, but biologically the joyous occasion does not signify a major shift in physical development. The one-year-old is in the midstream of a real physical achievement—walking. While some year-olds are not about to risk a first step without holding onto a parent's hands, furniture, or a railing, others will try walking by themselves. Still others have not discarded creeping and crawling. They are just beginning to employ trial-and-error methods to learn to stand erect; they lean backward and forward until they are able to stand alone. Once the infant masters the standing position, he practices it ceaselessly. He also becomes adept at sitting unaided. Most thirteen-month-olds still prefer to creep on all fours and to cruise and climb over barriers to get at a toy or other desired object." Many infants near the end of their first year walk on their hands and soles rather than on their hands and knees. This, according to Dr. Gesell, is the "last of a score of stages which finally leads to the assumption of upright posture. When the feet become the fulcrum in this ' human balance machine,' the hands will soon be emancipated."

"Early standing, sitting, walking, or running do not necessarily indicate that a child will be precocious in other areas of development (language, learning, social development, and so on). Children who begin to walk early have a very unsteady gait and usually continue to crawl a while longer. Walking or crawling, the year-old is an avid explorer of her environment and very busy with her hands. She is on the move all day, engrossed in a variety of activities: emptying ash trays (onto rug or floor), pulling things down, unrolling toilet paper, emptying drawers, clearing cans off available pantry shelves. She is driven to find out all she can about everything she touches: how an object feels and tastes, what will happen when it is dropped on the floor, and so forth.

"As you watch a child navigate through the house, feeling and handling every toy and household article in sight, three things become obvious. First, he is constantly in motion; second, he is completely absorbed in what he is doing; and third, he is beginning to use tools (an available stick, for instance) to get at out-of-reach hidden or blocked toys. At first he is awkward when it comes to conquering barriers. A toy blocked by a pillow may cause him to kick his feet or shake his head—as if these might remove the barrier. Some year-olds are challenged by such a barrier; others fall apart from the frustration. Whichever reaction occurs, the child is now beginning to exhibit some awareness of his limitations.

"Many children this age become more con-

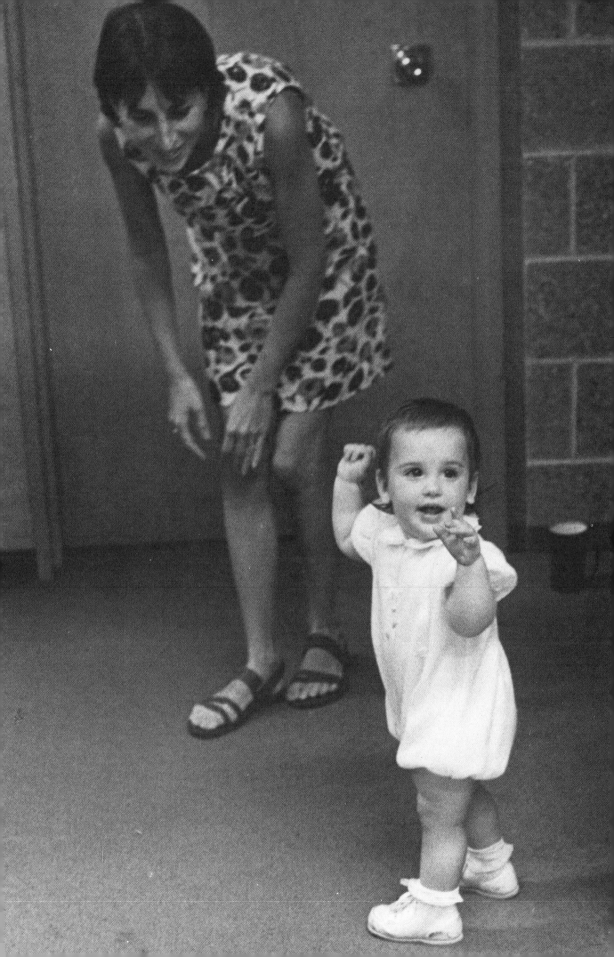

servative, relying on their parents for an awful lot of things. Learning to overcome obstacles will take several months of experience."

When your child's walking ability matures, she has a great inner urge to use it and practice it over and over again. Your toddler will walk, fall, walk, and fall—nothing will deter her. Trying to speed her up makes no sense. When her bones and muscles are ready, she will start to walk on her own accord.

Your intervention comes when you childproof the kitchen, living room, and bedroom—removing dangerous objects or protrusions, removing breakable antiques or valued objects, or training your toddler as to which objects are *no-no's* and which are safe to handle. This is the time to discuss with your doctor whether shoes will help correct his instep and to seek out toys and equipment that make walking fun—push toys, pull toys, a low, heavy-based carriage, and so on. This is the time when toys with noisemakers make a toddler feel "ten feet tall"; he feels he is making everyone take notice of him. Noisemaking appears to fuel the child's sense of power.

Fine-Motor Development

The thirteen-month-old is capable to a degree of fine-motor coordination in her daily activities; for example, she can grasp two cubes in one hand and build a tower of two cubes. She can remove small objects from a cup and put three or more cubes in a container. She likes to play with several small objects rather than with only one. She will pick them up one by one, drop them, and pick them up again one by one. According to Dr. Gesell, although this behavior appears to be disorderly on the surface, it probably is orderly as far as the child is concerned. In fact, it may even be a rudimentary kind of counting. Picking up and dropping is a way of practicing the newly acquired ability to release objects. Having learned how to grasp, the child now must learn how to let go.

The child appears to prefer one hand, but can hold small objects in both hands at one time. If you give the child a third object, he will look at both full hands, put one object in his mouth, and grasp the third one with his newly freed hand. He has a neat pincer grasp of pellets, using his thumb and index finger. He employs this skill in his eating and play activities. The child can pick up small bits of food and chew and swallow them with much less spilling than a month ago.

Language Acquisition

Children of this age group constantly learn a great deal. Imitation of adults and older siblings and playing games are some of the ways that body control is mastered. For the child who is beginning to walk, chasing after a large beachball lets him forget his balancing problems as he toddles to retrieve it and bring it back to a parent. Labeling the process with such words as *Catch the ball, Bring the ball back,* and so on are informal but important lessons in language acquisition. Using a favorite doll, a parent can point to the doll's eyes, ears, nose, and mouth and name them one by one. This will start a game of imitation and the process will be repeated by the child with or without naming.

Children observe sharply everything that their parents do and seek to copy what they see; for example, help weed the garden. Enthusiasm can lead to trouble when the child "weeds" favorite flowers. Intervening by teaching the child to *make nice* to the flower nearly always redirects the child's attention and corrects any misunderstanding.

By about the age of thirteen months, most children have no trouble making themselves understood without the use of words. Dr. Dodson points out that there are two phases of language learning: "passive language" (understanding) and "active language" (talking). Between a child's first and second birthdays, the passive phase predominates; between the second and third birthdays, the active phase becomes prominent.

Nonverbal Communication

"At the beginning of the passive phase, nonverbal techniques prevail. These take the form of gestures and sounds; scowling, kicking, flailing the arms when angry; bouncing, laughing, tumbling when happy. When feeling coy, the child may tilt his head to the side or drop his chin onto his chest; he will tug to indicate that he wants something or push away what he does not want. The thirteen-month-old understands commands and words best when they are accompanied by gestures and actions."

Language learning—at first the acquisition of words—is important to parents, but it does not seem important to the thirteen-month-old. As long as there is a parent around who understands her gestures and sounds, she sees no need to master words. However, in the latter part of the second year of life, when the child's walking ability has matured, making herself understood with strangers will require the active language of spoken words. Some children use intonation combined with gibberish, as well as pointing and gestures, all of which make it well nigh impossible to communicate with anyone outside their immediate family.

"Imitation is an important phase of language learning. The thirteen-month-old is adept at imitating intonations. His 'conversation' sounds are completely authentic except that the words are not recognizable. When the parent asks a question, the child responds with a babbled question. The child uses his sensitivity for intonation to interpret the meaning of adult language. Moods are picked up quickly. Even such prohibition words as *no!* or *stop!* are given feeling by different intonations. A matter-of-fact *no* does not produce the same reaction as a frantic *no!* and neither of these are the same as an angry *no!* A child may respond to a *no!* that warns of danger, but may challenge or ignore *no* in other circumstances.

"Many children toward the end of their first twelve months of life and the beginning of their second year make the sounds *dada, mama, bye-bye, car, cookie, bow-wow*. The child's language as he first uses it is very different from the adult's. It not only *sounds* different, it is *used* differently. Usually two types of language develop at the same time. One kind is imitation. If the parent says *tick-tock* when looking at a watch, the child will repeat *tick-tock* as he looks at the watch. However, the child also has a very special familiar language; for instance, *mama, dada, car* to cover a wide range of meanings. *Mama* often connotes a whole class of wishes for food, for toys, or to be taken out, as well as the wish for the parent to come. It is interesting to note that while the imitative words may come and then be forgotten, those that have real meaning for the child are apt to stay with him.

"This limited vocabulary may stay for weeks or months. The child's language will not expand until she has the concepts and a larger vocabulary to construct an organized and coherent view of the world around her. Language in this sense develops between the ages of fourteen and eighteen months, often quite a bit later."

Word Labeling

The thirteenth month is an important time for using words to label actions and objects for your child. Every time he handles an object or undertakes an action the parent needs to label it: *ball, smooth, it will fall, pick it up, bring it to me,* and so forth. Your child's vocabulary will grow and grow, and grammar, a most amazing accomplishment without any special training, will mature. Parents sometimes underestimate how much a child can understand when he does not talk. He is fully able to understand language long before he uses it, and shows in actions rather than words that he knows what his parents are saying. Nonverbal thirteen-month-olds understand their parents' simple questions or commands; for example, such prohibition words as *no!, yuk, dirty, messy.* Most understand and respond to "Give it to Mommy," "Do you want a drink?" "Are you hungry?" or even "Where's your tooth?"

You will find it a waste of time to try to teach your child grammar and other language constructs. What you can do is surround your child with an "envelope" of language that is properly and slowly enunciated. In talking with your child, keep these recommendations in mind: Use clear, simple speech; avoid "baby talk." Prepare your child for any future activity or trip by talking about what you are going to do beforehand, while you are doing it, and after it is all over. Make your child feel that she is part of what is going on and not merely an observer. Talk with your child and give her a chance to add her "two cents' worth." Give your child the feeling that what she says is important. Do not expect or demand perfection.

Listening

Listening is a skill that can help your child become sensitive to language. Call your child's attention to sounds all around him: the noises of engines running, trucks braking, leaves rustling, birds singing, the wind howling, doors closing, water running, teakettle whistling, clock ticking, and so on.

Let your child listen to people talking on the telephone and let her say a few words back.

Let your child play "follow the leader." Children in the family line up and the leader gives directions, such as "Pat your head," "Go behind the chair," and so forth.

Expose your child to children's records that offer sound differences and encourage imitation. An excellent recording is Woody Guthrie's *Songs to Grow On,* Vol. I. ("Put Your Finger in the Air," etc.)—Folkways.

This is the opportune time to teach your child that everything in his environment has a name and that he can learn what that name is. Knowing the names of objects gives the child a new kind of power over his world and enables him to manipulate the names of objects in his mind without having to handle the actual objects physically. This permits him to order the world, to play with it symbolically.

The Learning Capacity of the Brain

Pediatricians have long recognized that infants should not be closeted in drab, visually unstimulating nurseries. Research work with cats (try to read Roger Lewin's article in the October 5, 1974, issue of *Saturday Review/ World* entitled "Observing the Brain Through a Cat's Eyes") now gives that intuitive realization some scientific backing. But can we go further than this? Will a child become a musical genius if he is bombarded with Beethoven, Bach, and Berlioz from the day he is born? Will talking to a child in a variety of languages enhance his linguistic talent? Will a child become an outstanding mathematician if the parents teach him the elements of logic at a tender age? The answer to all of these probably is "up to a point."

Almost certainly, the learning capacity of the human brain has not been exploited to the full by current educational approaches. The essential point is the possible existence of sensitive periods not just for visual development, but for music, language, artistic talents, and logic. For instance, every normal child acquires the elements of her language between the ages of two and four. So why wait another six years before teaching her a second or third language? The brain clearly is

attuned to language acquisition in the early years and there is much evidence about the ease with which children pick up a foreign language to which they are exposed. It probably would be a mistake to try to teach children two languages at once when they are only two years old because there would be retroactive interference between the languages. However, a child of four could start on a new language.

Often musical talent runs in families. It may, of course, be "in the genes," but there undoubtedly is a large environmental element involved, too. Children exposed to a lot of music when young are almost always more talented musically than the average, but how much this development is due to encouragement and opportunity is difficult to tell. Evidence indicates that the "musical brain" does become keyed into its early experiences. This finding comes from the observation that people who develop perfect pitch while exposed to a slightly out of tune instrument always match their pitch to the instrument's. Although playing Beethoven to one's infant probably will not cause an environmentally-generated reincarnation of the great master, it may well produce a more than usually musically talented child.

Probably the most important skill that a child can learn is learning *how* to learn. A mark of intelligence is the faculty for solving problems. Too often adults give children answers to remember rather than problems to solve. This is a grave mistake. Unless children develop the art of problem solving, whether by analytical logic or by nonsequential intuition, their brains will remain underdeveloped. Everyone knows that infants go through a period of being intensely curious. This curiosity probably is a behavioral expression of the brain's most sensitive period for acquiring knowledge and learning techniques.

Researchers now are turning their efforts to discovering more about specific sensitive periods in the development of the brain, whether it be for language acquisition, enhancing musical talent, or simply learning how to learn. Unless these periods are exploited to the full at the right time, a child's potential may be forever lost.

Infant Intellect

Imitating people and reaching for things are more related than they seem. Both are major ways by which a baby adds to his "intellectual bag of tricks," says Dr. Roger A. Webb, former director of Harvard's Center for Cognitive Studies and now professor at the University of Arkansas in Little Rock.

Besides the more routine problems of research, such as the degree of reliability among observers judging the behavior of subjects, infant researchers must cope with subjects who sometimes break into tears or fall asleep during experiments. There also are difficulties associated with specific experimental methods. Dr. Webb himself, frustrated by his inability to interpret the behavior of the youngest infants, took the tack of using physical measures of infant response. He learned polygraphing, which yields penned-out records of such things as muscular tension, skin moisture, breathing, and heartbeat rate. Formidable titles of scientific publications, including "Cardiac Deceleration and Reaction Time," indicate Dr. Webb's earlier interest in the heart rate as an index of attention and learning. He soon discovered, however, that physical measures, despite having been a major breakthrough in the technology of the growth sciences, were "no pipeline to the soul."

For one thing, they require restraints, such as a gently placed band around the chest or lightly taped electrodes on arms and legs. Physically restrained infants are not always the most cooperative. There also is another, more serious problem. The researcher must find a more or less neutral period of behavior against which to measure changes caused by the experiment. Without this, it is impossible to tell which of any number of things is producing the behavior in which the researcher is interested. "You can't tell an infant to just sit there and not do anything," says Dr. Webb. In fact, some of his earliest work on depth perception through heart-rate recording featured many crying children just because he gave the baby nothing to look at.

The other set of Dr. Webb's studies at the Harvard Center for Cognitive Studies focused on imitation: how children learn from watching others. For this work, Mrs. Barbara Massar (a former actress studying at Harvard for her Ph.D. in education) designed a "supertoy" of wood and Plexiglas three feet tall and four and a half feet long. "The play frame," as it came to be called, "is actually a lousy toy," said Dr. Webb, "because it restrains creativity just like many toys sold today to be educational."

Twenty children aged fourteen to twenty-four months were asked to do four tasks. First, they were allowed to explore the play frame. After the child seemed comfortable, the experimenter called for his attention, blew on a marble, and dropped it through an S-shaped transparent tube of clear plastic. The marble was held between thumb and forefinger with the other fingers extended in a very exaggerated manner. As the marble emerged from the tube, the experimenter caught it with one hand, repeated the entire procedure, and then handed the marble to the child. The child's second task, putting a plastic triangle through a triangular slot, required correct orientation of the plastic shape. In the third task, a trapdoor covered a square hole into which the child had to drop a plastic square after he had beaten open the door with a tool. The fourth task was by far the most complex. The child had to reach in with a hook and pull a plug from a cylinder. After he had pulled the plug out, he had to drop it into a larger surrounding cylinder. He was "rewarded" when magnetically triggered lights along its inner surface lit up.

Obviously, the researchers were requiring much more from the children than mere imitation. The tasks demanded memory of object and place, spatial location, and sequencing behavior to solve a problem. Although they also demanded considerable manipulative skill, only the youngest encountered difficulty. The fourteen-month-olds, for example, lacked the coordination needed to catch the marble in the first task.

Despite these complications, even the younger toddlers, quite unsuccessful in completing their second through fourth assignments, had a marvelous time. For example, they thoroughly enjoyed beating the trapdoor to get it open and were completely unabashed by their occasional failure, i.e., picking up the square and forgetting the tool or forgetting all about the square. It was difficult at times for mothers to drag their children away from the experimenters. The delight was mutual. Dr. Webb and his team outdid themselves in designing colorful and imaginative equipment and ingenious tasks. Besides enjoyment, the researchers gained information. Dr. Webb easily found out what he wanted to know. All the children could imitate, for all of them tended toward the same solutions. Any mother who has had a thirteen-month-old studiously wipe a counter as she had or try stirring with a spoon in a mixing bowl might have told Dr. Webb that.

Imitation, an Early Learning Tool

Imitation, while it may be a very important kind of early learning, appears to be either a form of trial and error or a kind of play. ("Play," comments Dr. Webb, "is obviously important but we just don't know how to look at it yet.") The youngest toddlers, who had trouble with even the simplest task, often imitated some feature of the experimenter's demonstration, but not in the context of solving the problem. For example, a fourteen-month-old would blow on the marble, then hand it back to Mrs. Massar. The child seemed to be selecting a fragment of behavior from a sequence he did not fully understand.

Older children imitated some feature of the demonstration, but only after they had *solved* the problem; i.e., they would drop the marble through the tube and catch it, then hold it as the experimenter had or blow on it afterward, almost as if they were doing it for fun or "saying" to the experimenter that they could do something if they wanted to, even though they considered it pretty unnecessary. Dr. Webb felt that most of the children realized that matching of exact behavior did not pay off in this situation, so subsequent experiments will focus more on the child's ability to discern when imitation is and is not useful.

Research with imitation soon opened a line of investigation to "object permanence." Dr. Jean Piaget was the first to identify and describe the growth of this mental ability in the human infant. He postulated that for infants an object out of sight ceases to exist. It has no permanence. Each appearance or representation of it is a separate event. There is a brown-stuffed-bear-on-the-couch, a brown-stuffed-bear-in-the-crib, a brown-stuffed-bear-in-mommy's-hand instead of just one bear in different places at different times. In detailed observations of his own babies (Laurent, Jacqueline, and Lucienne), Dr. Piaget described how the infant completely loses interest in an object when it is hidden, despite engrossed play with it seconds before. He ascribed this "fickleness" to the child's belief that objects exist solely because of his actions upon them.

To understand that her ball or her doll exist independently of her, the child needs to be able to remember them. All children have memory of some type. The newborn probably remembers only what has gone on immediately before and can only respond to "change." For example, a new smell arouses behavior when the child has stopped responding to a familiar odor. The two-month-old "remembers" fairly complex events enough to become bored with frequent repetitions of them. Somewhat later the baby can imitate a behavior in the direct line of sight; i.e., she moves her hand in front of her face when another person does so. At about ten months, she can recall the location of an object if it is hidden immediately before she has to look for it. Usually, by the middle of her second year, the child has true representational memory: she can reconstruct an event sometime after she has seen it. According to Dr. Piaget, this ability is also a must for imitation of a behavior that is over and done with.

All of Dr. Webb's experiments say something important about infant intellect and relate to one another. Mental life begins from behavioral patterns with which a baby is born and from patterns that emerge early in the course of growth. Through practice in the first years of life, these early patterns become voluntary and differentiated. Through experience, they become internalized into the first patterns of thought.

Studies of infant grasping illustrate the very early *continuous* tie-in of motor and visual systems. Practice of these basic skills of reaching and grasping is under the guidance of the visual system right from the start. This ability to learn through watching is later applied to acquiring truly new skills. Imitation, an ability also included in a baby's basic equipment, means incorporating new activities by watching other human beings. This

ability, as with the realization that objects can be stable and independent of the child even if they are hidden, depends in turn upon representational memory, an intellectual and very special human skill. With sufficient experience, children learn that they can record sights, sounds, and objects in their mind and keep them there even though they may be out of sight, hand, or earshot.

How Infants Learn

"Play with your baby whenever you want to" is obviously an inadequate guideline for most parents today. They need to know *how*. Play with a parent is vital. All the games babies play help them learn the essentials of getting about in this world in a fun way.

The ten-month-old who plumps a block into a jar is delving into the notions of contained and container, empty and full, in and out. The thirteen-month-old who cruises to the stove and pokes it tentatively is ready to learn about hot and cold. The child who stretches his arms to the level of his head when his parent asks, "How big is _____?" is approaching the area of spatial relationships.

We have begun only recently to learn from psychologists, pediatricians, educators, and their colleagues that stimulation from the environment influences a child's development greatly. Babies whose parents play with, handle, imitate, smile, and talk to them, who provide things for them to look at, listen to, and explore with their mouths and hands, are advanced in their attentiveness, visual pursuit, and coordinated movements. Such children tend to carry their early advantage into later life.

A baby who during her first twelve months (and thereafter) lives in an environment charged with frequent, exuberant expressions of the good feelings of caring, laughter, and encouragement, as well as lots of face-to-face socializing with loved ones, is going to have far more than the average share of social initiative and get-up-and-go.

The Games Parents and Children Play

Parent-and-child games are a wonderful means to mutual fun, excitement, encouragement, and learning. Peek-a-boo may be a first token of humor. The baby plays a trick on someone; he had decided beforehand that he intended to play one. The game indicates that the baby is intrigued with human faces and the discrepancies offered by their partial concealment. Later on the game means that the child has a memory of someone he loves and that person's image is fixed enough in his mind and secure enough in his feelings for him to try a short separation under his control. He has a sense of his parent's permanence, as well as that of objects, and even anticipates the joy of recalling her or him.

At about the crawling stage, the infant will assay separations in other ways. The come-and-get-me game requires a pursuing parent and a scrambling, frantically pushing baby. The game should not be curtailed too quickly unless the parent desires a fussing, furious baby. Several runs before abducting him to something as run-of-the-mill as a meal or diaper change will promote a more resigned capitulation.

At about the same age, a child may begin to look over the edge of her highchair at objects that she has dropped to the floor. This is the pick-up-the-things-I-drop game. A variant during feeding times is dropping her spoon and cup overboard as she avoids the spoonful of food you proffer. When all dropable items are gone, the child probably will cry for mother, father, or a brother or sister to retrieve them.

Some tactile games emphasize toes and fingers. Often they are completed by a sensational tickling finish. In "This Little Piggy Went to Market," a parent takes each toe and recites what it does:

This little piggy went to market,
This little piggy stayed home,
This little piggy had bread for his (or her) supper,
And this little piggy had none
And this little piggy cried "wee, wee, wee,"
All the way home.

At "wee, wee, wee," the mother or father tickles the child.

In China, the baby's toes are cows:

This little cow eats grass,
This little cow eats hay,
This little cow drinks water,
This little cow runs away,
This little cow does nothing,
But lie down all day.

"The Beehive" rhyme highlights fingers:

Here is the beehive.
Where are the bees? (Hold hand in a fist)
Hidden away where nobody sees.
Soon they come creeping out of the hive, (Relax fist)
One, two, three, four, five! (Extend thumb, index, second, ring, and small fingers)

Months later, when the child grows more aware of his body parts and his distinctness from other people, he can appreciate the separateness of his toes and fingers. In a few more months, the child will grow aware of yet another facet of these games: the counting and stringing together of similar items in a series, a basic in numerical reasoning.

At about her tenth to fourteenth month, the child spontaneously imitates the behaviors of her parents. She tries to feed a parent pieces of food in the same manner as she has been fed. If the parent accepts the tidbits, the child is thrilled; she laughs gleefully if the parent smacks her or his lips appreciatively. The child watches the chewing and swallowing process intently. Besides enjoying herself, the child is learning something about the way people take food into their mouths, chew, and swallow.

In imitation of your washing him, your child may dab at his face with a washcloth and laugh if you imitate his posture and movements. When you take him from the tub and say *brr* and shiver as you dry him, your child will laugh and try to imitate you. As he imitates, he learns some things about cold—the feeling of being chilled and the way people react to it physically and vocally.

Your imitation of your child's movements is most important for her physical abilities, mental skills, and social behaviors. Watching you imitate her adds a consciousness of her own movements. A mirror hypnotizes her for the same reason. She laughs at the smiling image, pats and tries to kiss it. She presses her forehead to the mirror to see if perhaps the image is real or she tries to reach for it. She sights the image of her hand and compares it with the real thing, staring at its changing shapes. The portrayal of her own body movements enhances the kind of perception (called visuo-motor) that your child needs in learning physical skills.

Imitation is a real teaching tool if it is used subtly instead of pushed. Try it to teach your child to manipulate and drink from his cup. Give him a cup while you use one. Then give him some milk to experiment with. Let him play with it in the bathtub where he cannot create a mess, even though he may sample the bath water, too. If you make using a cup a game, your child will learn more easily how to use it.

A Game for Every Skill

As you have probably guessed by now, games that mothers and fathers and children play foster different kinds of skills. They can strengthen muscles, stretch attention spans, prompt vocalizing, and promote self-awareness. You can use physical games to motivate a quiet child or relax an active one. Above all, these games are great fun.

Accompanying words with actions and singing songs and nursery rhymes can help make speech interesting and pleasant, introduce your child to music, and teach her basic mental concepts at the same time. *All-gone,* which some parents sing out and accompany with a dusting off of each hand, signals the disappearance of an object that may have vanished quite naturally (food) or by design (a hidden toy). *Up-and-off,* as the child is being undressed, highlights the ideas of direction and the removal of objects from another object, in this case from the child herself.

After he has learned a new gesture or word, your child may spend days rehearsing it and offering it to every question of yours. It becomes a companion of play, a sound to fill in silence, or a ploy to draw your attention away from elsewhere. It lasts as a focal point in time as long as you react. When he senses you are growing bored, the child discards the mangled word and moves on to a new one. By imitating your gestures and words, he may learn to *look sad,* to *snuggle and kiss,* and to say *bye-bye*, waving as you leave the room or house and clapping and giggling when you return.

Naming games involving the child's nose, toes, feet, hands, eyes, and mouth emphasize body parts and self-concepts. Your cue for such games comes from the child herself. As part of exploring and comparing herself to her world and the people in it, the child will poke at her facial features—yours, too—and may even compare the feel of your features with her own. If you suck her exploring finger, she may try sucking it again herself, then offer it to you for an encore.

Action of a favorite nursery rhyme contrasts the size of the child's and the parent's hands while showing their similarity in shape. The parent takes the child's hands and claps them together. Then the child may clap his hands against the parent's:

Pat-a-cake, pat-a-cake bakerman,
Bake me a cake as fast as you can.
Roll it and pat it and mark it with a "B"
And put it in the oven for baby and me.

In fact, parent-child clapping games the world over show that people recognize a basic feature of human education: the awareness of a physical self. The Egyptian variety features a doting father:

Clap, clap, now clap your hands,
Hands like a little doll's
For she (or he) who claps her (his) hands
Father will bring
A roll of finest silk
To make a pretty gown (or robe).

The father also plays such a part in the lovely American lullaby:

Hush, little baby,
Don't say a word.
Papa's going to buy you
A mockingbird
And if that mockingbird don't sing,
Papa's going to buy you a golden ring.

If you ask your child to point to your eyes, nose, or mouth, she may show that she understands your request by looking at the right feature, but turning away chagrined. Do not be too disappointed at the refusal; her initial behavior may mean that she recognizes how different you are from her and her doll. In time she will learn the similarities. While playing this game, the Chinese say:

Little eyes see pretty things
Little nose smells something good
Little ears hear someone sing
Little mouth tastes luscious food.

The interest of the child who is old enough to have a total self-concept will extend to body parts and the construction of animals as well. Point at and label a picture of a cow (then substitute other animals and pertinent descriptions):

> There's a cow on the mountain
> The old saying goes
> At the end of her legs
> Are four feet and eight toes
> Her tail hangs behind
> At the end of her back
> And her head sticks out front
> At the end of her neck.

Ring Around a Rosy is another game that has a surprise element in it and connects large muscle use with hearing. When your child can walk securely, join hands, and walk in a circle singing:

> Ring around a rosy,
> A pocket full of posies,
> Ashes, ashes,
> We all fall down!

(When both parents and older siblings join in the activity, it is even more fun.) Gently press down on your child's hand and plop to the floor as you sing "we all fall down" until you see your child collapse of his own accord. When you are sure that he has associated the signal "we all fall down" with falling, vary the rhythm of the rhyme so that he has to listen to the expected signal at unexpected places in the song.

In your interaction games with your child, bear in mind that all children are natural-born players. All children at play are learning and working very hard.

When you are so maddeningly busy with dressing, feeding, diapering, bathing, and safeguarding, you may wonder how you can be expected to try all these games, too. You are right! You cannot possibly do them all. Just pick a few at each stage of your child's growth—the games that appeal to your child and you most.

Emptying Containers

"The thirteen-month-old's favorite activity is centered around handling and emptying baskets, plastic containers, trash cans, refrigerators, clothes out of the dryer, dishes from the dishwasher, and so forth. If not restrained, she will try to climb on top of the dryer or dishwasher. Whenever she hears the refrigerator door open, she will run to the kitchen and try to get a few items from the inside. All toddlers like to get into pots and pans cupboards, which some mothers discourage because of the noise and confusion. There seems to be a general pattern in children this age of emptying things that no one else wants emptied. Some parents recognize this activity, as inconvenient as it may be, as a necessary stage in the child's development. Other parents become frantic and create negative encounters with their child.

"As the child goes about his active explorations, it is inevitable that he engages in some activities that are stopped by a *No!* For example, tormenting an older sibling who is trying to put together a complicated jigsaw puzzle, playing with an electric cord or outlet, tearing pages out of a book, playing with the water in the toilet bowl, trying to climb upstairs unattended, yelling loudly, and so on. The meaning the toddler gives to the command *No!* can have considerable significance for his relationship with his parents. If he hears *No!* too often, he may interpret it to mean *Don't try!* or *Don't find out!*

"The delicate balance between learning through exploration and disciplining a child makes this beginning of the second year of life a nightmare for many parents. The curiosity that triggers the desire to explore and experiment makes the toddler a fun companion, but one who requires constant watching. Even alert parents are not prepared for the whirlwind shifts of interest and movement of the energetic thirteen-month-old."

Social Development

Soon after the first birthday, especially when he is "creeping on all fours" (hands and feet) or mastering walking, the child begins to reach out for active social contact. Chasing and hiding games are the thirteen-month-old's idea of a good time. He hides behind a

favorite chair and gets some adult into an endless game of "Where's baby?" He delights in throwing things on the floor from his crib or high chair or out of his playpen and waits for them to be retrieved by whomever is on hand. He also will give back objects that are offered to him, a kind of social game.

"The thirteen-month-old relishes noisy, active tokens of affection: being nuzzled, hugged tightly, thrown up into the air and caught securely, and so on. Imitation is the child's natural way to learn social ways. She will imitate coughing, nose blowing, "talking" on the telephone—anything to win attention, especially the ready smile of approval from her parents. She may throw a kiss as she waves *bye-bye* to her father leaving for work or as an adored older sibling goes off to school.

"During this period, toddlers have a way of getting adults to help them get at things or to do things for them. The child begins to consider parents a resource who can help him achieve his objectives; i.e., give him a piggyback ride, get a picture book down from a high shelf and 'read' it to him, push the swing in the playground, and so forth. He is starting to have a *very vague* notion of his powers and his limitations."

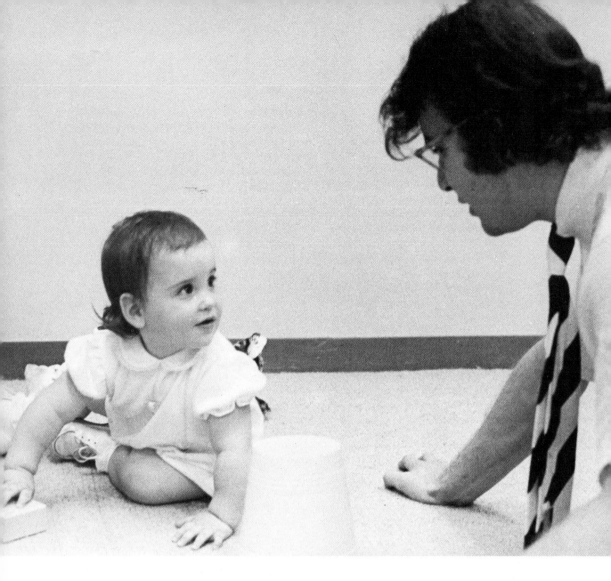

Stranger Anxiety

Reacting to unknown people with fear is a common response among thirteen-month-olds who have been raised with a mother, father, and siblings in the "nuclear" family. Actually it is a sign of growth because the child now can distinguish between whom he knows and whom he does not know. He is learning to establish a meaningful relationship with those who care for him.

The traditional psychoanalytical viewpoint emphasizes the fear of separation from or loss of the "love object" as the major determinant of stranger anxiety. Fear reactions usually take the form of whimpering, crying, a screwed-up face, looking or turning away, drawing back, lip trembling, running or crawling away, and hiding the face.

Research has shown (Schaffer and Emerson, 1964) that the mean age of the onset of fear of strangers is eight months.

"The thirteen-month-old is apprehensive toward strangers, but intrigued by them at the same time. In the beginning of social contact with a new person, the toddler seems to need to stay close to either parent (or other caretaker). The child uses her mother or father as home base to which she can return. Before she is able to accept a stranger, the child goes through a ritual of being close to the parent by sitting on the latter's lap or clinging to a leg and intently studying the visitor. As the child becomes more at ease, the distance between child and parent increases, but frequent return trips to the security of 'home base' will continue. Once the thirteen-month-old is certain that the parent is not going to leave and that the stranger will not harm her, the visitor may try to make friends at the pace set by the child. Usually the child should make the first move. She may hand something to the visitor (a small toy the child was holding, for example) and take it right back. Subsequently the child may bring everything movable and pile it all on the stranger's lap. However, no matter how involved the child may become with the visitor, part of her attention is always riveted to the parent. Despite eventual acceptance of the stranger, the disappearance of the parent from the room can have disastrous consequences."

Most pediatricians believe that some babies accept strangers in a casual way up to the end of the first year of life, but that then everything changes. Thirteen months appears to be the most suspicious age of all. At the doctor's office, for instance, the child may scramble to his feet when the doctor approaches and try to climb off the examining table and onto his mother. He may cry furiously. Even so, every once in a while the child will peer at the doctor with baleful looks. He will stop crying when the exam is over and then even permit the doctor to make friends with him.

Many adults do not have the good sense to leave a thirteen-month-old alone when he is sizing them up. They rush up to the child full of talk and movement and force the child to retreat to his parent for protection. Then it takes longer for the toddler to work up his courage to be friendly. Parents might tell visitors in the beginning that it makes their child bashful when attention is paid to him at once; that it would be better if the adults talked together for a while because then the child would have time to become more at ease and, therefore, more receptive to the adults' overtures of friendliness.

When your thirteen-month-old is walking, give her plenty of chances to be exposed and so get used to strangers. Take her to the shopping center when you market. Take her to the playground. Although she is not yet ready to play with her agemates, she will enjoy watching the other children. If she gets used to playing near other children, as she grows more mature, she will be ready for cooperative play.

Fear of Strangers Can Make Babysitting a Problem

"Some parents do not go out when their child is awake. Other parents take their child along when they go out. Still other parents leave their child with a relative. Marilyn M. Segal, Ph.D., director of the Institute of Child-Centered Education at Nova University in Fort Lauderdale, Florida, suggests a few ways to solve the babysitting problem: Although it is sensible to familiarize the child with a babysitter over an extended period of time, even with a familiar person the child may cry when the parents first leave. When parents wave goodbye in a casual way and the babysitter engages the child in a favorite activity, usually the crying spells are short-lived. Given the choice of playing or crying when their parents are away, most children choose the option of playing. A well-meaning babysitter who hugs a frightened, screaming child may be increasing his anxiety because he may interpret this holding as restraint rather than comfort."

Relations with Other Children

The thirteen-month-old is completely egotistic. He has not established his self-identity firmly enough to be able to consider others. Watch a few creepers or beginning toddlers playing in the same play area. They notice each other—you can be sure of that—but the toy the other child has always looks better. A child is liable to throw his own toy down and grab for another child's plaything. Actually it is more than the toy that interests him. He obviously enjoys the presence of other children.

A thirteen-month-old may greet an agemate with a smile, accept a proffered toy, and then give his friend a hug that knocks him down and causes him to cry. He looks at the crying child, but seems unconcerned when his parent tells him that he hugged too roughly. Although he may go over and embrace the crying child, in another moment he is just as likely to be biting him or bopping him over the head with another toy. The thirteen-month-old regards another child as an object rather than as a person with feelings and desires much as his own. From your appropriate handling of each situation, and with experience, your child will learn acceptable social behavior.

"The thirteen-month-old plays better with her older sibling or siblings. The toddler will follow

a sibling and join in any game that the older child starts. Although siblings usually fight over toys, the thirteen-month-old is easily distracted by the parent's giving her something else to play with. Most thirteen-month-olds are not especially possessive about their toys. However, they usually want to play with their sister's or brother's favorite toys, which invariably leads to conflict.

"The child of thirteen months is very determined. If he has older siblings, he will use them as models of behavior and try to do everything they do. This often leads to serious predicaments; for example, climbing too high on a playground slide and 'freezing' at the top, sliding down a five-foot slide and not knowing how to stop at the bottom, and so on.

"All parents claim that older siblings are extremely rough with meddling toddlers and many parents are driven to distraction by the frantic, seemingly inevitable back-and-forth shrieking. However, older siblings can be helpful in 'supervising' the younger child for short periods, enforcing rules the parents have set for the toddler.

"Thirteen-month-olds do have tempers. They show their aggression mainly by yelling or crying. Usually they do not hit grown-ups, but they will hit objects or other small children who frustrate them."

Contact with Animals

The toddler's social interest extends to animals also. She considers everything that moves of its own accord to be vaguely human. If the child has not been frightened or made anxious by the people around her, she will handle and respond to small animals with enthusiasm and to large ones with some caution. Small puppies brought up at the same time as infants make good companions (with little supervision) for a toddler. Cats, however, are usually too unpredictable with their claws. Although an older cat may take the punishment a young child gives (mauling, tail pulling, and so forth), eventually it will stalk off when it has enough.

Sometimes a thirteen-month-old may have to be protected from the enthusiasm of a young dog. Puppies especially will treat babies as another pup and will paw at them to restrain them if they should try to creep away. To offset the dog's behavior, the undaunted child will push the dog out of her way. (More often it is the child who requires parental supervision because she treats the dog as if it were placed there for her amusement. She pokes its eyes, yanks at its coat, pulls the dog's tail, or tries to use it for locomotion.) Dogs that have not been mistreated take special delight in babies and both come to terms early. An adult needs to be on hand at the first meeting of child and dog to prevent one from overwhelming the other. The child who becomes acquainted with a dog early is less likely to fear dogs and other animals later on.

Freedom of Movement

"A common characteristic of thirteen-month-olds is a genuine dislike of being re-strained. Freedom of movement is very impor-tant to them. When a parent wants to keep a child away from an appealing but forbidden object, it is necessary to distract him with another object. Holding the child only makes matters worse. The child will stiffen his legs, arch his back, and succeed in wriggling free."

The thirteenth month is a critical period for self-assertion. Walking has given the child a taste of "being on her own." She is no longer willing to play the role of the helpless baby or to let you be the boss all the time. She tries to tell you by her actions (refusing or pushing food away, for instance) that she wants you to respect her and her ideas.

All kinds of erratic behaviors begin to reveal themselves at this time: screaming at the top of the voice, playing with the water in the toilet bowl, trying to climb out of the crib, biting, and pulling down a tablecloth with your best china may be considered antics that test all parents' patience and skill. In reality, they are serious undertakings by the child who is trying out his own "wings," beginning to explore his envi-ronment more thoroughly, and trying to assert his power over himself—and other people and things. Power does not mean being destruc-tive or turning into a bully; rather, it means learning to become a competent, independent individual. Stephen Lehane, in his book *Help Your Baby Learn,* points out that during the second twelve months of life, beginning with the thirteenth month, it is well to remember that the things the child needs to do in order to develop and thrive are the very things that drive parents mad.

Personality/Psychological Development

Despite the process of separation that takes place throughout the second year, the thirteen-month-old likes a lot of mother or father contact. If the parent spends too much time at the sink, the child will wedge himself between parent and cupboard or tug on the mother's apron to get her to stop working. Most toddlers seem to like to play face-naming games with mother: patting the mother's mouth or cheek, pulling her nose or the skin of her neck, or putting fingers in her mouth. While most parents feel that these activities are acts of endearment, many psychologists believe them to be part of the separation process that goes on during the second year.

Most people believe that self-concept, ego, and confidence are traits one is born with. No-thing could be further from the truth. At birth, the notion of the self does not exist. It devel-ops with experience and maturation. The child who lacks confidence and self-esteem spends so much energy fighting anxieties within that he has little if any left over for learn-ing tasks.

If during the early weeks of life a healthy concept of self is laid down, if interaction be-tween mother and baby gives bodily satisfac-tion, the infant is off to a good start in the long, difficult zigzags between dependence and independence. During the first year, the infant experiences the world through his senses and reacts to it by moving his body and adapting to the environment. This early self might be called the sensori-motor (or bodily) self. How-ever, self-confidence in itself will not guaran-tee a competent, happy personality. An im-portant aspect of self-esteem is learning to express and control one's emotions and to adjust to the feelings of others. It means being able to give and receive affection.

Dr. Gesell calls this the *I, me, myself stage.* The child is straining at the bit; the playpen has become passé. He wants to tackle the whole world. To the untutored outsider, the thirteen-month-old may appear to be a mis-chievous child, but adept parents will recog-nize that this tumultuous period is a neces-sary part of the child's emotional and intellec-tual growth and will change or baby-proof the environment rather than the child.

Fear and Anxiety

Between one and two years of age, children begin to exhibit fear and/or anxiety over a number of objects and situations. As the child's imaginative capabilities increase, so does his awareness of potentially frightening situations. As he becomes an increasingly competent walker, he finds himself in situations not encountered before. Loud noises, the bath, nighttime, strangers, and big animals are some of the common fears at this age. It is helpful to understand what causes these fears and what parents can do to help the child overcome them.

Loud Noises. A child may be frightened by such sounds as the roar of the vacuum cleaner, the rush of water down the toilet or bathtub, train whistles, sirens, or even a plane overhead. If she is curious about the object making the noise, let her touch it or play with it if it is feasible or safe. Do not force the object upon her if she wants no part of it.

The Bath. Fear of the bath also is common at this age. It may stem from the child's having gotten soap in his eyes or slipping under the water, or from the not so rational possibility (at least from the adult's point of view) of going down the drain with the suds. There are easy ways to relieve some of the foregoing reactions. To avoid soap in the eyes, use only a damp washcloth to soap and rinse the face. Find a nonirritating shampoo that will not sting the eyes. If your child is afraid of sitting in the tub, give him a sponge bath standing up in the tub for a while. Then you can gradually turn on the water while he is standing and finally allow it to fill the tub. Washing can be introduced in a nonthreatening way at mealtime. Set a pan of water in front of your child while you wash his face and let him play in it with his hands.

Remember, your child has just gained the important ability to remain upright. She will be especially aware of the slipperiness of a soapy bathtub at this stage. Too, she is striking out for independence at a greater rate than ever before. Perhaps one reason for disliking the bath is resistance to being handled by an adult. Just have patience with your child—this stage, too, shall pass!

Nighttime. Fear of the dark, of bed-wetting, or just of being alone can make nighttime a terrifying experience for the thirteen-month-old. His developing imagination can cause stories, TV shows, or bits of adult talk to take on frightening aspects. As much as possible, try to explain the reality of things to your child. Do not try to make him brave by leaving him alone. It may help to leave the light on or the door to his room open. Comfort him if he wakes up crying and, if necessary, sit with him until he falls asleep. Do not let him get into the habit of coming into your bed. In the long run, this only has the effect of disturbing everyone's sleep.

Strangers. Fear of strangers reaches a peak at this age, with eye-to-eye contact an especially difficult situation for the child to handle. Be on the alert for well-meaning relatives and friends who force themselves upon your thirteen-month-old. Allow your child to maintain his distance until he is ready to interact on his own.

Animals. Can you imagine what it feels like to meet a German shepherd dog when you are only two feet tall? Many children are quite reasonably afraid of animals during this period. Do not resort to the shock method of forcing your child to get close to a pet in order to overcome her fear. Let her see you pet the neighbor's dog, but do not make your child do this. Perhaps through playing with stuffed animals or looking at pictures of animals with children, your child will gradually overcome her fear. At the same time, it is important that you teach your child not to make indiscriminate advances toward all animals. Teach her that she is to pet only the animals she knows.

Self-Help Routines

Eating, dressing, bathing, sleeping, playing—all are ego-building activities that are part of a child's daily routines. What distinguishes the child's attitude between the first and second years of life is that during the first twelve months, meeting health, hunger, and sleeping needs were basic to rapid growth and had to be satisfied completely and on time. During the second twelve months, there is not the same immediacy; i.e., there is greater flexibility of time and quantity.

Eating

"Acceptance at the family dining table requires the ability to sit up securely and the mastery of tidiness and table manners. If the thirteen-month-old wants to be like an adult, he has to adapt to family-imposed restrictions. Every home has to work out its own accommodations to the limitations imposed on the child by his immaturity. At the same time, the thirteen-month-old's strong drive to stand interferes with sedentary eating habits. For the moment, upright posture and locomotion are more important to the child than meat.

"To be a part of the family dinner means that the child must wean himself from the bottle to a cup, learn how to handle a spoon, resist grabbing a bowl, stop dumping food, and so on. The surge for independence is an integral part of the growth phenomenon. It is slowed down to some extent by the complexity of feeding implements, the immaturity of the child's fine-motor ability and nervous system. Pediatricians think that the child feeds himself best when he handles only part of the meal and the foods that he especially enjoys. Given too much range, the child messes, mixes, and even dumps food. It is not a good idea to complicate the thirteen-month-old's task of coordination of eating tools and adjustment to have him participate too soon in family mealtimes. He should eat in relative seclusion unless he is an exceptional child who will benefit from such a gathering."

Changing Attitudes toward Food

Your child may change her ideas about food. She may become more choosy and less hungry. She may lose her interest in food altogether. According to Dr. Spock and other pediatricians, this is not surprising. If a thirteen-month-old continued to eat and gain the way she did when she was a little baby, she would turn into a mountain. At the same time, now that she sees herself as a person separate from her mother, with ideas of her own, she becomes more definite in her likes and dislikes. Moreover, she is testing her power to refuse and make you angry. Likewise, her year of experience with mealtime has convinced her there is no danger of her going without food.

Now that his growth has slowed down and his interests have broadened, you must stop comparing your child's present appetite to that of his earlier months. Generally a thirteen-month-old has a good appetite for all meals, although somewhat less for breakfast. During the first year of his life, he gained about sixteen pounds, which is as much as he probably will gain during his next four years. There will be one meal a day when he eats very little. (At about eighteen months, it will not be unusual for your child to go several days without eating what you consider a normal amount of food.) Sometimes teething can interfere with appetite and your child will eat only half his usual amount and occasionally even refuse a whole meal.

Some parents insist that their child take one bite of every food that is offered. Violet Broadribb, R.N., and Henry F. Lee, M.D., claim that such tactics will only increase obstinacy. If offered wholesome foods, a healthy child will take care of his nutritional requirements. Of course, a child's appetite can be spoiled by making mealtime an unpleasant time. If the father says, "Carrots again; you know how I dislike them," how can you expect your child to accept carrots with enthusiasm? Also, how would your appetite be if the entire mealtime was spent criticizing your table manners? Your child will learn good table (and other) manners through practice and imitation, not by nagging.

The thirteen-month period is an opportune time for your child to learn to take fluids from a cup, use a spoon, discard pacifiers, wash her hands, undress, and cooperate in dressing.

You certainly can spoon-feed your child faster, but if you do not give her a chance to feed herself, you are losing an expedient time to let her develop initiative, self-confidence, and dexterity. If the toddler has been permitted practice with both finger foods and holding a spoon, she is becoming a good manager. However, you may expect unintentional messes now and again. Some children will eat certain foods by themselves, but allow parents to feed them others. When this occurs, the child may start discriminating between the foods she wants and the foods you want her to eat. During this period of self-assertion, such a practice could develop into a toddler/parent tug of war with the possibility that the child may not have an appetite for foods you want her to eat.

Pediatricians recommend that toddler snacks or finger foods at the table should be chew foods, especially thin slices of raw rutabaga, carrot and celery strips, raw apple slices, crumbled yellow cheese, tiny green peas, whole seedless raisins, whole seedless grapes, cubes of cooked liver, and so on. Chicken legs are excellent for emerging teeth and exercising the same muscles in the mouth that are used in speaking.

Health Care

Health care is becoming a joint effort of parent and child. The child is learning that hands are washed after toileting and before meals. Parents need to keep children away from sick people because they can spray into the air with a cough or a sneeze germs that are harmful. Some diseases invade the body from hand to mouth, especially when one eats. Some other diseases come from polluted water and contaminated foods.

Immunization against measles and rubella (German measles) should not be delayed beyond twelve months of age. Recent studies reveal that if taken too early or delayed too long, the immunity wears off and a booster shot may be required by the second year. If you keep a record of the dates of first immunizations, you will find it easier to cooperate with your doctor or health clinic.

Measles are highly contagious. The period of communicability (date of exposure to first signs) is about ten to twelve days. Springtime usually is the season for incubating the disease. Parents should isolate their child until seventeen days after the appearance of the rash. Reaction (five to twelve days) to the inoculation shows up in fever, coughing, and red eyes. Usually immune globulin taken three to six days after the appearance of the rash can lighten the attack. Inoculation consists of a shot in the arm or buttocks of a safe, live-measles vaccine.

Play and Playthings

Parents cannot play for their child, but if they are skillful, they may be able to play well with him. In addition to providing safe and adequate play space, suitable play materials, and enough storage space (low open shelves are recommended; a toy chest encourages the rough handling and even breakage of toys), parents need to make sure their child has ample opportunities for the various kinds of play activities he needs and enjoys.

When a thirteen-month-old wakes in the morning, he may be able to play contentedly in his crib for about twenty minutes with a small assortment of his toys before yelling to be picked up.

The child who has just passed her first birthday keeps on doing what she has been doing heretofore, except that she is becoming more and more adept. Soft stuffed toys are greatly enjoyed because the toddler likes to hold something in each hand as she locomotes. A doll—for girl or boy—should be of rubber or soft vinyl without hair or moving eyes so it can be taken into the tub with the child.

The thirteen-month-old can be very selective about the toys he plays with. He may ignore a big truck and shape-fitting toy and spend a while rolling rollers or chasing a big ball around the room. He may even try to kick the ball as if that were part of the game he was playing.

Putting things back is another game. The child will try to put the dish towel back on the rack, empty mother's purse and then stuff the disarrayed contents back, and so on. A favorite toy is a nest of blocks (whether of wood, heavy cardboard, or soft vinyl). Parents need to give their child only one plaything at a time because otherwise he may rush from toy to toy and tire of each quickly without having explored its possibilities.

Rolling a ball back and forth (or any rolling toy for that matter) is a popular pastime of the thirteen-month-old. Prior to this time, the child would watch as a parent or older sibling started to roll the ball. Usually she chased it, picked it up, mouthed it, and then surrendered the ball in an ill-defined manner. Now the child is able to release the ball by rolling it back.

This starts a game going with parents or older siblings that is enjoyed by all for a good part of the second year of life and even longer.

If your toddler will not or cannot play with a toy, it has not been well chosen. Parents need to make sure that every toy they buy or their child receives as a gift fits in with his current interest and level of skill. Playthings that are not appropriate discourage rather than stimulate exploration and enjoyment.

Your child's toys should be able to take hard use; edges and parts of all her playthings should be rounded and smooth; all paints should be lead-free and nontoxic; woods should be free of splinters; brittle plastics need to be avoided. First books should be of heavy cardboard or stiffly starched cloth (limp pages are well nigh impossible for the child to handle). The pictures should be bold, colorful, and of familiar, everyday objects.

The thirteen-month-old has a great urge to express her ego by pushing everything in sight. This appears to give the child a sense of power. She will push big and little objects, sometimes accompanying her actions with engine and other noises: a tiny plastic cup, a rocking chair, a vacuum cleaner, a platform on casters (the kind used by moving companies), a toy automobile, and so on. She likes, too, to pull a Snoopy dog and a small wagon. Emptying a wastebasket or a fit-together egg or a drawer is a preferred activity.

Toys and books should be stored on low, open shelves. A basket will enable you and your child to put away the many odds and ends that defy neat storage. The floor of your child's room or play corner should be covered with linoleum or asphalt tiles that can be washed easily. Wherever possible, the furniture should be placed against the walls so that the maximum amount of floor space is available for the child's unobstructed play. Toys left scattered on the floor after the play period has ended are potentially dangerous to both children and adults.

Felt toys should be avoided because their dyes usually are not colorfast. Check all plush toys to make sure that the eyes and ears are firmly attached. All components that might be pulled off by the child—ribbons, bells, string, and so on—should be removed by the parent.

The thirteen-month-old is not ready to manipulate any kind of hammer toy, but she will enjoy stacking rings on a large peg; she will try to take apart oversized plastic or wood nuts and bolts; stacking and nesting toys are challenging and fun; a few different-sized balls are always welcome; sponges in assorted colors and sizes are great for water play in bathtub or pail; a toy broom and carpet sweeper will get happy, active use; and a drum or tambourine will delight the toddler, who likes to listen to music and dance in rhythm to it. The child enjoys simple story recordings, too. Her favorite play companions are her parents and older siblings.

THE THIRTEENTH MONTH

Motor Development

Gross Motor

Stoops to pick up object from floor while holding on with one hand

Climbs on a low ledge or step

Backs down stairs and slides down from one step to the next

Dislikes all forms of restraint. Can stand alone without support for at least 5 seconds

Sits down from free-standing position

Moves to rhythms

Walks in a side-step pattern along furniture (cruises)

Fine Motor

Can grasp 2 cubes in one hand

Uses index finger to point

Removes small object from cup

Drops toys and watches them fall

Builds tower of 2 cubes

Puts 3 or more cubes in cup

Neat pincer grasp of raisin, using thumb and index finger

Pokes, bangs, pulls, turns, and twists everything within reach

Language Acquisition

Vocabulary of 3–4 words, in addition to "Mama" and "Dada"

Says "ta-ta" for "thank you"

Gives toy on request or gesture

Looks in appropriate place when asked, "Where is daddy?"—"ball?"—"kitty?"

May use sounds to indicate specific objects that are understood by the parents

Responds to own name

Jabbers with expression

Understands gestures

Obeys command: "Give it to me"

Attempts new words

Has begun to understand the names of people, objects, and animals that are important to child

Will listen for 3 minutes or so to rhymes and jingles

Comes when beckoned

Has learned to respond to speech by acts

Indicates wants other than by crying

Sensory Powers/ Learning

Will look at pictures in a book for a few seconds

Is a prodigious imitator; ability to copy all kinds of actions increases

Tries definitely to sing

Looks in correct place for toys that roll out of sight

Puts small objects into container; dumps; repeats

Tries out movable parts of environment: light switches, stove knobs, etc.

Begins deliberately to invent actions not tried before and explore the novel features of objects

Combines objects with other objects to create new ways of doing things

Uses trial-and-error method to discover new solutions to problems

Has not yet learned to recognize danger

Investigates the parts of the face of teddy bear or rag doll

Will empty anything she or he can get to—dresser drawers, kitchen cabinets, trash cans, hampers, purses, ashtrays, bookshelves, sewing baskets, etc.

Tries to manipulate any dial that he or she finds

Inserts round block into form-board

Can retrieve a hidden toy

Beginning concept of "up" and "down"

Dear Parents:

Do not regard this chart as a rigid timetable.

Babies are unpredictable individuals. Some perform an activity earlier or (as much as six months) later than the chart indicates, while others skip a behavior altogether (e.g., walking without crawling).

Just use this information to anticipate and appreciate normal child development and behavior. No norms are absolutes.

Growth Chart

Social Development

Loves an audience

Enjoys applause

Will repeat any performance that elicits response

Plays pat-a-cake

Will follow if left alone by an adult

Shows or gives toys to adults

Reaches for, pulls on, and vocalizes to familiar persons

Laughs when chased or found hiding

Demands personal attention

Definitely prefers certain people to others

Still wants to keep mother or father in sight while exploring

Reacts to each parent in a special way

Is more aggressive toward objects than people

Offers toy to image in mirror

Imitates housework (dusting, etc.)

Begins to adjust to babysitter

Still fears strangers

Personality/ Psychological

Gives affection to humans and such objects as toys and clothes

Will hug or kiss parents either spontaneously or at their urging

Expresses many emotions and *may* recognize feelings in other people

Shows anxiety at separation from mother (gradually masters this)

Differentiates personalities and trusts differently

Distinguishes self from others

Fears strange places

Negativism increases

May have tantrums

Is gradually realizing that the parents are separate individuals with their own personal interests

Self-Help Routines

Holds cup with assistance for taking fluids

Enjoys taking off hat, shoes, socks, pants, etc.

Takes 3 meals a day, usually insisting on self-feeding

Washes hands and face with help and tries to dry them

Tries to use a spoon

Fights sleep

Morning nap getting shorter; still takes a long afternoon nap

Picks up small bits of food with fingers and eats them

Discards pacifier

Cooperates in dressing: puts arms into coatsleeves, etc.

Is establishing more regular bowel movement patterns

Stays dry for longer periods of time

Play and Playthings

Can play a simple game of ball, grasping it and letting it go

Likes to listen to music and dance in rhythm to it

Enjoys playing with several small toys, picking them up and dropping them one by one

Interested in playing with people

Enjoys active peek-a-boo and chase games

Usually plays happily with older siblings

Likes to push a rolling toy

Enjoys stacking rings on a spindle toy

THE FOURTEENTH MONTH
Challenge and Practice

Review of Motor Development

How do toddlers develop physically? Can they be trained to do anything or must they follow an inflexible timetable of development predetermined by their genes and the inherent characteristics of the human species?

Two of the foremost child psychologists of our time took sides on the issue. During the 1930s, Dr. John Watson, one of the first psychologists to study infants experimentally, contended that through environmental conditioning a child could be molded to adult wishes. Watson's considerable impact and his big "if" imposed a tremendous burden on parents who followed a regime inspired by him of arbitrary schedules, laboratory sterility in the nursery, and rigid formulas. Because parents were told that instruction was solely responsible for development, they tried such things as toilet training their infant at three weeks of age, never rocking or picking up their crying baby, and metering out love by the clock.

Dr. Arnold Gesell alleviated some of this parental pressure with his maturation theory; i.e., he advocated waiting for the baby's nervous system to mature. He claimed that training before the baby was ready was futile and, therefore, a waste of time for parents and infant. But Gesell created new worries by his creation of standardized tests for measuring development, tests that checked whether the baby showed the "right" physical, mental, and social behavior at the appropriate time. This normative approach made parents seek in their own infant's development the milestones or specific events described in Gesell's timetable of infant achievement. When babies did not come across with the "right" behavior at the "right" time, parental panic often ensued.

Dr. Myrtle B. McGraw, retired director of developmental psychology at Briarcliff College in New York, is one of the few survivors of that generation of psychologists who devoted themselves to infant and child physical development. She does not and did not agree with either of her former contemporaries. Just why her voice of reason was not heard with equal attention is the kind of question being addressed forty years later by the Women's Liberation Movement.

According to Dr. McGraw, the limits for the appearance of behavior and even thought processes depend upon both the maturation of the nervous system and environmental influence. An infant will not acquire certain skills until certain hookups are established between nerves and certain muscles are strong enough. Within the limits set by these factors, a rich and challenging environment can and does make children use their senses, and walk and talk more efficiently. Unlike Watson, who said *conditioning,* or Gesell, who said *wait,* McGraw advocates *challenge and practice.*

In over thirty years of research, she has proved her point. She has worked with great success with infants and young children to develop their bodies and their sense of what they can do with them. She taught babies to roller skate at twelve months, swim at ten months, climb almost vertical inclines before the first birthday, and to push pedestals of various heights into stairlike progressions to attain the enviable position of being "at the top." The consistent enthusiasm and glee of these children as they leap off precipices into waiting arms and swoop down slopes on roller skates do not emanate just from the physical exploits themselves. Equally important are the children's own sense of accomplishment and their interaction with adults who encourage them and are supportive when they tackle the complex movement problems of standing, crawling, and walking.

Gaining Confidence via Body Control

According to Dr. McGraw, "If a child of a year or two gains confidence in handling his own body, then it is reasonable to assume that that confidence will subsequently serve him well in other areas." She advises mothers and fathers who want to work with their babies on certain essential but little-known facts about human growth: (1) Behaviors need not occur at a specific month, although they probably will do so within a span of months. For example, according to standard norms, North American children crawl at seven months; some delay until ten months, while others start at six months. Infants in Uganda often crawl at five months. (2) The order of growth events is not rigidly prescribed. Most developmental charts detail *creeping* (getting around with arms and legs, tummy on the ground); *crawling* (moving on hands and knees); and *standing*. Some infants creep and stand, and then, as if the experience were a bit overwhelming, flop down for more ground practice and crawl. (3) Some aspects of development are performed individualistically and not at all according to the books. An infant is supposed to sit up alone by rolling

from back onto side and pushing up with the arms. Actually many infants get into a crawling position, then flop their legs between their arms and out in front, landing adroitly on their bottoms.

Often old skills are being realigned with new awareness so that parents can be pleased rather than dismayed by a sudden reversion to old behavior. A baby who could balance very well standing may constantly lose balance and topple when he starts walking. However, when the two aspects of walking (stepping and balancing) mesh, the baby will balance well—standing or walking.

Fear or disorganized behavior often results from such a temporary dysfunction of growing systems. A baby may fear being thrown into the air until a new awareness of the situation matches consciousness of the father's ability to catch her. Newborns swim by reflex, but in about five or six months babies lose this ability. They cannot crawl through the water, they ingest it, and they cough after they are taken out. Rather than loss, this seeming regression means development because the baby is gaining a different kind of control. At about twelve months of age swimming movements reappear.

Critical Periods

One of the most critical features of human growth is learning readiness. Behaviors appear at certain optimum time periods, optimum with respect to the baby's personal learning readiness, not that of his contemporary down the street. Development in one area actually can interfere with development in another. Dr. McGraw found, for example, that infants learning to walk could not get out of a corral she had put them in. They tried, but could not climb over a bar placed at their chest level. They did not try crawling under it, although they had "learned" to crawl several months before. Their single-minded "devotion" to their new learning task—maneuvering upright—interfered with their ability to sense what their bodies could do. For this reason, an infant learning to walk will swagger right off a table's edge, about which he had shown great caution as a creeping infant.

With the utmost energy expended by the child, the least amount by the parent, and the least distraction from other learning, the baby will most efficiently learn a *particular* ability. An opportune time to teach a child to roller skate is when the child is learning to walk. In two months, Dr. McGraw taught a twelve-month-old to stop, start, and whip around corners. The brother at twenty-two months had difficulty. The twelve-month-old learned more readily because Dr. McGraw caught the child before he had learned a specific way to displace his body weight forward, but after he had learned to balance. After a child has learned to walk well, the tendency to *lift* the feet when moving forward interferes with learning to *roll* the feet when skating.

Each baby signals the readiness to learn. For example, around twelve months of age, after the phase of swimming "disability," the child will again make swimming movements when placed on the tummy. These are parents' cues that the child is ready and willing to swim.

Trial and Error in Gross-Motor Development

"Some fourteen-month-old children explode into walking. They master creeping, pulling up, cruising, hand walking, and independent walking in two months. For most toddlers, learning to walk is a highly complex art that takes time and much trial and error. Alert parents will want to set down the numerous movement steps that are involved. It means pulling oneself up from a sitting position, grabbing the rail of the crib, and moving around the crib holding on with one hand for support. When out of the crib and standing by a chair, the child has to learn how to support herself against a chair with an elbow so that both hands are available for play or picking up objects. The child may, of course, rise alone in the middle of the floor, put her hands forward, straighten her legs, and stand for an admiring audience, only to flop down on her

bottom without taking a single step. It will take much more practice—cruising from one piece of furniture to another, walking with one hand held, crawling on hands and knees (often with knees off the ground), climbing onto chairs, and so on—before walking develops. In the course of carrying out this demanding procedure, the fourteen-month-old may suddenly find that she has forgotten how to sit down from a standing position. This elicits a piercing scream that brings mother or father to the rescue. As the child is sat down, she pulls up again and starts all over to practice these new gross-motor movement skills until they are mastered.

"Sometimes the final plunge into walking by oneself can take an interminable period of time. The child walks holding two hands, then one hand, then one finger. Clutching one finger can be another drawn-out affair. When independent walking is accomplished, the toddler invests undivided attention and full energy in perfecting this physical milestone.

"Whether walking, crawling, creeping, or rolling over, the desire to explore the environment is overpowering. To climb a flight of stairs is an irresistible challenge to fourteen-month-olds. Going up is no problem and conforms to the crawling techniques mastered earlier. However, getting down is a difficult matter. Most parents, noting the early frustration, rush in to teach the child how to climb down. This type of parent intervention usually is unsuccessful and may delay the self-discovery process. Left to his own resources, the child works out the gross-motor skills needed to accomplish the task. Some children back down, others sit on each step, and still others slide down backward.

"Learning to sit in a chair is another important gross-motor technique. Some children take considerable time to learn how. First attempts are clumsy. Fourteen-month-olds either fall into a small chair or climb up onto it, turn around, and then sit down. Backing up into a chair and sitting down directly require considerable awareness of a body in space, distance judgment, and knowing up from down.

"Many fourteen-month-olds find it easier to climb than to walk and more often are better able to get themselves into overstuffed chairs than into child-sized rockers. Climbing does not use the same techniques as walking. Some babies are able to climb from floor to chair and from chair to table before they can stand alone. Still others show no interest in climbing before they walk. Whether walking is accomplished slowly or suddenly, the desire to practice is overwhelming. Nonetheless, in the early stages, the beginning walker may resort to crawling to get somewhere fast."

Patterns of Physical Development

By now it must be clear to you that there are "patterns" of physical development, as well as "ages and stages" that provide insight as to how you can work best with your child at her current level of development. From the uncoordinated movements of early babyhood to the control necessary to pick up a pen, certain predictable patterns emerge. Development occurs in an orderly sequence. There are certain steps a child must go through before she goes through others. Large muscles develop before small fine muscles. Control of the arm comes before control of the hand and fingers. Muscle control develops from head to toe. Babies use their arms to pull themselves up rather than their knees.

Many child development specialists claim that a child's self-concept (how he feels about himself) is directly related to his motor skill development. A child who has awkward use of the body may shun physical activities with other children and become socially gauche as well. Although the precise reasons are not known, most children display poor motor coordination to some degree. There are researchers who claim that skipping a motor development stage (creeping and crawling, for example) results in left-right learning and reading trouble in later years. If your fourteen-month-old appears to have any lag or deficiency in motor accomplishment, it would be to your child's advantage to discuss this with your pediatrician.

A "Love Affair" with the World of Objects, Space, and People

As soon as toddlers are really sure of themselves as walkers, they initiate an active and systematic exploration of their physical world—its objects, people, and spatial design. They develop a "love affair" with the outside world and with this comes danger, prohibitions, limitation of freedom, excessive use of playpen, reclining seat, protective gates, and so on. Researchers find that during the period from thirteen to fifteen months, children spend more time on interactions with physical reality than they do trying to affect people; for instance, 82 percent of their time is spent on nonsocial tasks as against 18 percent for social activities.

Gaining information is the single most devoted effort both in the first and second twelve months of life. During the first year, children spend time on sensory experiences: listening, staring, feeling, tasting, and manipulating (shaking, banging, grasping, dropping, and twisting). From all these encounters, children develop what Dr. Piaget calls "schemata," which they use in the second year to find out even more about the physical world.

"Confronted with a new object, a shoe box, for example, the fourteen-month-old will bang it, turn it over, taste it, explore it visually, shake it, and throw it down. During these investigations the toddler discovers that the box has a top that can come off. He centers his attention on taking it off and examining its contents. In a few months, the child may want to stuff the box with things, but not at fourteen months.

"Ambulatory fourteen-month-olds like to combine emptying with transporting things. They find favorite spots or hiding places:

under the bed, in the wastebasket, or even in the sink and toilet bowl. Because emptying can be a nuisance, parents put things 'off limits' or temporarily out of reach. A better way to counteract a toddler's emptying game is to provide baskets that can be filled and emptied endlessly.

"Tearing paper or pages out of a telephone book or discarded magazine is a favorite pastime for fourteen-month-olds. Unfortunately the tearing schema is applied to more desirable objects (pictures in a calendar, favorite posters, pages of a book, etc.) and creates behavior conflicts with parents.

"Fitting small things into containers and getting them out is a preferred activity at this age. Filling a small container offers speedy achievement and builds ego. 'Oversized' is the key for selecting toys for this age level Stacking rings, nesting large cups or mixing bowls result in quick accomplishments and teach size discrimination. Large hollow blocks (five by five by five inches or five and a half by five and a half by eleven inches) are the type of blocks used in toddler nurseries for making big buildings.

"At this age fitting toys are favored because quick results are guaranteed; screwing caps on a film container, fitting varishaped forms in a sorting box or formboard. Some fourteen-month-olds have sensory preferences and enjoy carrying a textured blanket, pajamas, a soft bunny, or the like. This is a good time for you to create a texture box with hand holes for your exploring child. Include all kinds of fabrics and materials (fur, silk, velvet, cotton, wool, sandpaper)."

Toddlers Require Constant Supervision

The fourteen-month-old walker is an inveterate explorer. If your child is ambulatory, she will spend an inordinate amount of time wandering and exploring novel sights—new rooms, a shopping center, playground, construction site, and so on. The child does not have any particular interest or purpose in these spatial arrangements, but they are new

areas to be observed and every detail is "recorded" in her memory bank. Parents claim that wandering can be downright dangerous. If they live on a busy thoroughfare, toddlers will walk across streets without parental help. If they live on a beach, toddlers will walk into the water until it is over their heads. What to do about this endless wandering? Supervise it! Be tolerant of it and participate in it by calling attention to interesting features and objects.

Curiosity

"No one needs to teach a child to explore his environment. As soon as babies crawl or roll over or move their bodies in space, they harbor the strongest desire to touch, taste, and investigate the physical objects and mechanisms of their environment. They are obsessed with objects in motion. On the way to the supermarket, crawlers are the most behaved observers of cars, trucks, buses, trains, and construction sites. At home, they will spend endless amounts of time watching the flight of birds at the feeder or barking dogs in the backyard.

"At fourteen months interest in mechanisms consumes the child: knobs that turn on radios and television sets, doors that open and close, and so on."

Burton L. White, Ph.D., considers this curiosity extremely healthy and one of the cornerstones of solid education development. You can nourish it by giving your child access to all the rooms. Be supportive when she wishes to share an enthusiasm with you. Get your child out of doors; take nature walks together. Encourage explorations and let your child know that you approve of this kind of activity.

Child-Proofing the House

"When you child starts to walk, you will all derive great satisfaction from this tremendous achievement. However, once your fourteen-month-old can get around, expect all kinds of trouble and headaches. Toddlers are not

satisfied with exploring the kitchen only. Now the whole world is their territory. Do not be shocked if your fourteen-month-old learns how to maneuver the front gate latch and begins crossing the street unescorted by you. Do not become hysterical when you discover that your toddler has emptied all the ash trays onto carpet or floor, investigated the bottom shelf of your linen closet, and is carrying around a prized antique china teacup given to you by your loving grandmother. Remember to control your emotions when you suddenly come upon your quiet child playing with his stools or masturbating."

You are going to have to keep a healthy attitude about what is going on. Surely you will not want to squelch your child's eagerness to practice walking and to control and master the newly available shapes, textures, and objects in her milieu. You will want your child to feel free to explore and "grab life with both hands." At the same time, you are not going to let her touch everything indiscriminately. Some things are dangerous and some things are precious. You will remove the most valued things.

There are many things you can do. For example, you can set aside certain areas and rooms as definitely off-limits. You can even leave some fine china in place, but you will have to start training your child about the beauty of the china when he is beginning to crawl. Make sure your toddler has plenty of things to touch and carry around—pots, pans, measuring spoons, nesting boxes, and so on. Arrange for an area in or outdoors for sand and water play.

Spoiling

Americans have a fetish about spoiling a child. Spoiling, to Americans, means overindulging every whim, giving in to demands, letting children have their way and say. Most specialists agree that very young children do not spoil easily. The infant who is hungry or discomforted cannot wait, cannot share, cannot postpone basic needs. This means that you do not have to worry about spoiling in-

fants by holding them when they want to be held, feeding them when they are hungry, or changing them when they are uncomfortable.

Back in the 1930s and 1940s, some pediatricians suggested to parents that to build stamina and discipline in infants, they should let a baby cry for fifteen minutes, then pick her up for five minutes, feed her promptly every four hours and never in between, and so on. The foregoing procedures may be responsible in part for the generation of hippies and other "copouts" who have been searching in vain for a kind of immature love they never received in early childhood.

There is no danger of spoiling a one-year-old whose growth is so rapid that he becomes bored with the lack of problem-solving opportunities, "stale" toys, or an environment that is devoid of challenges. Child psychologists and early childhood educators believe that parents can spoil a child's excitement for learning by not providing sufficient problem-solving materials and challenges when the desire to learn is so completely pervasive.

Strange as it may sound, many younger children are "spoiled" or "blocked" because they receive too little of what they need for normal growth. Severe disappointments block growth; too little comfort blocks growth. Some parents are afraid to hug or touch their child for fear of spoiling her. What can stop growth is the lack of spontaneity in helping children when they ask for help and comforting them when they seek affection. All children need the security of knowing that they are satisfactory, that they are loved and valued (without any reservations). Interest, attention, praise, comfort, assurance—none of these slows down the growth process, and of themselves, none will spoil a child.

Handling Frustration

There is a considerable number of fine-motor tasks that the fourteen-month-old cannot do and so frustration begins to set in. The child will try to put a doll's stocking on its leg or even try putting her own shoe on. The fourteen-month-old recognizes that her action is incomplete and will gesture to any nearby adult for help, showing satisfaction when the task is completed. It is obvious that the toddler's intention runs far ahead of her abilities.

Toddlers work hard to solve all kinds of manipulative projects. When putting small blocks in a jar or container, they get impatient with the slowness of the filling activity and will try to dump the whole bag of blocks into the jar. They will pull out a large peg in a pegboard and encounter great difficulty putting it back. Child education specialists believe it is better to guide a child's hand so that the edge of the peg touches the edge of the opening. This will encourage the child to try again and eventually master the technique. If you perform the whole operation for your child, he learns only that you can do it and gains nothing in manual skill.

Lack of skill does not prevent the fourteen-month-old from undertaking intricate and even dangerous operations. The child will use bookcase shelves as a ladder to get at a desired book or sculptured figure, and may go from shelf to shelf pulling out a book and carrying it to another shelf where elaborate arranging and rearranging are undertaken. Although all this activity makes no sense to an adult, it gives the toddler a feeling of power and control over the environment.

Rather than curb the child, it makes sense to applaud her enterprise and try to direct it. Most toddlers respond to reasonable requests, such as "Bring it here" or "This is where it goes," but they rebel if *no-no* or *don't touch* commands are repeatedly used.

What does the foregoing tell parents about toys for toddlers? Obviously that you need to select those that give your fourteen-month-old the chance for fun and success. Patience is short at this time and your child is in no mood for intricate building projects. Pegboards should have large holes and thick pegs with sufficient clearance for easy fitting. Look for hollow plastic blow-up, oversized tools—a hammer, shovel, broom, balls—objects of play that tell your child that you recognize his desire to be considered an active member of the family.

Language Acquisition

"The fourteen-month-old's lack of language skills is often very frustrating for both parents and child. Although the child is able to point, which increases communication ability, the parent may be unable to tell what object the child is pointing at. Often it is difficult to figure out what the child wants when she is babbling, pointing, and waving her arms impatiently.

"The fourteen-month-old understands the names of many objects, animals, and people that are important to him. Your child's beginning use of words lags behind his ability to understand language. When a child learns to say a word, he seeks out opportunities to practice it. The child who has learned to say the word *ball*, for example, will be particularly interested in finding balls so that he can use this new word. Parents can share in their child's excitement by helping with the search. They can point out balls that the fourteen-month-old might miss: a ball used in play at the beach or the picture of a ball in a magazine.

"The fourteen-month-old has a meaningful vocabulary of three to five distinct words, in addition to *Mama* and *Dada*. Practically day by day your child is learning to understand the meaning of new words and phrases and building up a base of experiences that are the major source of language acquisition.

"By now your fourteen-month-old has acquired understanding of many of your verbal commands, requests, and prohibitions and may respond with her own grouping of sounds."

Children normally acquire language at varying rates, but usually in an orderly, systematic pattern. (The language-disordered child—i.e., the hard-of-hearing or deaf child—will not necessarily follow an orderly sequence of language development.) Language is *listening* and *understanding,* as well as speaking. It may take your child a long time to say what he wants or means. Do not rush him. Listen patiently. Use concrete examples whenever possible. It is much better to hold an apple than to see a picture of one. When talking to your child, vary your tone and facial expression. Remember to smile and nod appropriately. Maintain eye contact as much as possible when you speak with your child.

Social Development

The fourteen-month-old is somewhat less afraid of strangers—as long as mother or father is nearby. The child also is less afraid of the babysitter as long as the parents are careful to let her see the sitter before departing; i.e., they never leave while their child is asleep. Most children this age do not like to be excluded from a room and try to open the door if it is closed by someone else or by siblings eager to keep the toddler out of their way.

Prohibition Words and Misbehavior

The toddler has learned to walk and is beginning also to learn to talk. The trouble is that among the first words learned are *no* (more often than *yes*) and *mine. No* can mean all kinds of things. Toddlers will say *no* when you call them and run away. They will say *no* when you ask them to do something for you and run away and hide. They will even say *no* when they mean *yes.* There will be quite a bit of this throughout the second twelve months of life. So be prepared!

If you can see this type of stubbornness as part of early attempts at ego building, "feeling their oats," and testing out their power to say *no* to adults, it will be somewhat easier for you to cope. If you regard such negativism as sheer disobedience in a toddler, you are inviting an encounter in which parents invariably lose. Of course, you do not want to let the child "get away with murder." But if you make an issue out of everything, you and your child will be setting up barriers that will hinder the growth of self-esteem. James L. Hymes, Jr., Ph.D., offers two helpful tips. The first is the business of time and planning ahead. If you want a toddler to come in from the outside or to get ready for bed or get out of the bath, plan

ahead so that there are extra minutes in the timetable. For example, five minutes for fussing and refusals and five minutes to get the job done. Stay away from questions that invite a *no* answer, such as "Do you want to come home now?" or "Do you want to wash your hands?" Flat statements, such as "It's time to go home now" or "It's time for bed," stand a better chance of getting results.

Attachment Behavior

Infant researchers have done a considerable amount of investigation of the attachment behavior that is manifested from nine to about fourteen months of age. These are the months when the child becomes disturbed by the parent's disappearance and most anxious about strangers. This behavior takes many peculiar forms: crying, touching mother, visual regard of mother (eye-to-eye contact), proximity to mother (distancing), and so on. Researchers are trying to ascertain which behaviors are good indicators of "separation anxiety."

If the mother decides to go to work during the "critical" separation period, she will be faced with a host of these behaviors that she cannot explain. The search to find predictable indicators of separation behavior have attracted such professionals as Michael Lewis, Ph.D. (of Educational Testing Service in Princeton, N.J.), John Bowlby, Ph.D., Lois Murphy, Ph.D., and others. "Distancing" (proximity to mother) and "touching" (staying close) are two of the most steady indicators. Visual regard, vocalizing, as well as crying, looking at the door through which the mother left, and so forth were not always good indicators. Dr. Lewis' research confirms that boys distance further from their mothers than do girls. (This behavior is described in much detail in a subsequent chapter.)

Social Competency

Child researchers have been searching also for behaviors that produce social competency in later life. Social competency in infancy usually is discussed in relation to crying, communication, and maternal responsiveness.

In a longitudinal study of crying conducted by Mary D. Salter Ainsworth, Ph.D., and Silvia M. Bell, Ph.D., of the department of psychology, Johns Hopkins University, it was found that crying seems to be the earliest and most effective way in which an infant can signal and communicate with the mother. Entitled "Mother-Infant Interaction and the Development of Competence," their report did not confirm the common beliefs that to respond promptly to a baby's cry strengthens his tendency to cry on subsequent occasions and that babies who cried little had a wider selection of techniques of communication.

Parental responsiveness to a toddler's social signals apparently supports the development of social competencies insofar as it promotes the development of a variety of communicative behaviors that are easy to read and, therefore, more likely to influence others successfully. Parental behavior also may play an indirect role in developing competence.

In 1971, Donelda J. Stayton, Robert Hogan, and Mary D. Salter Ainsworth,* all of the department of psychology, Johns Hopkins University, reported that a study of the relationship between maternal behavior and infant I.Q. showed that mothers who are sensitive to infant signals and permit their babies freedom to move about to explore the world on their own account tend to have babies who are relatively accelerated in psychomotor development. Floor freedom and a harmonious infant-mother attachment were found to be highly correlated with I.Q. The amount of time that adults or other children spent playing with the baby also was related positively to I.Q.

One significant outcome of mother-infant attachment seems to be that the infant can use the mother as a secure base from which to explore. Infants who had frequent, harmonious transactions with their mothers in the course of an observed play session and whose mothers were generally responsive to their initiations of interaction, tended to explore more toys and, more importantly, to display more behavioral schemata (ways of relating things) in the course of play. In short, the quality of an infant's attachment to the mother (or father) also affects learning development in the first two years of life.

Sometimes this toddler becomes angry when he does not want to leave a particular place; for instance, the play group that he attends two afternoons a week. At this age, he begins to show anger, sometimes by hitting one or the other parent. The father thinks it is half-amusing, but the mother thinks it should stop. If the parent holds the child's arm down and says *No!* the child learns to stop all hitting.

Mother and child have their own games, such as getting down on all fours in order to make the chase more equal or blowing through straws at each other so that the air tickles the skin. When the mother asks the child how big she is, the child raises her hands above her head. A social game with the father is listening to his voice on the telephone at five o'clock every evening. The toddler smiles at the sound, but does not say anything.

Self-Help Routines

The fourteen-month-old wants to do more and more things without parental assistance. The child helps with dressing by putting his arms up or lifting each leg or foot. Other self-help routines include brushing the teeth, combing the hair while looking in the mirror, taking off short socks, and occasionally removing diapers (to the consternation of the parents).

If you want to help your child build independence, you will have to allow lots of time for the process of dressing and undressing. At fourteen months, the child's search for autonomy and independence ("I do it myself!") is manifesting itself. To encourage these first

*Their report, "Infant Obedience and Maternal Behavior: The Origins of Socialization Reconsidered," appeared in a condensed version in *Child Development,* 1971 (42, 1057–1069).

expressions of assertiveness, you will want to buy clothing with big buttons, zippers where possible, large armholes and wide sleeves, and big necks in slipovers. You will have to look for roominess and easy-to-manage features in toddler clothing. It takes longer when a child tries to learn to dress herself, but she learns more.

Dr. Hymes warns that your attitude is even more important than the clothing itself. The active, walking child who is using newfound motor skills is bound to get dirty. If you show great distress about dirty and torn clothing, that feeling will be communicated to your toddler and initiate a sense of guilt. For peace of mind, just get the toughest and simplest clothes you can buy and be happy you have a normal, active, inquisitive fourteen-month-old.

Today's modern parents share equally the chores as well as the affection of the toddler. When father is home, he takes over the management of the child. Baby is whisked away for a change of diapers. There begins a program of interactive play—wrestling, chase me–catch me games, and hiding-the-ball game. After some physical activities, such as jogging with father or swimming in the pool, the child is usually ready for supper. Throughout the activities, the child speaks to the father in a special tone—the inflection and accent are quite close to regular conversation, but the words are not there yet.

Family Life—Fathering

Once upon a time in North America, father was a strong authoritarian figure with a handlebar mustache, the dispenser of discipline and (it was hoped) justice. On television shows of the sixties, he was transformed into the family's jovial buffoon, deferred to from pity rather than respect by his knowing wife and super-intellectual children. According to Dr. Frank Pedersen (of the National Institute of Child Health and Human Development), these bygone stereotypes are as elusive as "the father" of the seventies. The only clear thing about him is that mother and child need him, though he varies across time, between cultures, and even within social class.

The North American middle-class father varies tremendously. One reason, says Dr. Pedersen, may be the father's view that many aspects of his relationship with his child are optional; for example, his caretaking and play. Much of the mother's caretaking, however, is almost as obligatory as the mother's biological bond.

In his most recently completed research, Dr. Pedersen notes that some North American middle-class fathers diapered, dressed, bathed, and fed their babies daily. Others never did. Some fathers were patient, tolerant, and totally contained with their infants. Others openly expressed anger or annoyance with them.

Besides differences in these individual qualities of fathering, combinations of qualities also varied and one quality hardly presupposed another. For example, a father who enjoys roughhousing with his ten-month-old son might not want to change his diapers.

Scientific study, one thing that could order the apparent confusion, is almost nonexistent. The chief reason for this lack, Dr. Pedersen humorously comments, is that heretofore psychologists and psychiatrists have considered fathers unworthy of study. Possibly behavioral scientists, mostly males, are more comfortable scrutinizing the parental behavior of the opposite sex. Also, fathers who work the same hours as the scientists who would like to study them are less accessible. While the mother may in fact be the more critical parent, Dr. Pedersen feels that any understanding of her is incomplete unless complemented by more substantial information about the father.

The research on father that does exist addresses his absence: his desertion, divorce, death, and long-term separations, such as during military service. Such research orientation has been too simplified for the complexity of the problem. For one thing, the *reason* for the father's absence seems to affect his child differently. Absence because of divorce or desertion is often statistically associated with

juvenile delinquency in boys. Father's death is sometimes associated with personality disorders that involve the child's tendencies toward depression and feelings of worthlessness and/or guilt.

A culture's response to the father's absence, the child's age when separated from his father, and the mother's response and interpretation of it to the child also make important differences. The mother may castigate her child's father because he left her or act quite routinely if it matters little to her. Several studies show that the father's absence during the first five or six years is more likely to relate to his son's conflict over sexual identity than later absence. Father substitution through a woman's remarriage is an acceptable response in the United States to a husband's divorce or death. In India, it is not. In fact, the high rate of remarriage here means that many United States children have more than one father during their growing years. Father's desertion, on the other hand, is more socially acceptable in the Caribbean than in the United States and so may be less emotionally damaging to the child there. All these variations in separation and family response to it make simple generalizing difficult.

Drs. Pedersen's and R. S. Robson's "Father Participation in Infancy" is one of the early studies that deals with actual *father-infant interaction.* Father *is* important! His affection, concern, attention, and play foster his baby's affection for another human being, his emotional well-being, and his awareness of sex differences.

The father's behavior is definitely related to his baby's development of attachment. Baby boys with fathers who helped care for them, played with them often, and were relatively patient about their fussing became attached to them early and intensely as shown by their greetings as father entered the house. They smiled, vocalized, reached for, and tried hard to make physical contact with their fathers. Baby girls with anxious fathers were unlikely to be attached to them, although this quality did not seem to influence the boys one way or the other. Baby boys and baby girls differed very clearly on the bases for attachment, which might even be there from the first months of life. Dr. Pedersen conjectures that baby boys read action cues while baby girls respond to emotional ones. A baby's responses, if inborn, may actually condition a father's action emphasis, or with a girl, his concern. Whatever the basis, by nine months of age, 75 percent of the babies Dr. Pedersen studied were attached to their fathers; the balance, he felt, were simply delayed in forming the attachment.

Dr. Pedersen considers this attachment very valuable. He speculates that the father enhances his baby's independence, a quality valued in America, by being interesting and desirable enough to draw the baby beyond the mother-infant duo. He weans the child from her. The father may also promote his child's mental development. His more vigorous interaction and play seem to familiarize the baby with novel and arousing stimulation. This familiarity may increase the child's involvement during exploration and play with the inanimate world, which offers the same kind of stimulation. Such involvement has been found to promote certain mental skills best used in such professions as engineering and mathematics.

Dr. Pedersen also looked at that once so important facet of father, his authority. In the study, a father's authoritarian control, unlike his caretaking, play, and patience, did not relate to the baby's attachment to him. Its real impact comes at two to three years of age when setting limits for the child becomes so important.

Most intriguing of all, it was found that babies seem to learn sex differences from their fathers. While most theorists feel that masculinity is learned from the father and femininity from the mother, some (Dr. Pedersen, for one) are beginning to feel that the father is the key parent for establishing feminine identity as well. In 1963, Miriam Johnson, Ph.D., a United States psychologist, presented the theory that emphasized the father as more differentiating than the mother. Father stresses sex-typing of toys, for example, and girls discover feminine response from interaction with him; they learn how to be charming.

Dr. Pedersen's study revealed that baby boys whose fathers played vigorously with them responded differently to strangers according to their sex. Why? Because they had apparently experienced one kind of handling from men, another from women. In comparison, baby boys with fathers who did not initiate active physical contact responded in the same way to strange women or men; they either avoided or approached both sexes. The girls did not respond differently to strangers, possibly because their fathers treated them as gently as their mothers did.

Sex Differences and Preferences

This valuable finding suggests that the learning of sex differences comes from personal experience with men and women rather than anatomy, which is the thinking of Freudian psychologists. It suggests, too, that awareness of sex differences and sex preference appear as early as nine or ten months. By the end of the first year, babies show the rudiments of sexual identity; for boys, a quick recovery from a fall, preference for play with father at the end of the day, and the slow switching of imitation from the mother to the father.

If a baby at nine or ten months can distinguish men from women and if a model is needed to develop sexual identity, then boys without fathers may be less likely to develop male identity. Drs. Burton and Whiting, noted United States psychologists, suggest that a boy's conflict over his sexual identity is more likely to occur if the father is absent in his early years. Girls, too, may be handicapped in their relationships with the opposite sex. It may be that a little girl grows fearful of men because she is unfamiliar with them. As an adult she maintains her distance. Though she may procreate, she lives alone with other females or only briefly with men. Her daughter, again removed from an important, loving man, repeats the pattern of estrangement.

Father's influence on his child's mental, sexual, and emotional growth continues into childhood, adolescence, and adulthood. In the United States, Martin Deutsch found that in lower-income black families, young children without fathers scored lower on the Stanford-Binet tests of intelligence than their contemporaries with fathers.

Father is also being recognized as a real, full-time parent right from the very beginning. This budding recognition is part of a growing trend in the United States away from role stereotypes. An example is that girls wear slacks and shirts more and more places and boys with long hair are not (as frequently as before) labeled "queers." The Women's Liberation Movement, despite whatever else one might say about it, is demanding recognition for women as professionals rather than as mothers only and men are being recognized as parents. The father of an illegitimate child, for instance, now has a legal right to voice his opinion on placement of the child for adoption.

Today's women also seem less willing than the previous generation to tolerate careers that will keep their men away from home and parenthood. For example, retentions of naval officers who characteristically must work years of sea duty have dropped from 75 to 25 percent.

Among the educated upper middle class, father is involving himself more and more with pregnancy and child rearing. A tenet of the natural childbirth movement is the father's participation before and during the birth. He attends courses with his wife and often becomes emotionally involved with the pregnancy. Recently a few hospitals have allowed the father to attend his child's birth. Rooming-in for mothers in a few more hospitals allows the fathers to handle their infants.

In today's America, the demise of the extended family, which used to help insulate and support the young mother, has intensified her need for her husband, as well as added to the stresses upon him. But even in those bygone days, the husband was important to his wife. While a baby can love and interact with a father substitute, an uncle or a grandfather could never give a woman the intimacy and support of the husband-and-wife relationship. Clearly, a mother and child need the father, not least for the support and comfort he can render throughout the child's life.

Birth Order and Growth

If your fourteen-month-old is your first child, you may be thinking of having a second child. There is research that indicates that there are distinct advantages to spacing your first-born and upcoming baby about three years apart. Here is some interesting information that may help you make up your mind.

How close together should you have children? Dr. Akmakjian believes children would be given a decided advantage if they were spaced *three years apart* (better more than less). He believes that it is easier to deal with a newborn when the older child has learned to use the toilet, is gaining independence, and communicating fairly well. He thinks that if the gap is wide enough, the mother will not have to cater to two babies instead of one. Baby can be put to sleep and fed earlier than the older sibling. It also can provide the older child with a block of time with either parent. With the psychological separation of the first-born from the mother that normally is accomplished by age three, the birth of a new sibling is easier on the older child. The arrival of a newborn is less of a threat to an older child who has some mastery of her emotions.

There are others who believe that spacing children *two years apart* permits them to become playmates and there is less of a chance of their becoming rivals. Dr. Akmakjian and other psychologists and pediatricians disagree. They believe that sibling rivalry is inevitable in families. No young child can understand why a second child is needed and interprets the birth of a newborn as a rejection by the parents. Afraid of further loss of the parents' affection, the older child takes his hostility out on the baby instead.

Although there are difficult periods ahead for Number One son or daughter (with behavior regressions and other manifestations of disturbance), sibling rivalries ultimately work themselves out. A three-year difference does not appear to create problems as sharp as four- and five-year differences. For an infant or toddler to keep up with a five-year-old is potentially physically dangerous and emotionally stressful. If you are planning to have three or four children, know that the middle ones will never feel quite so well loved.

Mothers treat their baby boys differently than their baby girls, just as they act differently toward their first-borns than toward later babies—so says Dr. Lewis, director of the Infant Laboratory at the Educational Testing Service. Since mother is so all-important in the early years, these differences in her behavior influence her baby's mental and social development. For example, first-born babies receive more of mother's attention and concern and tend to be more intellectual than subsequent children. The high correlation between being a first-born and occupational success in adult life is probably no accident. As young as three months of age, first-borns are more attentive.

They also are more oriented toward adults because they are their primary social contacts for at least the first year of life. Even after a second child is born, the first-born still patterns her behavior after that of the parents. This lack of orientation to contemporaries may explain the comparative inability of many successful professionals to have successful interpersonal relationships. First-borns may also be less innovative. A study of scientists who have made outstanding discoveries in their fields revealed that first-borns contributed to ongoing advances while latter-borns tended to disrupt the continuum.

Children born after the first child receive less *contingent* attention and stimulation from adults. *Contingency* is important. It means that mother's response is a result of the child's behaviors. The child does something and the mother does something back. The ghetto child often gets lots of stimulation— people bustling around; bright lights; loud, sudden noises—but not the kind that relates to him.

From their first month of life, second and third children expect to live with others. They see and mimic the behavior of peers and older brothers and sisters instead of adults. Infants, in fact, seem to prefer watching other youngsters. This difference in social models makes a difference in the baby's behavior. For example, latter-born children may be merrier than first-borns. Although parents are just as delighted as brothers and sisters with an infant's smiles, adult reactions are not as free and spontaneous as those of children.

Latter-borns also differ among themselves. The second child of three gets squeezed in the middle and usually receives less attention than the first or third. This child may have more difficulty than middle children in a family of four, who might tend to comfort each other. There are hundreds of pictures of the first baby. The second child is lucky if she has half a dozen. Parents can alter this disparity by being aware of it and consciously working to give this child "equal time."

The last child, the third in the average American family, receives stimulation from brothers and sisters and also gets contingent attention from parents. There are many reasons for this. First children are such a proving ground that few parents enjoy them fully. Also the final baby represents the end of the child-producing function. To mother, and perhaps to father, too, he is a constant reminder of their earliest adventure in child rearing. Both parents now are more experienced and relaxed.

Spacing between children also influences the way a child is socialized and, therefore, learns. Twins on the average have I.Q.'s several points lower than those of single children. Pairs of children spaced further apart do better on intelligence tests than those born closer together. A last child born more than three years after the previous one is treated more like a single child. In the intellectual sphere at least, spacing makes this child more like a first-born. Mother has time to give contingent attention. The main disadvantage is from the parents' viewpoint: they seem to spend half their lives rearing children.

When the baby's sex is considered along with birth order and spacing, prediction of "results" becomes virtually impossible. The interaction of sex and birth order affects relationships between children and their parents, as well as among brothers and sisters. A middle child of a different sex has novelty going for him or her from the first.

THE FOURTEENTH MONTH

Motor Development

Gross Motor

Stands alone

Kneels on floor or chair

Crawls over low barrier

Climbs stairs on hands and knees

Creeps like a bear, hands and soles of both feet in contact with floor

Able to start and stop when walking, with equidistant alternation of feet

Stoops and recovers toys from floor

Fine Motor

Can pick up and hold 2 small objects in one hand (cubes, spools)

Can hold 4 cubes in hands at one time

Piles 2–3 cubes

Voluntarily releases and goes after object

Reaches for object by smooth, continuous movement with no spatial error

Language Acquisition

Likes rhymes and jingles

Indicates wants in some other way than by crying

Is putting all kinds of sounds together

Brings coat to indicate desire to be taken out

May bring parent a record to have it played

Tries hard to make self understood

Amuses self with vocal play

Attempts to say any word she or he hears

Knows through words or signs names of objects she or he uses: chair, cup, teddy bear, kitty, doll, etc.

Knows names of family members

Speaking vocabulary of 3–5 words

Repeats sounds of words without indication of understanding the meaning

Sensory Powers/Learning

Scribbles spontaneously with crayon or pencil

Tries to see, touch, and taste all the things around her or him

Imitates housework

Is discovering he or she can make things happen by his or her own actions

Searches for hidden toys

Understands relationship between a container and the contained

Bounces to music

Indicates likes, dislikes, and preferences; recognizes and remembers

Demonstrates awareness of the action of reprimand

May scream to show his or her power

Points to one named body part

Social Development

Demands personal attention

Adores an audience

Appears to be establishing own basic style as a social animal

Calls parent to be taken out of crib in morning

Drops objects from high chair to get parent to interact

Imitates housework

Upon request offers toys to others and lets go of them, but may immediately want them back

Dear Parents:
   Do not regard this chart as a rigid timetable.
   Babies are unpredictable individuals. Some perform an activity earlier or (as much as six months) later than the chart indicates, while others skip a behavior altogether (i.e., walking without crawling).
   Just use this information to anticipate and appreciate normal child development and behavior. No norms are absolutes.

Growth Chart

Personality/ Psychological

More self-assertive

May throw things when angry

May be afraid of the dark

May be afraid of strangers

Throwing things is a favorite pastime

Wants to do as much as she or he can alone

Self-Help Routines

Can hold cup for drinking

Uses spoon without help, spilling some

Likes to feed self; in process smears food on his or her face, bib, and high chair tray

May cooperate in dressing by extending an arm or leg when so requested

Sleeps undisturbed by noise

Pulls off socks

Play and Playthings

Engages in solitary play

Enjoys sitting on floor and rolling ball back to parent or older sibling

Relishes "Ride a cock horse" and somersault games

Delights in roughhouse play

Plays with materials, but discards or loses interest after a brief time

Babbles into toy telephone; may say "bye-bye" to signify end of "conversation"

Actively participates in "chase me–catch me" game

THE FIFTEENTH MONTH
Explorer of the Senses

Gross-Motor Progress

Fifteen months is another milestone in your toddler's development. For now your child has finished going through the stages of head balance and control, sitting balance, creeping, standing balance, and walking (upright locomotion). These steps often are called "developmental milestones" by researchers who use them to estimate an infant's overall rate of growth and development.

Although infants and toddlers do not progress evenly at a standard rate, they do move through the *same stages* of development and in about the *same order.* To make it easier for you to check your own child's development, the following is a listing of developmental milestones. The approximate ages at which 50 percent, 75 percent, and 90 percent of all children reach them are indicated. If your child has been slow (later than 75 percent of all children) in reaching more than three of these milestone behaviors, it would be well to discuss the matter with your doctor.

"The walking fifteen-month-old has graduated in a real sense from being an infant. Parents complain that when their babies start walking, they grow up all at once. They discard the nursing bottle. By gesture-language they may call attention to wet pants or a toy they cannot reach. Patterns of behavior and motor skills that were in the making now come to fruition. The toddler is in no

The Second Twelve Months
Developmental Milestones*

	Age Achieved by Percentage of Children		
	50 percent	**75 percent**	**90 percent**

Gross Motor

	50 percent	75 percent	90 percent
1. On stomach: lifts head strongly, face straight ahead	2 mos.	2½ mos.	3½ mos.
2. On back: turns head freely from side to side, head centered most of the time	2 mos.	2½ mos.	3 mos.
3. On stomach: raises head and chest, supporting self on forearms or arms	3 mos.	3½ mos.	4½ mos.
4. Rolls completely over: any direction	2½ mos.	3½ mos.	4½ mos.
5. Sitting, supported: holds head erect and steady	3 mos.	3½ mos.	4½ mos.
6. Sits alone for 30 seconds or more	6 mos.	7 mos.	8 mos.
7. Gets from lying to sitting without aid	8 mos.	9½ mos.	11 mos.
8. Prewalking progression: creeping on hands and knees or hands and feet; sit-and-hitch	7 mos.	10 mos.	11 mos.
9. Pulls self to stand by furniture	7 mos.	9 mos.	10 mos.
10. Stands alone: 10 seconds or more	10½ mos.	13 mos.	14 mos.
11. Walks well alone	12 mos.	13½ mos.	14 mos.

Personal-Social

	50 percent	75 percent	90 percent
1. Feeds self cracker, cookie, etc.	5½ mos.	6½ mos.	8 mos.
2. Indicates wants in some way other than by crying	12 mos.	13½ mos.	14 mos.
3. Drinks from cup: holds himself, cup without spout	11½ mos.	14 mos.	16 mos.
4. Uses spoon, spills little	14½ mos.	18 mos.	24 mos.

Fine Motor

	50 percent	75 percent	90 percent
1. Picks up small object (crumb, raisin) between tips of forefinger and thumb	10½ mos.	12½ mos.	14½ mos.
2. Scribbles spontaneously with crayon, pencil, etc.	13½ mos.	16 mos.	24 mos.

Language

	50 percent	75 percent	90 percent
1. Says 3 words other than *mama* and *dada*	13 mos.	15 mos.	21 mos.

*From *Growing Child,* 1973 (124 W. State St., Lafayette, IN 47902).

mood to settle down to a quiet existence. He looks older in the upright stance than when creeping. Now your child sees himself as a grown-up and tries to show this perception by doing grown-up things; for example, he seeks to drive the family car, talk on the telephone, start the vacuum cleaner, sit at the adult table."

Your toddler's gross-motor drive is powerful. She is continuously active—starting, stopping, clambering, climbing, and exercising all new-found powers to excess. Your fifteen-month-old is learning different ways of walking—trotting, running, or dawdling. When you take her to the supermarket, she is no longer content to sit in the carriage but prefers to stand up. Now there is open rebellion against being housed in a playpen. Your child is becoming very demanding and strains at the bit. At this age the toddler stands on a chair for things out of reach and wants to carry something in each hand while walking. She insists on doing everything without help or interference. The fifteen-month-old overturns wastebaskets and empties them with great delight, but rarely returns the contents to the basket. When parents dress or diaper their child, she wriggles and turns, probably because she is seeking the upper hand.

Keeping up with the toddler's whims can drive parents "up a tree" during this time. Some years ago a noted athlete tried to keep up with the gross-motor actions of a walking toddler. He literally fell apart by midday and gave up following the child about. The walking child's favorite physical activities are pushing objects around—chairs, furniture, wagons (the larger the better), opening and closing doors, crawling under tables, and so on.

"Manipulating and exploring mechanisms are a prime activity of this age level. Fifteen-month-olds continue to explore the immediate environment, but are more selective in the toys and objects they play with. These include articles and tools that older siblings or parents use; for example, wallets, keys, screwdrivers, lipsticks, pens, watches, matches, telephones, magazines, razors, and so on. In each room of the house, toddlers have favorite things and activities. In the parents'

bedroom, climbing up onto the parents' bed and pretending sleep; in the kitchen, opening the refrigerator door and removing bottles, or opening cabinets and hiding toys, or (if the cabinet is large enough) himself.

"This is the time when toddlers explore hardness and softness. They tap the floor with an object or tap two objects against each other; or they mouth such things as mud, a can, a rock, hair clippers. It is a primitive type of trial-and-error exploration that can sometimes lead to destructiveness and accidents—and family hysteria—if things are scattered about and not picked up.

"All the exploratory play and the persistent demands of the toddler to use the household articles that adults use is a healthy sign of the emerging awareness of the toddler as a person," points out Dr. Marilyn Segal of Nova University." Whereas one-year-olds try out a schema on all objects in their environment, the fifteen-month-old prefers those objects that adults use in their daily life. They stand and watch their father shave and later seek to reach the sink and shelf area where razors are kept.

"What are parents to do when conflict develops? Many parents set certain defined areas for play the moment their child becomes ambulatory. Bathrooms and libraries are off-limits because these afford a child easy access to hair sprays, toilet paper, interesting items in wastebaskets, and other forbidden items. Other parents provide a special drawer or open shelf with aluminum pots, pans, jar covers for plastic bottles, and so on. To avoid constant up- and downstairs traffic in a bi-level home, some mothers provide a basket of toys upstairs and one downstairs and try to limit exploration to these baskets and open shelves. At this age level, parents feel that a toddler can be taught what things can be touched and those items that can be played with. Such teaching takes much time, but parents must play the part of teachers or retard their child's learning. Actually stamping an item as forbidden encourages rather than discourages a child. Letting a child touch something or hold it while you are there is the kind of rule setting and compromising that has to take place if children are to learn about freedom."

Fine-Motor Development

In the area of fine-motor development, the voluntary ability of a fifteen-month-old to pick up and release hold of an object or wooden cube does not appear to the average adult as a great achievement. Dr. Gesell called this "casting," actually an elaborate development of controlling nerve cells of the brain. It takes time to master this skill. The child has to learn how to modulate her release, to time it accu-

rately, and to make it obedient to her intentions. Like any other physical development, it needs to be practiced over and over again. Whereas the year-old child can only try to pose one cube on top of another one, the fifteen-month-old can let go of the block to build a block tower of two units, or release a pellet into a bottle. This achievement provides the schema for releasing a ball when the toddler throws it and enables her to play a primitive back-and-forth ball game.

Trial-and-Error Learning

The fifteen-month-old begins to use objects as if they represented something meaningful. Whereas the twelve-month-old is satisfied with banging a spoon, the fifteen-month-old uses it to stir in a saucepan. Provide a broom and your child will sweep the floor; present a brush and he will brush his hair. (Sometime at the end of the second year, the toddler will begin to pretend that blocks are food or a pillow for sleeping.)

This new approach to playing with objects is closely correlated with the toddler's beginning use of words to express ideas and the ability to handle ideas.

Watch your toddler as she plays in the bath with floating toys and other objects. Your child continues to push them under the water and watches them bob up; then splashes them to start them moving. By trial and error children become more skillful at repeating *a sequence of actions*. Ultimately they become able to try out new variations without going through the original trial-and-error manipulations. To put this another way, the child begins to try to think things out in her head instead of with objects in such a way that she can foresee what to do and what the results will be.

In a study of children this age, all were given a long stick to get at a toy out of their reach. The fifteen-month-old was able to get the toy by means of trial and error and by imitating adult behavior. Eighteen-month-olds knew how to do this without trial and error or imitation. They were able to "figure out" how to reach the toy and did so successfully.

The fifteen-month-old is also learning about space, shape, and size and how things are related to each other. The toddler drops a ball and it rolls out of sight. At eleven or twelve months of age, the child would try to retrieve it by looking at the point where it disappeared. Now he will search for it in the back of the sofa. The fifteen-month-old comprehends that even though it was invisible as it rolled, it must have reached the back of the sofa.

An interesting change takes place, too, in how the toddler plays with some of her toys. If given a Playskool Post Office or a shape-sorting box, the twelve-month-old would open the top and put in or take out some of the varishaped beads. The fifteen-month-old is challenged by the shapes and tries fitting the shapes into the corresponding holes. If given a color cone with different-sized discs, the one-year-old would place them over the long dowel stick without regard to size. At fifteen months, size differentiation is important. The child considers the job well done if she stacks the wood or plastic discs in perfect conical order, the largest at the bottom and the smallest at the top.

Now your child is using ideas in much more complicated ways—studying and mastering the relationships between things without having to see or handle them. The fifteen-month-old begins to put together bits of knowledge about all kinds of things and their relationships and puts them into his memory bank. The toddler's ability to store sequences of actions, to recall and compare events is fantastic. He likes order and repetition and repeats a song, rhyme, or a record over and over again until the sounds or rhythms have been mastered. As the end of the second twelve months are reached, your child will have begun to use words for things and will describe wants with words. Whereas every intellectual or problem-solving project was once worked out with actions, the child now has ability to use schemata (images and ideas of things) and to label them with words instead of resorting to gestures, intonations, or gibberish.

"Although most fifteen-months-olds are preoccupied with walking, they find time for manipulating the adult tools around the house. They poke, pull, and twist any part of an older brother's motorcycle or father's lawn mower. Even if these are too difficult to move, they try anyway. This is the time when the toddler insists on pushing the carriage as well as being transported."

Urge to Climb

The strongest urge in fifteen-month-olds is the desire to climb. They have little trouble with climbing and scrambling on today's soft-textured covered-foam furniture. Since they have few inner structural supports and are usually low in height, parents do not seem terribly upset with this type of exploration. However, hardback chairs, rocking chairs, or circular staircases sometimes present insurmountable barriers because there are no toeholds. Sooner or later these "incipient mountain climbers" accomplish their objective only to come face to face with another movement problem; for instance, how to limit the rocking chair's action so they will not fall.

On the playground, the toddler has to contend with and master large-sized swings, jungle gyms, and slides without sufficient bottoming-out leeway for lightweight fifteen-month-olds to slow down. As a result, a child may fall with a thud on a hard surface and refuse for many months to tackle the slide again. Following a four-year-old sibling up such a slide, the fifteen-month-old will usually freeze at a five-foot height and cry for help. Usually a firm parent pats or supports and reassures the child, who is helped to reach another physical milestone.

No toddler can be left unsupervised during these critical climbing periods because every task is fraught with danger. Keeping the child away from such play is not the answer. Learning to manage danger is an art that is mastered in time—if parents' supervision is unobtrusive, if anxiety is hidden from the child, and if reassurance and support are freely given.

Of course, there are alternatives to constant supervision of toddlers who are discovering their climbing powers. One is to plan and build a small play yard either cooperatively with neighbors or by yourself. Such a play yard should have a substantial sandbox (to last throughout early childhood), covered with two opening and closing doors to keep out dog or cat excretions. Water play is an important activity for this age level and a fiberglass or concrete wading pool imbedded in the ground will ensure many happy hours of water play—filling and emptying containers. Of course, you will have to supervise your toddler's outdoor play. A four-foot-high platform with climbing ladders or climbing holes on all sides makes a fine playhouse. An attached fifteen- to twenty-inch slide without handrails will become your toddler's first "encounter with danger." To minimize falls, the area should be covered with a four- to six-inch surface of large (three-fourths inch) smooth beach pebbles. Pebbles give way and cushion a fall. Enterprising parents could try making four twenty-two-by-twenty-two-inch wooden tote boxes (plastic ones also are available). Walking boards eight inches wide, small barrels, and sawhorses can be purchased at school supply houses. Hollow wooden blocks, a washboard, and wash basin also are fine props for water play. Pails, shovels, sand toys, large lightweight "water-painting" brushes, and so on will keep any toddler busy for long periods. Swings, seesaws, and metal jungle gyms require a great deal of adult supervision.

Games Toddlers Play

When a child walks, she develops a series of games to involve mother, father, or other caretaker. Playing peek-a-boo and being chased are perennial favorites. The most popular one is to bring toys to mother and then take them back. This type of game goes on endlessly. Hiding a toy and later discovering it is a self-directed activity in which the child hopes to involve mother or father. Emptying toy baskets and methodically placing the toys or household articles in favored positions is another game that expresses emerging ego powers. Do not expect your fifteen-month-old to learn to put back all the toys she has scattered. Develop a singing game that involves you both in putting toys back. *Mine, yours, I give, I take* are techniques developed by toddlers to draw mothers and fathers into their play.

Imagination

Imagination or fantasy turns the mundane into the magical. You nurture imagination when you permit your child to explore, when you trust his ability to master a skill, create a song, or simply sit and dream. In these ways, you give your child the right to think for himself.

Your own inventiveness can stretch your toddler's imagination. The child who is asked to shut her eyes and listen hard enough to describe every sound she hears—the blue jay, the dryer tumbling clothes, the scissors clicking—will not only have a better awareness of sounds, but a richer reservoir of words.

The music your child hears and the stories you tell also broaden his ideas. Your toddler will get even more from an activity if he takes part in it—singing, dancing, making believe. Imagination gives wings to the intellect.

Sensory Powers: Vision

The fifteen-month-old may not be able to talk, but uses every sensory power to "digest" the experiences offered by the environment.

Your task as a facilitator of your child's learning starts at birth, when your infant hears sounds and works at distinguishing one from another. You encourage your baby to follow moving objects. You change the views from the crib regularly: pictures, wall murals, window stickers, mobiles, "stars" that glow in the night, and so on. Your baby will be interested in picture books that fit on the crib. At age one

your baby will delight in seeing her image in a full-length mirror and will enjoy the game you play on the recognition of bodily parts.

Have you ever wondered why you cannot in your adult drawings or paintings recreate a blossoming cherry tree that you have been eyeing for twenty years while a four-year-old can recreate the tree in almost exact detail? Sensitivity to fine detail is a learned activity that requires parent initiative during the critical first two years of life when the infant and toddler can give sharpest attention. Children need parental input and stimulation to point out hidden surprises: the white, black, and gray squirrels, the horse weathervane on a barn, spiders in their webs, the different types of animal gaits. Marguerite Kelly and Elia Parsons put it this way: "Once you help a child see the unseen he will always see it again."

Touch

Touch is a quickly developing sensory power. Nature gives the newborn a "reflexive" (inborn) ability to grasp your finger and, in due time, to put her thumb in her mouth and to discover her fingers and toes. The walking child "sees" with her fingertips. As a child locomotes, she fingers the gate along the walk, the bumps on a rubber tire, the water out of a garden hose. The toddler cannot resist the bark on every tree because each is a different texture and she wants to touch them all. Parents of toddlers soon discover their child's sensory patterns and habits and try to respect these touch-and-feel sensitivities. Your child loves to go barefoot on the rug or in the sand.

When you begin to understand your child's sensory responses you can help him develop the necessary skills to enrich this growing sensitivity. When your fifteen-month-old handles a crayon awkwardly at first and has difficulty making bold strokes on a sheet of paper, you may notice that his hand is cramped and stiff. You can intervene and help your toddler relax his grasp by playing finger-and-touch games, playing the piano, and so forth.

Toddlers can be irritating when they want to finger everything—the bannister of a stairway, the edge of a table, the contours of your face. Actually most people and *all* children must feel and finger an object before they can incorporate its schema into their memory. There have been many heated discussions among educators about whether very young children learn verbally at all and there are differing points of view about translating concepts into laboratory approaches with tangible materials. Dr. Maria Montessori was a pioneer educator who contributed all kinds of didactic materials for stimulating sensory awareness on the part of young children.

To be able to touch in freedom requires your cooperation. Minimize the constant *no's* by assigning some time during the day for playing a matching textures guessing game. Into a big paper bag you can put two of all kinds of textures—sandpaper squares, felt, macaroni (yes, uncooked), pebbles, nails, corduroy, and so on. Whoever pulls out a nail has to find the matching object. Later in the year you might want to add "naming the objects" to your game play.

If you must curb your child's sense of touch, do it with reasonable "rules" rather than with threats and warnings. Hands have to be washed after playing with mud or clay; you ask a visitor's permission when you want to touch her fur coat, and so on. As your child develops into young adulthood, you will see your encouragement paying off in heightened perceptual abilities.

Sound

Sound starts very, very early—in the fifth month of pregnancy when researchers have found that the fetus responds to sounds of all kinds. Sound is one of the most developed abilities in a newborn child. Researchers believe that a musician who practices continually during pregnancy gives birth to a child with a natural rhythmic sensitivity. Of course, such a newborn still has to master a whole new set of sounds: her own cry, your voice, and the soothing sounds and lullabies

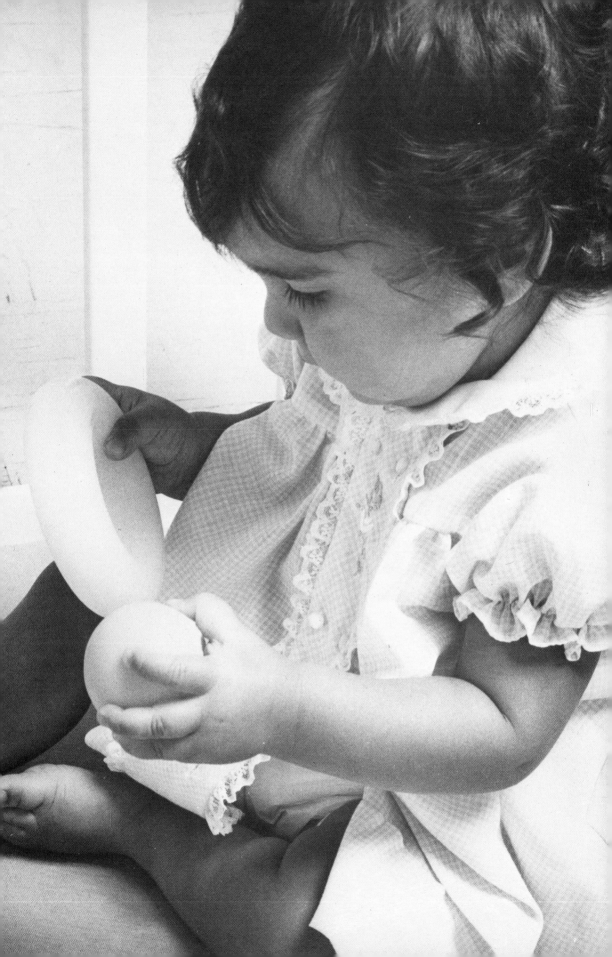

you sing. Through records, radio, wind chimes, bells, music boxes, and so on you can enrich the environment with a variety of sounds for your child to distinguish. You can expand the listening skill by games—filling two sets of cylindrical containers (with caps) with rice, lentils, gravel, sand, and so on and asking your fifteen-month-old to match and pair them by the sounds. Try not to get upset when during this period she makes every possible noise and starts a regimen of screeching at the top of her voice simply to play with sounds or to test your response.

Smell

Smell as a distinguishing tool is often neglected. At birth, the sense of smell is completely developed. The infant's first contact with smell in his contact with you and the rest of the world should be a pleasant one. Hospitals are beginning to take seriously a French gynecologist's advice (Frederick Leboyer) to burn incense in the delivery room. The emergence of your and your child's love affair—building a sense of trust—can be encouraged with the use of sweet-smelling lotions, as well as body odors. Encourage this sense of smell with a walk in a flower garden; introduce your child to the marvelous smells and ingredients in the kitchen: onions, garlic, celery salt, bread baking, soup cooking, and so on. Let your fifteen-month-old help you pulverize a cinnamon stick, mix allspice, and so forth. Odors have their own curriculum and vocabulary. Practice them with your child throughout the first two years.

Taste

The sense of taste is another area where little if any "education" takes place. When a new food is introduced, your child will examine every surface of it with his tongue. In the

second year, introduce him to all kinds of foods by allowing him to lick the spoon of anything you cook or bake. Make a game out of it by asking your toddler what it is. Of course, your child will enjoy it more if you let him taste only the foods he already enjoys, but remember that you are trying to teach your toddler to be a more experimental eater. (You will have to make sure your child does not interpret this as a trick to introduce new foods.)

Stimulating the sense of taste should be a slow process. Fifteen-month-olds fixate on a food they like and keep asking for it throughout life. You will have to be careful about introducing candies and cookies, dishes with more than one flavor (stews), or food with peculiar textures, such as fish roe, raw clams, bagels and lox, and so on. Cultivated tastes in this critical second twelve months of life can bring you an adventuresome eating companion or can result in a poor eater. It all depends upon how you introduce the new foods.

Social Powers

"Although the investigation of objects and their uses occupies a major portion of a toddler's 'working' hours, it is only one aspect of his exploratory behavior. A second area of exploration is social. The child is becoming more and more interested in exploring the effects he has on other people. Can the child get attention by shouting, showing off, or imitating the gestures of others? Can he make people react in an interesting way by pinching, poking, shoving, or hugging? Can he make people do the things he wants by pulling, hitting, whining, crying, or smiling?

"A child whose parents set up consistent and reasonable limits learns several things through his explorations. The fifteen-month-old learns that he does have the power to affect other people, but that this power is not without limits. The child can get the father to let him taste his dinner, but cannot get the parent to give up his whole meal. The child can play and kick and fuss for a while during a diaper change, but if he acts up for too long, the parent will hold him down firmly and the diaper will be put on.

"The child also is learning that certain techniques for affecting people work better than others. He may learn that he gets things faster when he cries than when he hits, or that people pay more attention when he laughs than when he screams. Some toddlers learn that different people react in different ways; i.e., crying may produce a desired outcome with a grandfather, but not with a father. Hitting may bring a laugh from daddy, but may make mommy very angry. It is much easier for the child to learn effective social techniques when parents are in agreement on what the limits are.

"At the same time that children explore their power to affect other people, they exert themselves to the limits of their own power and ability. They push and pull, lug and carry, open and shut, climb up and slide down in a constant effort to find out just what they can do. Eventually they reach the limits of their endurance, but they are too keyed up to agree to a nap or to go quietly off to bed. The end result often is a temper tantrum or a burst of uncontrollable tears. Some children fall asleep after a few seconds of crying. Others need help in settling down before they can fall asleep. Again, each family finds its own way of helping its child handle his exhaustion. Relaxed pacing during the day and establishing a workable routine help prevent the buildup of tension."

Growing Sense of Humor

"While the fifteen-month-old presents the family with many new challenges, he also is an entertaining companion. A delightful aspect of your child's self-awareness is his growing sense of humor. Your toddler realizes that he can become the center of attention and enjoys the role. Your fifteen-month-old dances to music now, not just because he can, but because he enjoys the applause. After a performance, your child looks around the room to see the effect he has created. Once the attention of the audience has been captured, your offspring will perform his entire repertoire. This repertoire may consist of a bouncing up-and-down dance step, a tilt of the head, a halfway somersault, swinging the arms, turning around in a circle, or perhaps crawling on the floor. This reversion to crawling as a joke shows your toddler's awareness that he is really too big to crawl. In other words, your child is making a distinction between the baby he was and the child he is now.

"Living with a fifteen-month-old is never a dull experience. For some parents, it is a favorite age. They enjoy the opportunity of interacting with their child in new and different ways and are fascinated by their child's new discoveries and growing sense of humor."

Self-Help at the Dinner Table

"Fifteen-month-olds are not only demanding of others, they also are demanding of themselves. In short, they are asserting the beginnings of self-dependence. They want to get out of the high chair and sit at the dinner table just like the rest of the family. They insist on feeding themselves with a spoon or holding mother's cup of coffee. They can grasp a cup with both hands, but then tilt it and, of course, 'bring the house down' by spilling its contents. They will thrust a spoon into their cereal and then put it in their mouth upside down."

If a fifteen-month-old walker who is meeting new locomotion challenges is suddenly hospitalized or goes through some other stressful situation, be prepared for some regression of all learned physical skills. Your child will tend to become tired more easily, and toward the end of the morning, will regress to creeping instead of walking. If traumas result from the birth of a new baby, the supposedly normal child will suddenly start to hurt himself, show a marked increase in crying, or continually climb into the mother's lap. As time goes on, he may become restless and hyperactive. The child also may show signs of wanting to be a baby, climb into the playpen, become less responsive to the mother's verbal instruction, and begin to show aggressive behavior, i.e., throwing things or running around aimlessly.

Nightmares

With growth in the toddler's ability to play out roles and events, with fantasy and imaginative play, comes the ability to play out scary characters in dreams and in nightmares. The child talks to herself before and after going to bed. Then suddenly after a period of sleep, she lets out a scream and frantically kicks. It takes the parents about a half-hour to quiet their child and reassure her that they are present, that it was only a bad dream. Nightmares are an outgrowth of a child's ability to think on a symbolic level, to transform reality into fantasy, to control the direction of imaginary characters. Such distortion of reality sometimes becomes so powerful that a preschooler becomes confused by what is real and what is made up. To calm your child it is best to search out the "monster" and go through the motions of tossing the monster out the window. (Sometime around four years of age, your child will be able to distinguish between dreams and reality.)

Feeding Problems

If you asked parents of fifteen-month-olds what they considered a major child-rearing problem, fully 80 percent would answer "feeding." All mothers of children this age complain about "picking" and poor eating habits. Even though it is natural for eating to slow down in the second year because walking, climbing, talking, locomotion, and communicating seem more important to the toddler, parents cannot make the adjustment from an enthusiastic feeder in the first year to an impossible eater in the second.

More feeding problems start between one and two years than at any other period. The more the mother frets and urges, the less the child eats—and the less the child takes, the more anxious the mother is. Mealtimes become agonizing contests of wills and the problem may go on for years.

No child will become a feeding problem if the parents do not force eating. Feeding can become a problem when the parents (mother or father) attach an inordinate importance to the child's eating. This difficulty may begin when a child has been sickly or has lost weight during an illness. Then the child is exposed to a pressure that is rather mild at first, but eventually develops into violent coercion just short of war. Generally, a child exposed to this kind of pressure reacts with resistance because he has the impression that eating is not for its own sake, but for his parents' sake. Thus eating becomes a weapon to be used against parents if the child feels neglected or slighted.

Young children have very few ways of getting back at their parents. Refusing to eat is one of them. As soon as a child moves from passive dependence upon the mother to active use of his or her body to pursue self-help and independence, the whole push for independence becomes involved with food habits. Most eating problems in the mid-second year would vanish within a few weeks if parents permitted their child's natural impulses to exert themselves.

Dr. Fitzhugh Dodson claims that all this tension is completely unnecessary. Why? Because parents have a great ally on their side if they use it wisely: *the natural hunger of the child.* Dr. Dodson writes, "Let them go hungry and after a while the child will ask for food. Children lose nothing if they miss one, two, or occasionally three meals. Sometimes they refuse two meals, but eat so fully at the supper meal that they make up for any nutritional loss. The child's eating is no subject for discussion or commotion. The child will not starve if you refrain from meddling."

Think of all the attention a balky child gets from the parents. Such a child is even in a position to overpower you, to render you completely helpless, just by not eating. Nor should you sit quietly at the table glaring at your child.

The late Dr. Rudolf Dreikurs advocated that children should experience the natural consequences of their refusal to eat. When children do not eat a meal, they must wait for food until the next meal—no snacks, no candy, no bread and butter in between. At the next meal, they should have the same food that the rest of the family is served. You must be firm, resist all promises, temper tantrums, or other tricks. As soon as your child gags and struggles with his food, just remove the plate and calmly tell him that he probably is not hungry and should not force himself.

How do you handle the child who will eat only hamburgers and bananas or some other combination of two or three foods? Use the same technique as above. Give him the full meal you had planned, including a *small* amount of the hamburger and banana. If only the last two items are eaten, your child will be mildly hungry afterward. Do not give him anything to eat until the next meal. If you keep up this routine for three days, your child will be sampling and eating all the foods served.

Obesity: Feeding Fat Cells

Most Americans suffer from overeating and are forever dieting—with little or no success. What is wrong with being fat? Everything! It shortens the lifespan and can lead to a high incidence of serious diseases: heart disease, high blood pressure, diabetes, gallstones, and so on. Fat people are more prone to accidents, fatal and nonfatal. Excessive fat makes people miserable because they not only feel and look unattractive (by American standards), but they are discriminated against and persecuted in countless ways—socially, psychologically, economically.

Exactly what produces the tendency to be thin or fat is still conjecture. Many scientists believe that the regulatory center in the brain is genetically set higher or lower in different people. Genes may determine the way in which a person absorbs or digests foods or a higher number of fat cells may be inherited.

Alvin N. Eden, M.D., in his book *Growing Up Thin,* suggests that while inherited tendencies to be overweight are certainly of great importance, we should use them as warning signals. Once parents realize that their child is susceptible to being overweight, they should take a firm stand against it by not overfeeding or underexercising him or her.

Parents cannot do a thing about their children's genes, but they can prevent obesity if they start at the very beginning of the child's life. A few years ago, Doctors Jules Hirsch and Jerome Kittle made an amazing discovery in their research with rats. They divided twenty-six newborn rats into two groups, each with a normal nursing mother. The first group of newborns numbered only four and they grew fat. The second group numbered twenty-two, and because they had to compete for food from only one mother, they grew up lean. After weaning, all the young rats were offered a normal rat diet. The lean rats remained thin and the fat rats stayed fat. Throughout the tests, the rats' fat cells were counted and weighed. They concluded that the rats that grew fat soon after birth had developed an abnormally large number of fat cells that they never shed. Experiments and studies of humans at the Mount Sinai Medical Center in New York and at the University of London in England indicate that the earlier in life obesity begins, the greater the number of fat cells that form and need to be fed. Dr. Kittle deduced that the *critical period* in the development of fat cells occurs between birth and five years.

Dr. Eden believes that "it is important for parents to know that the fat baby and the child with excessive numbers of fat cells will never shed them, but will carry them around the rest of her life. She can shrink the fat cells by dieting, but they are always there to be filled up when the diet is over." If you do not want your child to grow up fat, his or her number of fat cells must remain normal. This can be accomplished by keeping a child thin right from the start in the first and second years of life.

The third factor leading to overweight (after the genes and fat cells) is eating habits that are set in the first two years. Many of us grow up without ever learning how to eat properly. We have a tendency to overfeed our children and ourselves. By the time children are five and six years old, they have lost most of their opportunity to grow up to be thin adults. They eat the wrong foods ("junk" foods); they are overfed with milk; they are fed solid foods long before they are necessary; and they are bribed with candy or cookies to eat everything on their plate—or even to behave.

The last factor contributing to obesity is our failure to exercise. Most of us just do not burn off enough calories. Children also benefit from exercise: walking, climbing, swimming, and so on.

Play and Playthings

Generally, favorite indoor playthings are a Kiddie Kar (with two wheels on the steering post) or the Playskool Tyke Trike, large five-by-five-inch hollow wooden or foam blocks, balls, spoons, cups, clothespins, and such fitting toys as a color cone, formboard, and postal station. Also enjoyed are bean bags to toss, large pop-it beads or blocks, and ride 'em toys (large, foot-propelled tractor, horse, locomotive, and so forth). Blowing soap-and-water bubbles is great fun.

Fifteen-month-olds enjoy playthings that challenge fine-muscle control: a large peg-board with thick pegs, a hammer and peg bench, large wooden or plastic beads to string, simple take-apart toys, beginner jigsaw puzzles, a screwing rod (oversized nuts and large bolts).

This is not yet the time to provide nursery school building blocks. Fifteen-month-olds lack the ability to manage them. Instead give your child a floor train or floor boat without wheels (usually found in school supply house catalogues and educational toy company catalogues). Because these are flat-bottomed and sturdy without complicated connectors, they can more easily be moved about on the floor. We call this type of toy an "unstructured" plaything because (1) a child can manipulate it any way and without frustration; (2) unpainted, each toy can be rearranged without a child's being distracted by matching colors; (3) sturdily built, such a toy can take punishment without child or parent anxiety about breakage.

Structured playthings are metal trains and tracks, trucks, cars and planes with fragile detailing, and so on. Normal rough handling by toddlers usually results in breakage. Children should not have to be subjected to restrictions by parents when they play with their toys. If toys are fragile and poorly made and can only frustrate your child, do not buy them. If they can be used for one purpose only and lack interchangeability, avoid them.

Indoor gross-motor playthings are especially enjoyed on rainy days. One of the better pieces of equipment is the Toddler's Climbing Gym. Made sturdily of hardwood, it has low steps that lead up to a platform, safe wide slide, and openings in the framework that are large enough for climbing into.

Below are other suitable playthings that will be enjoyed now and throughout your toddler's second year of life (and even beyond). Remember that toddlers play with toys differently as they go from one stage of maturation to the next one:

- Nesting blocks and nesting cylinders
- Jumping Jack
- Shape-sorting box (with cover that opens)
- Cardboard books with brightly colored pictures of animals and their babies, children doing familiar things, cars and trucks
- Small, sturdy four-wheel wagon (to pull or ride in)
- Small rocking chair
- Heavy-based wood doll carriage (to push or ride in)
- Stacking toys (Fisher-Price Donuts, and so on)
- All kinds of empty boxes
- Rocking horse
- Pots and pans of all sizes, an aluminum tea set, child-sized aluminum cutlery
- Pull toys (make sure string is strong and there are no loops that can slip over the child's head; these are best with interesting movement and sound)
- Washable, nonallergenic, soft stuffed animals
- Doll (an eight-inch all-rubber or vinyl one is recommended—without hair or moving eyes so it is impervious to water)
- Large kindergarten crayons and large sheets of paper (provide one color at a time and encourage large sweeps and bold strokes)

A Few Helpful Hints about Toys

If a child is bored or angry with a toy, it probably is too old for him or it serves no useful purpose. Remove it. Inappropriate toys make a child unhappy, as well as careless.

When a toy breaks, put it aside until you can repair it. If you cannot fix it, discard it.

Too many toys will overwhelm a child. Rotate all but a few of your toddler's favorite toys (about one-third of the toys) every few weeks. This will add freshness and revitalize play activity.

Choose toys without sharp points, thin edges, or protrusions. Look out for objects that may come off: bells, wheels, nuts, knobs, and so on.

Make sure ride 'em toys are tip-proof, well made, and sturdy.

A satisfactory toy will be returned to by your child throughout the years of childhood and be used in many different, interesting, and enjoyable ways.

Musical Toys

Fifteen-month-olds adore rhythm toys and playing with sounds, music, and rhythmic movement. A tambourine, musical triangle and striker, five-inch brass cymbals, rhythm sticks, and small drum can be purchased at a music store or educational toy shop. All can be used to accompany the beat of folk dance records, mother's or father's piano playing, Woody Guthrie's children's recordings, and rhythmic classical music.

This is the time to purchase a good record player, but one that is simple to operate, so that your toddler can learn how to manage it without any help. Dr. Dodson cautions parents not to confine themselves to records marked "children's records" only. Highly rhythmic music can be found on all folk recordings. There is a tremendous library of excellent classical recordings that will delight your child.

You must be prepared for the enormous amount of repetition that is characteristic of recordings for toddlers. Woody Guthrie understood that young children learn by repetition and repeated each theme over and over and over so that it could become a part of a child's memory. "Dance around and around and around" may tire and bore a parent, but never a fifteen-month-old.

A music box will be used with pleasure. Get the hand-cranked model so that your toddler can turn it to make music without help from you or anyone else.

Fantasy Play

Although toddlers this age are not ready to carry on extensive fantasy play, nonetheless they should be given a soft doll to play with (those without removable button-eyes; embroidered eyes are best at this time). Such dolls are plentiful today because local craft-oriented youth are building small businesses around well-designed soft toys. Each child finds security in sleeping with a good-sized cloth doll. Included in this category are such popular figures as Raggedy Ann or Andy, Snoopy, a teddy bear, and so forth. Since you, too, will be living with it for years to come, it makes good sense to purchase a fine, attractive, washable one.

Vague Stirring of Fantasy—Pretending

Somewhere between fifteen and twenty months, at the exact time when your toddler begins to use language more, she starts to manifest the glimmerings of imagination and pretending. It may start simply as "drinking" out of an empty cup or considering a block a "delicious food" to be "eaten." The toddler is beginning to use symbols; i.e., to play with the *idea* of something.

At fifteen months these bits of make-believe play are bound up with the child's self and own actions; the child may pretend to go to sleep and may pretend eating something. In the next two years, this make-believe play becomes less tied in with the child's own actions: she plays that a block is a car; that sand trickling through the fingers is rain; a stick is a horse, and so on. The child makes an imaginative jump into the preschool world of fantasy by playing at being something or someone other than herself. The imitations get more complex, more elaborate, and less closely tied to some real event.

Planning a Cooperative Playground

If you are ambitious and community-minded (especially if you live in a city), you may want to bring together mothers and fathers of toddlers and plan a playground for fifteen-month-olds.

Most park or recreation departments do not make provision for toddler playgrounds so they will welcome any initiative on your part. In the cities, especially in older neighborhoods, there are many empty lots that can be had if your group is willing to rent the lot for a minimal yearly lease, take out adequate accident insurance (about $100,000 worth, which would cost well below $100 a year), and maintain and supervise the playground.

Toddler playgrounds should have a shady area for hot weather and an eight-foot hill for practicing scrambling and running (such a hill might also discourage older children from using the area for a baseball field). Of course, your group will have to maintain the cleanliness of the playground. Among other things, you will need several sturdy, foolproof garbage containers and you will have to find a way to keep dogs out.

To equip a cooperative toddlers' playground, you may have to get contributions (a minimum of $500) to buy selected climbers. You might try to get gifts of three-foot cement conduits that can be set on their sides in cement so they will not roll. You might ask the telephone company for unwanted old telephone poles that can be fashioned into horses with funny faces and fancy tails. Other telephone poles might become the beginning of a three-foot-high playhouse. Railroad ties could enclose a sandbox (covered at night to protect it from garbage and dogs). With considerable group effort, a railroad tie could become the stanchion for a rope and leather seat-swing. You can purchase a ten-foot walking board, eight inches wide, with cleats, and a twenty- to twenty-four-inch sawhorse from a kindergarten supplier. These will make a perfect seesaw. With two sawhorses and a board, toddlers can enjoy the game of "walk-the-plank."

If the foregoing interests you, you can visit your local public library to find out what books are available on this subject.

THE FIFTEENTH MONTH

Motor Development

Gross Motor

Climbs up stairs on hands and knees

Sits on small chair for short periods

Walks a few steps sideways and backward

Picks up object from a standing position and flings it

Can climb on chairs, sofas, tables

May climb out of crib, high chair, or stroller

Has discarded creeping

Is ceaselessly active—starting, stopping, starting again, climbing, and clambering

Uses rapid "running-like" walk

Throws ball standing or sitting; extends arm at elbow joint

Fine Motor

Puts a pellet in a bottle and then pours it out

Can open a small, hinged box

Tries to turn doorknob

Wants to hold and carry something in each hand

Language Acquisition

Speaking vocabulary of 4–6 words, including names

May also say "there" and "bye-bye"

Uses jargon and gestures

Says "ta-ta" or equivalent for "thank you"

Points to shoes or clothes on command

Vocalizes and gestures to indicate wants

Points to familiar persons, toys, and animals on request

Follows simple commands: "Give me the ball," "Get the teddy bear," etc.

Combines jargon and words in conversation

Asks for objects by pointing

Understands such directions as "no," "come," "show me," "look"

Delights in dogs and often says "bow-wow"

Recognizes names of major body parts

Identifies pictures of a few named objects or the objects themselves by pointing or vocalizing

Can respond to a few key words and phrases

Points to one named body part

Sensory Powers/ Learning

Pats pictures in a book

Incipient imitation of stroke in drawing with crayon or pencil

Scribbles spontaneously with pencil

Places round block in formboard

Will look at a picturebook with the help of mother or father

Removes pegs, one by one, from pegboard

Can place a peg in hole in pegboard, with some help

Rubs fingers across all kinds of surfaces, sorting out the textures that please, amuse, or displease her or him. (Most toddlers like smooth, soft things, are intrigued by unusual textures, and dislike substances that stick to their fingers)

Can fit a round block into round hole in formboard

Enjoys imitating coughing, nose blowing, sneezing, and blowing out lit matches

Imitates simple actions

Shows interest in picturebooks

Turns object right side up

Growth Chart

Social Development

Looks for adults when left alone

Demands personal attention

Likes to go out for a ride by auto or baby carriage

Recognizes the absence of familiar persons

Is easily diverted and entertained

Shows or offers toy to mother, but wants it back again

Likes to empty wastebaskets

Imitates housework; will help in simple household chores

Personality/ Psychological

More demanding and more self-assertive

Has shifting moods

Exhibits affection in imitation of parents

Recognizes self in mirror or photograph

Is beginning to learn to distinguish own body and its limits in space

Onset of negativism

Temper, while quickly aroused, tends to be short-lived

Is starting to learn what compromise means

Self-Help Routines

Holds cup and drinks, still with some spilling

Spoon-feeds self with some spilling

Likes to take off shoes and socks and other garments

Discards bottle

Sits on toilet or potty chair

Indicates wet or soiled pants

Begins to insist on doing things without help

Indicates desire for more food by pointing and grunting

Enjoys bath and washing

Play and Playthings

Flings toys in play

Enjoys pushing little cars along

Likes to listen to music and dance in rhythm to it

Can manage a Kiddie Kar

Enjoys play with colored rings of graduated size that fit on a spindle

Likes to pound on things

Plays an improved to-and-from ball game

Favorite playthings are balls, spoons, cups, clothespins, boxes, some fitting toys

Likes to push a carriage, toy horse, etc.

Manipulative play is full of experimentation

Dear Parents:
Do not regard this chart as a rigid timetable.
Babies are unpredictable individuals. Some perform an activity earlier or (as much as six months) later than the chart indicates, while others skip a behavior altogether (i.e., walking without crawling).
Just use this information to anticipate and appreciate normal child development and behavior. No norms are absolutes.

THE SIXTEENTH MONTH
Up, Up, and Away

Motor Development

Most researchers consider toddlerhood as beginning at fifteen to sixteen months and continuing to two and a half years of age. Thereafter, the preschool period begins. All agree that for physical development, self-esteem, learning, and autonomy, toddlerhood is a critical period, as vital as the preceding and following ones.

At sixteen months, a child may already have been walking for a few months, but probably with great uncertainty because he was so involved with problems of balance that his hands could not be used for any other purpose while walking. If the toddler really wanted to get up some speed, he reverted to creeping and crawling. But now your six-teen-month-old really is up and away—with feet spread wide apart and pushing hard. The legs are still short for the body in comparison with adult proportions, giving the toddler a bottom-heavy look. Part of this is due to the fact that most sixteen-month-olds wear two bulky diapers (which will give way to slimmer training pants in another few months).

Toddlers this age are quite low to the ground and see most of the adult-scaled world in terms of the undersides of things. They are babies still in terms of what they do. Sixteen-month-olds explore objects by seizing them, inspecting them, stuffing them into their mouths. They continue to be content to sit on the floor for some time banging pots and pans in the kitchen, as long as mother is nearby or within call. They are more motor-driven than verbal in their encounters.

The Drive for Autonomy

All healthy sixteen-month-olds attempt to move away from toddlerhood while remaining bound to much immaturity. The single most important development phase, according to Erik H. Erikson, is autonomy—becoming aware of oneself as a person among other people and wanting to do things for oneself. The drive for autonomy is best demonstrated in the child's mastery of her own body: walking, climbing, jumping, and the beginning of control of the sphincter muscles. It is also manifested in the mastery of objects: pushing the stroller instead of riding in it, carrying oversized parcels and objects from place to place, removing her clothing.

In their social relations, sixteen-month-olds begin to refuse parental commands, requests, and offers of help. Understandably, the drive for autonomy is not "up, up, and away" all the time. These toddlers vacillate between dependence and independence (a pattern that will persist right through adolescence). When trying some new feat, such as

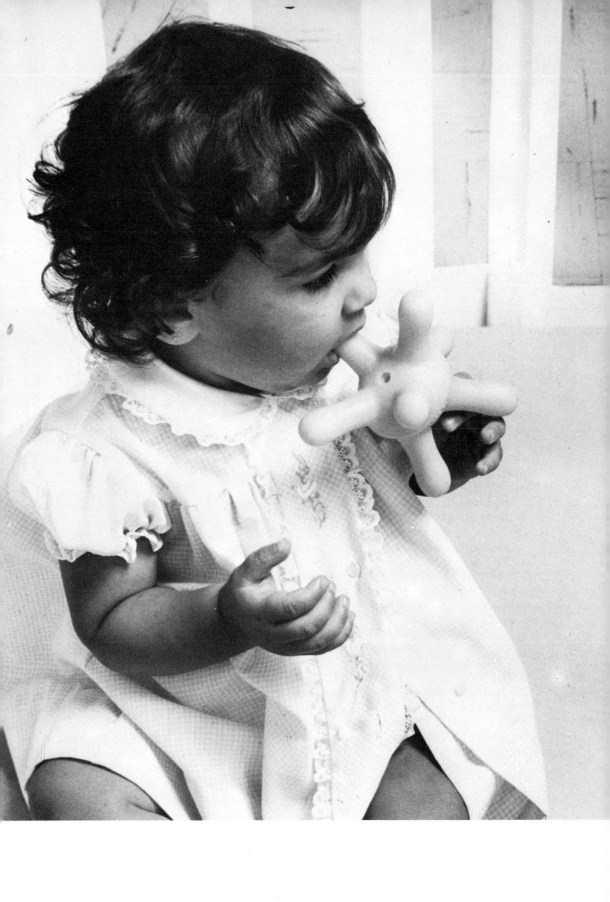

jumping from a step, the sixteen-month-old will make a great show of boldness, but cling tightly to an adult's hand.

Sixteen-month-olds seem to be compelled to move and explore; to affect their environment. However, their attention span is short and their tempo slow. Their information is scanty and unorganized and their language acquisition remains inadequate for communication.

When the sixteen-month-old first rides a Kiddie Kar, he pulls forward or pushes backward with both feet at once before learning to adopt the more mature rider's pattern of alternating steps. The child's unsureness also is evident in the way he needs to use two hands when carrying objects.

Re-creating Missing Stages of Physical Development

By the sixteenth month, most children will have reached the stage of physical development where they can roll or fling a ball, crawl over a low barrier, creep on hands and feet, kneel on both knees without support, climb stairs on hands and knees, stand and walk several steps alone, and pick up an object on the floor from a standing position. Sometimes, however, because of illness or hospitalization and the lack of practice, a child will miss a stage or regress. We know so little about the effects of missing a stage on body control or learning that it may be a good idea to have the father incorporate some of these physical skills in the games he plays with his child. At the very least, it will give you some idea of the physical skills your child has mastered, those she is currently developing, and those that are not yet in her repertoire.

The activities below were taken from a development test explored by a group of researchers working with developmental lags in young children:

Roll ball forward	Assume position sitting behind your child. Sit 2 or 3 feet from wall and roll ball against wall. Sit opposite your child and encourage him to roll ball to you. Place 3 empty milk cartons about 3 feet in front of your child and encourage him to roll ball and knock them over.
Project or fling ball	Give your child things to drop: blocks, balls, balloons. Place a ball in your child's hand and manually guide her hand in throwing motion. Tie a hoop up so that it makes a large circular target. Have your child drop a ball or balloon through the hoop a foot or so away and encourage her to throw the ball at the hoop.
Crawling over low barrier	Make a low barrier (such as a rolled pillow) and have your child creep or crawl over the barrier. Place your child with back in corner of room and place barrier and a toy in front. Call your child to come and get the toy.
Kneeling on both knees without support	Have your child assume a creeping position on hands and knees. Then have him raise right hand in balance with a 3-point balance; repeat with left hand. Then your child can kneel with both hands free and, finally, kneel and throw a ball.
Climb stairs on hands and knees	Place your child in position at bottom step. Place a favorite toy 2 or 3 steps above your child's reach. Encourage her to go up (if necessary, put one knee on first step and urge child to pull herself up). Spot your child for safety.
Walk with one hand held	After your child stands alone and cruises, encourage him to push a chair, Kiddie Kar, or doll buggy along the floor. Lead your child as he holds a round stick or rope. Hold rope so that your child's arms are no higher than his shoulders.
Stand and walk several steps alone	Have your child stand against the wall with you 2 or 3 feet away. Encourage your child to reach for your hand and take 1 or 2 steps. Repeat this process and encourage steps forward each time your child grasps your hand.
Walking without support	Let your child experience walking on a variety of surfaces: grass, sand, up-and-down inclines, and so on (you may have to hold your child's hand for a while). Let your child carry objects while walking alone. Encourage solo walking and provide a variety of interesting toys to pull.

Child-proofing the House

Experienced parents offer the following hints on child-proofing the house:
- Plug all unused electric sockets with blanks.
- The kitchen is the toddler's favorite playroom. Keep pot handles turned inward; fry or boil foods on the back burners. It is not too early to teach your child that *hot* can be dangerous and hurt.
- Teach your toddler that streets are not playgrounds, whether you reside in a city or suburbia.
- Block the top and bottom of any stairs; use a barrier in any doorway you do not want your toddler to cross.
- Keep matches or cigarette lighters out of reach.
- Band with foam tape the potentially head-splitting edges of low tables.
- Lay scatter rugs over skidproof pads.
- Jam books into their shelves so that a child cannot possibly remove them.
- Keep your treasured bric-a-brac well out of reach until you are ready to teach your toddler how to handle delicate things.

Of course, all medicines, household cleaning agents, and pesticides must be kept out of the inquiring hands of small children.

Socialization

Socialization skills are those acceptable behaviors that involve living and interacting with other people. During early childhood, social behaviors are reflected in the manner in which the child relates to her parents, siblings (if any), other adults, and playmates. Living with other people is the basis of most behavior; in fact, it is difficult to think of a behavior from infancy to adulthood that occurs and is repeated in isolation from other people.

Socialization is learning to live with others and requires that the child differentiate "right" from "wrong." The child learns this by being rewarded when he behaves in a way that other people decide is "right." The reward—hugs, smiles, praise, goodies—ensures that the behavior will be repeated. Behavior that other people decide is "wrong" will be punished or ignored and will tend not to be repeated. However, which behaviors are rewarded and which are punished differs according to the people and the environmental events surrounding the child; i.e., he will need to know the difference between what mommy, daddy, grandma, and siblings require of him and learn to act accordingly.

In the process, the child will learn to work for the most positive of all social rewards—attention, the response of other people in the environment to him. All behaviors in self-help, language acquisition, socialization, motor development, and cognitive areas are strengthened in this way.

Children learn through pleasure (rewarding experiences), through imitation (copying rewarded behaviors of adults and other children), through participation (active involvement), and through communication—all social skills. Examples of appropriate social behaviors during toddlerhood include waving bye-bye, following simple directions, smiling, playing peek-a-boo, and so forth.

The sixteen-month-old is working hard to become a social animal; in fact, her personal social style is beginning to be established. (Actually it becomes so well established by two years that to undo some inappropriate behaviors may require remedial therapy.) To put it another way, from eleven months to two years, children acquire many of the social skills that they exhibit by the time they enter the first grade. In the latter part of the second year of life, children also develop the ability to fantasize and play social games with their parents and siblings.

Social Skills

Dr. Robert White, in a Carnegie Institute and U.S. government-supported study of well-developed and competent three- to six-year-olds, lists the following social abilities and dimensions of competence that a child must acquire between sixteen and thirty-

playmates and full opportunity for play. Children, if left alone, will seek play and playmates as if their lives depended on it—and perhaps they do!

Children learn to relate to life and the people and things in it when they are not isolated from the world and its goings-on. Their first attempts at wider socialization come when the family includes others in its activities. People of varying ages, temperaments, relationships, and occupations stimulate a child's feelings, curiosity, and thinking. Parents who are alert to the need for building social acceptance between varying age groups take steps to organize an environment that fosters social interchange.

Throughout their social development, children spend less and less time with their

six-months of age, and many are not observable until age three.

- Getting and holding the attention of adults
- Using adults as resources after determining that a job is too difficult to do alone
- Expressing affection toward adults
- Leading and following peers
- Expressing affection or mild annoyance toward peers
- Showing pride in accomplishments
- Engaging in role-playing and make-believe activities

Some of the skills that are acquired as a child learns to relate to others are giving, receiving, and sharing; expressing feelings and ideas; and making choices. Social competency also includes techniques for expressing interest and friendship; for welcoming and including others in play; and for initiating and carrying on group activities. No child enjoys an adequate social life unless he acquires the ability to play with other children.

Consideration for others is a learned social skill. How well a child relates to other children and adults depends on his ability to get to know and accept other people. However, if a child is to attain optimal development, he must also have suitable playthings and

Cheer up—such periods of withdrawal usually are temporary.

As children become more aware of themselves, they learn to use *no!* in the ways that their parents use it—chasing a cat off the table by yelling *no!*—or to defy their parents' requests. Children will use *no!* when they want to play longer in the park or when they do not want a particular food.

Handling Encounters with Toddlers

"The sixteen-month-old's ability to use *no* correctly inevitably brings on difficult encounters with the parents. There is no ready solution to the demands of toddlers. Parents can limit their requests to those that are important and thus make fewer requests and demands. Parents can grant their toddlers some of their requests, but be consistently adamant about not allowing others. For example, 'You cannot pick leaves or flowers from a house plant, but you can pick dandelions in the backyard.' 'You can pour water in the bathtub, but you cannot pour water on the rug.' "

Mutuality and Social Bonds

A child has to learn how to function as a social being or she will not survive. Living with and communicating with others aids a child's socialization process. In the beginning, the mother and father are the infant's entire world. The baby learns to love because the parents love her. The quality and intensity of this earliest experience indelibly imprints itself on every infant.

Much can happen during the earliest months of life to make a child fearful of society, shy, hostile, or indifferent to others. You can see this vividly in infants who are adopted after their seventh month of life. If they are typical examples of the adoption procedure, they have been given up by the biological mother who could not rear the baby she never wanted. The infant is turned over temporarily to a foster home while a social caseworker and the biological mother "talk it over." The

families. Well past their second birthdays, children spend more time in play with their agemates. This gradual transference, which extends over several years, is a major process in social sophistication. Positively, there is more independent behavior and increased participation in peer-group activities. On the negative side, there is a growing revolt against parental control and often a critical attitude toward the parents and the home. The peer group is a child's very own social milieu, with its special language, mode of interaction, loyalties, values, and acceptable forms of behavior—many of which grown-ups cannot understand. The child has equal and at times even superior status with others in this child-sized dominion, not the subordinate role she invariably has with parents and other adults.

Progress in social relations is not smooth. After illness or separation there is regression and the child is less willing to interact with others and becomes more dependent upon the parents because he is afraid of losing their support. Some children become whiny and cling to their parents; others become aggressive and try to strike out at their parents.

mother may decide to try again to accept and adjust to her baby. The foster parents hardly have had time to make contact with the infant when they are obliged to follow the caseworker's instructions to return the baby to the natural mother.

The baby then is sent to a different foster home—with new faces and new voices to adjust to. Having had four or more caregivers during the critical period for establishing a bond of affection with *one* caregiver, the baby no longer trusts anyone—not even the new caring, affectionate parents, who eventually sign final adoption papers for the baby. It will take years of warm, understanding attention by the adoptive parents to help pave the baby's way to a spirit of basic trust—without which no one can function well.

The human newborn is completely helpless, much more so than any other species in the animal kingdom. Humans have the greatest need for sustenance, protection, love, and encouragement. Not only do human babies need caring adults, they need them for more years than do baby animals. Everything children master during their earliest years (to be an individual, to speak, to become independent, and so forth) they learn within the bonds of parental nurturance.

Erikson describes infancy as the period during which the baby learns his attitude of basic trust or mistrust. The amount of trust a baby develops depends on his relationship with his primary caregivers—the mother predominantly and the father. The infant's first act of socialization depends upon his willingness to let mother out of sight without screaming in anxiety. Babies can do this only when they trust the mother to come back soon. It is at this point that infants learn that the mother is a separate person. This discovery makes it possible for the baby to return the love the mother has given from the very beginning and sets the stage for the interpersonal connections the child will make later on with other people.

Defective Human Ties

What happens if human ties are fragile, defective, or ruptured during infancy and early childhood? Children who have had little or no experience with consistent and responsive caregivers in infancy and early childhood or who have not established strong bonds become seriously impaired emotionally. They show varying degrees of inability to make human attachments in later life. Remedial efforts at four and five years usually do not succeed even if such children are placed in substitute families whose members genuinely love them.

In the last twenty years, researchers have been studying the bonds of relationships between parents and child. Leon Yarrow, Ph.D. (of the Social and Behavioral Science Branch of the National Institute of Child Health, in Bethesda, Maryland) specifies the stages for social attachments during the first two years of life. First comes social awareness: the discrimination between people and objects. Then comes active recognition of the mother, followed by preference for the mother over other available figures. Then confidence relations ensue whereby the child accumulates a sense that the mother will always return. Next come the beginnings of stranger anxiety (at eight to nine months and thirteen to fourteen months). After this there is active differentiation of strangers by the toddler. Finally, the toddler shows marked stranger anxiety.

Many early childhood researchers have been pleading for a primary caretaker during the early most critical years—the mother. Other researchers who have studied mothers during their children's second and third years of life seem to suggest that we may be overestimating the significance of one continual caretaker for the healthy unfolding of a child. However, even they admit that parents who have had contact with a child from birth on may be more sensitized to his or her personality, activity level, quirks, and so forth and so may be better able to engage in productive transactions with the child. In recent studies of the problem of separation during the day only for toddler (day care and other group living experiences), it is being shown that there is *no* loss of attachment to the mother or other primary caretaker and that there is a decided need for young children to enter into many happy, reciprocal relations.

Social Development and Competency

Dr. Selma Fraiberg warns that parents must not confuse two types of development in children. A child who learns to crawl will outgrow this motor technique and proceed to walking. This maturing power follows an innate tendency and a certain type of order of development. However, social development—the acquisition of standards of behavior, the control of one's impulses—will not develop without teaching. "The toddler will not control his impulses unless we require him to."

Building Self-Esteem

Every infant is born without a sense of self; each one must learn to be human. Without a sense of identity, without the need for others, without language for communication, the child would be human in appearance only.

The sense of selfhood is not easily taught. It is an awareness that is learned mainly from living with others. Having been one with the mother and the uterine environment through nine months of the mother's pregnancy, the neonate does not discriminate between where she ends and the rest of the world begins. The newborn does not know that she is a person. From the very first day of life, she starts to explore the strange, new world outside the mother's body. New sensations arouse the infant—touching and being touched, listening to sounds, smelling, tasting, blurred objects to discriminate. When the baby touches her body, there are sensations in her fingers and body. When she touches a stuffed toy, the sensation is only at her fingertips. In time, the baby discovers that her body is part of her, but the stuffed toy is not.

As time goes by, infants learn to differentiate objects from people. People come and go, make sounds, cuddle them, and make them more comfortable. Babies discover the difference between themselves and the mother and then use the mother as an extension of themselves. They push her hand in the direction of a cookie so that she can give it to them. They can get her to transport them home or to a play yard, and so forth.

Language Acquisition

As the brain and vocal chords mature, the child learns to talk. Language, all psychologists agree, is the tool that enables the child to feel fully separate. Children discover by imitation that certain sounds stand for particular objects and then that objects can be labeled qualitatively—*stove hot, Dada big, cookie,* and so on. Once they master their own names, they have a symbol for thinking of themselves as apart from others. This comes tentatively to all toddlers at around thirteen to eighteen months (full awareness does not come until children are about two and a half years old). First through their senses and later through language, children build up a picture of themselves and their world.

Even before they have language ability, babies and toddlers gain impressions about themselves from how they are handled and treated by others. They know how parents feel by how close they hug them or by whether their hunger is respected or ignored or by the kinds of games their parents play with them. The touch, body movements, and facial expressions of those around them tell children how much they are admired, loved, and valued. "Children value themselves to the degree that they have been valued."

Psychologists say that the degree of responsiveness provides the foundation for a positive view of self. This responsiveness (gained from thousands of impressions of the body language of others) starts children off on their way to high self-esteem. Parents who never play with their infant or toddler or who care for their child with unresponsive, cold efficiency fail to give their child a feeling of worth. Equally pertinent is the fact that when parents describe their toddler as "bad" and unmanageable, their child gains a dim view of himself. Parents need to keep in mind that words have power; they can shred or build a child's self-respect.

To recapitulate, each child's view of himself is built upon reflections that come from many sources: parents, siblings, grandparents, and so forth; the treatment the child is accorded; the physical mastery of his body; his degree of achievement; and recognition in areas of accomplishment that are important to the child. These actions become the basis of the child's self-concept or self-image. They are the child's personal answers to "Who am I?"

Personality—Ego Development

Sixteen-month-olds reach that stage of development where they are aware of themselves. Everything they do is intensely personal. Their keenest interest lies in any activity that puts them on center stage; in short, they are highly egocentric. This self-centeredness shows up in their greetings to strangers or to relatives. "I have a new dress." "I have new boots." They will interrupt a story or conversation with "My mommy is an artist." "My daddy is an architect." "My daddy shaves."

When they were infants, they depended so much on their parents that they were not aware of themselves as separate individuals. Now that they are walking, they are overwhelmed by this awareness and expect everyone else to be equally amazed. They want to make choices—and even though they are not yet good at this, they do have preferences. They love to take the initiative; to have an idea and to carry it out.

Several years from now, your child will develop a strong social sense and will be able to think in terms of family, group, nation, the world. However, now you must teach your child to take first steps and to learn to love herself. Parents need to make the time to listen to their toddler, to offer rightful praise, and to build their child's ego.

Dr. James L. Hymes, retired early childhood educator, plugs for supporting a child's ego during toddlerhood when it counts so much. Success matters very much to the toddler: "I tied my shoes myself." "I know how old I am." "I fell and didn't hurt myself." For all this boasting, toddlers are unable to deliver what they boast about. A hundred times a day, their smallness and their limited capacities bring them face to face with reality. Invariably they confront things they cannot reach, things they cannot see but want to see, and things they cannot lift or carry.

Manmade failures really hurt the ego of toddlers. The environment is adult and not child-sized. Toddlers cannot participate in putting out the fire, driving the bus, delivering the milk. They know that they are too small to be part of the action in which they want desperately to be involved. This is the time to bring the action down to their size with child-sized playthings, blocks, and so on—where their participation is appreciated. At this stage, it is wise to stay away from competition, from games with winners and losers. Toddlers cannot stand losing.

Drs. Joseph Stone and Joseph Church, in their fine book, *Childhood and Adolescence,* point out that the toddler's "awareness of himself and his environment increases as he becomes more differential from his surroundings, as he is able to distinguish between external events and internal ones, as he learns to suspend action in favor of thought and feeling."

Motivation to Learn

An important issue in the study of the intellectual growth of infants and young children is the relationship between a healthy personality and intellectual achievement. From research with older children (and adults), it is clear that maximum intellectual development can take place only when the personality is sound. It is, therefore, important to discover what personality and social factors are most effective in promoting intellectual growth.

One aspect of personality about which there is increasing information is the motivation to learn. This motivation is closely linked to the child's belief that she can affect the environment and it has been shown that this belief is acquired very early in life.

The intellectual growth of the infant is closely tied to the responsiveness of the people around her. In many studies, attention has been given to the nature of the maternal response to the infant's behavior as the basis for her intellectual growth. These studies indicate that there are two dimensions of the mother's response that are important in affecting the infant's development: (1) the total amount of stimulation provided and (2) the relationship between the infant's behavior and the mother's response.

The latter dimension is of greater concern because it is in this interaction that the infant's expectation that his behavior has consequences is established. For example, if an infant cries when hungry and the mother immediately feeds him, the baby has learned that he can, indeed, affect the environment. The positive maternal response has reinforced the baby's behavior and, therefore, is a motivation for the infant to continue his efforts to affect the surroundings.

A study of institutionalized infants produced some interesting results concerning this issue. It has been found that institutionalized infants gained skills at about the same time as infants raised at home, but since the skills were not reinforced promptly because of the many demands on the staff, there was little motivation for the babies to use them, and the infants showed little desire to practice their new achievements.

The greater the belief that one's actions have consequences, the greater the motivation to learn will be. This fact emphasizes the importance of the relationship between the infant and consistent caretaker in promoting intellectual growth.

Sensory Skills

Sixteen-month-olds develop sensory skills through their daily contacts with new objects. By touching, feeling, and examining things, they learn to distinguish the different qualities of various objects. They learn that some things are soft and others are hard, scratchy, or rubbery. Many activities can be planned to stimulate children's senses. Sounds heard or things seen in their surroundings should be called to their attention. Opportunities to be

mobile can arouse their curiosity as they explore the world they live in.

As your sixteen-month-old engages in sensory experiences, use language as you describe, point out, touch, or see objects. One simple way is to name the sounds your child hears in her everyday experiences; the knock on the door, water running from a faucet, or the telephone ringing, to name a few. When your toddler has heard a sound or seen an object, it is a good idea to make her aware of it by asking, "Did you hear that?" Or saying, "It's water running" or "Let's look out the window at the cars going by." Name often the sounds your toddler hears or the things she sees so that she can become familiar with them. Learning to listen and observe are invaluable sensory skills.

Blowing Is Great Fun

"Most sixteen-month-olds are able to blow out matches, blow up balloons, and blow bubbles in a glass through a plastic straw. Blowing through a straw may have begun as imitation with your toddler copying an older sibling sipping a beverage that way. Once the technique is mastered, toddlers will continue to blow just because it is fun. Toddlers do not make much of a distinction between the functions of mouth and nose and very often you will find your sixteen-month-old blowing on a flower when asked to smell it."

Exploring Muscle Power

"Watching a sixteen-month-old struggle to lift up a heavy suitcase or push a chair through the door makes the adult wonder why the toddler has to do everything the hard way. Why must he carry a teddy bear, truck, and cigar box all at the same time? Why must he go after the book that is at the very bottom of a pile of books? Apparently the toddler needs to find out and challenge his own physical limits just the way he has to find out and challenge the behavioral limits set by the parents."

Freedom to Climb

"Once sixteen-month-olds learn to climb on things, they are ready to use their climbing skill to accomplish other goals. They climb on a living room table in order to get a hand in the fishbowl or on the corner chair to investigate the telephone. Toddlers cannot understand why their parents—who formerly were supportive of all their efforts to practice new skills—are now curbing their explorations. This is a good time to offer your child many other alternative 'research' activities."

Expressing Affection

"Between twelve and sixteen months, children develop greater ability to express their affection. Much of this imitative. If the child's mother tends to express her affection by kissing, her child will begin to nuzzle in return. The father who often wrestles with his toddler discovers that the child likes to embrace him.

"The ability of sixteen-months-olds to imitate all kinds of actions increases. They become especially adept at imitating hand movements. A wave from familiar adult produces a wave in return. By the same token, when adults clap their hands to reward a toddler's accomplishment, the child will clap also.

"As well as imitating specific gestures of the parents, the toddler is beginning to observe and imitate some of the things that the parents do. When eating, the sixteen-month-old wants to hold her own spoon. The spoon is not used much, but holding it is very important. Similarly, the child puts her feet in the parent's shoes, tries to hold a parent's coffee cup, or insists on holding the car keys. The toddler does not assume the adult role in a sophisticated sense, but the attempt to use adult objects is a first step."

Nonverbal Communication

"Although sixteen-month-olds usually use six or seven clear words, they still resort to

nonverbal messages; i.e., they will point to indicate specific desires, to call attention to events. A fascinating nonverbal message that the toddler learns to send is "Look at this!" If the toddler finds an intriguing object lying around, such as a pincushion, he will proudly bring it to his parents. It never occurs to him that his parents will be horrified and grab the object away. The sixteen-month-old does not appreciate his parents' perspective; he wants to share his own."

How Do Babies and Toddlers Learn?

If you live with or work with infants as parents or caregivers, you have an opportunity to guide and challenge them through a time when some of the most dramatic influential changes in all of human development take place.

In a brief sixteen-month period, the infant is transformed from a being who cannot turn over in her crib to one who with help can climb stairs; from a being unable to grab an object in front of her to one who can poke a thin wire into an electric socket; from a being who communicates only with cries to one who can recognize and name pictures of animals or familiar objects in a storybook. It is fascinating to observe that infant learning truly is play— the enjoyable practice of new skills (making sounds, nesting boxes, and so forth) not because someone else rewards the child, but because it gives her a sense of deep satisfaction to be able to do it.

Let us explore this sense of competence and its expression in the infant's feelings of curiosity and involvement as a problem solver. The infant develops competence with regard to (1) physical objects around him, (2) his body and sense of self as a person, and (3) the people around him (parents, other caregivers, peers).

According to Catherine Cooper, who wrote an article entitled "Competent Infants and Their Caregivers" that appeared in a 1976 booklet published by the Association for Early Childhood Education, there are four major principles covering how babies learn:

1. Competent babies and their caregivers are individuals with distinctive needs and styles of interacting who are able to tune in to each other in mutually responsive ways. Caregivers need to have a general idea of the typical sequences and rates of development so that they may be alert to any indications that an infant may need special attention. This is particularly true of the first two years of life when the normal course of development includes very broad variation.

One infant may be placid, observing quietly the things and people in the world, while another is active to the point of exhausting herself in practicing gross-motor skills. With such differences, the infant and caregiver need time to get to know each other.

2. Competent infants are able to develop a basic trust in their parents or other consistent caretakers and to build on this trust a foundation for becoming confident, self-sufficient toddlers. Infancy is the period when babies learn or do not learn that the world is one in which their needs for food, warmth, affection, and encouragement are met and in which they feel safe and sure.

3. Competent infants thrive on varied stimulation that is appropriately timed, linked to their actions, and presented in the context of basic trust.

Many people have believed that a quiet infant is a happy one; that an infant should be left alone in the crib if he does not mind. We know today that infants left in their cribs except to be fed and changed show signs of declining intellectual development as early as eight weeks of age. In contrast, a high level of interest in exploring and manipulating the environment and a longer attention span have been directly linked to the stimulation that a capable parent or other caregiver provides.

4. Infant learning is built on action cycles; i.e., an action produces a result that in turn becomes a new kind of action. The competent parent or other consistent caregiver encourages and helps to extend and elaborate these cycles.

The infant begins a new learning sequence by performing some action; for example, banging a rattle on the side of the crib. The action has an effect that interests the baby: it makes a noise. When that result intrigues the infant, she repeats the action to make the interesting result happen again. The older the infant, the more elaborate the action cycle becomes.

A young child's capacity for intelligent reasoning begins to emerge sometime in the second year when the toddler begins to use tools. You will recognize this growth stage when your child has learned to use a stick to pull a toy or other object toward him. How did this power to reason come about? From the ability to coordinate the body, arms, and hands, and from the new connections the child is making between means and ends, he has graduated from solely trial-and-error learning to the beginning of reasoning.

The Roots of Intelligence

In order to develop self-confidence and drive, the child has to feel able to control her environment of things (and people) through successful actions. These processes, which free the child from the domination of the environment and show the greatest independence, are indications of the most advanced learning abilities of humans.

Learning theorists consider these capacities worthy of the term "intelligence." Intelligence is considered to be the capacity of the child to structure internally the results of her own actions. Interaction with the environment gives rise to schemata that alter the way the child perceives and responds to the environment.

Just as there is a definite progression in the "ages and stages" of the maturing of physical and sensory capacities, so there is a definite order in the acquisition of schemata for relating to objects. Maturation alone cannot account for motor development. Retardation in such development often is due to the absence of specific kinds of learning opportunities. In short, because of body deficiencies or temperament, some children have trouble engaging in actions on the environment and encounter difficulty in their development.

Most U.S. children, because of our culture and social behavior, are pretuned to bind themselves to people. However, they are not without particular temperaments and preferences; i.e., some learn better than others through tactile experiences. Since infants are programmed from birth for such tactile stimulation, if they do not get it, they will not develop learning ability.

Obviously, playful mutuality between parents and child and actions on things in a "responsive environment of things" are essential for optimal development. An enriched, provocative environment has to be planned for each maturing physical and sensory power. One cannot provide *average* care for young children and expect to promote good growth and superior learning.

Behavior Conditioning

Behavior results from a combination of environmental and hereditary influences that act upon the human organism. A change in behavior that occurs as the result of practice on the environment is called learning. Since parents possess the ability to manipulate many conditions of their child's environment, they can determine to a large extent the behaviors that their child will acquire.

Many common child-rearing situations provide circumstances in which the techniques of conditioning can be applied. The following is an example of one such circumstance. Two children want a toy that is out of reach. The parent of the first child runs to get the toy as soon as the baby stretches his hand toward it. The parent of the second child does not respond immediately, but allows the infant to practice crawling toward the toy.

In the first case, the behavior being reinforced is that of sitting still and reaching with the hand. In the second, the behavior being reinforced is that of crawling. The parent in both instances has manipulated the environment in some way to condition the child's behavior.

Legs and Feet

Most children's legs and feet do not look "normal" until the children have been walking for several years. The feet seem to turn in or out in the first year of life. The legs look bowed by the time the child is twelve to eighteen months old. Almost all of these funny-looking feet and legs are perfectly normal and will gradually straighten out as their owners run, climb, and play.

If you can move your toddler's foot easily into a normal-looking position and if the foot moves freely when your child kicks and struggles, it is almost certainly a normal foot that developed a bend or twist while your baby was sitting on it during your pregnancy.

You will not cause bowed legs by pulling your baby into a standing position or letting him walk or stand "too early." Also, your child will not learn to walk any sooner by being placed in a walker—which usually is not much fun for him anyway.

Buying Shoes

There is no need to buy a child a pair of shoes until she is walking out-of-doors. Remember that shoes are a human invention. Walking barefoot around the house or in the sand or grass where there is no danger is good for the child's feet because it provides excellent exercise.

Shoes become necessary when the child starts to walk on injurious surfaces. Most pediatricians prefer that you buy sneakers or soft shoes with rubber soles. Buy the cheapest pair that fits properly because the shoes are bound to be outgrown quickly. Buying shoes a couple of sizes too big makes for foot trouble! There should be a half-inch space beyond the toddler's big toe and the tip of the shoe. Dr. Virginia Pomeranz points out that if you cannot feel the big toe, the shoe is too hard.

Striving to be Grown-up

"Emerging awareness of herself as a person is apparent in much of the sixteen-month-old's play activity. Although the child continues to explore the immediate surroundings, she is becoming more selective about the things she gets into. The articles or tools that parents or siblings use take on special value and the toddler tries to get hold of such things as wallets, keys, screwdrivers, lipsticks, pens, matches, the telephone, records, magazines, razors, and so forth. Constantly on the alert, the sixteen-month-old watches how adults use things and waits impatiently for a turn to try. Whereas year-olds try out all their manipulative schemes on every object they find, fifteen- to eighteen-month-olds are most interested in imitating adult use of objects.

"As sixteen-month-olds expand their field of exploration and become more keenly interested in copying adult activities, the question of limits comes up. Each family is faced with a series of decisions to make. What sorts of things will they allow their toddler to do and what sorts of things will they stop? How will they keep their child from getting into things that he can destroy or things that might be dangerous? Should they put everything fragile or potentially harmful out of reach, watch their toddler at all times, or try to teach their sixteen-month-old what she can play with and what she cannot? Usually parents opt for keeping things that are dangerous or valuable out of reach. At the same time, they leave a few 'safe' things within reach that they do not want their child to touch. In this way, their toddler can have opportunities to learn the meaning of *no* without the risk of an accident."

THE SIXTEENTH MONTH

Motor Development

Gross Motor

Trots about well; rarely falls

Can walk sideways (does so while pulling a pull toy)

Hurls ball without falling

Tries to take steps on a walking board

Climbs and descends stairs with help

Attempts to kick a ball, but steps on the ball instead

Stands on right foot with help

Actively uses arms, legs, and all parts of the body

Tries to walk on tiptoe

Squats down smoothly

Seats self on chair

Recovers standing position after stooping

Fine Motor

Builds tower of 2–3 cubes

Turns pages of a book a few at a time

Scribbles in imitation

Can put round block in formboard

Puts beads in box

Language Acquisition

Uses 6 or 7 clear words

Brings a familiar object from another room upon request

Points and gestures to indicate desires and call attention to events

Responds to "Give me that" when accompanied by gestures

Indicates wants assertively; will use one word to make want known; e.g., "Up"

Combines 2 different words

Points to one named body part

Most toddlers at this age do not like having a whole story read to them; they prefer to pick out and point to pictures or listen to adult talk about pictures

Responds to verbal directions, but must still be managed mostly by actions

Interested in watching children's shows on TV ("Sesame Street," cartoons, singing commercials)

Sensory Powers/ Learning

Scribbles more freely

Likes to smell different odors

Handles things in order to find out what they are like

Identifies 2 or more objects from a group of familiar objects

Ongoing imitation of simple actions

When shown a picture book, takes interest in the pictures and will turn pages, but several at a time

Still likes emptying things, but is beginning to be occupied with fitting things inside other things

Identifies simple pictures in book; "Find the ball," etc.

Growth Chart

Social Development

Demands personal attention

Is definitely making self a member of the family

Has learned to get from room to room in the house and knows how to hunt for a missing parent or sibling

Expresses refusals with bodily response primarily; occasionally says "no"

Follows simple command with less or no gestural help

Hands object to parent and awaits reaction expectantly

Imitates housework: sweeping, setting table, etc.

Behavior varies according to emotional reaction of parents

Personality/ Psychological

Narcissism is at its peak now through 18th month

Male toddler discovers his penis

Female toddler envies male's having a penis

Increasing awareness of own separateness from parents and others

Happy and talkative

Smiles at everyone in sight

Self-Help Routines

Uses spoon, spilling little

May resist going to bed

Enjoys self-feeding

Drinks from cup; hands empty cup to mother

May accept toileting routine

Unzips large zipper

Indicates when pants are wet

May insist on choosing own clothes

Tries to blow own nose

Play and Playthings

Pulls and pushes toys

Enjoys pile-up toys

Carries or hugs soft doll or teddy bear

Likes to play in sandbox

Relishes roughhouse play

Still enjoys playing rolling a ball with parent

Dear Parents:
   Do not regard this chart as a rigid timetable.
   Babies are unpredictable individuals. Some perform an activity earlier or (as much as six months) later than the chart indicates, while others skip a behavior altogether (i.e., walking without crawling).
   Just use this information to anticipate and appreciate normal child development and behavior. No norms are absolutes.

THE SEVENTEENTH MONTH
A Period of Consolidation

Seventeen-month-olds are at the threshold of being "grown-up." They have mastered the problems of balance and walking. They have learned how to creep up and down stairs (with a little help) and to open doors. They have mastered many complex physical tasks; for instance, holding something in one hand and throwing a ball with the other. They walk well and seldom fall. They are able to climb onto an object at chest height, turn around, and sit down. They can stoop and recover standing position after stooping. Seventeen-month-olds are developing considerable fine-motor skills. They are able to drink from a cup (with some spills). When eating soft food, such as custard, they can get the food onto a spoon. They amuse themselves daily with arranging and rearranging both toys and nontoys. A major pastime includes strewing the house with various objects, picking up a portion of them, and then finding new locations for them. They are especially fond of picking up small items, such as cigarette butts and blown-out matches. They love to handle pencils and to distinguish the eraser from the lead end. They enjoy scribbling.

Rituals and Routines

Most seventeen-month-olds are creatures of routine and enjoy following rituals. Bedtime usually includes bathing, brushing teeth, put-ting cap back on toothpaste tube, finding a favorite blanket or love object. The child may be permitted a few minutes' playing on the parents' bed, whereas the child's bed is clearly defined for sleeping. When this quiet playtime is over, the toddler may sit beside the father, expecting a story to be read. Then the child may say good night to his animals, take the favored one along, and go to bed with few problems.

If the mother is separated from the toddler for a long period of time (being hospitalized or because of death in the family), the child regresses, all good conduct goes out the window, and the routines of feeding and bedtime can become something of a hassle. The toddler may refuse to be fed and even throw the dish on the floor. Bedtime can become a prolonged event, with long periods of crying, calling out, and refusal to quiet down. Nights for toddlers and parents can become a nightmare, with traumatic waking periods, episodes of bottle throwing, and angry tears.

Discovering Daddy

Seventeen-month-olds begin to "discover" daddy. They greet him fondly with a "hi" and jump into his arms when he returns from work. When the father leaves in the morning, there is considerable unhappiness and tears.

Children at this age are still plagued by the

fear of separation. They will wander about a new house they are visiting, explore its decor and objects, open doors, then turn around to look at mother. The farther they venture forth, the closer they get to mother on the return trip. When they wander around corners, they come back in a wobbly run and rub their cheeks on mother's dress.

Most seventeen-month-olds seem to have trouble adjusting to parents' leaving and to having to stay with babysitters. They continue to show concern about strangers visiting the home, but now they take only a few minutes to adjust and include them in their play by handing them objects.

Seventeenth-month-olds show aggressiveness toward a younger sibling. Even when they are encouraged by their parents to give the baby a bottle, for instance, they are unhappy. Toddlers have been seen pulling a pacifier out of the baby's mouth, tasting it, spitting it out, and then tossing it back to the baby.

"Seventeen-month-olds can be taught to live with limits. Parents usually establish a long list of forbidden household objects, including dangerous electric sockets, certain drawers, the telephone, glass tables, and so on. If necessary to get compliance, some mothers use a quick swat on the rear. Child-proofing the milieu of the curious, active toddler would make better sense.

"One of the most exciting accomplishments of seventeen-month-olds is the way they understand and follow simple instructions, including turning off the television or radio, throwing things into the wastebasket, getting ready for bed, and so on. Another is the beginning of the amazing 'telegraphic' language they devise for getting adults to help them achieve their objectives. With each new accomplishment they will say 'See,' and then enjoy the limelight to the full. Upon rising early in the morning, toddlers of seventeen months will call our 'My mommy' or 'My daddy.' If they get no response, they will shout out 'Mommy up.' When the parent arrives, a particular toddler asks for 'Becky-apricot-bread' that translates to the mother as 'I am ready for breakfast and would like to have apricot

juice and toast.' Usually daddy joins the breakfast table. When the father leaves, knowing the routine, the child is ready for a diaper change. If mother is too busy, the child might take off the diaper and say to the mother, 'Wet' or 'Die' for dirty, and ask for Pampers. Occasionally, the toddler will place the dirty Pamper in the pail and come to the mother with a clean Pamper in hand.

"Sometimes after dinner, a father may announce that the family is going for a ride. The toddler will announce, 'Keds, bye-bye' which means 'Put on my socks and shoes.' If a seventeen-month-old is hungry, he will pull mother or father into the kitchen and say 'Apple juice, gimme'—and that needs no translation.

"Toddlers love music and songs that involve responding, clapping, finger gestures, and putting words in appropriate places. When the mother or the father sings 'Eensy, Weensy Spider,' for example, the child will add words and gestures after demonstration, and will twist her wrists to show the spider climbing. For the song 'Row, Row, Row Your Boat,' the toddler will fill in the words and, after demonstration, will spread her legs far apart so that she can rock with the rowing.

"Most toddlers enjoy watching television, but reflectively. Not all like cartoons, but many will respond to programs with animals, puppets, and children.

"Between fifteen and eighteen months, the toddler's ability to manipulate other people becomes quite apparent. It is easy to emphasize the negative side of this behavior. The first real tantrums appear when the child learns to use tears to get her own way. Of course, the child is just starting and will keep refining the techniques of interrelating into adulthood.

"At the same time, there also is much joy and humor in the toddler's manipulative efforts. During this age, the child learns to tease. A favorite game is running away from the mother or the father in the hope of being chased. The child runs off when the parents are trying to dress her; runs behind counters in a department store or aisles in a supermarket, and so forth. All the while the toddler laughs and crows in delight. The toddler learns to show off and often takes center stage, and makes a deliberate attempt to play for the gallery by clapping, giggling, or swaggering. Showing off has negative overtones for adults, but the show-off behavior of seventeen-month-olds is universally loved. The toddler is so alive and trying with all her might to be a person. There is genuine communication between her and her admiring parents; they share the feelings of excitement and good humor. For the moment everyone is on the same wavelength and it is a wonderful experience."

Achievements

Seventeen months is in some ways a period of consolidation. The toddler is consolidating walking skills and using these to increase his understanding of the physical layout of his world. Although still apt to walk with legs apart and arms held up, the toddler's balance is definitely better. A remarkable sign of agility at this age is the ability to squat down on the floor, play with whatever is there, and pop right up again.

Climbing

Infants who learn to walk at a year often reach the climbing stage by the time they are fifteen months old. As soon as the child has performed her first climbing feat, there emerges a strong desire to practice on a variety of barriers: chairs, sofas, tables, and so forth. At this age children often overestimate their strength and start to climb out of cribs, high chairs, and strollers without realizing how hard the floor is. This is the time to lower the spring and mattress and keep the sides of the crib up at all times. As toddlers get closer to two, they become so adept at climbing out of the crib that it is time to change to a bed. (The Federal government recommends getting all children out of cribs by two years of age.)

Restraints

In the mastery of climbing, toddlers begin to get into areas that are downright dangerous. They now climb on chairs to get into fishbowls, stairs leading to the basement, onto the table to get at the telephone, and so on. For the first time, parents who heretofore

have been understanding about their child's need to practice maturing skills begin to fence her in by using gadgets, barriers, and *no-no's.* The basement is "gated," the bathroom cabinet is locked, the telephone and chairs are put out of reach. The frustration that evolves, combined with the toddler's lack of language to make her needs felt, make this a tough time for parents and child.

Exploring Textures—a Safer Activity for Toddlers

"The exploratory interests of seventeen-month-olds can be redirected from dangerous pursuits to safer territory, exploring and sorting textures around the house, for example. Toddlers like smooth, soft things (silk, fur, hair, polished stones, and stuffed animals). They are upset with things that stick to their fingers, such as glue, mud, chocolate pudding, and so forth. Not liking dirty fingers has nothing to do with the toddler's desire for cleanliness. More likely, he wants clean fingers to carry on texture explorations.

"Exploring food textures is particularly important at this age. Now that they can chew and swallow, toddlers begin to develop tastes and dislikes. Seventeen-month-olds' dislikes are usually determined by texture rather than smell or taste. On their dislike list are strawberries, tapioca pudding, spinach, Jell-O, unstrained orange juice.

"Textures underfoot are also important to toddlers. Some refuse to walk on grass, others do not like cement, and still others do not like the touch of sand on a beach.

"In his explorations of space in the home, the toddler now can get from room to room and increase his understanding of objects in these rooms. If there are two entrances to a room, the child learns how to get back to his starting point. This kind of circle game can keep him busy for several minutes."

The Struggle for Autonomy

The struggle for autonomy is a major thrust of the second year of life. It seems to reach a high point between seventeen and twenty-one months. We have talked about the conflict that arises when toddlers are unable to do something by themselves, but do not want to ask for help. Other conflicts arise when toddlers test their power to make decisions for themselves or to make other people do what they wish. Often toddlers use *no* just because they can. The parents may ask their child to show Nana where her ear is. The toddler shakes her head and says *no* in an angry voice. Actually the child has no objections to touching her ear, but is driven to say *no* in order to establish her power.

"Another power struggle takes place when the toddler's insistence on doing something without assistance interfers with family plans. For example, Janet's family may be ready to go on an outing, but Janet is standing in the doorway screaming at the top of her lungs. The problem is that she is not able to get the zipper up on her jacket and does not want anyone to help her.

"An almost equally exasperating aspect of the autonomy struggle is the toddler's inability to make choices. The parent asks whether the child wants a cookie or a lollypop. First the child says, 'Cookie,' but as soon as he gets the cookie, he wants a lollypop. The parent patiently takes away the cookie and gives the toddler a lollypop, but now the child wants the cookie again. The problem is that the child wants the right to choose, but does not want to make a choice. From the child's point of view, he does not have a choice unless he can choose them both.

"This period of development can be difficult for the whole family. The toddler is struggling both to be independent and to control people. She does not have a realistic idea of her own capabilities and does not know how to accept help when it is needed. Her new demands for autonomy, her constant *no's,* her refusal to accept help, and her inability to make choices produce some trying moments. However, if the family can tolerate the difficult moments, this is an especially exciting period. Suddenly, the toddler has developed a sense of self, a recognition of her personal rights and privileges. In a period of just a few months, the toddler becomes a competent, self-willed child who must be dealt with on her own terms."

Self-Awareness

"The self-awareness that develops during this period lays the foundation for the child's efforts to be autonomous. *Autonomy* is a large word that means getting your own way, being able to realize your wishes. Often autonomy is identified with independence and power. However, autonomy also involves dependence and limitations. In the real world, a person's desires must be adapted to the needs of other people and to physical limitations. True autonomy is a balance between feelings of independence and dependence. A child needs to learn to depend on other people, as well as to be self-sufficient; to recognize both his own power and its limitations. Obviously a child does not acquire autonomy overnight. The balance between independence and dependence continues to be an issue between parents and children at all ages.

"Feelings of autonomy, of being in control, are often negative at this age. Seventeen-month-olds assert themselves by resisting someone else. They refuse to obey their parents; they fight with their brothers and sisters over toys. Encouraging a child to assert herself by making a choice helps the child develop positive feelings about autonomy. Naturally parents do not ask children to make choices they cannot understand. Even more important, they do not offer children a choice once they have already made a decision. For example, if they have decided the child should wear a blue shirt, they should not offer a choice between blue and red. Giving a child some choices does not eliminate conflict; on the contrary, it may increase conflict.

"There is no magical solution that will resolve these conflicts. Both children and parents are going to lose their tempers from time to time. However, parents can keep the word *no* from turning into a highly-charged symbol. Sometimes they can ignore a child's *no*. For example, suppose a parent suggests a new way to play with some blocks and the child says *no* and pushes the blocks away. The parent can ignore this invitation to argue and more than likely the child will try the parent's suggestion a few hours later.

"On other occasions parents can turn a child's *no* into a game. Suppose the toddler does not want to eat a piece of cheese. The parent can ease the tension by handing the child a toy car and asking whether he wants to eat *that*. When the child shouts *no,* the parent can suggest eating a pillow or the TV—the more absurd the better. Usually the toddler recognizes the joke and has great fun yelling *no* amid peals of laughter. In the end, the child still may not eat the cheese, but he has broadened his understanding of *no*. It does not always have to instigate a battle."

Self-Help and Rituals

"From a parent's viewpoint, independence means that the child is learning to take care of herself. Unfortunately, however, the child's idea of independence does not always match the parent's. Many children this age learn to remove some or all of their clothing. They strip off their shoes and socks or their diapers. Parents would be happy if the children were learning to dress themselves, but this is not the way it happens. Undressing precedes dressing and parents are faced with a child who wants to run around the house naked, but is not 'toilet trained.'

"Another common problem is children who refuse to let parents hold their hands while walking down stairs. On a shopping trip, when the parents want the toddlers to be independent and walk by themselves, they may ask to be carried. But when the parents want to hold their hands because of a dangerous situation, the children insist on being independent. In such cases, parents must weigh the value of encouraging a child's independence against the risk it entails.

"Sometimes a conflict arises over a daily routine, such as washing, bathing, eating, or bedtime. The resolution may be brought about through the development of a ritual. A child may have a bedtime ritual, a changing ritual, rituals in the bathtub or at the table.

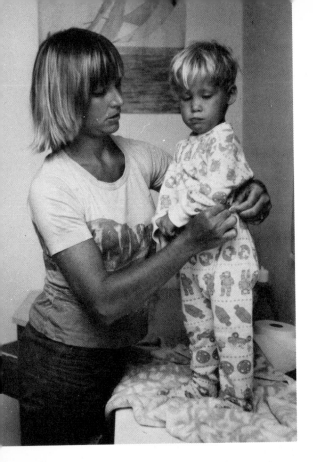

Rituals are a *compromise*. Parents get what they want, but the child feels that he is an active participant and not a passive victim. For example, the bedtime ritual helps get the child to bed—which is the parent's objective—but the child feels he has some control because he makes sure that the parent completes it. The child is the keeper of the ritual.

Rituals may be quite short and still effective. A child may want the blanket arranged in a particular way or insist on an ice cube in her hot soup. Some of the most effective rituals are verbal. The child is old enough to understand the parents' language and can be soothed by a familiar verbal game. For example, the parent may sing a short song such as "Baa, Baa, Black Sheep" when putting the child to bed. Or the parent may sing a simple song to the child while dressing her—"Put your little, put your little foot in your shoe." When washing the child's face, the parent may pretend to paint different parts of the child's face with the washcloth.

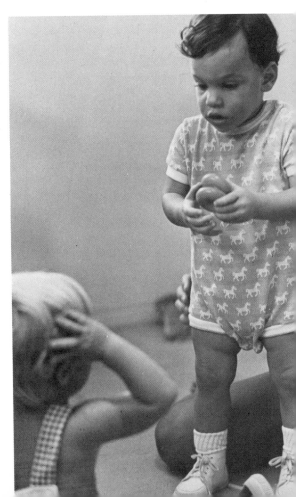

"Toys are more than desirable objects to toddlers—they are symbols of their autonomy. All parents have been exasperated by children who keep on taking toys from other children. They do not want these toys; they want to keep other children from using them. Every time the other child picks up a new toy, he takes it away. The toddler who guards his toys so protectively is trying to protect his sense of power. The toys are important symbols to the child, and the more toys the child has at his disposal, the more he feels in control of the situation.

"A child's sense of autonomy is nurtured very much by her increased ability to use language. Between seventeen and twenty-one months, many children develop a large vocabulary of labels. As they point and name objects or pictures, there isan obvious feeling of pride in their voices. To name an object is to gain a kind of control over it."

Self-Control

Parents have a lot of trouble trying to teach their toddlers self-control. Lack of self-control assumes many guises—aggression toward children and adults, unwillingness to wait even for a moment for some treat without tears or scenes, even to the point of destructiveness. Children are not born with self-control; it is something they have to learn. Learning to control oneself is basically a matter of learning to accept delay and frustration.

The infant brooks no delay. When hungry, he wants food immediately. This works for the infant simply because there is an adult on hand to cater to his needs. Left alone, the infant would, of course, starve.

The toddler, on the other hand, when angry or frustrated, lashes out at everyone. When adults are angry, they realize that when they lash out, they will suffer undesirable consequences. As a result, adults control their impulses, sacrificing immediate gratification in the interest of a long-term solution. The mature person has a sense of the future and thinks in terms of it, as well as of the present. Rational control of our emotions and impulses

depends upon our ability to wait and see; to take into account all the consequences for ourselves and others.

Rationalizing with a toddler does not work. It is insufficient to say to a toddler, "If you hit John, he will hit you back and that will hurt you." Toddlers do not operate on a rational basis. This develops only through long experience with reality. As children grow older, they begin to understand the consequences of their acts. The ability to postpone our impulses is based on two repeated experiences: the knowledge that control pays off in positive affection and consequences and that the absence of control is not rewarded.

Temper Tantrums

Dr. Virginia Pomeranz and Dodi Schultz, in *The First Five Years,* offer the following advice for handling temper tantrums:

If you are at home, ignore your child or calmly pick her up and place her in her room.

If you become visibly upset or offer a reward for stopping the behavior, or give in, your child will have achieved his aim, and the performance will be repeated because he knows it "works." On the other hand, once your child knows that this form of behavior does not shatter you, he will stop it.

Some children use breath holding as a type of tantrum. The act can be terribly upsetting. The child practically says by actions that "he is going to hold his breath until he turns blue." The breath holder starts to lose consciousness and rapid breathing takes over. Unfortunately, the child can go into convulsions.

"It is wise," write Dr. Pomeranz and Ms. Schultz, "to put an end to this type of behavior. How? By calmly and suddenly slapping his face. There will be an involuntary intake of breath and that will be that."

The worst way to cope with a tantrum is for the parents to respond with a tantrum of their own in a screaming match that escalates into inevitable violence. The best way to deal with physical assault is firm and soothing restraint. Envelop your toddler in an embrace that keeps him from continuing the attack.

Aggression

Aggression in childhood is universal and learning to control it is an important part of the socialization process. Aggression often develops because the child discovers that she can secure compliance with her wishes by hurting. Anger and aggression may be expressed in many ways.

In a study of the expressions of anger in the homes of some forty-five mothers, 1,878 instances were recorded of angry outbursts from children from seven through eight months of age during a period of one month. Among children from one to two years of age, denial of permission to carry out some desired activity or verbal or physical restraints were the reasons for outbursts. Being forced to remain on the toilet, restrictive clothing, or being put to bed triggered the beginning of total aggressive outbursts. Disagreements among playmates accounted for only 10 percent of all manifestations of anger.

In attempting to socialize their children's aggression, the mothers used a great variety of techniques. Ignoring, spanking, removing the source of trouble, diversion of attention, and coaxing were most frequently used by the mothers of children under two; scolding, threatening, and isolation were most typically employed with older children. "Giving the child his or her own way" led to more frequent temper displays. In other words, when the child finds that his aggressiveness is rewarded—i.e., he gets what he wants—the aggressive behavior will be repeated.

It was concluded that the control of anger is best achieved when the child's behavior is viewed with tolerance and serenity by the parents, when the standards set are within the child's ability to achieve, and when standards are adhered to with sufficient consistency to permit the child to learn. Self-control on the part of parents is most likely to be the best guarantee of self-control in the child.

Socialization

Socialization teaching by parents ordinarily begins in earnest during this period. At first it is centered on the inhibition of undesirable behaviors: curbing tantrums and destructive activities, restricting free exploration, and so forth. The effectiveness of socialization teaching depends on the child's relationship to the parents, as well as the motivation to please them, and the desire to avoid the unpleasant feelings generated by rejection or punishment.

Learning bowel control, for example, will proceed with minimum conflict if the parents are warm and loving and encourage gradual understanding and performance from their child. If toilet learning is begun too early, too rigidly, or too severely, the child may become intensely anxious or feel highly aggressive toward the parents.

Also, parental acceptance and a *reasonably* permissive attitude toward the child's explorations and emerging autonomy are likely to foster the development in the child of self-confidence, increasing independence, as well as spontaneity. The overprotected or overrestricted child is more likely to become anxious and dependent, avoiding novel and challenging situations.

During early toddlerhood, attachment to the mother is still intense, reaching a peak at about eighteen months of age. The child will manifest strong "separation protests" when she is absent. Long separations from the mother during toddlerhood may result in enduring emotional maladjustments.

More About Negativism

At seventeen months of age, a difference of opinion or contrariness should be considered a matter of the child's doing something her own way, however ineffective it may be. If your child is in a foul mood, she will brush aside any suggestion or help you may offer. If the project is relatively simple and not earthshaking, you may decide to allow it, and by so doing, you will be telling your toddler that you are two separate beings. This behavioral technique will emphasize independence by permitting your child to make a few mistakes and then correcting them. What is most important is that although your toddler's

choices may be poor ones, at least they will be independent ones.

One form of contrariness at this age is to defy a command before complying. (Although we have discussed the problem of negativism before, we are discussing it again because all children go through this phase as they develop.) You may say to your child, "John, no-no, don't touch," as you remove a favorite cut-glass bowl from his grip. To John your behavior and threat become an irresistible invitation to defy you and touch the bowl again. So, looking at you, he deliberately lifts it up and puts it down. What should you do? Dr. Akmakjian urges that you do nothing. You know that your message got through, and once your child has satisfied his need to assert his autonomy by defying your order, he has attained his objective and you have attained yours.

Fighting contrariness in a child of seventeen months only makes contrariness a habit and could interfere with his social development. If you accept the idea that these ex-

pressions of contrariness (as tough to take as they are!) are growth promoting, it may help you not to overplay your hand.

As we have pointed out, defiance can sometimes trigger a temper tantrum. Frustrated by the lack of words, the child cannot explain or make her wish come true in a world of unyielding reality and thus resorts to actions, and often a tantrum results. At first, a tantrum looks like a sit-down strike. Dr. Akmakjian explains that "the tantrum is a stormy release and the child would like nothing more than to have it stopped." If you allow the tantrum to go on and on, your child becomes anxious and begins to believe that she possesses terrible power over you—and this scares the child almost to death. If you react calmly, you reassure your child that she may feel destructive, but really is not.

If the tantrum is an attempt to get you to do something, do not give in, but do comfort your child. Comforting does not mean that you have given in; it serves to soothe feelings and makes your stand easier for your child to take. If your child angrily orders you to "Go away!" respect his wishes. This saves face. Children resort to temper tantrums when they are ordered about too much. Are you treating your seventeen-month-old toddler like a baby?

Language Acquisition

Children learn to use language in different ways. Some go from one clear word to another clear word and the language begins to build up. Others start using a real word in the middle of a pattern of babbling. Sometimes a word the child used constantly is dropped and not used for a time. During the next eight months, you as your toddler's teacher will have countless opportunities to help increase her vocabulary; to name everything she sees and touches. Give your seventeen-month-old a new word every time she experiences a new feeling (for example, the first time your child gets hiccups); discovers a new object (the toilet bowl, for one); or touches the freezer compartment and feels the cold.

Of course, this labeling can be used when you are looking through books or magazines together. Your child will show you things he sees every day and that is your cue for identifying each with a name or a short phrase. Your toddler may need to hear things said over and over again; that is because children learn to *understand* words when they can use them in a meaningful way.

Whereas the one-year-old rocks the crib and screams at the top of her voice to communicate with her parents, the seventeen-month-old uses a word or two to get what she wants: *a cookie, milk, a toy car,* and so forth.

How important is the intervention of parents in the word-labeling period? Research with thousands of toddlers by the U.S. Office of Child Development shows that when counselors visited the homes of deprived children and began reading picture books to them and labeling their actions, the I.Q. scores of these disadvantaged children were increased by as many as twenty points.

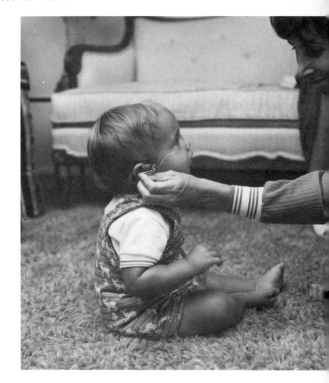

Fifteen to twenty-eight months is the opportune period for vocabulary building. A study of toddlers who spent fifteen minutes a day with their mothers labeling and identifying objects produced interesting results. These children were far more advanced in their speech than children who had not had the additional stimulation. When you consider the importance of verbal skills in our world today, it certainly was time well spent. Here are some suggestions for your role as "language master":

- Speak in short sentences when giving your toddler directions. If your child appears confused, shorten the length of the phrase; i.e., change "Drink the juice" to "Drink juice."
- Stress the use of pronouns and your child's name in referring to him or her. For example, "Bobby rolls the ball." "He rolls it back to me." "Who has the ball?" "Susan has it." "She has it."
- Demonstrate high and low with musical instruments (the piano or violin, and so on) or by voice.
- Take walks in your community. Name as many objects as you can for your child. Point out and label a police car, trucks, telephone poles, a fire engine, dogs, cats, and so forth.
- Use a tape recorder to listen to voices and help your toddler learn to listen. Record your and your toddler's voice on tape.
- Use puppets to gain your child's attention (remember his attention span is still very short). Get him to respond to *yes* and *no* questions. Tell simple stories with the puppets that deal with subjects and experiences that are within your toddler's ability to relate to.

"Seventeen-month-olds continue to add the names of objects to their speaking vocabulary and their ability to imitate words becomes more precise. Children vary widely in their language acquisition. It appears that girls generally develop this earlier than boys. For the most part, however, the explosion of new words that characterizes language development does not occur until eighteen months of age or later.

"Sometimes parents are concerned when a new word is dropped and seemingly forgotten after several weeks of use. It is believed that a child's vocabulary is very unstable at this age because word meanings are not yet fixed. The child seems to change the meaning of a word from one situation to another. Whether or not this is the reason, it is normal for children to drop words they previously have learned."

Combining Words in Meaningful Phrases

"Parents also are surprised by how long it takes most children to combine familiar words into a sentence or phrase. It is not unusual for a child to have a hundred-word vocabulary before combining two words at a time. There is no clear explanation for this fact. Apparently a great deal of organization must take place in the child's mind before she can link two familiar words.

"Some children learn whole phrases between sixteen and seventeen months of age. Through imitation a child may learn to say 'Catch the ball' or 'Pick me up.' These phrases involve more than one word, but they are fixed. The child cannot change the phrases or use the words in other phrases. Each phrase is like one big word to the child. There is some evidence that children develop language by expanding either their single-word vocabulary or their phrase vocabulary. Children who use language to express their needs and desires are thought to speak in phrases, while children who use language to comment on objects around them tend to use more single words.

"Between fifteen and eighteen months, the toddler learns that other people have distinct names and he may begin to call the members of the family and the family pets by name. A favorite activity is looking through a photograph album and picking out familiar faces. Many toddlers this age recognize their own pictures and are likely to begin noticing baby pictures on food boxes."

Playing with Toddlers

Parents may not be able to do much about their child's eagerness to master language, but once she becomes a talker, they can surround their toddler with an "envelope of language." They can label their child's actions with words. For example, during playtime, they can talk about what they are doing.

Collect a batch of cans of different sizes. You can name some of the foods that come in a can and say, "This is a big can," "This is a middle-sized can," and "This is a little can." Line the cans up in sequence of size and show your toddler how you can place one in another. "I am putting the little can into the middle-sized can." "Find it for me." "Let's take them out and you try again." Make it exciting by expanding the learning; i.e., trace the bottoms of the cans on paper and ask your child to find the biggest one. Be approving when your toddler finds the right one.

Collect three different-sized balls (tennis ball, volley ball, beach ball) and have your child sit on the floor with legs spread apart. "This is a small ball." "It is round." "I am going to roll the ball to Johnny." "Can you roll the ball to me?" "I roll the ball slowly." "Can you roll the ball slowly?" "I roll the ball fast." "Now you roll it fast." "This is the biggest ball." "This is the smallest ball." "Roll the biggest ball to me." "Now roll the smallest ball to me." You can sometimes transform the learning activity to other settings; i.e., rolling balls down a playground slide.

Speech Disorders

Some infants are born with a deficiency in sound-making or develop speech disorders. Such children need special help to acquire a level of speech development that others normally reach earlier. A program instituted in the early life of such a child and carried out by the parents at home under the guidance of a speech therapist will avoid later frustrations and failures and enable the child to become a functioning member of the family and society. Check local Councils for Exceptional Children, Schools for the Deaf, and public elementary school offices for full information. Such remedial programs include helping children develop:

- an awareness and responsiveness to sounds in the environment
- an ability to localize sounds
- the ability to discriminate among sounds
- the ability to reproduce nonverbal sounds, sound sequences, and repetition of sounds
- habits of listening and attending, as well as primary modes of communication

"Learning about Self and Others"

"Seventeen-month-olds begin to develop personal relationships with a wider circle of people. Although the mother and father still are the most important people in their lives, they associate special games and activities with other relatives and family friends. Perhaps the toddler likes to climb on the grandfather's lap and retrieve a pipe from his inside vest pocket or maybe the child encourages the aunt to sing to him by calling her 'la la.'

"The seventeen-month-old also is less afraid of strangers. It is common for toddlers this age to hand a toy to a stranger. Sometimes the child extends the toy and then decides not to give it to the stranger after all. At the other extreme, the toddler may bury a friendly visitor with favorite books, trucks and stuffed animals. This is one way the toddler uses to invite the stranger to talk with her. A less direct way to attract a stranger's attention is to scatter toys around the room. The toddler may not be bold enough to ask the guest to admire the toys, but she communicates the same message by scattering."

Eating Should Be Fun

With grown-ups, mealtime usually is a happy time. We serve food at our parties. We go to banquets to celebrate an event. We have tea and cake with our good friends. Too often, unfortunately, mealtime with children is a battle. It does not have to be. There are many things you can do to make it a time of good feeling.

Leave a lot of time. Do not feel that you have to hurry your seventeen-month-old through a meal. Do not worry too much about his dawdling. Let your child play with the food *a little.* Let him spill it, if he must. Let your toddler use his hands, if he wants to. Keep in mind your two big aims: you want your child to like to eat and to like to do things independently. You cannot achieve either of these if you rush him.

An attractive setting also helps—quiet, not too much else going on, no confusion, a pretty table mat, sometimes a flower. Good color in the food helps, too. The consistency of the food also is important. Things that stick together, for example, are much easier to handle (soups and runny dishes are the hardest). Bland rather than sharp flavors are preferred by seventeen-month-olds. All children enjoy variety: something raw, something crisp, something chewy, something they can hold in their fingers.

Most important is your attitude. During these early years, you will be introducing your child to many new foods. This is a big part of your job, as important as helping your child to meet different people and to see many things. Start with the conviction that your toddler is going to like the foods you serve. After all, eating *is* fun. (If you have many food dislikes yourself, your job is harder. You can try to overcome them.) It helps if you introduce new foods one at a time. Serve a very small portion the first time and serve it at the same meal with foods your toddler already knows and enjoys.

Remember that no one food is all-important. Fussing over milk or mashed potatoes or eggs, or demanding that the spinach be eaten, is not worthwhile. In the long run, you want your child to like all the good foods. However, he does not have to like all of them right from the start. It takes time to cultivate food tastes.

If your toddler is off milk, you can supply

what she needs in puddings, soups, and cheeses for a while. If your child fights a particular vegetable, you can provide essential vitamins and minerals in other forms (your pediatrician will tell you how). Do not make an issue out of any one food. Everyone should be entitled to a dislike or two.

Your seventeen-month-old may want so deeply to be a self-feeder that he will seem angry if you offer to help. Then when you are feeling good about your toddler's independence, he turns right around and with contrariness wants your assistance. The rough turns in child rearing are all par for the course!

Of course, your toddler will want you to help most when she is tired. Sometimes this comes after she has made a real effort at self-feeding. Do not insist too much on your seventeen-month-old's finishing the job. Just pitch in and give her a hand as needed and accepted.

Most children want more help when they are becoming ill or convalescing. (Almost everybody seems to like a little more service when not feeling up to par.) Do not worry about these occasional requests for help. If your toddler has been manifesting a real urge to be independent, you will not hurt him by being mildly indulgent when he is sick or overly tired. When your child feels better, he will snap back to the usual self-help stance.

Consistency

Much has been written about consistency with children. Some people feel that all the food must always be eaten every time; a clean plate with never an exception is their rule. Some believe that if you help feed children, you will always have to. This is the "bugaboo" of bad habits.

If you think back to the first year of the life of your child, this will not bother you too much. You know that children want to grow, they want to do things for themselves, and that basically they want to please. You do not have to be stubbornly consistent to make this come true—it is true anyhow. So do not be afraid of *occasional* exceptions. If it looks to

you as though your child would make out better with a little help on certain occasions, do not hesitate to offer it.

"In many families, the dinner hour is the best time for toddlers to see father. After all, most fathers are not home all day. The toddler's need for attention conflicts with the family's normal routine. The normal fifteen- to eighteen-month-old knows that she can get attention by being mischievous with food, or by demanding that father feed her, or that father share his food. If the going gets tough and the toddler is removed from the table or high chair, she may start some other disruptive activity to get father to stop talking with mother and pay attention to her.

"Each family needs to find its own solution to these early typical misbehaviors. Some parents feed their toddler first and dine later. Others allow the child to play, but teach him how to use a spoon. Still other families allow toddlers to stay up later to see father after dinner."

Sleep Problems

"Few children go to sleep without some fussing, but the toddler's ability to say *no* and get desired results from parents now becomes a bothersome bedtime technique. Bedtime can become a battleground and parents have to try all kinds of supportive techniques: reading stories, singing lullabies, and, if these do not work, setting a pattern of letting the child cry herself to sleep for a while. It is amazing how quickly children can learn that their parents 'mean business' when it is time for going to sleep.

"Parents should recognize that the toddler's sleeptime revolution is but another tussle for gaining control. A compromise can be worked out between the feelings of the parents and their offspring."

"Negative" Trust

"The ability of the toddler to say *no* certainly is negative in a real sense, but in another, it is a sign of trust. The typical toddler who is learning to defy his parents is quiet and docile with other people, even relatives.

"At this age, the child's anger or frustration may take the form of hitting the parents, but the child does not hit other adults. Seventeen-month-olds show that they are not afraid to say *no* or to defy their parents because they can trust them and know that they will not hit them back. Obviously, striking out at parents is part of a larger pattern of independence. Perhaps much of this defiance could be eliminated if the toddler had better command of language with which to express his conflicting feelings."

The Power of Play in Learning

Intuitively, most United States parents consider the span of eight months to six years a period for physical growth, playing, and social development. They prefer not to "educate" a child until of school age. The work of animal and human infant researchers is proving the intuition of parents to be correct: play is a powerful tool for learning, self-expression, exploration, and satisfaction. During the preschool years, attitudes toward learning and patterns of thinking gel and guide a person's thoughts and personality for the rest of his or her life.

Learning is not merely memorizing facts and giving them back on an academic test. It is a period for playing with ideas, building self-confidence, taking the raw materials of play and combining them, and making them do one's bidding, as in block building, painting, collage, clay modeling, drawing, and so on. It is a time for handling, manipulating, and experiencing in a physical way complex mathematical, scientific and social ideas before giving them a fancy name; i.e., ordination of numbers, gravity, architecture, and so forth. Play is the way a child learns to attend, concentrate, exercise imagination, role-play, practice grown-up social behavior, and develop a sense of control over the world.

Just think of the projects United States infants learn *without going to school, just by*

playing. They master by two-and-a-half years the speech and grammar of the English language (and probably a second language if it is spoken in the home). They paint pictures by the sixth year of life that express a spirit of creativity and freshness that artists spend their lifetimes trying to emulate. Through play, they learn to respect differences in others, share, cooperate, love—traits that endure throughout life. Young children at play combine a seriousness of purpose with an enjoyment that adults envy.

Jean Marzollo and Janice Lloyd, writers of *Learning Through Play,* put it this way: "Nature has always been on the side of early learning. When children are born they are graced with an insatiable sense of curiosity. They want to touch, smell, taste, see, and hear everything. The more they learn, the more they want to learn. They want to talk, they want to imitate other people, they want to explore."

Because of this innate drive, young children are imprinted by environmental influences. In a home where exploration is discouraged, children most often learn how not to learn—a tragic waste, to say the least. In a home where discovery is encouraged, the child's mind and personality grow and approach the potential that is her heritage and right.

What can parents do to support their child's sense of wonder and daring? They have to know the kinds of play activities and materials that stimulate play, discovery, and learning. They need to learn when and how to intervene in children's activities in order to be able to enlarge their child's experiences. They have to be patient and supportive of his efforts and praise him for efforts and accomplishments.

Play and the Practice of Sensory Powers

Adults regard play as a way of relaxing from the serious business of working. Although they allow their children full opportunities to play, most are inclined to consider play unimportant. However, most psychologists and educators regard early play—during the first two years of life—as practice for the emerging motor-sensory powers.

Whether the infant is snuggling against the mother's breast, shaking a rattle, playing with the fingers, kicking the legs, shouting, masturbating, or sucking her thumb, she delights in learning about her capacities for feeling. *Sense-pleasure play*—reveling in the experience of physical movements, tastes, sounds, touch, and so on—continues throughout life, usually in increasingly complex and patterned forms. Even during infancy, sense-pleasure play branches out into a somewhat less self-contained *skill play,* the exercise of one's capacities for action. It is remarkable how at the point of near-mastery of a skill, children will drill themselves in it over and over again. Once mastered, the skill serves other ends, but during the period of acquisition, it is fun for its own sake.

The infant crawls and creeps, cruises endlessly from one piece of furniture to another, and so forth. The toddler pounds and pounds a pegboard, undoes and recombines nesting blocks, climbs over furniture again and again, loads and reloads a wagon with the heaviest things he can pick up. When the toddler begins to feed his teddy bear or doll, there emerge the first signs of *dramatic play,* the enactment of scenes from the child's everyday life.

Make-Believe Play

In effect, children have two ways of getting to know their world: they can interact with it or they can act it—in other words, *be* it. In make-believe play, children try out by identification what it feels like to be other people and other things. As children begin to become aware of other people with an existence apart from their own, as they start to break loose from their egocentricity, they attempt to comprehend the style, the attitudes, and the activities of others by putting themselves—often literally—in their shoes. We see children dressing up in adult clothes, playing the mother or baby, serving tea, pretending to be a rabbit or a tiger, acting simultaneously as airplane and pilot, and so forth. Make-believe play serves not only as a means of learning about the society of which the child is a part; in play, the child's feelings of participation and identification afford the sense of power, consummation, and accomplishment that are not yet his in the practical scheme of things.

In all early play, we can see a trend from variable, impulsive play that is largely under the control of external stimulation toward more sustained and deliberately planned activity. The toddler is highly distractible and very much subject to the pushes and pulls of the environment; i.e., she responds to whatever catches her attention, promptly forgetting the activity just engaged in. Concentration and sustained interest come with maturation.

Scribbling—Art of the Toddler

Drawing is a human capacity that many adults avoid because they never had the opportunity to draw when they were children. Or they may have been "taught" rather than allowed to develop the skill at their own pace. Here are some guidelines for helping your toddler begin the developmental process of learning to draw:
1. Place a piece of sturdy drawing paper on the floor in front of your child. Give him an oversized hexagonal or round kindergarten crayon. Make a stroke on the paper. Then pass the crayon to your child and say, "Now you do it."
2. When your toddler comprehends that the crayon is to be used for drawing and gets

the knack of using it, just provide paper as needed. If your child has trouble holding the paper down with one hand and scribbling with the other, tape the paper to table or floor with masking tape. If you have trouble finding drawing paper and oversized crayons, check your local art store, educational toy shop, or the yellow pages of your telephone directory for the school supply showroom nearest you.
3. Seventeen-month-olds (and younger toddlers) love to scribble with a crayon on paper. Encourage this activity. Scribbling helps toddlers practice their fine-motor coordination. It is the child's first direct exposure to the graphic arts.

Children learn to draw by scribbling first and then drawing, *not* by being taught.

Scribbles and Drawing

Drawing does not come spontaneously to the toddler. He does not pick up a pencil or crayon and begin drawing. Rather he needs to be shown that if he maneuvers a pencil in a certain way, he can make a mark on the page. When he discovers that he is capable of scribbling, he is so fascinated that he practically blackens the entire paper with his scribbles.

This type of aimless activity starts at about a year and continues throughout the second year of life, taking the same forms for most children (see Figures 7 to 10). First the lines are wavy, probably the result of swinging the arm backward and forward. Then a little later, they take the form of circular scribbling; the lines go around and around in spiralling movements. Then toward the middle and end of the second year, the wavy and circular forms are mixed. Finally, instead of the scribbles being a single mass all over the paper, there now are various separate blocks of scribbling.

After the twenty-fourth month, the toddler starts to draw single lines, spirals, and circles and begins to name them. Eventually these scribbles begin to take organized form with schematic images. Thus within one year the child has learned to control her pencil and now is able to systematically copy forms she sees in nature. A period of endless repetition of these schemata follows, causing the toddler to "sharpen" her scribbles and place them with patterns that are more different and distinguishable from one another. The child's developing ability to force forms apart from one another is the beginning of the creative process.

The ability to bring something into existence—to create—gives the child a sense of self that permits him to experiment in a climate of security and helps him to become a strong and autonomous person.

The role of the parent is to "stoke the fires of imagination and creativity through the exercise and stimulation of the senses—eyes, ears, nose, muscles, skin." According to Polly McVicar, in an article, "The Role of the Parent in Art for the Primary Child" (Washington, DC: National Art Association, 1972), the ways of doing this are endless:

- Hang balls of yarn in doorways where moving air makes them change with shadows of the room
- Hang a prism through which light rays dance
- Collect a basket of stones, small and big, and have your toddler see the glistening specks and feel smoothness and roughness
- Take your toddler out into the night to see and feel the sounds, lights, reflections
- Bring in a clump of grass to smell, feel, and see; a pocketful of leaves, shiny on one side, fine "suede" on the other, to feel and see
- Collect things of nature and put them in a "nature bowl"—pine cones, pieces of bark, empty birds' nests, empty hornets' nests, dried seed pods, and so on

There should be a place that is private for each child to store her own things and interact in her own personal way. No matter how strange the things are, they have a special meaning for the child and must be respected by the parent. Encouragement can also come in the form of art books borrowed from the library.

Children are spontaneous "makers" and derive great joy from combining materials; mixing water and sand, hammering nails in a board and winding yarn around them in intricate patterns. The interest in combining materials requires parents to provide such things as paper, scissors, cardboard, wire, string, water paints and different-sized brushes, and moist clay kept available in a plastic container. Parents who value creativity will be willing to tolerate some messiness.

Imaginative Play

"A seventeen-month-old sits on the floor and holds a telephone up to the ear of his stuffed dog. The child is recognizing that a telephone is something that talks to you, that the ear is the part that does the listening, and that the flap on the side of the dog's head is an ear. In his imaginative play, the child has indicated that he is aware of very sophisticated generalizations; that he has, in fact, been able to hold an idea in his head. For example, an ear is not just his own ear; it is a thing that you hear with. This level of symbolic thinking becomes increasingly evident and more complex with each passing month. However, further developments are but a refinement and extension of this capacity. The mind's functioning at seventeen months is truly phenomenal."

Using Tools

"As seventeen-month-olds become more skilled at using a variety of tools, they naturally want to do more things for themselves. They want a key to open daddy's briefcase, to put the record on the phonograph, to push the vacuum cleaner, to pour their own milk, to cut their own piece of meat, and so forth. Sometimes there is a conflict between the toddler's intense desire to get something to work and her equally intense desire to do it without help. The shoe's strap will not go in the buckle, the zipper refuses to be pulled up, the flap will not go down on the raisin box, and so on. The toddler is torn between wanting an adult to help and wanting to do it alone. Parents find themselves in a 'no-win' position. The child gets angry if the parent withholds help and gets angry when the parent tries to provide assistance. It takes much ingenuity on the part of parents to furnish toddlers with opportunities to do things for themselves within the limits of their capabilities. No matter how hard the parents try to find household tasks or playthings that the toddler can manage alone, inevitably the child will be thwarted by a challenge she just cannot manage.

"The same kind of drive that puts toddlers in awkward predicaments makes them fun to watch. They are constantly performing new feats that show how much they have observed of adult behavior and how very well they are able to mimic. A toddler may come out of a closet wearing the mother's wig or shuffling along in the father's shoes; or pick a dandelion from the backyard and 'plant' it inside the pot of ivy. These acts are more than simple imitation; they are the toddler's interpretation of what adults do."

As a result of the growing independence of seventeen-month-olds, the parents' role becomes that of managers who keep their child's learning environment stocked with suggestions and activities, all geared to the child's interests and present capabilities. Managing from the sidelines offers parents a perspective for observing the development of their child's learning styles or preferred ways of dealing with various challenges.

THE SEVENTEENTH MONTH

Motor Development	Language Acquisition	Sensory Powers/ Learning
Gross Motor Stoops and recovers Tries to stand on a walking board Likes to lug, tug, and drag things Physically venturesome Can walk upstairs with one hand held Rejects baby carriage Can stand on right or left foot, holding on Constantly testing own strength—how big a box she or he can pick up or push, etc. **Fine Motor** Builds tower of 3–4 cubes Begins to show hand preference Has difficulty in coordinating hands and feet Hands not agile at wrists	Long, babbled conversations with some clear words Enjoys picture books Points to one named body part Says 6 words in addition to "Mama" and "Dada" Ability to imitate words becomes more precise Words used rather than gestures to express some wants and needs Understands more words than able to say, but even this understanding is extremely limited Combines 2 different words Extensive vocalization and echoing	Pulls aside paper or cloth to get at a hidden toy Points to one named body part Gets into everything Continuing spontaneous scribbling Is into, on, over, around, under, and part of everything Imitates strokes in drawing Imitates adults by "reading" a newspaper, crossing legs, simple household chores Learning takes a great spurt forward with the mastery of language Explores cabinets, wastebaskets, and drawers

Dear Parents:
   Do not regard this chart as a rigid timetable.
   Babies are unpredictable individuals. Some perform an activity earlier or (as much as six months) later than the chart indicates, while others skip a behavior altogether (i.e., walking without crawling).
   Just use this information to anticipate and appreciate normal child development and behavior. No norms are absolutes.

Growth Chart

Social Development

Demands personal attention

May begin to hit parents in anger, but does not hit other adults (is not afraid to say *no* or to hit parents because child trusts that they will not retaliate)

Waves "bye-bye"

Responds appropriately to emotional content of parent's verbalization

Responsive to social stimulation from strangers

Helps in simple household tasks

Especially enjoys sociability with father before bedtime, with a little roughhousing

Interpersonal relations are almost completely dominated by ideas of taking, not giving

Personality/ Psychological

May be afraid of thunder and lightning

Is unable to make choices

May be afraid of large animals

Is struggling to be independent and to control people

Is increasingly aware of "myself" as a separate person, with power, potentials, and limitations

May be willful, stubborn, hardheaded, negativistic

Self-Help Routines

Manages cup well, half full

Can take off shoes and socks and simple garments

Tries to put shoes on

Helps put toys away

Uses spoon, spilling little

Enjoys bath

Blows on food when hot

Likes to turn on faucet

Plays with food

Play and Playthings

Constructive play with boxes or other materials

Maneuvers a 3-step ladder

Likes to play with nesting toys

Intrigued with water and pouring toys

Beginning to enjoy hammering toys

Plays ball and other interactive games with verbalizations

Concentrates intently when playing with toys

Pulls and pushes wheel toys, large toy boxes, etc., around the floor

Likes to play hide-and-seek

Likes to chase and be chased

Loves to play with sand

THE EIGHTEENTH MONTH

Growing Up "All of a Sudden"

The ability of year-and-a-half-olds to walk well changes their perspective in remarkable ways, all greatly affecting their various accomplishments and behaviors. In addition to their clearer sense of themselves and more defined moves toward independence, their improved locomotor skill enables them to try to satisfy their healthy drive to explore and so to learn more about their world. Above all, eighteen-month-old runabouts are insatiable in their desire to master language, to attempt to do all the things that grown-ups do, and to affect the people in their environment. They are dynamic, exciting, entertaining, and rewarding. At the same time, they often are exhausting and exasperating "whirling dervishes" to their parents and other caretakers.

Gross-Motor Development

Eighteen-month-olds constantly try out variations in their locomotor skills as if to test all the components of their gross-motor equipment. They will walk backward partly because they are learning to shift the gears of their nervous systems (which are still far from mature). They start walking and stop quite smoothly, but are not yet able to turn corners well. They walk with feet wide apart and run stiffly. They enjoy the sense of control of their bodies that squatting affords them and so

squat a great deal. They can pick up a toy from the floor without falling—another measure of improved muscular coordination and balance.

Now your toddler can seat herself in a small chair without your help. In fact, she can even climb into an adult chair and seat herself by turning around while standing and then lowering herself into sitting position. Your child uses whole-arm movements in ball play because her hands are not yet agile at the wrists.

Your toddler is perpetually testing his strength by seeing how big an object he can pick up, what size chair he can push, how many toys or other objects he can carry at the same time. Climbing is a favorite activity. Your intrepid explorer will try to climb out of the crib and will move a chair to a cabinet in an attempt to climb on top of it. To avoid accidents because your child has difficulty coordinating his hands, feet, and whole body at this time, you need to make sure that his environment is completely safe.

Your "gymnast" can jump off the floor with both feet. Holding on, she can stand on either foot, but the ability to balance unsupported on one foot comes much later. It takes sufficient growing time to achieve full physical control of one's body. However, your toddler can walk upstairs, one step at a time, with one hand held. (If you have a stairway in your home, now is the time to install a handrail.) This is

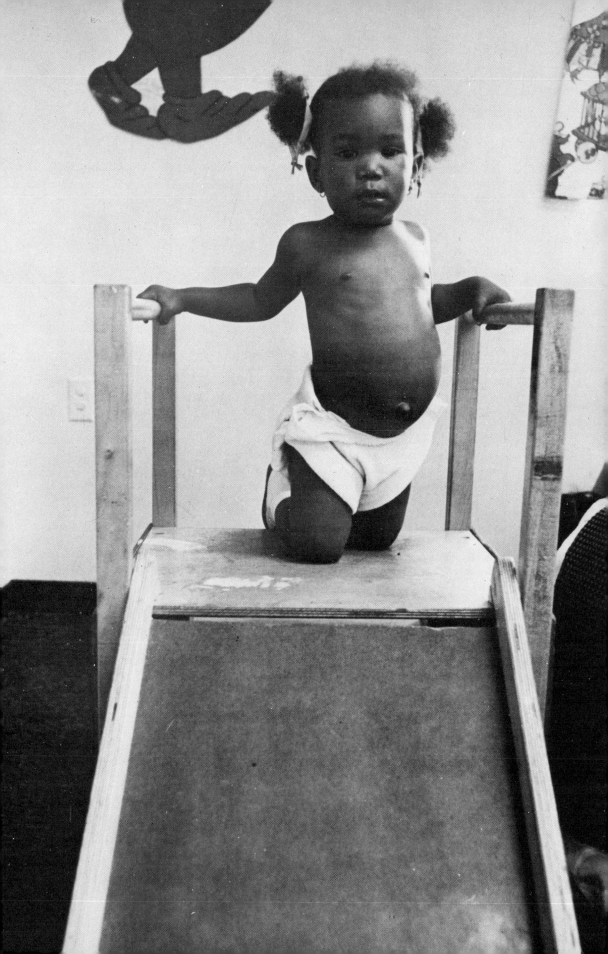

spoon or cup, handling of a crayon or pencil in scribbling, and so on. Inasmuch as their jaw muscles are not fully coordinated, eighteen-month-olds masticate their food crudely.

Your child can build a firm tower of three or more cubes—evidence of improving eye-hand coordination. Included in this growth are interest in turning the pages of a picture book, albeit two or three pages at a time; turning a knob to open a door; and trying to turn a water faucet on. Fine-motor improvement is reflected, too, in your child's ability to dump raisins from a bottle (a test used by child psychologists to appraise the manual dexterity and thinking ability of very young children).

the onset of your child's creeping backward downstairs. (Gates at the top and bottom of stairways are especially important once a child becomes mobile, whether creeping, crawling, or walking.)

Walking is a tremendous milestone in every child's push toward independence in every area of upgrowth. Do not be perturbed if your child rejects his baby carriage in favor of walking on many occasions. For quite a while, however, he will be ambivalent about walking, being carried, and riding in a carriage. (What patience and understanding are required of parents throughout their child-rearing years!)

Right now your toddler's gross-motor development and activities take precedence over her fine-motor abilities. Keeping up with any active eighteen-month-old is no mean feat. In addition to physical stamina and emotional calm (not possible for anyone always to maintain), parents need infinite tolerance, affection, and humor as part of their child-rearing equipment. It can be tiresome and even impossible on occasion for you to give your toddler the complete attention that she demands.

Fine-Motor Development

Year-and-a-half-olds begin to show preference for one hand, either right or left. This tendency shows up in their play, holding of

Language Acquisition

Understandably, walking extends the environment of children and their communication needs. The process of the growth of meaning is a highly complex interaction of learning and social factors. For example, when the mother asks her child, "Where's auntie?" the child imitates ah-tee, pointing in the right direction. To "Where's Timmy?" the child replies Tee, again pointing in the right direction. But to "Where's mommy?" the child points in the right direction, but remains silent. Subsequently from the baby carriage, as he catches sight of a picture of a smiling woman on a poster, the child immediately says "Mama, Mama."

At about their eighteenth month, normal children, according to linguist Noam Chomsky, begin to use language in ways that suggest existing innate abilities just beginning to emerge. Chomskian linguists maintain that a child comes equipped with very specific principles concerning the nature of sentence structure and that these enable her to deduce the details of the language to which she is exposed. Linguists who use the environmentalist approach to language acquisition believe that the speech in the child's environment serves as the model upon which the child bases her own speech.

Modeling has been found to be the most effective means of helping a child expand his

use of language. A child learning to talk probably feels like an adult trying out a foreign language for the first time. Modeling is the kind of response in which the child's idea is incorporated by the parent into a new expanded phrase; for example, "Juice gone" might be followed by the parent's saying, "Yes, because you drank it all."

Year-and-a-half-olds also indicate their desires by inflection and a combination of body actions and single words (their command of words is still very limited). For instance, *cookie* uttered loud and emphatically conveys *I want a cookie* to the parents; *up* may mean *pick me up.*

As in so many other aspects of language development, children begin their rudimentary questioning before they adopt conventional speech. A child eighteen months and three days old was looking at a picture book with his mother. She asked, "Where is the egg?" whereupon he pointed to the picture of an egg. Coming to a picture of a horse, he looked up inquiringly at his mother, who said "horse." Coming then to a picture of a jug, he pointed to it and looked up at his mother. She remained silent. Then he said "Eh-eh-eh!" urgently, pointing all the while until she answered, "Jug." When the child's mother asked him questions, he replied by simple pointing without language. Then he imitated her to the extent of looking at her interrogatively and this evoked her reply. When he tried again, however, his mother deliberately refused to respond until he made a spoken interrogation. Her approach and the urgency of his need to secure a response brought him to the point of utterance. His "Eh-eh-eh!" is as yet hardly a question. It is perhaps no more than a demand that she reply. However, it does have the rudiments of questioning in it. It is manipulative in that the child is using a kind of speech as a means of securing action from another person. The important development here is that the action he hoped to secure was a reply, an act of speech. (Try in your public library to borrow a copy of *Language, Thought and Personality in Infancy and Childhood* by Morris M. Lewis. It is listed in our bibliography.)

Eighteen-month-olds think with their bodies rather than with their sound systems. With only about a dozen words, including some names, at their command, they rely on their more abundant "vocabulary" of expressive gestures, odd sounds, and jargon. Favorite words at this time are *bye-bye, all gone, thank you,* and *oh, my*—all indicating the child's notion of completions. Although they can respond to a few simple verbal directions, they still must be managed mainly through actions or things.

Now that your child has good movement of the tongue, lips, and palate, it is becoming increasingly easy for her to form words. Although continuing to rely on extensive vocalization and echoing, your toddler is able to ask for some of her wants by naming objects; for example, *milk, cookie, car.* Your child also has begun to refer to herself by name, another sign of a keener sense of self.

A favorite game of many toddlers this age is attaching a name to a thing—what educators call *labeling.* The connection between name and thing may be punctuated by the child's touching with his index finger the object that he names (a ball, teddy bear, doll, cat, dog, and so forth).

Frequently toddlers use a question form (such as *whatsat?*) when they want to know what something is called. The labels the children are learning help them separate the objects in their world into categories: animals are cats, dogs; foods are cookies, meat; drinks are milk, juice; toys are balls, teddy bears, and so on. Most importantly, they are learning that everything has a name. It delights parents the first time their child gets her coat or hat and says *bye-bye*—and so it should! Using language to express thinking is a dramatic developmental hallmark.

Eighteen-month-olds comprehend the meaning of many words before they are able to use them. At first, they indicate their needs or desires by gestures and utterances. They identify objects by pointing and imitate simple sounds upon request, another indication of their language learning. They are able to follow simple one-step directions; for instance, they can point to a few body parts: their hair, eyes, nose, or mouth. They will sit down upon request and will extend their arms, if asked to do so, so their sweaters or jackets may be put on by their parents.

Most toddlers this age do not like having a whole story read to them. The ability to sit still or concentrate for too long is not yet established. They prefer picking out and pointing to pictures in a book or magazine or listening to an adult tell them short stories about familiar "here-and-now" happenings.

Now your child may be interested in watching children's shows on television ("Sesame Street" and cartoons) and trying to sing along with the commercials. Actually if your toddler attempts to sing, it is by repeating one word only. His humming is more spontaneous. Your child has a wide range in tone, pitch, and intensity of voice and is keenly aware of the sounds of bells, whistles, and clocks. He enjoys hearing such repetitive songs as "Old McDonald Had a Farm" and listening to short rhymes with interesting sounds, especially when they are accompanied by pictures or actions. A record player and recordings of rhythmic folk songs and repetitive nursery rhymes are appreciated by the eighteen-month-old, who will respond with his whole body to the beat of the music and listen to the words.

No! is the chief word of the year-and-a-half-old, sometimes meaning *no,* but more often connoting *yes*. This proclivity, which is perfectly normal at this age, can be upsetting and confusing to parents.

Two-Word Sentences

Eighteen-month-olds begin to use two-word phrases, "telegraphic" versions of adult sentences without junction words; for example, *Catch ball, Me up, Want cookie, Eat now.* They chatter volubly—verbally or nonverbally—in imitation of the conversations they hear. It can be said that your child is now on the threshold of speech.

Children whose imperfect speech is corrected too often and too intensely may become frightened or frustrated. They may

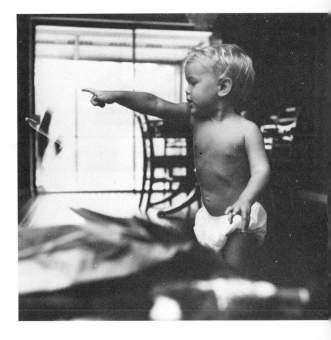

stammer or even stop talking until the atmosphere is more amenable to their efforts. Many speech therapists believe that stuttering may begin because of too much correction. Even when children speak incorrectly (calling all men *daddy,* saying *pitty* instead of *pretty* because they have not learned to pronounce *r*, or telling someone that one food is *gooder* than another), they have made a great effort to accomplish communication with as much skill as they possess.

Acceptance and encouragement for what a child achieves rather than overcorrection for what she cannot yet do are the best possible responses for parents. Of course, language development can be inhibited when parents are so responsive to signals that their eighteen-month-old does not have the need to speak. All children will benefit from having parents who listen to them, encourage them, and talk to them as they do to each other.

Speech Difficulties

Sometimes after a child begins to talk it will seem that he hesitates and has trouble saying certain words. Should this happen, you can be helpful. Wait for your child to get the word said. Do not rush him. Do not correct him. Show your child that you are interested in what he is trying to say, but do not attempt to help him say it. Above all, do not transmit to your toddler the idea that you feel sorry for him or are perturbed.

There are times when an eighteen-month-old will repeat a word or phrase a few times. This is not necessarily stuttering; the child may just be practicing by repetition, one of a child's important ways of learning. (Real stuttering, a speech defect that is apparent as a speaker starts the same word many times before being able to produce it vocally, requires professional evaluation.)

Thought Symbols

Learning takes a great spurt with the beginning mastery of language at eighteen months, but at this time the child also is learning a great deal by watching. Even though the toddler's spans of attention are short, they do mount up and, during them, the child adds to her storehouse of useful information. However, her limited attention spans cause the year-and-a-half-old to be easily distracted, which operates for and against parental child-rearing practices.

Although he still needs objects present, the eighteen-month-old is starting to build thought symbols for them, commencing to figure some things out in his head (in very crude ways, of course). The symbols help the toddler to create "new ideas"; i.e., actions that he had not seen or practiced before. For example, the child begins to understand that a telephone is for hearing someone's voice talking out of one part and then talking back in the other.

Eighteen-month-olds can associate a tool with its function—a broom is for sweeping, a hammer is for banging—and will try to imitate the way adults use objects. They will copy the actions of adults by "reading" the newspaper, crossing their legs, trying to sweep the floor, dusting, and so forth. They like to blow out matches and blow on balloons to get them to move. These toddlers will learn to blow through a straw before they will be able to sip through it.

Although eighteen-month-olds have no real notion of time (yesterday, tomorrow, next week, last month, and so forth), they are beginning to grasp the meaning of *now;* for example, the mother's saying "It is time for lunch now" takes on specific meaning and may even cause the child to go for her bib. Each child has her own internal time clock for all her growing and learning. Your love, interest, praise, and assurance will go a long way toward making your child's unfolding easier and smoother.

Scribbling and Drawing

An eighteen-month-old may react to a crayon or pencil the first time he sees it by merely holding it, or he may use it to make marks on paper and other surfaces—the walls, table, telephone directory, address book, his own clothing, face, and hands. (This is a time for close supervision of your child's "artistic" efforts.)

The initial stages of scribbling may emerge by accident when your child makes a mark on an object. The first marks usually are done hesitatingly. With practice, your child will gain confidence and make repetitive marks with increasing force. Most eighteen-month-olds are just beginning to initiate definite strokes in drawing. Children who see others writing and drawing in the home and who have crayons or pencils and paper available to them will acquire competency before children who have no opportunities to observe and to practice drawing skills. It may be that more than with other skills, scribbling and drawing are shaped to a large extent by conditions in the home.

The "Explorer"

The year-and-a-half-old is an avid explorer of wastebaskets, drawers, cabinets, and closets. Mother's pocketbook and father's briefcase are especially inviting. Although toddlers this age still like emptying things, they are beginning to be preoccupied with fitting things inside other things. Nesting cylinders are great fun, also nesting boxes.

The adventuring and repetitive behavior of eighteen-month-olds helps them to remember where objects in the home belong. They become great assistants to their mothers by helping put groceries away, fetching and carrying a newspaper or small tool for their fathers, and so forth.

Because children this age relish fitting challenges, they enjoy putting shapes into a shape-sorting box. They also have learned to place a circle and square in a formboard. Year-and-a-half-olds can gain much from simple puzzles: recognition of shapes and sizes, the experience of trying to solve a problem, and learning the names of objects. At the same time, they are learning to use their fingers more skillfully. Picking up puzzle

pieces and putting them in their proper places in the board entails fine eye-hand control. The first puzzle should have only three or four separate pieces, each one being the picture of a whole object. The large wooden puzzles with colorful pictures are easier to start with, although simple heavy cardboard puzzles will suffice.

The eighteen-month-old's interest in Sesame Street may extend to simple, very colorful picture books. Your child will delight in identifying pictures of single objects in a book and will respond to "Find the ball" by searching for it and pointing to the ball. Also relished are tactile books—*Pat the Bunny,* for example. Right now your toddler needs supervision while looking at books because frequently she tears them. Cloth and heavy cardboard books are recommended until such time as your child can be more careful.

Social Development

In the normal course of events, children become more actively social as they grow older and walk. Then they begin to build relationships with other people. From the very beginning, they have a streak of individuality, and as time passes, they become increasingly aware of themselves as separate beings.

Among the earliest experiences that influence the development of a child's view of himself are those with other people, especially with the significant people in his life (at first, the parents or other primary caretaker). If children are accepted, respected, and liked for what they are, they will be helped immeasurably toward a healthy attitude of respect for themselves.

Linked to their affection should be the ability of parents to truly *enjoy* their child. In the main, parents derive great pleasure from being with their children and helping them to mature. Nonetheless, most parents will admit that their enjoyment of their child's individuality has its limits. While they may admire their child for having a mind and will of his own, they often are annoyed by overt expressions of willfulness.

The capacity of year-and-a-half-olds for acquiring various forms of social behavior changes as they mature. They constantly explore the effects they can have on other people and learn that different people react in different ways. Most toddlers are skillful in dealing with older persons before they learn to interact with their agemates.

Long before they can walk or talk, infants take notice of other children. Actually they begin to throw in their lot with their own generation at an early age. At first, however, they tend to treat another child as an object rather than a person. They resort to experimental poking, pulling, pinching, pushing, stroking, and sometimes hitting or hair pulling as though the other child were merely a'thing to be manipulated. Although eighteen-month-olds do not play directly with their peers, they do like to be near them. Of course, the more people of all ages a child is exposed to, the more her social skills will increase.

The Play Group

One way to expand a toddler's social sphere is to have him participate in a small cooperative play group. Such a group can consist of from three to five toddlers and their parents. The parents take turns caring for the children, often from 10 A.M. to 2 P.M., two or three days a week. The parents provide lunch, milk, juice, and carefully chosen toys, as well as diapers or training pants and tissues. They take the toddlers on suitable little outings and break up any fights that may ensue (knockdowns, biting, hair pulling, and so forth). You will have to decide whether your eighteen-month-old would benefit from such an experience and whether you would enjoy being involved. (If you are interested, you may wish to borrow from your local public library a copy of *The Playgroup Book* by Marie Winn and Mary Ann Porcher, which was published in 1967 by The Macmillan Company.)

Many eighteen-month-olds demand a goodly amount of personal attention from their parents. Certainly children are entitled to friendly interest and reasonable amounts of attention, but many children remain demanding because they have been encouraged to develop that way.

Forever on the go and intrigued by everything, the year-and-a-half-old learns where things are kept in the home and likes to put them back where they belong (but do not set standards for undue cleanliness, neatness, and efficiency right now). Your toddler cannot resist getting into things and upsetting them (this is one way of learning!). When tired, she is especially resistant to inhibitions.

At times when a toddler knows that he is taking something that is forbidden, the child will run away and drop the object while trying to escape the expected admonition. At the same time, your child often will do what you ask. A mixed bag of behaviors, to say the least!

With her great penchant for getting into "tight spots," your eighteen-month-old will seek your help when she gets into real trouble. Despite your toddler's "do-it-myself" stance, there are many occasions when your direction and assistance are needed and relied upon.

Personality/Psychological Development

As in all areas of child growth and development, there are wide variations among

person—with potentials and powers as well as limitations. Eighteen-month-olds are as ambivalent as their parents. The latter want their child to remain their loving, compliant baby, but to behave in more and more grown-up ways. For the child's part, it is hard for him to want to be self-reliant and want to control people at the same time.

Your child's own temperament, the balance in her between dependence and independence, determines the way she reacts and behaves. Aggressiveness may be triggered by frustration and anger, as well as your toddler's limited experience in control and self-discipline.

The least aggressive children are those whose parents do not tolerate abusive, uncontrolled behavior and are not aggressive themselves—who do not resort to aggression to stop outbursts in their children. While it is hard for parents (and children) not to be irritated and impatient when they are feeling exhausted or strained, they must try to keep in mind that eighteen-month-olds are constantly learning from their parents and patterning themselves after them.

A child watches what the parents do and attends to what they say, not only when being pleasant, but also when being disagreeable. When parents understand that their year-and-a-half-olds see themselves as being like them and are trying to confirm this perception by attempting to do grown-up things, they are more likely to call upon their sense of humor and deep love in many hectic instances and to muster their good nature and fortitude.

Ambivalence of the Eighteen-Month-Old

Energetic, busy eighteen-month-olds try persistently to succeed without the help of their parents and others. Far from mature, they may be willful, stubborn, hardheaded, and negativistic. Their testing of themselves, their parents, and the environment often is met with less than complete success. Growing in all directions at the same time, they find it hard to make choices. They want to ac-

children in personality and psychological development. Normal, healthy one-and-a-half-year-olds are delightful, entertaining show-offs—except when plunged into dark moods by the many restrictions and frustrations that often are their lot. They are daring and exploratory because of their innate drive to satisfy their curiosity, unless deterred by too many no's! from well-meaning but apprehensive parents. They laugh easily and often when the most cherished people and stimulating elements in their lives help them in their quest for self-identity and competence.

The desire for autonomy propels eighteen-month-olds to try all kinds of antics, some of which may be dangerous or otherwise upsetting to their parents. One of the most telling forward strides is the increasing awareness of the child of being a separate complish everything at once, whether feasible or not.

This seems to be the period when both toddlers and their parents abuse the word *no!* Eighteen-month-olds' desire to be in control is often negative. They try to assert themselves by resisting someone else: fighting with a sibling for toys, refusing to obey their parents, and so on. As their confidence in their ability to direct themselves increases, they may resist their parents' requests even more frequently. Parents need to learn when to be firm and when it is wiser to release their hold on the reins.

Nagging toddlers when they "fail" or in other ways discouraging them is one of the chief reasons why children become timid. Parents can see to it that their children succeed a good part of the time in what they try to do. They can help their children feel that they will soon be able to do something challenging if they just keep on trying. (Many of the so-called behavior problems that arise in connection with child rearing are related to feeding, sleeping, and elimination and will be covered in the section of this chapter headed "Self-Help Routines.")

Fears

Children learn fears from their parents and other adults and children or from frightening experiences (having a bad fall or being scratched by a cat, or the like). It is not unusual for eighteen-month-olds to be afraid of large animals, but they will learn to be afraid of mice if the mother jumps up on a chair when she sees a mouse in the house. Normally children enjoy holding and playing with mice.

Children also learn fears by hearing them talked about. Adults can frighten a child just by describing situations in which they were afraid, whatever the reason. Self-control, understanding, and good sense on the part of parents can help their child *not to learn* to be fearful.

Of course, it is perfectly normal for a child to be fearful on occasion, but if her fears are too intense or too prolonged, they can be harmful, causing damage to her developing personality. For this reason, parents need to take their child's fears seriously (but calmly) and try to relieve them. Some fears are transitory and are easily forgotten; e.g., being afraid of a big dog or loud noise. Others that are lasting and injurious include fear of soiling from too rigid toilet training, fear of dirt from constant harsh scolding for getting dirty during play, and so on. Whatever seems to make you withdraw your love will worry your child because she loves and needs you so very much.

You can avoid the growth of needless fears in your child by being tolerant and friendly about his progress—or lack of it—in eating, playing, or keeping dry. You need to praise your child for all his efforts, even if they are uncertain and clumsy. If you make your eighteen-month-old feel a failure, he is bound to be full of fears.

Fear of being alone in the dark at bedtime is common. The usual cause is the child's lack of self-confidence or sense of security. A toddler also may be afraid of wetting the bed. A pleasant bedtime routine can help eradicate fears that may be connected with going to sleep at night.

Discipline

All too soon the toddler is under pressure to conform to external standards of behavior. These pressures may be imposed with a heavy hand or through a series of gentle nudges. Both approaches constitute the beginnings of discipline.

In brief, discipline is any kind of influence that is designed to help the child learn to deal with the demands of her environment (home and society). What children do or refrain from doing by virtue of the discipline they receive is something they would not at first do of their own accord. For instance, eighteen-month-olds will try to feed themselves, but it usually is as a result of discipline that they learn to use a spoon rather than their fingers.

The aim in discipline should not be to curtail freedom, but to give children greater leeway within limits that they are able to manage. All children need freedom to grow and learn in their own way. However, they cannot thrive on unlimited freedom. They need discipline because without it they would have a hard time surviving in the world. Through reasonable restrictions, young children are spared dangers they might otherwise encounter while they are too young to perceive the consequences of their actions (running into the middle of the street, playing with matches, and so on).

Good and proper discipline relieves very young children of the responsibility for deciding matters over which they have no choice or control, thus freeing them for action where they do have a choice. This is especially important for eighteen-month-olds who often cannot make up their minds because they are not yet able to resolve their "dependence/ independence struggle."

Unhealthy, mean discipline is punitive, restrictive, or coercive and teaches the child to be angry and rebellious. Temper tantrums may be triggered by harsh discipline. Negative behavior also may arise from fatigue, aggressive feelings, or frustration, as mentioned previously. Parents want to do all the right things for their child, but no one succeeds all the time, and unless there is something seriously wrong, your child will keep on growing well and have an exhilarating *joie de vivre.* You can help your toddler achieve psychological well-being.

In spite of all their "ups and downs," eighteen-month-olds are delightful and joy-giving. They express their affection by hugging and kissing their parents and other beloved persons and lugging and hugging their favorite doll, stuffed animal, or other valued toy. They are not yet ready to feel affection for their peers; that will come with their ongoing experiences in sociality.

Self-Help Routines

Eighteen-month-olds are consolidating their growth and learning from birth to this point in their maturation and are beginning to show glimpses of burgeoning new skills. Their trying *no!* stage reflects a developmental stride ahead rather than a regression. Think about this! These toddlers are striving to assert their increased individuality and to express their urge to become self-reliant. They get into all kinds of situations that tax their parents' ingenuity and stamina. They are torn between wanting parents to help them and wanting to do it by themselves. They get angry both when their parents withhold help and when they proffer needed assistance. In the main, however, they get angry because they are not big or strong enough for the tasks they set for themselves.

Because year-and-a-half-olds do not possess realistic notions of their capabilities and limitations and do not know how to accept help even when they need it, parents are placed in an uncomfortable "wire-walking" position. This may be considered a transient "no-fault—no-win" interim for both children and their parents. But parents need not despair! A lot of love, laughter, and child-rearing expertise can help all concerned through all the phases of child development even when the going is neither smooth nor easy.

From the parents' viewpoint, independence means self-help: learning to eat with a spoon, drinking from a cup or glass, washing oneself in the bath, making an attempt at brushing one's teeth, and so forth. Of course, the ideas of independence held by eighteen-month-olds do not match their parents'. For instance, toddlers this age are becoming more actively interested in the process of being dressed. They will hold their legs so their parents can pull on their overalls. They even try to put on their shoes, but without success. Of course, eighteen-month-olds are more adept at undressing than dressing themselves—it is easier to learn. They are able to take off their socks, caps, mittens, and other simple garments. They can unzip a large zipper (the ability to zip will come later).

Sleeping

On the average, healthy year-and-a-half-olds sleep about thirteen and a half hours per

own accord. During this period, it will not cause misshapen teeth or mouth. Ignoring this passing habit is a good "rule of thumb"; nagging only heightens tension.

Mealtimes

Although year-and-a-half-olds may accept breakfast feeding by a parent, they will insist on holding the cup while they drink. They are able to lift and hold the cup between their hands. They are more insistent on feeding themselves at luncheon and are able to handle a spoon fairly well. Having engaged in a degree of self-feeding at the noon meal, they appear to be willing to accept help at suppertime.

The eating of toddlers is erratic at this time; they eat a lot or a little. Their food preferences and refusals are fluctuating and not yet clearly defined. Your pediatrician can decide with you what foods are essential to your child's physical well-being. Pushing food is positively a *no-no*! Remember, healthy children do not starve themselves.

Eighteen-month-olds have a tendency to play with their food. Without undue pressure, you can teach your child that food is for eating, not playing. Your example at table will help implant your message. One evidence of advancing learning is the fact that your child now places only edibles in his mouth—a great advance over his behavior of only a few months ago.

Another indication of your toddler's mind at work is her blowing on food when it is hot. Also, your child now will hand you the dish when finished eating. (Of course, you have to get there in ample time or the dish may well land on the floor.)

Your child's verbal/gestural vocabulary enables him to ask for food and drink (and even the need for the toilet if he has been started in this learning). When an eighteen-month-old unintentionally spills his food, throws up, or has an accidental bowel movement, competent parents do not welcome the mess, but they do not treat their child as a "juvenile offender."

day. Most awaken between 6 A.M. and 8 A.M., but will usually stay under the covers talking to their bed companion—a doll or teddy bear—for a while. When they feel it is time to get up, they may fuss or call and are overjoyed to see their parents and to be picked up. Normally these toddlers awaken happy and cheerful from their afternoon naps, which may last anywhere from one and a half to two hours.

In many families, bedtime for toddlers comes sometime between 6 P.M. and 8 P.M., depending upon the routine that has been established. Often the child will bring a teddy bear or other favorite toy to show the parents that she is ready for bed. (Should night walking occur, the toddler is easily quieted by being talked to gently, given a small drink, or toileted if that is required.) Many toddlers turn to thumb-sucking when they go to sleep (or when they are experiencing difficult times; i.e., when they are tired, excited, afraid, or hungry). Normally thumb-sucking stops of its

Self-Feeding

Eating habits can become a prime cause for belligerency. This is one of the first ways for children to learn that they can please or defy their parents. The child can turn her head quickly, push food away, or even spit it out. An impatient parent may shout at the child and take over the whole business of feeding. In addition to establishing an unhappy emotional tone at mealtime, the parent is depriving the child of a new skill at precisely the time when she has just found out about it and is eager to use it. Overly concerned about messing, a parent may so restrict the child's use of a spoon that she becomes awkward or rebellious. Frustrating a child in her clumsy attempt at self-feeding and stampeding her with anger or disapproval will impede learning.

The normal child learns to eat in a socially approved manner eventually even if his experiences have been disagreeable, but not without a trace of resentment about how the process was handled by the parents.

Bathing

Most parents bathe their eighteen-month-olds before or after their evening meal and most toddlers enjoy bathtime. There may be occasional short periods of resisting the bath, the cause of which may be hard to determine, according to Doctors Gesell and Ilg. Perhaps a child bumped her head on a side of the tub or was frightened by the noise of the water rushing down the drain.

The child who is stimulated rather than calmed by a bath just before going to bed might benefit from having the bath at an earlier hour. Your child will enjoy helping wash himself with a small washcloth. Of course, you have to make sure your toddler gets really clean, but encourage him to be an active part of the procedure. Eighteen-month-olds want to begin to try to brush their teeth and comb their hair "like Mommy and Daddy do." It makes sense to encourage children to learn to do for themselves what they can manage.

Toileting Is Another Learning Experience

Most child-rearing specialists are in agreement that parents should not rush or push toilet learning. The most recent findings indicate that control depends upon the physical maturation of the sphincter muscles and the sensory centers of the brain. Psychologists note in their researches that the success curve begins at about the time when the child starts to pay unmistakable attention to the act of eliminating and to the result.

Eighteen-month-olds have greater awareness of when a bowel movement is coming or going on—a sign of more definite *readiness* for learning to use the toilet. The child may indicate to the parent by sounds or actions that he has soiled the diaper and would like to be cleaned. Usually it is not until a few months later that most toddlers are able to notify their parents soon enough to be helped to the toilet in time. Toilet learning for bowel movements may begin at eighteen months if the parents are gentle and reasonable and expect their child *eventually* to perform as suggested, but most experts indicate that it is better to wait a few more months.

If you are aware that a bowel movement is about to begin, you might suggest, "Would you like to go to the bathroom and have a B.M. the way big people do?" This is one way to help your child make the connection between her bowel movements and having them in the toilet. According to Dr. Akmakjian, this is how toileting starts.

The period of helping a child to learn to use the toilet is a lengthy one because there is no way to speed up physical maturation. By the age of about eighteen months, many parents start using training pants on their child, which seems to make the toddler more aware of bowel movements when they occur. This seems also to make the toddler feel he is getting older and more is expected of him. If the child can remove the training pants without help, this provides another opportunity for self-help behavior.

It might be best to begin the toileting routine with a safe, sturdy, comfortable, child-sized seat placed over the adult commode rather than with a potty. This avoids the need for the child to have to go through two phases of adjustment: from potty or potty chair to a chair on an adult toilet seat. If you explain simply that it might be fun to sit on the toilet seat when your child feels the approach of a bowel movement, you might place your child on the seat at once to try it out. However, you can expect your child to continue to eliminate anywhere, at any time, for many more months. (Although it usually takes children longer to achieve urethral control than bowel control, there are some children for whom the order is reversed.)

Of course, parents become impatient with diaper changing; it is a mess and a bore in any language (for those parents who can afford disposable diapers, patience appears to come easier).

Toileting can be easier for child—and parents—if it is not started too early and if there have been no previous developmental problems straining the relations between parents and child. There are no absolute rules or timetables for toilet learning. Children vary in their readiness and parents differ in their willingness to keep on changing diapers.

There seem to be two types of bowel movement behaviors in children: one has a close meal association; the other is more irregular and occurs sometime between meals. Children who have a meal association appear to learn to use the toilet more easily; the two daily movements usually occur after breakfast and after supper. Eighteen-month-olds who have an irregular functioning commonly have their movements when alone, most often in midmorning, and preferably standing at their playpen or crib rail. They usually want to be changed and, therefore, may tell afterward by making a meaningful sound (perhaps *uh-uh* or *k-k*) or they may merely gesture by pulling at their pants.

If your child does not seem to get the idea of the process of elimination or shows signs of resenting sitting on the commode, do not press her. Most behavioral psychologists recommend against strictness with regard to a child's learning to use the toilet; no standards should be presented until the child can understand what is required of her. The maturing child is willing to learn to have bowel movements in the toilet because it is your way of doing things and your child wants to be just like you.

Being wet is more noticeable to the child than the feeling of a full bladder. Studies of average children indicate that most of them have frequent accidents at two and a half and many are not able to remain completely dry until about the age of three. Most eighteen-month-olds do not object to the toilet if they are not put on too often. Some children take the initiative by occasionally asking in advance. All children seem to respond best when asked whether they want to urinate *before* they are taken. If a child is in training pants and makes puddles on the floor, he will point to them saying, "See" or "Pee-pee," and enjoy mopping them up. Unfortunately punishment and shame often are introduced by parents because their child's awareness makes them feel he could have done better.

An indication of readiness for learning bladder control comes when toddlers are able to connect their puddles on the floor with something they did themselves. If they have seen their parents or older siblings use the toilet, they will begin to see a connection there. Girls seem to achieve bladder (and bowel) control a little earlier than boys. Complete night control comes later than daytime control. It seldom happens before the age of three and may come much later.

Since bladder control takes longer than bowel control, keeping the toddler in padded training pants and rubber pants makes good sense, especially during the child's play periods when she does not like to be disturbed and during the night when they may keep her from feeling wet and waking up. Training pants plus rubber pants are more comfortable than diapers at this time. Your toddler may need them especially when away from home because she may refuse to respond to a strange toilet.

Toileting need not become a pitched battle of wills between parents and children. Only those parents who forcibly try to "train" their children find toileting a hopeless chore. The more the parents insist, the more their children assert their newly-felt power over them by refusing—especially during their strong *no!* phase.

Punishments, shaming, or other unpleasant associations with learning elimination control can have an unwholesome effect upon a child. All children learn more easily and well when they are praised and encouraged rather than demeaned and harangued.

Play and Playthings

Eighteen-month-olds are not mature enough socially for play with an agemate even though they are interested in other children. If exposed to a peer, a toddler may engage in solitary play for a short period, perhaps back to back with the other child. These toddlers are not yet able to share their toys. Their possessiveness makes them hoard and hide all their playthings, even those of their siblings.

Because they locomote well, they enjoy walking with a pull toy either forward or backward. The more movement, color, and noise it has, the more the pull toy is valued. A toddler may even take pains to keep the toy upright.

In their play, eighteen-month-olds like to carry objects from one place to another, and in so doing, they learn what a place is. They use their energy to push and pull large toys and boxes around the floor. They express their feelings of affection by carrying or hugging a favorite stuffed animal or doll. They can maneuver a small indoor wooden steps and slide. However, because they do not yet estimate distance well, they must be caught at the bottom of a playground slide if they are not to hurt themselves. They require constant, close supervision at a playground to keep them from running into a swing in motion. Although you want your child to feel free and to use all his muscles, and to have a happy time, it is up to you to safeguard him from possible harm.

Eighteen-month-olds are able to hurl a ball without falling, but their catching remains crude and fumbling. They like to play more involved peek-a-boo games now, to hide and be found. They love to chase and to be chased. They may show a marked preference for certain of their playthings: a teddy bear (to hug and take to bed), toy drum (to make noise), soft doll (to cuddle), or small wagon (to push or pull).

During social play with a parent or older sibling, this toddler may enjoy piling up small blocks and knocking them down. Banging blocks together or lining a few up to make a train is fun, too. Eighteen-month-olds especially enjoy hidden object toys (postal station, simple inset puzzles, hammer-peg toy, and so forth). They can string a few large wood or plastic colored beads and manipulate a pounding bench crudely.

Eighteen-month-olds are beginning to play "pretend" games; for example, they will use a toy telephone expressively. They even may attempt to feed their dolls. They are able to point to the eyes, nose, and mouth of a doll upon request.

They respond to music joyfully and with abandon, using their whole bodies, and will turn the knob of the radio to get music to dance to.

Out-of-doors, your eighteen-month-old will adore playing with sand and can sit for long periods filling a container and dumping the sand. For this activity, your toddler needs a pail, shovel, sieve, measuring spoons, nesting cans, and so on. A small wagon will enhance the play.

THE EIGHTEENTH MONTH

Motor Development	Language Acquisition	Sensory Powers/ Learning
Gross Motor	Follows one-step direction	Remembers where objects belong
Onset of creeping backward downstairs	Can point to own body parts: hair, eyes, nose, mouth, on request	Beginning to "figure things out in head" in very crude ways
Picks up toy from floor without falling	Asks for some wants by naming object: milk, cookie, etc.	Explores cabinets, wastebaskets, and drawers
Moves chair to cabinet and tries to climb	Attempts to sing	Still needs objects present; but is beginning to build thought symbols for them
Tries to climb out of crib	Refers to self by name	Places only edibles in mouth
Walks fast; seldom falls	Gets coat or hat and says "bye-bye"	Places circle and square in formboard
Runs stiffly; falls	Enjoys songs such as "Old McDonald Had a Farm"	Has short attention span
Can climb into adult chair and seat self by turning around	Imitates simple sounds on request	Uses stick to reach toy
Uses whole-arm movements in ball play	Identifies objects by pointing	Tries to imitate the way adults use objects
Walks with one foot on walking board	Names or points to familiar pictures in a book	Spontaneous scribbling
Jumps off floor with both feet	Speaking vocabulary of about 10 words, including names	Enjoys putting shapes into a shape-sorting box
Walks into ball; not able yet to make definite imitative kicking motion	Understands simple questions	Likes to blow out matches and blow on balloons
Fine Motor	Uses 2-word phrases, "telegraphic" versions of adult sentences (*and, at, the* are lacking)	Can put together a very simple inset puzzle
Dumps raisins from bottle spontaneously	Favorite words may be "all gone," "thank you," "bye-bye," "oh, my"—all of which register completions	Beginning to grasp the meaning of "now"
Turns pages of a book, 2 or 3 at once	May hum spontaneously	Imitates vertical line in drawing within 30 degrees
Shows hand preference	Is now on the threshold of speech	
Builds a tower of 3–4 cubes	"No" is chief word	
Scribbles a circular stroke	Chatters in imitation of conversation, verbally or nonverbally	
Turns knob of radio or TV	Enjoys playing the question-and-answer game with parent	

Growth Chart

Social Development

Temper tantrums may be triggered by fatigue, anger, or frustration

Claims desired objects as her or his own

Demands personal attention

Beginning to do what asked to do

Explores the effects she or he can have on other people and learns that different people react in different ways

Pulls, pinches, pushes, and strokes other toddlers as though they were objects for manipulation

Seeks help when in trouble

Slaps back if slapped

Opposes parents with *no*

Shows everybody when she or he gets something new

Has not even a glimmer of the concept of sharing

Imitates housework, helping in simple tasks

Personality/ Psychological

Cannot tolerate any frustration

Looks at own photograph and says own name

Sees self as being like the parents and attempts to confirm this perception by trying to do grown-up things

Is less afraid of strangers

Is a delightful, entertaining show-off

Hugs and shows affection for doll or teddy bear

Persistently practices the mastery of own autonomous capacities (independent of mother and others)

Self-Help Routines

Is more skillful at undressing than dressing

Likes to undress and walk around without clothing on

May indicate readiness for beginning of toileting for bowel movements

Handles spoon fairly well

Likes to put things back in place

Wants to "do it myself!"

May complain when wet or soiled

Can unzip zipper

Lifts and holds cup between hands

Tries to brush teeth

Asks for food, drink, the toilet

Drinks from cup or glass unassisted

Feeds self partially

Eating is erratic; eats a lot or a little

Brings pillow or favorite stuffed toy to show readiness for bed

Play and Playthings

Likes to lug, tug, dump, push, pull, and pound

Throws and catches a ball crudely without falling

Walks with pull toy

Shows preference for certain toys

Can string large colored wood beads

Can manage small indoor steps and slide

Manipulates pounding bench crudely

Uses play phone expressively

Enjoys blowing bubbles

Loves hidden object toys (Postal Station, simple inset puzzles, hammer-peg workbench, etc.)

Engages in solitary play, albeit back to back with an agemate

Dear Parents:
Do not regard this chart as a rigid timetable.
Babies are unpredictable individuals. Some perform an activity earlier or (as much as six months) later than the chart indicates, while others skip a behavior altogether (i.e., walking without crawling).
Just use this information to anticipate and appreciate normal child development and behavior. No norms are absolutes.

THE NINETEENTH MONTH
Motor Driven

Motor Development

"Nineteen-month-olds are completely physical. They continue to walk much as a person aboard ship in turbulent seas; feet are held wide apart, toes are turned out, and the body has a slight forward tilt. These toddlers roll from side to side as they propel themselves forward. Since their balancing ability is still precarious, they may be toppled easily from their feet. Nineteen-month-olds seem to derive great satisfaction from their repetitive practice of the basic gross-motor skills of walking, climbing, and running."

Of course, your physically active child will have his share of inevitable spills, bumps, and bruises during this period. If you do not overreact to minor accidents, your child will be able to regard them merely as annoying but temporary interruptions, and this attitude will accrue to his store of self-confidence.

Gross-Motor Activities

Do not be surprised if your child decides to walk backward on occasion. Locomotion in every possible way remains a thoroughly challenging and pleasurable repetitive pursuit. Now your child is able also to do a little walking sideways without crossing her feet—a new refinement. Running is not yet smooth and easy, but there is some decrease in your

toddler's falling. Especially important are her positive feelings about herself. Take time out of your busy schedule to really look at your child's face as she pushes, pulls, throws, or carries toys or other objects while walking. The glow of mastery is special indeed. As with adults, each accomplishment registers yet another degree of self-confidence.

Your toddler likes to walk up and down stairs, which can be done now in an upright position with your help. In fact, the nineteen-month-old will climb stairs endlessly if permitted to do so. As mentioned in the previous chapter, you need to put a gate at the top and bottom of every stairway in your house to preclude the possibility of a bad fall. Toddlers have no sense of distance or danger. They will try to climb up onto everything that appears promising to them—nothing is sacrosanct! They are not dismayed by tables, bookcases, cupboards; you name it, they will try to scale it. Without adequate supervision, life is full of incipient danger for all normal, healthy children of this age.

Your toddler can stand on either foot holding onto you or a stable piece of furniture, but his not yet mature sense of balance precludes standing without support on only one foot. For the same reason, he will be unable to jump well with both feet for a few more months.

The arms and legs of the nineteen-month-old tend to function in unison rather than in balanced opposition. Greater maturity will

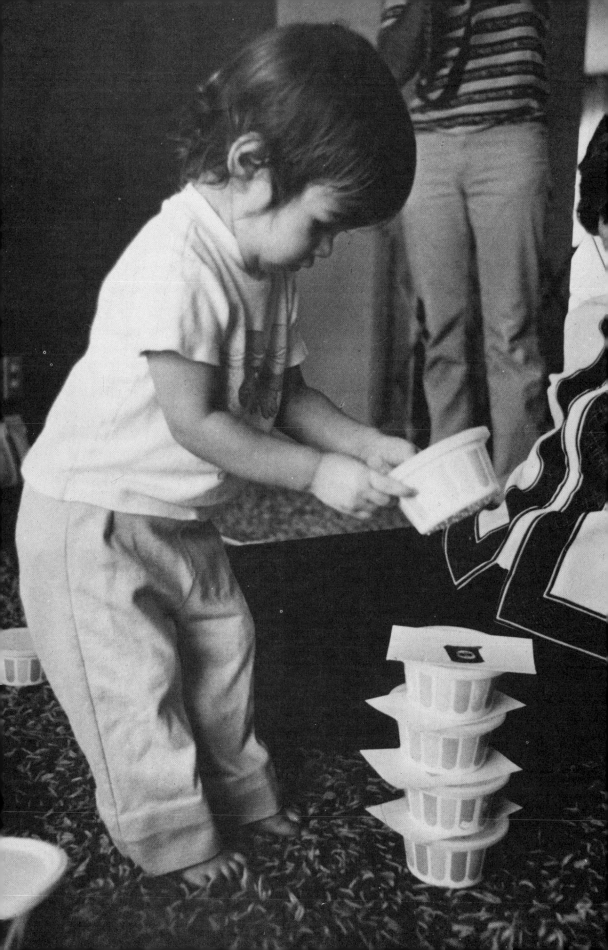

banish this temporary shortcoming. However, your toddler can throw a ball overhand, which is something she could not do a while ago. The increasing improvement of this skill will make it more fun to play throw-and-catch with your enthusiastic "athlete." Your toddler can also kick a large ball on the ground without stepping on the ball.

Have you noticed the agility with which your nineteen-month-old squats from standing position to pick an object up from the floor? Getting back up again is less smooth, but adequate. Grandparents (and even parents) wish they possessed such flexibility of movement.

Your toddler undoubtedly has a child-sized chair by now. The many clumsy maneuvers of a month or so ago are gone, as evidenced by your child's sitting on her own chair with fair aim. Muscle maturity and sufficient physical practice produce increasingly smooth gross-motor functioning.

As was the case in previous months, the nineteen-month-old will move to music with his whole body—joyously. You can encourage this wonderful form of body movement and self-expression by participating when invited to do so by your child. If your child does not respond to music this way, then you can gently initiate various kinds of actions: walking, swaying, running, and so on, as dictated by the rhythm and mood of the music.

Fine-Motor Skills

Although the nineteen-month-old can use thumb and fingers to pick up small objects—a raisin, for example—for the most part the fingers act in unison and manipulation remains less than precise. However, the child does possess fully developed grasp, prehension, and release. You will find that your toddler likes to hold two small objects in one hand and continually tests this skill.

Now your child can build a firm tower of at least three to four or even more cubes, another indication of maturing eye-hand coordination. The nineteen-month-old can hold a container with one hand, release a small object into the container with the other hand, and then dump out the object. This is another big step forward in manipulative control.

Language Acquisition

Dr. Morris M. Lewis, the British speech authority, believes that the key to language acquisition lies in the baby's babbling. He calls this the "beginning of delight in language for its own sake, the rudimentary beginning of the enjoyment of the art of language." Learning language is one of the most important developmental tools for a child. Professor Eric Hawkins, of the York University Language Center in England, likens the process of language learning to "teaching human songbirds to sing." Those who fail educationally often are, in his words, "the human songbirds who never learned to sing."

If there is a total lack of external stimuli, a lack of viable contact with a caring adult—someone with whom to identify, with whom to speak—a child will not learn to talk, for speech is a skill one cannot acquire on one's own. Every child needs meaningful interaction with a regular, responsive caretaker during the early formative years. (It appears, as documented by Benjamin S. Bloom, a Chicago psychologist, in his technical but interesting book, *Stability and Change in Human Characteristics,* that a child's most important intellectual development—more than half of what will be attained during a whole lifetime—occurs before the age of four. Dr. Bloom believes that the loss of development in one period cannot be fully recovered in another period.) Research indicates that if the opportunity to verbalize during the crucial early years is lost, a child can never fully attain this most essential skill.

Labeling or Naming

A child learning words will point to objects and pictures so the mother or father can name them. Astute parents will not only tag each object and picture; they will explain simply and clearly what it does, where it came from, and how it feels. The parents also will sense when their child is ready for a new experience and be imaginative enough to think of an activity that will be interesting to all of them.

Labeling (attaching a name to a thing) is a favorite game of nineteen-month-olds. The labels for things, actions, and people the toddler is learning help her separate the elements of the world into categories. For example, when a child learns the word *car,* she begins to find cars everywhere—in picture books, magazines, and television commercials, in toy shops, on the road, and in used car lots. Your child probably has recognized cars for a long time, but the word helps her to know what a car means in general. At the same time, your toddler is learning to label actions or qualities. Parents usually know that when their child says *up*, this indicates she wants to be picked up, and that *on* means "turn on the light," because the toddler joins body actions to her labels.

On the average, nineteen-month-olds have a speaking vocabulary of more than ten but less than fifty words. There still is much babbling, but now several syllables with an intricate intonation pattern embroider the design of their verbal communication. The child this age omits most prepositions and will say "Come me," "Roll ball," "Sit lap," and so on. Most nineteen-month-olds understand such spatially-related words as *up, down, on, under, in,* and *out* and use them in their speech.

Your nineteen-month-old is beginning to respond to speech by speech; i.e., the remark of another person evokes a spoken response (when a departing visitor says *bye-bye*, your child will say *bye-bye*). Your toddler also is using speech as a means of securing action from another person, usually the mother, and can respond appropriately to requests for simple, familiar bodily action: "Throw the ball," "Pick up the book," and so on.

Toddlers enjoy listening to rhymes—in small doses—and the Mother Goose rhymes are fun if you choose those that have some meaning for today's children. Many nineteen-month-olds are able to repeat some of the words of simple nursery rhymes; most can fill in words left out by the parents.

Two picture books that are especially helpful in teaching toddlers to label their environment are Richard Scarry's *Best Word Book Ever* and Dr. Seuss's *Cat in the Hat Dictionary.* Both are vocabulary expanders. At first you can point to a picture and say the word for it. As your child learns, he will be able to "find the dog, find the fireman, find the tractor," and so on. Then you can point to a picture and your child can say the word that describes the object or person. Inasmuch as nineteen-month-olds still "explore" books by tearing pages out of them, you will have to supervise the use of all but cloth or heavy cardboard picture books until your child is mature enough to treat all books carefully.

Sensory Powers/Learning

The nineteen-month-old is primarily a "motor learner." By moving objects from place to place, your child learns about size, shape, and weight. By trying to pull, push, stack, and insert all kinds of available things, your child finds out that large and heavy objects cannot be budged and that small, light things slip readily from the fingers. Your child learns, too, that square objects do not fit into round holes and that oblong shapes do not fit into triangular spaces.

The perception of *relative* size depends upon learning. It is not an inborn ability. There appear to be two independent acts involved in mastering this concept. First, the child's ability to place small things into much larger ones implies a perception of a relationship between container and the thing or things contained before the child is able to judge things solely on the basis of size. Second, when two objects are nearly the same size, they seem to the nineteen-month-old to exist vaguely as potential containers of each other.

Learning by Imitation

Some theorists see imitation as a basic learning tool with which children come to understand and adopt that which is initially in the environment (imitation seen in its social-relatedness form). Others consider imitation as a form of play in which children use their repertory of skills and behaviors for self-development and entertainment (imitation seen in the framework of a child's autonomy). When imitating, the child must be relating to other people who are present in the immediate environment or whom the child has seen in previous encounters. An act of a child cannot be called an imitation unless it has some correlation with the action of another person. At the same time, the child who is imitating must be utilizing, too, that which is a part of himself or herself. The child's imitation of others is not haphazard; each child selects what he or she wants to try out. With sufficient experiences, the child will create new learning and behaviors out of prior imitations.

The nineteen-month-old continues to scribble spontaneously, still gripping a crayon or pencil in the fist. Large sheets of paper are needed, plus your supervision to make sure all markings land on the paper and not on walls, tables, your child, and so forth.

Your toddler is learning to associate a tool with the function it performs: a hammer is for banging, a vacuum is for cleaning, a telephone is for listening and talking, a spoon is for eating, a cup is for drinking, and so on. You can help your toddler expand such associations by indicating more and more correlations between tools and their practical uses.

Putting Things Together

Your nineteen-month-old is in a tough albeit exhilarating spot—and so are you. On the one hand, your toddler is becoming more competent; on the other, he is not yet really skilled at many manipulative tasks. Just as was the case last month, you do not quite know when your child wants you to intercede or when he must learn the hard way that it takes time to mature and experience to become skillful. No one is born with manual dexterity. Smooth coordination comes from innumerable interventions with objects of all kinds.

Having gone through the stages of emptying, pulling things apart, and filling and refilling containers, your nineteen-month-old is now investigating various ways of piling, building, and putting things together. There is insatiable interest in stacking containers in huge

piles or arranging assorted things in very long rows. You will note that your child is curious about the kinds of things that can be fitted together.

"As toddlers go about their self-imposed task of rearranging the objects in the house, they are hard at work. They enjoy lining up all sorts of things across the floor or making a pile of things. As they pile cans of food on top of one another or make a tower out of blocks, they are concentrating on the problem of balance. What will happen if they put a big block on top of a small block or place a large can on top of a pile of blocks? Most children will cheerfully say *oo-oo* or *oops* as their structures tumble down. The exclamation is an announcement of the event, not an expression of displeasure, because to nineteen-month-olds the toppling is as fascinating as the piling up."

Effects of Nutrition on Learning

Although we believe that our readers feed their children proper and adequate foods, we wish to present in passing a few thoughts about the effects of nutrition on learning. Severe malnutrition creates in children patterns of apathy, environmental unresponsiveness, and irritability, all of which behaviors are inimical to physical and emotional well-being and hence to learning.

Research indicates that depression of intellect occurs in children hospitalized for severe malnutrition between the ages of six and thirty months—a critical span for the development of competence. According to Myron Winick, M.D., associate professor of pediatrics at the New York Hospital, an infant is especially vulnerable to "chemical brain damage" during the first year of life. Even when not terribly severe, early malnutrition will induce certain permanent changes in the brain (exactly what the relationship of these changes to mental function is, is not yet known, however). Although it is not known for certain that severe malnutrition retards intellectual growth, evidence suggests that malnutrition can cause changes within the brain that are functionally

significant and that may be manifested by faulty intellectual growth. It is known that if significant malnutrition occurs during crucial periods of rapid brain cell multiplication, there is a reduction in the number of cells produced. Furthermore, such cell deficiency is irreversible regardless of subsequent nutritional sufficiency.

The psychological and social deprivation common among severely malnourished children can directly affect intellectual performance. Nonstimulating home environments and lack of incentive due to repeated discouragement are some examples of such deprivation.

Nurturing Creativity

Toddlers are not only completely physical, they are wholly creative, a wonderful quality that usually is diminished or deadened as they grow older by the strictures of society. You need to provide enriching indoor and outdoor environments that will enhance the natural curiosity, exploratory needs, sensory perceptions, and imagination of your child. Creativity can be served well by places to explore, all kinds of materials to handle, various objects to manipulate, and especially by opportunities to experience the world through *all* the senses. You can help your nineteen-month-old's creativity blossom by your sensitive responsiveness to her feelings, interests, questions, awareness, and so on.

Parenting

Parenting is one of the world's most difficult and demanding professions—and also one of the most exciting and rewarding. With sufficient child-rearing knowledge and commitment, and in spite of occasional doubts and times of physical and emotional stress, parents are able to nurture the growth and development of children as no one else can.

Limited instruction in developing skills for avoiding or changing negative child behavior in the home is available to parents today. The

natural love and warmth they have for their offspring are not enough to help their children develop the necessary social attitudes and behaviors. Increasingly, child psychologists and educators are seeing the importance of identifying and presenting the major skills required in child rearing, as well as the environmental factors that determine child-rearing practices. Unfortunately, there still is a paucity of reliable child-rearing data.

The earliest example of systematic behavior change in the home, as presented by D. C. Williams in a 1959 edition of *The Journal of Abnormal and Social Psychology,* in an article entitled "The Elimination of Tantrum Behaviors by Extinction Procedures," demonstrated the effectiveness of teaching parents how to apply the *principle of extinction* to bedtime crying and temper tantrums. Study revealed that the child obtained too much parental attention for his negative bedtime behavior by keeping one or both parents at his bedside for from one-half to two hours every night. The parents were instructed to put their child to bed in a relaxed manner, to share some pleasantries while their child was settling into bed, and then to leave the room and close the door. They were directed not to return to the room when their child began crying and screaming. The stimulus event—parental attention—that had been maintaining a negative pattern of behavior—crying and tantrums—was eliminated, resulting in the decrease and finally the elimination of the negative behavior. (Crying lasted over forty-five minutes the first night, but dropped to zero after the next several nights.)

Instructions to parents should always include *when* and *how* to interact with the child and must emanate from information obtained through observation of the child's behavior and the events occurring in the environment.

Research indicates that a parent's social interaction with the child can develop and maintain acceptable or unacceptable behaviors. Changing the parent's behavior toward the child can change the child's pattern of behavior in prescribed ways. Often the parent is trained to direct attention (social reinforcement) to the child's cooperative rather than demanding behaviors and to independent rather than dependent acts.

Parents need to avoid the temptation to try to break up undesirable activity with the distraction of a treat of some kind, because although this may check the undesirable behavior temporarily, in the long run it strengthens the undesirable pattern of behavior. When a child has a temper tantrum at home, she should promptly be put in her room without attention and the door closed. In this way the child is removed from all events that may strengthen this negative, annoying behavior. As soon as the tantrum ends, the door should be immediately opened by the parent. This firm but unemotional response to the tantrum will eventually teach the toddler that no satisfaction can be derived from screaming and carrying on hysterically. (See page 280 for a discussion of temper tantrums in a public place.)

Good child rearing does not come about accidentally; it requires planning and effort on the part of both parents. The following are a few child-management procedures you may find of interest: Parents need to decide standards for acceptable and unacceptable behaviors in their child. They need to pay attention to their child when he is doing what is acceptable to them, and to ignore his unacceptable behavior—unless there is a possibility of destruction or damage to the child, others, or property.

Nineteen-month-olds are still in the grips of "separation anxiety" and so do not part easily from the mother or father (whoever is the primary caretaker). These toddlers remain more interested in adults than in their peers. However, as they get older, they begin to approach each other more, although they will not be able to play cooperatively for several more months. With experience and maturation, your child will learn to get along with others, both adults and children.

The nineteen-month-old indicates awareness of the absence of a loved or well-known person by saying *gone* or *bye-bye*. The child this age is responsive to cuddling and sensitive to overt signs of approval or rejection.

After being scolded, a nineteen-month-old may go over to the parent, place head into lap, and say, "Love, Mommy" or "Love, Daddy," as the case may be.

Your child delights in helping you with simple household chores: dusting, sweeping, and so on. Welcome and encourage all such friendly efforts. Skill will come with practice. In the meantime, your nineteen-month-old is learning what it means to be a part of the family and to be a contributing member in good standing.

The healthy, happy nineteen-month-old is completely relaxed in sleep. Your toddler may become a midday napper at this time (from about 12:30 P.M. to 2:30 or 3 P.M.), finally giving up the morning nap. When a child this age has a disturbing dream, parents need to offer loving attention as they soothe the child back to sleep.

Personality/Psychological Development

We are discussing normal children in this book, but we would be remiss if we did not mention that there are children who show a combination of temperamental traits that include more than average nonadaptability, withdrawal responses, and highly intense negative moods. Although such children are not necessarily nonadaptive, they find it hard to come to terms with new demands that are made upon them. These slow adapters make extra demands on their parents. However, if the parents of such a child are able to "roll with the punches" and to create productive interactions despite all the difficulties, the child is less likely to develop serious, lasting behavior disorders.

Discipline

According to child psychologist Fitzhugh Dodson, Ph.D., in his highly readable book *How to Parent,* "One teaching method which unfortunately tends to be heavily used by some parents during the toddlerhood stage is

that of spanking. Apart from a few very, very extraordinary occasions, there should be no need to spank a child under the age of two. If a toddler persists in running across the street, you may have no alternative but to administer a swift whack on the bottom. But ordinarily you should be able to handle the behavior of a toddler by arranging a home environment without the need for thousands of *no-no's;* by distraction; and by physical restraint where necessary, without resorting to spanking . . . If you find that you are losing your patience and your temper so frequently with your toddler that you are spanking him a good deal of the time, then you need professional help to work out your own emotional problems in handling a child this age."

Parents often think of discipline as meaning "How can I make my child stop doing what he's doing?" or "How can I get her to do what I want her to do?" A better approach is to direct your child so that she learns to live by acceptable modes of behavior while still being able to maintain a normal amount of self-esteem.

Constructive discipline would seek to help a child develop into a responsible, independent person. Below are some suggestions that you may find helpful:

1. Build a sound foundation for discipline. Love and accept your child even when his behavior annoys you. Offer praise whenever possible so your child can keep on building self-confidence and self-worth.
2. Establish clear-cut rules, but not too many of them. Make sure your requirements are consistent and feasible.
3. Do not expect too much. Do not require your nineteen-month-old to act like a "little lady" or a "little gentleman."
4. Try not to make big issues out of little things.
5. Maintain an active, working sense of humor.
6. Keep in mind what you are trying to teach your child and what she appears to be learning.
7. Spanking—a physical assault of a bigger person on a smaller one—does not teach

inner conviction; it teaches fear, deviousness, and aggression.

8. Scolding, another device for control, attacks a child's self-esteem because it blares out shame, humiliation, and rejection.

9. Withdrawal of love for control is another boomeranging negative behavior on the part of parents because it tells the child that his personal value is strictly conditional.

Of course, none of the foregoing precludes appropriate reaction on the part of parents to unacceptable behavior. The important point is that the parents try to keep their calm and maintain an atmosphere of mature objectivity and understanding.

Many nineteen-month-olds can become suddenly upset by changes in their routine or their environment, or by other unexpected events. They appear to suffer from sharp mood swings, moving unpredictably from feeling great to being "down in the dumps." Some of this may be due to the fact that their self-concept is not yet firmly established. A toddler this age may experience a gamut of feelings that range from omnipotence to complete self-denigration and abysmal self-doubt. Small wonder then that one of the hardest things for many children this age is to make a decision. Of course, there are children who are able to cope with the demands made upon them by themselves and/or their parents with less strain. However, all nineteen-month-olds experience a variety of pressures. It is almost as if every time a great step forward is made, several steps backward occur. Parents can provide incalculable support by being keenly aware of their child's developmental signals of what is needed at specific times and providing ameliorating affection, understanding, and attention. At the same time, parents need to be alerted to the possibility that sometimes what may appear to be a fixed temperament actually reflects a physical problem, i.e., sensitivity to many different allergens. An allergic child in the hands of a competent physician and under a proper health regimen will stop whining, lose tenseness and overexcitability, cease having tantrums, and even become able to tolerate frustration.

Your toddler is continuing to practice the mastery of her autonomous capacities. The nineteen-month-old does pretty much what she did a month ago, but with increased awareness of her individual self, a pursuit that goes on into one's adult years.

Self-Help Routines

At mealtime, your nineteen-month-old now handles a spoon quite competently, but still continues to do most of his eating with his fingers. Milk, juice, and water are drunk from a cup or glass without any help from you. If you keep the cup only half-filled, there will be limited spilling.

Lest you forget on those occasions when you are pressed for time or are growing weary of your child's mealtime sloppiness, it is only with sufficient practice that your nineteen-month-old will become an adept self-feeder. Children cannot learn to manage their food neatly unless they try. They will learn before too long if they are not scolded when they spill—and if their hands are not guided by well-meaning but misguided parents. One approach is to let the child use the spoon for one mouthful and then the parent presents the next one, and so on alternately. It is best to offer praise when a child does well and not to scold when he does not. If you have allowed your child to try to feed himself with some help and encouragement from you, by now he probably will be able to manage cup and spoon quite well.

Avoid Disease-Producing Foods

"Junk" foods should be avoided. Included in this category are all-white-flour products, most packaged dry cereals, foods containing large amounts of sugar (confections, ice creams, sweet bakery products), soft drinks of every kind, synthetic fruit "ades" and "fruit" drinks containing sugar, dyes, and chemical flavors and little or no fruit juice, gelatin

products, processed cheeses, hydrogenated cooking fats and foods cooked in them (potato chips, corn chips, and so on).

Parents who desire to raise healthy children will have nary a one of the above on their pantry shelves. According to the late Adele Davis, "The foods children are allowed during their first years usually become their favorites throughout life." Nineteen-month-olds usually accept new foods easily.

More About Toilet Learning

The attitude, tone of voice, and response of the parent to success or failure are vital aspects of the child's learning of sphincter muscle control. The first great loss a child experiences is the birth of a baby brother or sister. The older sibling rationalizes that if he became a baby again and relinquished all signs of independence, then the mother would have to take care of him the way she cares for the baby. The child then acts out the feelings of loss in an effort to force the mother to respond. Illness, hospitalization, or a period of absence from the mother are other crises that can trigger regression. Fortunately, in almost all instances, the older child resumes all previous habits and level of development.

Many child psychologists and pediatricians strongly recommend that a child not be expected to learn control of the rectal muscles until about two years of age. However, a toddler who is neuromuscularly able to control her sphincter muscles may achieve this complex learning task anywhere from the twentieth month onward. If mishandled by the parents, stubbornness, anger, defiance, and fear may be aroused in the child rather than learning.

Your child's bowel movements may be reasonably well established by now. During the daytime, many nineteen-month-olds will often (but not invariably) indicate when a B.M. is about to occur. Bladder control usually is achieved later, but the toddler will indicate the need for dry clothing after getting wet. Since your child likes to flush the toilet, let him do so after each evacuation in the toilet. Remember to praise success and ignore accidents.

If parents do everything for their children, they are not helping to start them on the way toward self-help. They get through dressing and undressing routines much more quickly, but they deny their children the opportunity to experience early independence and competence. Parents need to let their nineteen-month-olds help all they possibly can right from the start. If they are patient and encouraging, their children will succeed in learning to do things independently and with much less frustration and bad temper experienced by all concerned.

Nineteen-month-olds still cannot dress themselves, but are becoming great undressers. They can take off their socks, shoes, hat, mittens, and other simple garments. They are whizzes at unzipping zippers; the ability to zip is yet to come.

Care of the Teeth

Toddlers this age want a toothbrush to brush their own teeth. A child-sized soft natural or nylon bristle toothbrush is best because it can clean the teeth better than a hard one and will not harm the gums. Let your child try to squeeze some toothpaste out of the tube onto the toothbrush, but do not let your toddler chew on toothpaste tubes because many contain lead.

Preventive dentistry should begin in earliest childhood when it is most effective. Your child should see a dentist as soon as all twenty baby teeth have erupted. With your help and the dentist's, your child can learn to take proper care of her teeth so that both the baby and the adult teeth will be healthy. Of course, you will have to be in complete charge until your child is about four or five years old. Even after your child can care for her teeth unaided, you should still make sure that a thorough job is done for a few more years.

In the beginning, have your toddler stand in

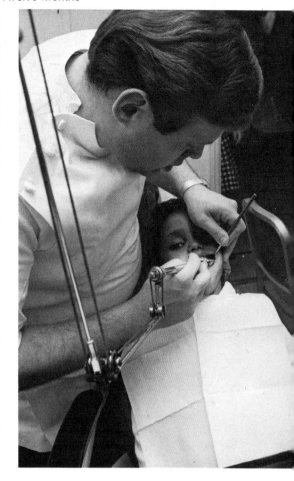

front of you with the back of his head against you. Using one hand to brace your child's head, you brush with the other. Simple up-and-down brushing is the easiest to teach. Show your child how to brush the teeth the way they grow; i.e., the upper teeth should be brushed down and the lower teeth should be brushed up. Children should use a nonabrasive fluoride toothpaste. Your dentist can recommend the brand of toothpaste that is least abrasive. The goal of brushing the teeth is to remove *plaque* (bacteria, plus food debris, plus saliva—found in everyone's mouth). If not removed, *calculus* forms (a hard deposit that coats the teeth above and below the gums), which causes tooth decay. Brushing twice a day usually is enough.

Flossing helps to keep the teeth clean. You will have to do this until your child is at least seven or eight years old. The critical areas are between the back teeth, especially the adult six-year molars. Proper flossing removes food debris and plaque, too. Floss also polishes the teeth, making it more difficult for the plaque to adhere to them. Your dentist will show you how to use floss on your child's teeth.

Foods most responsible for tooth decay are the easily fermentable carbohydrates. You should keep them to a minimum for all members of your family. They include soda pop, condensed milk, chocolate milk, cocoa, sweet sauces and syrups, imitation fruit juices, white bread, refined flour in all baked goods, jams, and jellies, ice creams, pies, cakes, cookies, dried fruits (including nutritious raisins), heavy-syrup canned fruits, candy of any kind (especially sticky ones—caramels, Lifesavers, lollipops, and so on), gum, processed cereals, marshmallows, graham crackers, macaroni, and spaghetti. The foregoing are all quickly changed to acid in the mouth. It is this acid that destroys enamel, causing cavities.

To help keep the teeth healthy, dentists recommend for children and adults such "detergent" foods as raw celery, carrots, cabbage, lettuce, cucumbers, radishes, green peppers, cauliflower, tomatoes, cantaloupe, watermelon, oranges, apples, plums, pears, and so forth. You will introduce these to your child one at a time over a period of time when she is able properly to chew them. Of course, you should discuss your child's proper diet with your pediatrician.

Play and Playthings

When you play with your nineteen-month-old, let your child take the lead. According to Stephen Lehane, in his book *Help Your Baby Learn,* "Be a companion rather than always being a coach, policeman, or teacher. Enjoy your baby. Follow up on what he wants to do, not on what you want him to be."

Importance of the Selection of Suitable Playthings

We keep bringing this up because countless numbers of toddlers (and younger and older children as well) are involved in serious toy-related injuries each year.

Parents and all others who buy toys for children need to take into account the dexterity, maturity, and interest of the child. Playthings that are safe for older children are hazardous in the hands of toddlers who are unaware of the dangers of sharp points and edges or of brittle plastic.

The Bureau of Product Safety of the U.S. Department of Health, Education, and Welfare presents the safety checklist below in their DHEW Publication No. (FDA) 73-7012:

When choosing a toy for a toddler (or infant), make sure it—

- is too large to be swallowed
- does not have detachable small parts that can lodge in the windpipe, ears, or nostrils
- is not apt to break easily into small pieces or leave jagged edges
- does not have sharp edges or points
- has not been put together with easily exposed straight pins, sharp wires, nails, etc.
- is not made of glass or brittle plastic
- is labeled nontoxic
- does not have parts that can pinch fingers or toes or catch hair
- does not have cords or strings over twelve inches in length

The nineteen-month-old is apt to spend more time playing with toys than he did earlier. Favored playthings tend to be a soft stuffed teddy bear or dog, balls, simple puzzles, blocks, a small wagon, a doll, toy cars and trucks, a toy telephone, and fitting-together toys. Your child will play happily alone for as many as twenty to thirty minutes if you are nearby or at least within earshot.

There is no real block-building play at this point. Your toddler may carry some blocks around the room, bang them together, pile some into a wagon, or just dump them in a heap. Pulling a loaded or empty wagon around the house is considered great sport by a toddler.

A toddler this age may play alongside other children, but is not yet able to play interactively with agemates.

Your child will now watch the path of a ball that is rolled to her and squat down on the floor to catch it. Your child may attempt to throw the ball back to you, but is not yet successful at this. You might want to buy a supply of tough balloons because toddlers like to play catch with a balloon.

Greatly appreciated is playing a crude form of hide-and-seek with parents or older siblings in which the toddler waits in delighted terror to be caught.

Toy Storage

Low open shelves that are wide enough to store the largest toy your toddler has will permit your child to get at the toys easily, thus encouraging independent action. A raised lip on the front edge of each shelf will keep toys with wheels and balls from rolling off.

An indoor piece of equipment that is good for large-muscle development and lots of fun is the indoor wooden climber/slide. A toddler can walk up its steps, slide down its low slide, and climb on it.

Toys for small-muscle development include bean bags, a pegboard, hammer-peg bench, large beads for stringing, simple take-apart toys, very simple puzzles, a coordination board with large screws and nuts and colored squares that screw on and off. A few oblong building blocks will be enjoyed. They can be used with wooden cars and trucks in floor play. The unit building blocks are not used extensively by the nineteen-month-old.

Toddlers adore rhythm and playing with sounds. They can handle a drum, cymbals, musical triangle, and toy xylophone.

Outdoor Play

The best type of outdoor play equipment for the nineteen-month-old is the stationary kind on which the toddler does the climbing rather than the movable type (swings, for example). The Dome Climber, based on the principle of the geodesic dome developed by Buckminster Fuller, can hold safely as many children as can climb on it. It should be set up on grass or sand so that if your toddler does take a tumble from it, he will have something soft to land on. The Dome Climber is excellent for large-muscle development, climbing ability, fostering self-confidence, and for sheer fun.

Sand play is relished now and will be for many years to come. You need to provide a sandbox that is large enough for several children to use at the same time even though your nineteen-month-old is still quite a "loner" during his playtime. Your toddler will enjoy having such sand toys as pie pans, assorted

nonbreakable plastic or metal cups and spoons, a sifter, a sieve, and small boxes, as well as cans of various sizes.

Water play also is important. Of course, your toddler can play in the bathtub under your constant supervision. Needed are plastic boats, cups, measuring spoons, balls, funnels, and other water toys. You will have to closely supervise your child's water play out of doors as well. A plastic tub filled with water would be fine and a small plastic sprinkling can would add immeasurably to the fun. Learning to blow soap bubbles with a bubble pipe would be a great adventure.

Large hollow blocks are good for climbing indoors or out. Together with one or two three-quarters inch by ten inches by three to four feet, smoothly-sanded hardwood planks, such hollow blocks can be used by your nineteen-month-old for all sorts of activities that help develop the large muscles. (They are standard equipment in day-care centers and nursery schools.)

Nineteen-month-olds continue to scoot about merrily on their kiddie kars. Some are able to maneuver minitricycles. The more gross-motor control, the smoother the pedaling.

Of course, the way to supplement your own play yard is to take your toddler as often as you can to a nearby park or playground that has play equipment geared to very small children. This is especially true for parents who live in city apartment houses.

THE NINETEENTH MONTH

Motor Development

Gross Motor

Walks up and down stairs, with help

Squats from standing position to pick objects up from floor

Walks with one foot on 2″-wide walking board, one foot on and one foot off

Can kick large ball on ground without stepping on the ball

Climbs up onto everything

Likes to move to music

Runs without falling too frequently

Can stand on either foot, holding on

Pushes, pulls, throws, and carries objects while walking

Walks sideways without crossing feet

Fine Motor

Fully developed grasp, prehension, and release

Builds tower of 3–4 cubes

Holds 2 objects in one hand

Holds container with one hand, releases small object into container with other hand, and then dumps out

Language Acquisition

Touches 3 or more body parts or items of clothing on command

Still much babbling, but now of several syllables, with intricate intonations

Speaking vocabulary of more than 10 words but less than 50

A favorite game is attaching a name to a thing (labeling)

Likes to be read to

Responds appropriately to requests for bodily action

Points to most pictures of familiar objects named by parents

Uses speech as a means of securing action from another person, usually the mother

Beginning to respond to speech by speech; the remark of another person evokes his or her spoken response

Combines 2 different words

Responds to "Where is your nose?" by correctly indicating nose; also to "Where are your eyes?"

Sensory Powers/ Learning

Is learning to associate a tool with the function it performs (a hammer is for banging, etc.)

Imitates simple actions

Examines pictures in cloth or cardboard picture books

Scribbles spontaneously holding pencil in fist

Imitates vertical line in drawing within 30 degrees

Social Development

Helps with simple household tasks (dusting, etc.)

Demands personal attention

Indicates awareness of absence of well-known person by saying "Gone" or "Bye-bye"

Responsive to cuddling

Enjoys change in environment

Growth Chart

Personality/Psychological

Is continuing practice and mastery of autonomous capacities

Recovers readily from hurts

Desire for autonomy impels him or her to try all kinds of antics

Self-Help Routines

Wants toothbrush to brush own teeth

Can unzip a zipper

Likes to flush the toilet

Is torn between wanting an adult to help and wanting to do it alone (zipping a zipper, buckling a shoe, fitting a key into the keyhole, etc.)

Will often but not invariably indicate when a bowel movement is about to occur

Washes and dries hands with assistance

Sound sleeper

Indicates need for dry clothes

Accepts new foods readily

Uses spoon, spilling little

Play and Playthings

Plays contentedly alone if near adults

In imaginative play, sits on floor and holds play phone up to ear cf stuffed dog

Likes to ride a rocking horse

Enjoys swinging on a swing

Is apt to spend more time playing with toys than at an earlier age

Can fill a wagon with toys, rearrange the contents, and pull it around the house

Enjoys challenge of a shape sorting box

Will play alongside other children; does not play interactively

Dear Parents:

Do not regard this chart as a rigid timetable.

Babies are unpredictable individuals. Some perform an activity earlier or (as much as six months) later than the chart indicates, while others skip a behavior altogether (i.e., walking without crawling).

Just use this information to anticipate and appreciate normal child development and behavior. No norms are absolutes.

THE TWENTIETH MONTH
Doing What Comes Naturally

Gross-Motor Development

Throughout this book, we are trying to make you aware of the sequential development of the initial "primitive" steps that are the cornerstones of all finalized skills. The twentieth month is not a dramatically different milestone. Your child is improving in all her gross-motor actions. She still likes to carry a large stuffed animal or doll while walking and will avidly push and pull all available boxes and large toys around the floor.

There is smooth walking backward and sideways. The twenty-month-old can walk up and down stairs with one hand held, but often will creep downstairs backward without anyone's assistance. Hanging from a low bar, holding on with both hands, is both a challenge and a delight at this time. Your toddler enjoys running, but still does so stiffly. There is improved coordination in throwing a ball overhand and kicking a ball on the ground in a forward direction. You will be pleased by the smoothness with which your child now seats himself on a small chair by sliding onto it.

You might enjoy the following gross-motor activity with your child: Hold onto your child's hands and help her bounce up and down on a bed, pillow, piece of foam rubber, couch cushion, or small trampoline. Give your child only minimal support. Encourage verbalization of all actions—*up, down, high, low,* and so on. You might chant in rhythm to the jumping and encourage your child to try to do the same. Of course, you can play music on the radio or a phonograph recording and have your child try to bounce in time to it.

Fine-Motor Development

Your toddler can build a tower of four to five cubes and continues to manifest a decided hand preference. Twenty-month-olds are able to throw a small rubber ball in play with a parent or older sibling with a bit more finesse than a month ago. However, eye-hand coordination with regard to turning the pages of a book remains at two or three pages at one time. If the radio suddenly goes on, you may be sure your toddler turned the knob to get music to move or to listen to.

Language Acquisition

Your child may be attempting to talk in short sentences by combining two different words. These two-word phrases usually express some kind of association between the words used; for example, perhaps the child points to the mother's hat and says, "Mommy, hat," or indicates that the ball is on his chair by saying, "Ball-chair." Verbs your child learns, such as *gone, fall, broke,* and *eat*, can be combined with many labels to produce two-word

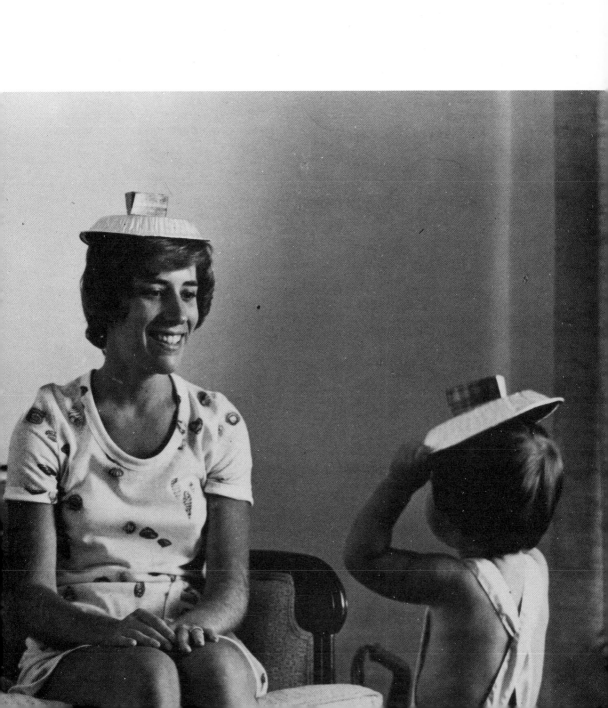

sentences: "Daddy-gone," "Juice-gone," "Ball-gone," and so forth. These simple combinations indicate a giant step forward from the single-word stage and are very exciting for parents who have been waiting months to hear them.

From the eighteenth to twenty-first months, most toddlers continue to imitate readily the language around them. They repeat whatever is said to them and they also repeat themselves. Such children can learn to repeat nursery rhymes. However, there are other toddlers who seem to stop imitating phrases during this period.

"No" and "Yes"

Your child's understanding of the concept *no* leads to the understanding of *yes*. As René A. Spitz points out in his book *No and Yes,* there cannot be a *yes* without a *no*. As expressed by Hiag Akmakjian in *The Natural Way to Raise a Healthy Child,* "If events happen because the person is incapable of saying *no* to them, they are not the result of a decision *(yes)* but merely a yielding. When your child begins to shout 'No!' at you, take it as a confirmation that you are doing a good job. Your baby's 'No!' is one of those surface indications that great internal organization is silently going on, thanks to your 'good enough' parenting."

Twenty-month-olds usually have a speaking vocabulary of twelve, fifteen, or more words. Of course, as heretofore, they understand many more words than they are able to use, and language acquisition continues apace just below the surface of your child's spoken vocabulary.

Twenty-month-olds indicate their needs and desires mainly by gesturing and utterances.

Naming Body Parts

Encourage your toddler to name body parts as you dry her after a bath. Progress to requesting your child to perform an action with familiar parts; for instance, "Wave your hand," "Blink your eyes," "Open your mouth," and so on. In the beginning of this activity, it would be helpful if you demonstrated each action. The twenty-month-old is able to point to several named body parts: eyes, nose, mouth, hair, ears, and so forth.

Talking on the Telephone

To stimulate the use of words, let your child talk to someone familiar on the telephone —grandma, grandpa, dad at work (if feasible), and so on. Conversations on the real telephone are one-sided at this time, with the child mutely listening. A toy phone for make-believe conversations will get lots of happy, expressive use during your toddler's fascinating upgrowth.

Language Games

There are many games one can play with young children to help them become aware of sounds. Most of these involve the improvement of listening skills:

1. Have your child listen to the everyday sounds in your home. Give words to describe the sounds: "pop" goes the toaster, "whoosh" goes the vacuum cleaner, "tick-tock" goes the clock, and so forth. Encourage your child to make up words for some sounds.

2. Listen together to sounds outside your home: "wee-eee-eee" goes the siren, "beep-beep" goes the horn, "tweet-tweet" goes the bird, "bow-wow" goes the doggy, and so on.

3. Introduce animals and the sounds they make to your child. Show her pictures of the animals or take her to a farm or zoo and listen to and then imitate all the sounds you hear.

4. Following instructions: Start by giving your toddler one simple direction to follow; for example, "Close the door." If your child responds well, you may increase the number of directions to two at a time.

5. You can make a "sound" book with sheets of construction paper stapled together

to form the book. You and your child can look for magazine pictures of objects that start with a specific sound—*S,* for example—and cut them out and paste them into the book. If you like, you can make separate books for each sound.

6. You can make your own picture books of similar objects; for example, animals, household items, clothing, all kinds of children, and so on. Finding the subjects in magazines will be fun for both of you.

7. Your toddler will enjoy your reading nursery rhymes and other simple, lilting poetry to him.

8. When you and your toddler look at a picture book together, encourage her to turn the pages (which will still be done two or three at a time; but no matter, soon they will be turned singly) and name two or three familiar objects. Do not discourage interruptions by your child (pointing, jargon, and so on). Then ask your toddler to point to less familiar objects that you will label clearly. Right now it is important to have your child repeat two-word verbalizations. This activity, as well as any other pursuits, should be ended by you before your toddler grows disinterested and restive.

Sensory Powers/Learning

Your twenty-month-old continues to imitate all kinds of simple, familiar actions: daddy shaving, mommy brushing her teeth, dusting the furniture, sweeping the floor, making toast, talking on the telephone, and so forth. The toddler continually places in "live" storage new words, events, and experiences for ready reference in ongoing living and learning.

An indefatigable fetch-and-carrier, the twenty-month-old can obtain familiar objects from a different room upon the request of the mother or father.

Scribbler par Excellence

The child who has been lucky enough to be exposed to crayon or pencil and paper is a spontaneous scribbler, which is all to his benefit. Eye-hand coordination is improving so that markings are now a bit less random. It takes the fine-motor muscles longer to mature than it does the gross-motor muscles.

You can give your toddler a large crayon and a large piece of paper. Demonstrate making a vertical line and ask your child to try to imitate this. Most twenty-month-olds are able to imitate a vertical line in drawing within thirty degrees. (At later sessions, you can progress to demonstrating a circular movement.) Name each stroke as your child makes it. Encourage imitation. For variety, provide different shapes of paper to draw on: square, circular, oblong, triangular, and so on. With maturation and practice, your toddler will learn to grasp the crayon with thumb and fingers in opposition rather than clutching it in the fist.

Give your child a shape-sorting toy (postal station, shape-sorting box, and so on) that has circular, square, and triangular shapes that fit into corresponding openings. Encourage her to examine each piece and then to release the shapes into the matching holes. If your child tries to put them in the inappropriate holes, describe the problem. Have her name the shapes as each is deposited in its proper opening. After this task is mastered, you can ask her to place two consecutive shapes; i.e., "Put a circle in and then put a triangle in the holes," and so on.

The twenty-month-old is able to place a circle, square, and triangle shape in a formboard with less adaptive turning.

Social Development

We believe that when parents bring out the best in their children they have called upon the very best in themselves.

It is not our intention in this book to discuss the complex social, psychological, medical, economic, racial, educational, political, and other issues that face today's parents and their children. What we are trying to do is to make parents more keenly aware of the natural "ages and stages" of child development that apply to all areas of growth so that they

will be better equipped to deal with child-rearing problems as they may arise. There is no such thing as completely concern-free child-rearing, even with caring, competent parents and perfectly normal children.

The majority of parents are perplexed by the often conflicting advice of experts and the admonitions of doctors, psychologists, and educators. What they seek and need are sensible, practical guidelines in order to cope as well as possible with "the hardest job on earth." Unfortunately, even knowing "what to do, when" does not ensure an answer to every question in bringing up children. Many factors (social, economic, and so on) and influences are beyond the control of parents.

Although there are some parents who do not love their children (an idea that is shocking, but is a fact of life), most parents love and want to do right by their children, according to Catherine Mackenzie, who wrote an interesting book, *Parent and Child,* based on her columns in the *Sunday Magazine* section of *The New York Times.*

With regard to child-rearing approaches, Joseph Church, in *Understanding Your Child from Birth to Three: A Guide to Your Child's Psychological Development,* says, "Spock helped, in the direction of getting parents to appreciate that their baby is a person who can be a source of pleasure as well as headaches, but Spock's training was in medicine, not psychology, and much of what he has had to say about psychological development does not match the evidence."

"Learn to understand your baby's language of behavior," counsels Dr. Church. "Long before he can talk, your baby gives you cues for appropriate action. There is a certain amount of trial and error involved, but in a short while you should be able to guess—from his posture, movements, tone of voice, and from the way he reacts to what you do—what his needs of the moment are. You will be able to tell when he is ready to sleep, when he is hungry, when he needs company, when he is about to have a bowel movement, when he wants a particular plaything."

The dissemination of knowledge today, incomplete though it is, should heighten parents' awareness of child growth and care without thwarting their ability to function effectively.

The first twelve months of an infant's life are relatively calm except for occasional feeding, sleeping, or special health problems. It is the second year that ushers in all kinds of difficulties for inexperienced parents—especially the mother. The toddler is beginning to have a mind of her own. Usually food needs change. Pushing ahead toward independence, the toddler becomes sharply aware of her dependence upon the mother. Hence, she will clutch desperately at her when a stranger approaches—the same person the child had accepted wholeheartedly at eight or ten months of age. The toddler is afraid not only of strangers, but of the loud noises of moving objects. At the same time, the child this age has no fear of heights or any notion of real danger.

Children differ in temperament and in rates of growth, but they appear to develop according to a regular pattern. Understanding this can be of help to parents and enable them to enjoy their children as they move from one age and stage of development to the next plateau of accomplishment.

Discipline

Often toddlers say *no* in a spirit of play, as a form of teasing. They do not expect to be taken seriously. In fact, they are shocked if they are. Of course, there are many occasions when toddlers mean their *no's.* Although distraction may help in some such instances, most often calm but firm parental authority needs to prevail.

Twenty-month-olds are becoming more organized. They are better able to follow orders and seem to gain pleasure from the parents' expressed appreciation when they complete their commands. These toddlers show more awareness of the things around them and continue to like to imitate adult actions and tasks. For example, when the mother cleans the house, the child will follow her with a cloth trying to dust the furniture.

Toddlers enjoy short walks with their parents, rides in the family car, and other outings of not too long duration. However, the twenty-month-old does not always regard going to the supermarket with mother a pleasant experience.

Babysitters

Never leave your child in a house alone, not even for a few minutes, and not even if your child is asleep. This applies equally to babies and all young children.

When you need a babysitter, it is a good idea to have the sitter come about an hour in advance of your departure the first time so you can size up the sitter's personality and maturity. A capable sitter has empathy with children and should be able to spend time with a child if the latter should awaken during the parents' absence. The sitter you hire should be able to talk to your child or play with him and then get him back to sleep. Of course, you will let the sitter know what your child's habits are, where you keep clean diapers, and so on. You should try to use the same sitter each time.

Your toddler should not be asleep when the sitter arrives the first time because if your child should wake up after you have gone, your unexpected absence would be frightening. An experience of this kind could lead to sleep disturbances and fear of the dark because your child would equate sleeping and nighttime with losing you.

Personality/Psychological Development

The development of independence can be inhibited or prevented, but it cannot be forced. It is best to permit independence to grow at the child's own rate, but never so fast that it results in harm to the child or to his environment. According to Marguerite Kelly and Elia Parsons, writers of *The Mother's Almanac,* "If necessity is the mother of invention, frustration is the grandmother. Every child needs a

little of this frustration, but the smaller the child, the smaller the dose. This is not only to establish his place in the pecking order, which it does, but to force him to figure out other ways to accomplish a job. In this way you show respect for his ability."

Through *no* (with a frown from you) and *yes* (with a smile from you), even the very young child begins to understand that some actions are considered acceptable and others unacceptable by the parents. Many consider this to be moral education in its most elementary form.

The need for the child to submit her growing control of the body and of the world to social and cultural pressures often produces frustration and anger in the child. Temper tantrums, breath-holding spells, and less dramatic but disturbing outbursts are common consequences. All such negative emotional episodes respond best to management by a firm and loving parent who is able to set the necessary limits for the child.

We all know that telling a toddler that he cannot have or do something can result in yelling, loud whining, throwing things, hitting, running, and thrashing about on the floor. This emotional fireworks may last from a few minutes up to half an hour's harassment of the parent. Tantrums can occur anywhere—at home, in the home of a relative or friend, at the supermarket or the playground.

Temper Tantrums in Public Places

Because every young child is apt to have a temper tantrum at one time or another, we are discussing this bothersome subject again in this chapter. This violent outburst indicates that a child's frustration and/or anger have overwhelmed her. Psychologists indicate that tantrums do not take place frequently *if* a child's emotional needs have been met well by the parents and if frustrations have not been permitted to percolate.

Should your toddler plop down on the floor and start caterwauling and thrashing about —whether at home or in a public place— resist your strong temptation to scold or spank.

After a few moments, try to quietly hug your less than appealing child while speaking as calmly as you can. Although your child may continue to carry on for a while longer, the core of his eruption will cool because your understanding response tells your child that you have control over the situation and want to help. Writes Dr. Akmakjian, "The original feeling of frustration will diminish with your show of concern. As the rage subsides, the child realizes you have not been destroyed nor the world annihilated by the tidal wave of feelings, and that too feels good."

Never give in to a tantrum because this turbulent, negative behavior might become your child's way of getting things from you. However, do offer comfort because this will help your child to come to grips with her feelings more easily.

If you can control your anger and impatience when your child misbehaves or is unreasonable, he also will learn control.

Learning Sex Roles

"One of the major distinctions that the toddler learns between eighteen and twenty months is to identify the sex of other people. The toddler may learn to label a person as a

'lady,' a 'man,' a 'boy,' or a 'girl.' During this time span, toddlers identify themselves as a boy or girl and start to form sexual stereotypes. Many female toddlers become sensitive to new clothes. They show them off and notice when other members of the family wear new clothes. 'Pretty,' a frequent word in their vocabulary, is used to describe themselves and other people. Male toddlers, on the other hand, may show off by demonstrating their strength. When visitors arrive, a little boy may push a heavy stroller around the house with boastful shouts. It is a controversial issue in our culture how much of this sex differentiation is necessary or desirable.

"Part of the toddlers' exploration of roles is dressing up. Although these children do not engage in elaborate dress-up activity, it is usual for them to rummage through a closet for the parents' shoes. Children will drape ties and jewelry around their necks. They adore all sorts of hats and even invent new kinds of headgear. Perhaps a wastebasket or a salad bowl will be converted into a hat. As toddlers experiment with new clothes, their interest in mirrors is rekindled. These children may spend considerable time admiring themselves in a mirror—an expression of their self-esteem and ego satisfaction."

Fingering the Genitals

Twenty-month-olds find their genitals and finger them. They enjoy the sensitive spots that respond to their touching. Adults most often are concerned that this casual fingering of the sex organs of the young child will lead to masturbation, about which they may have some feeling of guilt themselves. It may be that the child needs something to do. Play and playthings are bound to be more interesting than touching any one part of the body.

Masturbation is most prevalent at bedtime. Ordinarily there is no reason to do anything about masturbation. However, if it becomes an all-consuming preoccupation, it signifies that there are deficiencies in other areas of the child's life that should be examined.

Some parents react to their toddler's masturbatory gestures with shock, disgust, anxiety, or embarrassed guilt, according to William E. Homan, M.D., despite the fact that at this age the children have not attained "the sophistication of enjoying masturbation." Unfortunately, there are those who still believe the myth that masturbation leads to physical deterioration, impotence, lunacy, sexual problems, loss of memory, visual impairment, or other dire consequences in later life. Although early-childhood fondling of the genitals is considered perfectly normal by pediatricians and psychologists, if it is actively engaged in to excess, it may require parental redirection, but without tension or other stressful behaviors.

Children masturbate a great deal more when they are tired, bored, or unhappy.

To Share or Not to Share

Because of their growing sense of autonomy, twenty-month-olds are more possessive about their toys and many hide them from their siblings or other children. But be of good cheer, your child's ability to share is slowly aborning.

Fears

Your twenty-month-old may express fear of the water by refusing to take a bath. She may be fearful of large dogs or dogs that bark. This is the time when fear of thunder and lightning may appear. Calm reassurance from you will help your child resolve these fears.

Self-Help Routines

Enlist your toddler in the role of "helper" when you do your housework. Try to make requests that involve two directions and include prepositions; e.g., "Get the spoon from the drawer. Put the spoon on the table." Your child loves to please you and helping you is one tangible way to show you this. Your directions will serve to help expand your child's speaking vocabulary.

Undressing and Dressing

Encourage your child to undress completely, including taking off shoes. Provide minimal help when there is difficulty removing a complicated garment or unbuttoning very small buttons. The twenty-month-old unzips zippers quite expertly, pulls socks off, puts shoes on (but cannot yet tie laces or do buckles), and can pull on simple garments unaided.

With your child sitting in front of you and facing away from you, enlist his help in putting on simple garments. For example, putting his feet in openings and helping pull his pants up, finish pulling his shirt down, and so on. Gradually your child will increase his active participation.

By now you must have an established daily routine for your toddler. It is important that mealtime, naptime, and bedtime be maintained on schedule, with exceptions being made only on very special occasions. Toddlers are creatures of habit. They do not behave well or enjoy themselves when they are hungry, fatigued, or overstimulated.

Some children get very upset when food spills on them or their fingers get sticky. Such a child may be quite content to play with mud because she chooses to play with it and, therefore, the activity supports her feelings of autonomy. Soup on the shirt, however, upsets the child because it happens despite her wishes. A toddler may become so upset with spills that she wants to be fed by the parent. This child will not go back to eating with her hands, but neither will she use a spoon.

Feeding

A very young baby being introduced to new foods, such as canned vegetables, meats, and fruits, is expected to adapt to new flavors, colors, and textures. As the child grows older, he is expected to adapt mainly to a change of texture (chopped and minced rather than puréed foods). The final adaptation the child is expected to make is to the food from the family table.

Your twenty-month-old lifts and holds her cup between both hands and drinks without spilling (if you have only half-filled the cup in the first place). Your child now can pour water from one cup into another. (The bathtub is a perfect place for this kind of water play—under your supervision, of course.)

Your child uses a spoon well now and is a self-feeder for the most part. Food is chewed quite well, but it is advisable to present only bite-sized morsels of meat, fish, vegetables, and so on.

Help your child to learn to wash and dry his hands. Turn the water on and help rub soap on his hands. Then help him rinse the soap off. Encourage your child to dry his hands. Then you can finish the drying process. You may need to continue turning the water on and off for a while longer.

See that your toddler brushes her teeth morning and evening. Of course, you will finalize the cleaning.

Sleeping

Some toddlers—who have been "spoiled" —will not go to sleep, even in their own beds, unless their mother stays with them until they have fallen asleep. Children need to learn early to sleep in a room by themselves or with other children. Some parents complain that their children wake up and wander about at night. Sometimes this comes from sleeping too much during the day (which may please the mother because this keeps the child from being "underfoot"). Undoubtedly, also, children sometimes have bad dreams that wake them up and they want to be reassured and make certain that they are loved before they go back to sleep—in their own beds. Children, no matter what their age, should *never* be encouraged to go to sleep in their parents' bed!

Play and Playthings

Your twenty-month-old will play contentedly alone for fifteen to about thirty minutes at a time if you are nearby. Toddlers this age enjoy sitting inside a ride 'em toy—auto, fire engine, and so on—and pushing it along with the feet. A Kiddie Kar gets good use also. Still completely pleasurable to your toddler is playing tag or any interactive game with you or an older sibling.

Some of the most popular play materials are things with handles. The toddler is learning to use a handle as an extension of his hand. The harder the tool is to manage, the more determined the child becomes to put it to use. In part, the toddler is trying to do the things that big people do, and in part, he is intrigued with the doing itself. When a child manipulates a long-handled tool, such as a rake or a broom, he is more interested in the activity than the outcome. He could not care less how many crumbs are left on the floor or how many leaves remain scattered. However, when using a short-handled tool, a hammer, for example, the child is more apt to focus on results. He hammers a peg down on a peg bench and checks to make sure it went down.

Other small tools that the toddler uses with some concern for the outcomes are a toothbrush, hair brush, comb, spoon, paintbrush, scoop, and sand shovel.

Filling containers is another early scheme that is becoming more elaborate at this time. For several months your child has been interested in pouring water from one container to another. During such play her concentration was centered on the pouring action. Now your child is beginning to take notice of the container she is pouring into and is learning to stop pouring soon after the second container overflows.

The twenty-month-old is concerned, too, about having enough water in the bathtub or having a cookie for each hand.

Hidden-Object Games

Children this age enjoy hidden-object games; for instance, the Postal Station (by Playskool)—a wooden box with an assortment of varicolored and shaped painted wooden blocks invites the child to place the blocks into the corresponding openings in the box. In a jack-in-the-box, a turn of the key makes a clown pop up. In a hammer-and-peg pounding bench toy, the pegs reappear when the bench is flipped over. The twenty-month-old has improved eye-hand coordination and is beginning to play more successfully with this toy.

The toddler's fascination with the phenomenon of hidden objects is evident in many of his investigations, as well as in his choice of toys. This is the age when your child is apt to look down your mouth to see where the food went, stare at a dribbling popsicle, or peer down the bathtub drain to find the missing water. It also is the time when a toddler begins to notice his shadow.

Challenging toys have more than one element to capture a child's interest. This is especially true of simple jigsaw puzzles. In a sense, an inset puzzle is a hidden-object game. When the missing piece is put in place, the hidden object reappears. At the same time, a jigsaw puzzle is a filling-the-container game where the object is to fill the puzzle with all the pieces. It is fascinating to watch toddlers when they first get interested in a puzzle. They find the spot where the piece belongs, but fail to orient the piece so that it slides into the spot. Often you will see a toddler pounding on a piece of puzzle in an attempt to force it to fit.

In a primitive way, your twenty-month-old is able to "think up" a plan and carry it out. Note how your child fills a container with water so that she can water the plants, or opens a safety pin in order to remove a diaper.

Discovering Space at the Playground

"As the toddler builds with blocks, intercepts a ball, and pushes cars or a doll carriage around the house, she is discovering more and more about spatial relationships. The child is learning, for example, that if she opens her legs and pushes a ball between them, she will be able to turn around and watch the ball roll away. She is learning also that she is an object in space. One little girl's sequence of activities shows this beginning awareness of oneself as an object in space. She was playing with a little car and some blocks. Her father made a tunnel out of the blocks and showed his toddler how to push a car through the tunnel. For several minutes,

the child pushed the little car under the tunnel, back around, and under the tunnel again. Quite suddenly she got up, scooted under the table, under her father's legs, and back under the table. She seemed to be saying, 'Look at me, I can go under things just like my little car.' "

"Several playground activities capitalize on a child's interest in exploring space. Slides, jungle gyms, seesaws, stepping stones, and so forth are designed to give children different kinds of spatial experiences. Although children enjoy this kind of equipment, they find their own substitutions when it is not available to them. A box to climb in and out of, a bed to scoot under, or a mattress to jump on provide ample opportunity for exploring positions in space."

Take your toddler to the playground often and encourage and help him to take a ride on a swing, play on a slide, climb on a jungle gym, and so on. Verbalize your child's actions. Encourage him to verbalize all his playground experiences. When you return home, you can help your twenty-month-old relate the experiences to another member of the family.

"Closely related to the toddler's interest in spatial relationships is a heightened interest in disappearing objects. Here again, the child is interested both in objects that disappear in space and in herself as a disappearing object. The twenty-month-old is ready for a grown-up version of hide-and-seek in which the mother closes her eyes and the child goes off to a hiding place. When it is time for the mother to look for her child, the latter calls out to her excitedly, not realizing, of course, that the sound of her voice gives away her location."

Because falls frequently occur from backyard or playground swing sets, slides, and teeters, toddlers should be taught the proper use of such equipment. Equipment should be the right size for the child and all pieces need to be assembled according to the directions of the manufacturer. The desirable placement is on level ground and away from fences, hedges, or buildings that might force children to walk or play too close to the moving rides. Backyard equipment should be checked often

for stability, excessive wear, loss of parts, and rust, and should be repaired before further use.

Music Box

If your child does not already have a music box, you should now procure a hand-cranked one with good Swiss musical works. This kind is better because the wind-up models go out of order easily from overwinding. There even is a see-through, hand-cranked music box on the market.

Dress-up Play and Pretending

Certainly dressing up is a kind of early pretending. The child is assuming the role of an adult by donning adult clothing. Shoes seem to be the most important symbols in such dress-up activity. The child is beginning to consider himself a child and not a baby. Babies usually do not wear shoes, but children do. Wearing shoes is a sign that the child no longer is a baby. By extension, wearing the shoes of adults is a step toward adulthood. We forget how important shoes are for children. A child periodically gets new shoes because he is "growing," so the connection between growth and shoes is a strong one. It is not unusual to hear preschool children arguing about whose feet are the biggest. Having big feet is a virtue in their world.

Although children like to dress up, young children often are afraid to wear certain items of clothing and accessories. They may resist a pair of goggles, for example, or an apron or a certain necklace. Toddlers have a new awareness of their bodies and do not want to wear anything that strikes them as strange. It is hard to predict ahead of time what a particular child will find strange, but parents should be sensitive to this new development.

Just as the toddler begins to pretend by dressing up, she also pretends to perform other daily activities that are important to her. The most common forms of imaginary play involve pretending to go to sleep or to eat

is covered with a blanket or fed from an empty cup. There is little elaboration of the activity, although the child will copy the more sophisticated pretending of older children or adults. The child does not talk much while pretending, but does enjoy listening to a simple dialogue supplied by the parent. If the doll gives the child a good-morning kiss and tells the child it is hungry, the child listens eagerly and often responds to the doll's request.

Much of the child's pretending is still imitative. The fantasy element is minimal, but the child has started to define autonomy in a more subtle way. Independence and power can be expanded through imaginary play. At the same time, the toddler is beginning to develop another use for imagination. Little incidents occur from time to time that show that the child can empathize with another person. When a sibling pinches his finger, the toddler helps kiss the hurt finger. When an older sibling gets a shot at the doctor's, the toddler cries, too.

If a child is given a small amount of water, she can mix it with dirt and have plenty of mud to roll into balls, to make mud pies, or just have great fun patting or squeezing the mud. Sand, water, and mud play have high priority with the twenty-month-old (and older child as well).

A child develops a sense of order through his own efforts, not the parents'. A child needs a place for everything and the responsibility for putting away some of his own treasures. Inasmuch as your twenty-month-old remembers where objects in the house belong, he will be able to help pick up and put toys away upon your request. Clean-up time should be announced by you before you expect it to begin. Your child may be expected to park his favorite car on the "garage" shelf. If need be, you can assist your child in a pleasant, relaxed manner.

something. The twenty-month-old likes to have the parents join her in these games. The child covers the parents up with blankets, pats them, and says, "Night, night." If encouraged, the child tries to feed them pencils, blocks, and other pretend foods. The child finds this kind of pretending a good joke, and if a parent pretends to eat the child's fingers or toes, the child laughs heartily.

Pretending can be extended to dolls, but again it involves very simple actions. The doll

THE TWENTIETH MONTH

Motor Development

Gross Motor

Jumps forward

Runs

Walks up and down stairs, one hand held

Seats self on small chair by sliding onto it

Hangs from bar grasping with hands

Kicks ball forward

Picks up object from floor without falling

Pushes and pulls around floor large toys, boxes, etc.

Fine Motor

Makes tower of 4–5 cubes

Can throw a small rubber ball

Fits related objects together appropriately by releasing, pressing, turning (ring onto pole, peg into hole, nesting, etc.)

Can put lid on oblong box

Language Acquisition

Speaking vocabulary of 12, 15, or more words

Is learning to label actions or qualities; *up* when he or she wants to be picked up, or *on* when she or he wants the light on

Enjoys hearing nursery rhymes

Attempts to talk in sentences; combines 2 different words

Points to several named body parts

Constantly asks "What's that?"; is discovering that everything has a name

Is beginning to use rudimentary questioning as a substitute for physical, nonlinguistic behavior

Enjoys playing a simple lotto game with parent

Sensory Powers/ Learning

Imitates simple actions

Is continually "placing in storage" new words, experiences, and events for ready reference in ongoing learning

Places circle, square, and triangle in formboard with less adaptive turning

Can obtain familiar object from a different room on command

Scribbles spontaneously

Imitates vertical line in drawing

Can put together 2 pieces to form a whole geometric figure

Can remember a familiar object without actually seeing it or holding it in hands

Social Development

Demands personal attention

Enjoys car rides, outings, walks

Likes to help with housework

Leads adult to desired object, even into another room

Likes to remove clothes and run around naked

Delights in helping put groceries away

Dear Parents:
   Do not regard this chart as a rigid timetable.
   Babies are unpredictable individuals. Some perform an activity earlier or later (as much as six months) than the chart indicates, while others skip a behavior altogether (i.e., walking without crawling).
   Just use this information to anticipate and appreciate normal child development and behavior. No norms are absolutes.

Personality/ Psychological

Is more possessive about toys and may hide them from siblings or other children (due to growing sense of autonomy)

May spend considerable time admiring self in mirror

May express fear of the water by refusing to take a bath

May be afraid of large dogs or dogs that bark; also thunder and lightning

Self-Help Routines

May have bladder control during the day

Can pour water from one cup into another

Feeds self

Helps pick up and put away toys on request

Likes to fetch and carry

Pulls on simple garments

Accepts going to bed without protest

Puts on shoes, but cannot tie laces or do buckles

Washes and dries hands with some help

Brushes teeth, with finishing cleaning by parent

Play and Playthings

Plays contentedly alone if near adults

Relishes sand and water play and making mud pies

Plays with pounding bench with increasing coordination

Continues to enjoy stringing large beads

Enjoys dressing up (is assuming the role of an adult by putting on adult clothes, shoes, hats, jewelry, ties)

Engages in imaginary play that involves pretending going to sleep or eating something

Can sit inside a wheeled toy (auto, fire engine, etc.) and push it along with the feet

Engrossed in take-apart toys

Enjoys playing interactive games; tag, for example

THE TWENTY-FIRST MONTH
Power Struggle

As soon as you think you have tuned in to your toddler's needs and behaviors, new conditions and considerations arise because, after all, growing children—and the rest of us—do not live in a vacuum; we are in a constant state of flux. The twenty-first month of life does not offer too many surprises, but now you must learn to understand and cope with your toddler's internal and overt power struggle. The conflict between wanting to be in control, to do everything unaided, and not yet being completely competent, makes life rocky for the twenty-one-month-old—and for the parents.

Children waver between their need for their parents and their burning desire to be independent. Dr. Church says, "There is nothing to be done about growth ambivalence except to recognize it, tolerate it, and lend the toddler your finger to get him over the rough spots." A toddler may be slower in developing independence due to overrestriction or underencouragement. Often when a child is ready to go forward, the parents hold him back—and when the child hesitates, the parents try to push him ahead.

More on Parent Education

Parental control and limiting are essential to every child's growing process. A child who is never frustrated or inhibited would be ill-prepared to cope in the real world. Just as having *some* fear and distrust protect a child, so the ability to handle frustration and conflict is absolutely necessary for survival in our less than perfect world. A major concern of parents is to restrain themselves from frustrating their growing child too much or in ways that are damaging. Much wise parental understanding and discrimination are called for. Each child is an unique individual and requires the stimulation, protection, and discipline that are best suited to his needs.

Parents need to be mature and capable of running the family because children cannot. Able parents persist in loving their children and in competent caretaking even when emotional rewards are not immediate.

Even parents who are doing a good job will be challenged by their offspring now and again and there will be conflicts. The child's personality emerges and takes shape in constant testing and perpetual pressure against parental authority. Although individual will and personal initiative may first be manifested in the second year of life with the toddler's upright mobility, the struggle for independence and a separate identity actually goes on until the child becomes an adult.

Overprotective parents may be affectionate and permissive when their children are infants, but they become overly cautious and, therefore, restrictive when their toddlers begin to show signs of independence. Then these

parents attempt to "infantalize" their children by curbing this independence and thus retard their gradual acquisition of mature attitudes and behaviors.

However, if parents are understanding and reasonably permissive, allowing moderate ánd practical degrees of autonomy (the freedom to explore, manipulate, and investigate), their children are likely to derive satisfaction from their own discoveries and from the pleasurable exercise of their nascent skills. Such children are likely to become self-confident and spontaneous in their behavior, approaching new hurdles without anxiety, and reacting with curiosity and gusto to novel and challenging situations.

"Children Learn What They Live"

A wise, albeit unknown author had the following to say about growing up:

If a child lives with criticism, he learns to condemn.
If he lives with ridicule, he learns to be shy.
If a child lives with shame, he learns to be guilty.
If he lives with tolerance, he learns to be patient.
If a child lives with encouragement, he learns to be confident.
If he lives with praise, he learns to appreciate.
If a child lives with fairness, he learns justice.
If he lives with security, he learns faith.
If a child lives with approval, he learns to like himself.
If he lives with acceptance and friendship, he learns to find love in the world.

Gross-Motor Development

Your toddler is doing everything she did last month, only with greater ease and coordination; i.e., walking forward, backward, and sideways, standing on either foot holding onto you or a stable piece of furniture, walking with one foot on a walking board, and so forth.

Twenty-one-month-olds are able to walk up stairs, with both feet on one step, and holding onto the railing without adult help. They can walk down stairs with one hand held by a parent or other caretaker. These toddlers love to jump, climb, throw, and run. They can pick up an object from the floor without falling and squat in play (mini yoga enthusiasts!).

No adult chair stymies the twenty-one-month-old, who can climb onto and get down from one adroitly without assistance. Sofas, tables, shelves, and so on continue to invite climbing exploits.

Your twenty-one-month-old throws a ball overhand a bit more accurately than heretofore and kicks a large ball on the ground in a forward direction without stepping on the ball. One mark of the toddler is carrying one or more favorite toys (teddy bear, doll, plane, and so on) while walking. The more variations on the theme of locomoting, the happier the toddler is. Yours may be pedaling a very small tricycle now or may still enjoy scooting about on the easier-to-maneuver Kiddie Kar.

Fine-Motor Development

The fingers are more nimble at this time, although still less than completely smooth in their coordination. Twenty-one-month-olds can make a tower of five to six cubes, which indicates improved eye-hand dexterity. If you fold a small piece of paper once, your toddler will be able to imitate your act.

Of course, you know that your child is able to turn the knob of your radio. She can also put the lid on an oblong box and enjoys experimenting with big and little boxes. Twenty-one-month-olds are able to fit related objects together appropriately by releasing, pressing, and turning; i.e., ring onto a pole, peg into a hole, nesting small blocks, and so on. Your child's hand preference is not yet clearly established, although she will use one hand more than the other.

Language Acquisition

The toddler begins to realize that single words are limiting and starts to use grammatical relationships; i.e., noun phrases *(Good girl)* and verb phrases *(Come here)*. The child may even begin to combine words and thus produce a simple sentence.

All children proceed with their speech development at a different rate. Some children show steady progress; others who seem to have a limited vocabulary for a long period of time may actually be storing words and suddenly express many new ones over a short span of time. Eventually both types become equal in their general learning. This difference applies to most kinds of learning.

Joining Two Words

It takes a while for a child to talk in real sentences. In the beginning, a single word represents a complete thought; for example, *mama* may mean *mommy come here.* As more words are learned, the child is able to communicate more needs and feelings. When the toddler begins to put two words together to make a sentence *(Get ball, All gone, Give cookie,* for instance) he is well on the way to piecing together a grammar that will grow more complex, paralleling increasingly sophisticated thought processes.

The average twenty-one-month-old has a speaking vocabulary of twenty or more words and now understands a few personal pronouns; for instance, the toddler can distinguish "Give it to *me,*" "Give it to *her,*" "Give it to *him,*" and so on.

If you have avoided baby talk and are speaking clearly and directly to your child all the time (without strain or tension), your child's speech will increase in clarity and in quantity of words being learned and put to use.

The twenty-one-month-old continues to indicate desires by gestures and utterances, but more words are being brought into verbal play. This toddler can accurately name three pictures of common objects and uses the names of some familiar objects. You may find your child trying to imitate a two- or three-word phrase. Encourage this without pushing. Language acquisition should be a wholly pleasurable experience.

Twenty-one-month-olds begin to use rudimentary questioning as a substitute for non-linguistic physical behavior; i.e., they constantly ask "What's that?" as a bid for parental attention and to learn. They are continuing to discover that everything has a name. If you have played naming body parts with your child, she should be able to point to five body parts (eyes, nose, mouth, ears, hair).

Toddlers this age enjoy listening to short nursery or Mother Goose rhymes with interesting sounds, especially when they are accompanied by pictures or actions. If the rhymes are sung, so much the better. Now the

child engages in spontaneous humming or singing of syllables. You need not possess an operatic voice to delight your offspring.

Twenty-one-month-olds love tactile books, *Pat the Bunny,* for one. However, they still need supervision while looking at books because they often tear them at this age.

Finger Plays

We hope you will enjoy with your child the words and actions for the finger plays we are providing below. These are great fun and will stimulate your toddler's language acquisition and thinking. You can test out one at a time over a period of time. There are sure to be special favorites.

Pease Porridge Hot
Pease porridge hot,
Pease porridge cold,
Pease porridge in the pot

Nine days old.

Some like it hot,
Some like it cold,
Some like it in the pot
Nine days old.

(slap knees, clap hands, slap child's hands)
(repeat above)
(slap knees, clap hands, slap child's right hand with
  your right hand, clap hands together)
(clap child's left hand with your left hand, clap
  hands together, clap child's hands)
(repeat sequence above)

Little Miss Muffet
Little Miss Muffet
Sat on a tuffet,
Eating her curds and whey.
Along came a spider
And sat down beside her
And frightened Miss Muffet away.

(thumb straight up)

(eating motion with other hand)
(twirling fingers from high)
(down toward thumb)
(as spider fingers reach thumb, quickly put thumb
  behind back)

Here's the Church
Here's the church,
Here's the steeple,
Open the door
And see all the people.

(fingers interlocked, palms down)
(index fingers raised to a point)
(keep fingers interlocked, but turn palms up)
(wriggle fingers)

Jack-in-the-Box
Jack-in-the-box
Sits so still
"Won't you come out?"
"Yes! I will!"

(hand closed, thumb inside)

(thumb "jumps" out)

Jack Be Nimble
Jack be nimble
Jack be quick,
Jack jumped over
The candlestick.

(hold closed fist with thumb standing)

(second hand hops over "candlestick")

Hands
Open them and shut them,
Open them and shut them,
Open them and shut them,
And give a little clap.
Open them and shut them,
Open them and shut them,
Open them and shut them,
And put them in your lap.
Creepy, creepy, creepy,
Up to your chin,
Open your mouth and
Pop them in!

The Little Mice
The little mice are creeping, creeping, creeping
The little mice are creeping all through the house
The little mice are eating, eating, eating
The little mice are sleeping, sleeping, sleeping
The old gray cat comes creeping, creeping,
  creeping
The little mice are scampering, scampering,
  scampering

(fingers creep on lap)
(fingers to lips)
(rest face on hands)

(one hand creeps slowly)

(fingers creep rapidly on lap)

Ten Little Fingers
I have ten little fingers
And they all belong to me.
I can make them do things—
Would you like to see?
I can put them up high,
I can put them down low,
I can make them hide,
And I can fold them just so.

Birds Flying
Up, up in the sky
The little birds fly,
Down, down in the nest,
The little birds rest,
With a wing on the left,
And a wing on the right.
Let the little birds rest
All the long night.

(fingers flying like birds)

(hands form nest)

(hands on each hip)

(head to one side as if tucking under wing)

Teensy, Weensy Spider
A teensy, weensy spider
Climbed up the water spout
Down came the rain
And washed the spider out
Out came the sun
And dried up all the rain
And the teensy, weensy spider
Climbed up the spout again.

(fingers climb upward atop each other)
(wiggle fingers to make rain)
(hands and arms flung downward and outward)
(hands form circle)
(hands open wide and outward)

(fingers climb upward as before)

Me
My hands upon my head I place,
On my shoulder, on my face,
On my knees and at my side.
Then I raise them up SO high,
Swiftly count to 1, 2, 3
And see how quiet they can be.

(bring hands down slowly and place them in lap)

Fall Leaves
Leaves are floating softly down,

They make a carpet on the ground.
When, swish! The wind comes whirling by
And sends them dancing to the sky.

(arms raised, fingers wiggling, gradually lower to the floor)

(move both arms quickly from one side to the other)
(wiggle fingers and arms in the air)

The Firemen

Ten brave firemen	(ten fingers straight up)
Sleeping in a row.	(fingers out flat)
Ding! Goes the bell!	(clap hands)
Down the pole they go.	(motion of going down a pole)
Jumping on the engine	(motion of driving)
Oh! Oh!	(hands shaped like hose)
Putting out the fire.	(hissing noises like water)
Back home so slow,	(driving motion, slow)
All in a row.	

Helping Mother

I help my mother.	
I sweep the floor,	(swing arms pretending to sweep)
I dust the table,	(make a circular motion with one hand)
I run to the store	(run a few steps, then run back)
I help her beat eggs	(hold hands together, moving one in a small circle)
And sift the flour for cakes.	(holding one hand closed, shake it back and forth)
Then I help her eat	
All the good things she makes.	(hold hands to lips pretending to take a bite of something)

Little Boy (or Girl)

This little boy is going to bed,	(index finger on right hand is child)
Down on the pillow he lays his head,	(thumb of left hand on palm of left hand forms pillow)
Wraps himself in the covers so tight.	(fingers of left hand close over index finger of right hand as blankets)
There he stays all the long night.	
Morning comes; he opens his eyes.	
Back with a toss the covers fly.	(fingers of left hand open up)
Up he jumps, he's off and away,	(index finger of right hand jumps up)
Ready for work and ready for play.	

The Flowers

When the flowers are thirsty	(both hands form cup, representing flowers)
And the grass is dry,	(hands spread out flat)
Merry little raindrops	(hands and fingers coming from sky like raindrops)
Tumble from the sky.	
All around they patter	(fingers tapping on floor or table)
In their happy play,	
Till the little sunbeams	(hands and arms form a round sun)
Chase them all away.	

If any of the foregoing seem too advanced for your child, you can make use of such finger plays later on. This activity is relished by children throughout early childhood. Of course, you can make up your own finger plays incorporating subject matter that is familiar to your child, as well as fanciful rhymes, but within his understanding.

Sensory Powers/Learning

Creativity is the opposite of imitating or copying; it is something new or novel. At the core of all creative activity is the ability to look freshly at an object or a problem. Creativity may be regarded as a genuine expression of oneself. It also may be described as having different kinds of ideas and carrying an idea as far as it will go. A truly creative person has to be willing to take risks. Healthy children are curious, flexible, inventive, spontaneous, playful, observant, and free—and so are creative people.

Writes Fredelle Maynard, Ph.D., "To say that all children are creative is not, of course, to say that all are or can be equally creative. Some children are born with a gift—for music, let's say, or mathematics. A favorable environment may cause the gift to blossom into greatness. But the most favorable environment in the world won't make a creative musical genius out of a child with a tin ear. So it's necessary at the outset to distinguish between two kinds of creativity—the special talent variety, which depends upon genes and chromosomes, and the instinctive urge to learn, grow, and develop, which exists in every individual."

The late Rachel L. Carson wrote, "A child's world is fresh and new and beautiful, full of wonder and excitement. It is our misfortune that for most of us that clear-eyed vision, that true instinct for what is beautiful and awe-inspiring, is dimmed and even lost before we reach adulthood. If I had influence with the good fairy who is supposed to preside over the christening of all children, I should ask that her gift to each child in the world be a sense of wonder so indestructible that it would last throughout life, as an unfailing antidote against the boredom and disenchantments of later years, the sterile preoccupations with things that are artificial, the alienation from the sources of our strength."

We are in wholehearted accord with Dr. Maynard, who writes in her book, *Guiding Your Child to a More Creative Life,* "I am not interested in attempts to turn out prodigies—concert violinists or literary geniuses. Or in trying to make a child brighter and more talented than the kid next door. My concern is with whatever helps a child to discover his own best self, and so to become a more complete human being."

You can foster your twenty-one-month-old's "sense of wonder" and natural creativity by providing opportunities for her free expression in your daily routine and responding with interest and enthusiasm to her questions and actions. Play with unstructured materials encourages being inventive, even during early toddlerhood. As your child grows older, there will be more and more materials to manipulate (including clay, finger paints, paints) that permit experimentation and provide great satisfaction.

Shape Discrimination

When presented with a formboard with round, square, and triangular holes and forms to fit these holes, the twenty-one-month-old can successfully fit the forms into the correct openings. This toddler can also put together two pieces to form a whole geometric figure and complete simple jigsaw puzzles of three or more large pieces. By now your child is able to place six round pegs in the holes of a large pegboard. It is as much fun to remove the pegs from the pegboard as to replace them.

You can introduce your toddler to playing a simple picture lotto game with you. You can buy this in a toy shop or make your own out of cardboard with colorful pictures of familiar items from magazines (you will need two of the same magazines out of which to cut matching pictures).

Twenty-one-month-olds are interested in very tiny things, especially bugs. Nature walks or trips to the park playground should provide a ladybug or other "safe" insects. In the summertime, the beach is a good source of interesting specimens. Comparing tiny and big seashells would provide a good preliminary lesson in size discrimination. Most twenty-one-month-olds understand and use the word *big.*

Toddlers this age can remember a familiar object without actually seeing it or holding it in their hands. During the first twelve months of life, this was not possible.

Scribbling

Toddlers like to make marks on paper with a big crayon. After your demonstration, your

mint, newly-cut grass, pine, and so on; and such pungent odors as leather and fur. You can make a simple guessing game for each particular kind of smell.

Social Development

Research findings suggest that the way for parents to produce a nonaggressive child is to make it perfectly clear that aggression is frowned upon; to stop aggressive behavior when it occurs, but to avoid punishing a child for his aggression. Punishment appears to have complex effects. While it undoubtedly often stops a particular form of aggression—at least momentarily—it seems to generate more hostility in the child and to lead to further aggressive outbursts at some other time or place. When parents punish their child, especially when they resort to physical punishment, they are providing an example of the use of aggression at the very time they are trying to teach their child not to be aggressive.

The most harmonious home is one in which parents believe that aggression is not desirable and rely—for the most part—on nonpunitive forms of control. Homes in which children show angry, aggressive outbursts frequently are ones in which parents have a relatively tolerant attitude toward such behavior, or where they administer severe punishment for it, or both.

We believe that although punishment sometimes eliminates a few specific aggressive responses, it leaves a strongly hostile, bottled-up feeling within the child—and there is evidence to support this belief. Of course, complete parental permissiveness does increase the amount of aggression in the home and it is worth considering what *this* does to the child. An angry child usually is unhappy and does not receive affection from others. Such a child is a constant source of discomfort to the parents.

A child is more likely to be nonaggressive if the parents hold that aggression is undesirable and should not occur. A child is more apt to be nonaggressive if the parents prevent or stop the occurrence of angry outbursts instead of passively permitting them to go on.

child will learn to draw a vertical line (a circular scribble, even a crude one, comes a bit later).

Twenty-one-month-olds are keenly aware of such sounds as clocks, whistles, and bells. You can expose your child to the various tones and qualities of the above, as well as other interesting sounds in toy shops, hardware stores, your own home, and elsewhere.

Your Toddler's Sense of Smell

It is not too early to expose your child to all kinds of smells: such floral scents as rose, lily of the valley, narcissus, jasmine, gardenia, honeysuckle, sweet alyssum, and so on; such fruit odors as lemon, lime, and orange; the spicy smells of ginger, allspice, cloves, cinnamon, nutmeg; such herb and woodsy odors as lavender, thyme, basil, oregano, sage,

They prevent them by means other than punishment or threats of retaliation.

The foregoing does not imply that parents do not have the right to be angry on occasion. However, since anger interferes with constructive action in most problem situations in a family, most parents are careful to keep their own feelings within reasonable bounds.

Although most psychologists are opposed to all but the most sparing use of physical punishment, there are times when a quick, angry swat on a child's bottom is very effective. Certainly this does much less damage to the child's sense of worth than the devastating withdrawal of love; for example, "If you do that, I will not love you."

During the second year, parents begin to impose restrictions on activities that are socially unacceptable, but that the toddler normally finds pleasurable. The child is asked to stop making so much noise at dinner, to stop messing with her food, to stop jumping up and down on the bed, and to delay defecation and urination until she can get to an appropriate place. The situation is complicated by the fact that many socialization demands are made at the same time.

Very early in life the child acquires certain motives that facilitate the socialization process. By the end of the first year, the child appears to be highly motivated to please his parents, thereby ensuring continued affection and acceptance, and to avoid the unpleasant feelings generated by punishment or rejection. These motives are very strong in the first two years.

Accordingly, parental rewards and disapproval are the major techniques used in early socialization. In a sense, successful socialization involves an exchange in which the child gives up the desire to do as he pleases in return for the ongoing love of both parents. This works best only if the child is receiving sufficient nurturance to make it attractive to him. Parents who have not been nurturant during their child's first year of life do not have sufficient reward value to motivate their child to adhere to their values. Parental warmth and acceptance are tantamount to effective socialization, as well as the child's feeling of

confidence in his ability to deal effectively with the home environment.

Even though twenty-one-month-olds respond less quickly to requests and are apt to do the opposite of what is asked of them (often as a form of testing and sometimes playfully), they will relinquish items that belong to others when requested to do so. They delight in helping put the groceries away—and do this very well because they have a good memory for where things belong in the house. They will pick up and put away their playthings, with a little help.

Along with your child's awareness of other people comes a glimmering awareness of "property rights." Your child knows which room is hers and which room is mommy's and daddy's. Your twenty-one-month-old likes to know that she has a drawer in your room and a place for her books on a bookshelf in the living room. It is important for your child to have something of her own in each newly discovered room. As soon as toddlers this age become bored with their things, they love to play with other people's possessions. It is advisable to watch a twenty-one-month-old when exploring in another room. A period of dead silence usually portends some kind of upheaval.

Personality/Psychological Development

According to Margaret S. Mahler, "By the age of twenty-one months, a general diminishing of the rapprochement struggle could be observed. The clamoring for omnipotent control, the extreme periods of separation anxiety, the alternation of demands for closeness and for autonomy—all these subsided, at least for a while, as each child once again seemed to find the optimal distance from mother, the distance at which he could function best."

Several elements appear to contribute to making it possible for the twenty-one-month-old to function at a greater distance from the mother: the development of language in terms of naming objects and expressing desires with specific words, which appears to give the toddler a greater sense of ability to control his environment; the internalization of parental rules and demands; and progress in the child's ability to use play for mastery.

Dr. Mahler indicates that the realization of separateness is affected by—and in turn affects—the mother-child relationship, as well as the father-child relationship and the integration of each child's total personality.

Parental Sex Typing

Psychologists know that parental sex typing in the United States begins even before the baby's birth. If parents wish for a boy, they paint the nursery blue and buy clothes in "male-related" colors. A mother in doubt of her baby's movement in utero is more likely to report activity if she thinks she is carrying a male fetus.

As soon as the baby is born, all kinds of differences occur. Mothers of boys as young as twelve weeks act differently toward them than mothers act toward their girl babies. At first, boys receive more attention and handling, probably because they cry and fuss more. However, by six months, the mother pays more attention to her girl, probably talking and interacting with her more. Just one effect of this different treatment is the far greater early language development of girls in comparison to boys. Girls also tend to be breast-fed more often and longer than boys. One reason for this difference is sexual. The female breast in North America is a sexual object (as far as the mother's subconscious goes)—even for a nine-month-old!

Pushing boy babies away from the breast and the decline in the mother's touching and closeness may be due, too, to her preparation of him for his role as a North American male. Attachment behavior for men in our culture is severely limited. Men are supposed to be independent. They should *never* cry. Kissing or embracing another male is suspect. The consequences of these kinds of attitudes and child-rearing practices are reflected in North American adolescent behaviors. Teenage girls touch hands and dance together; boys do not. The question is, what would we think if boys did?

Yet in other cultures physical contact between males is acceptable. In Italy, men embrace when meeting or leaving each other. In Greece, males may dance together, often to the exclusion of women. In these cultures, the mother's handling of her son quite possibly remains constant throughout his infancy. The fathers probably touch and handle their sons more also.

A parent who realizes how arbitrary and culture-specific sex roles are may want to rearrange them. Why shouldn't small boys play with dolls and why can't girls grow up to be engineers? Such parental rearrangement or thinking about sex roles is good. It belongs to a current trend of questioning and change that, we hope, will allow people more individual freedom. A particular danger, Michael

Lewis, Ph.D., cautions, is unconscious pathological motivation that can hopelessly confuse the child. A simple example is giving a male name to a female child because the parents are disappointed at having a little girl.

Parents are not altogether responsible; some sex differences appear to be inborn:

Girls are more sensitive to pain and touch

Girls at all ages have less muscle, but more and differently distributed fat

Girls are less active than boys

Girls follow a faster and more predictable timetable of maturation

Boys are larger and longer

Boys are biologically more fragile, which may be why they cry and fuss more

Boys of the same size as girls are less mature developmentally

There are more natural abortions of boys and boys suffer more birth trauma. Although many more males are conceived than females, by age ten females equal and thereafter quickly outnumber males.

According to Jerome Kagan, Ph.D., of Harvard University, the most intriguing sex difference is the more stable physical and mental growth of girls. For example, if you examined the number of teeth of one thousand boys and one thousand girls at the age of two, you would find a far greater range in the number for boys. Vocabulary at the age of three is a better predictor of a girl's adult vocabulary and I.Q. than it is for a boy.

While the mother may allow her little boy to explore more and spend more time away from her, a little girl may be less prone to be independent of the mother's influence and so less likely to explore actively.

Which sex differences are biological and which are sociological, and where the two interact, are fascinating and still unspecified distinctions. Increasingly clear is the earliness of their impact on behavior. By thirteen months, children may essentially be in the sex roles they will assume for life. Little girls sit and play; little boys roam around. Girls talk more and cling more. Boys like miniature lawn mowers and trucks. Girls like dolls and homemaking toys. Boys try to strong-arm their way around physical barriers; girls beckon and cry for help—and probably will do so for years to come.

More on Negativism and *No*

Although challenging to the patience, equanimity, and ingenuity of parents, psychologists view negativism, the *no* stage, as a transitional period between babyhood and childhood. They believe that parents should view this as a positive stage in their child's upgrowth.

If your twenty-one-month-old's contrary and contradictory behavior often leaves you bothered and bewildered, take heart—you are not alone. All toddlers and their parents go through this phase (not too much the worse for the inevitable ups and downs that accompany the child's faltering progression toward ultimate independence).

Your child will often say *no* even to things he wants to do or have. The use of *no* appears to be a natural part of every young child's growing up. You will learn that often when your toddler is saying *no*, he does not expect you to take it seriously. However, there are times when your child means exactly what he says. The example of the twenty-one-month-old saying *no* to having a bath while happily climbing into the tub symbolizes the child's always serious but sometimes amusing battle for autonomy. It is easy for us to suggest that you "keep your cool" during this exasperating time, but if you can, you will escape some bouts of impatience and ill-will between you and your toddler.

The building of self-confidence and independence impinges upon all the things children are able to do for themselves—so do not fence your child in; do not hold the reins so tightly that your child has no chance to become competent and self-sufficient.

Twenty-one-month-olds often try to make a stand for their own rights and attempt to make decisions on their own. Sara D. Gilbert, in *Three Years to Grow,* writes, "We shared the baby's delight when he discovered his hands and feet and his pride when he took his first step. *No!* and *Mine!* may be harder to take, but they are just as surely signs of progress toward independent selfhood."

Children from twenty-one to twenty-four months of age are very defiant of their parents and inflexible in what they will do. They want everything immediately and insist that things be done in the same way every time. They try to dominate their parents and often make unreasonable demands on them. In *The Magic Years,* Selma Fraiberg says, "To do just the opposite of what mother wants strikes the child as being the very essence of his individuality."

It would help if you ignored your child's *no* as much as possible. Lead your ambivalent toddler rather than ask what she wants to do or have. You might try to rechannel negative responses or behaviors by making games out of what you would like your child to do. However, limit your commands to a minimum, except in situations where her health or welfare are concerned, as well as the well-being of others.

Hitting and Biting

Some twenty-one-month-olds become very bossy and may attempt to hit or bite their parents when angry or frustrated. You can divert this by being firm (but gentle), letting your child know that you will not tolerate behavior of this sort. Hitting or biting the toddler back will not solve the problem. In fact, it would reduce the parent to the child's level. Diversion is a better tactic.

Dawdling

This is a subdued form of negativism that often is employed by two- to three-year-olds (and older children). When you are faced with this pattern of behavior, you can develop approaches to speed things up without causing your child to "lose face." Self-esteem is fragile indeed, especially during childhood.

Disobedience

Some disobedient behavior is normal in twenty-one- to twenty-four-month-old children. They are testing their parents to find out their limits and the fine distinctions of their rules and regulations. You should not be alarmed at occasional disobedience. On the other hand, total obedience is not normal behavior. Children who always obey probably have had too much and too severe discipline so that they are fearful and eventually lose their individuality.

Children who constantly misbehave have not yet set up acceptable standards of behavior in their own minds. Some children find that the only way they can get attention from their parents is by misbehaving. Usually a constantly disobedient child is not receiving enough attention and reward for *good* behavior.

Destructiveness

Tearing things down and building things up are common activities at this age as the child discovers things around him. However, a child who is always destructive may be searching for parental attention. If this is the case, do not undermine your child. Instead try to give your toddler more loving, relaxed, uninterrupted attention.

Most "behavior problems" at this age are really not problems at all; they are normal reactions to maturing. With affection, understanding, and patience, parents can ease and usually remedy most troublesome situations. Time itself resolves many of the normally transitory difficulties.

Of course, there are manifold happy occasions for toddlers and their parents to share and enjoy at this time. For one, the twenty-one-month-old will sit on the laps of and hug familiar adults, in addition to the parents. There are not too many interpersonal feelings that compete with the love expressed by the hugs and kisses of a twenty-one-month-old.

Your toddler's use of the pronoun *I* matches her almost constant declaration of *mine*. At the same time, the twenty-one-month-old is beginning to be able to sympathize with another person because she can now imagine—to some extent—the feelings of the other person. Your emotional input and example imprint your child's feelings of affection and caring. Toddlers this age continue to like to help with housework and should be encouraged to do very simple but real tasks. Enjoy this great spirit of cooperation because, unless nurtured by you, it soon shall pass.

Self-Help Routines

Twenty-one-month-olds have a new sense of self. They insist on taking on some responsibility for their own activities. You will find the partial listing below interesting and revealing:

- They delight in trying to put their own beds in order
- They turn on the radio or TV
- They participate in washing themselves
- They adore brushing their teeth (which usually consists of biting on the toothbrush)
- They like to sweep, mop, dust, vacuum, hammer, shovel, scoop, or rake (tasks they have seen performed)
- They will get a sponge or broom on own initiative to clean up spills
- They will ask for a tissue and blow own nose and then put tissue in a wastebasket
- They may often refuse proffered help when some project frustrates them
- They attempt to master tasks that are beyond their previous limits
- They will kiss their own hurts

A lot of growing and learning are reflected in the above "declaration of independence."

Ownership and possession seem important to twenty-one-month-olds. The assignment of ownership appears to be a classificatory device by which children this age make the world orderly and manageable.

Self-Feeding

Your child may now be a self-feeder and less dependent upon you. Inasmuch as you know just about how much your toddler is going to eat, it is best to put that amount on the plate. More than your child can handle will merely tempt him to play with the food. If he should begin to mess around, take the spoon away and offer a few bites to see if he is through eating. If he is surfeited, take the plate away quietly without fuss or fanfare.

According to Doctors Gesell and Ilg, "Since the child at this age is sensitive to peripheral stimuli, it is important not to have his meal interrupted by small or large distractions. The dessert within sight, too much interference on the part of the mother, or the father coming home—any of these may serve to interrupt and perhaps terminate his meal."

Twenty-one-month-olds have definite food preferences, especially regarding the amounts they want to eat. No doubt your toddler is beginning to ask you for a cookie or a drink on his or her own initiative.

Snacking

With regard to in-between meal treats, common sense is probably the best approach. If your toddler is eating well at mealtimes, she certainly should be given a nutritious snack (no "junk" foods, please) if she wants it. Generally, it is wise to establish a time (midmorning or after a nap) and a place for the snack to avoid continual wails for snacks and to prevent her from consuming food all over the house.

Although snacks usually are given more than an hour before a meal, some children seem to need a quick pick-me-up just before they eat or they become cranky and irritable. A small glass of juice often helps such a child to relax and eat better.

Now what of the child who is not eating well at meals and yet constantly requests food between meals? Most pediatricians agree that this usually happens with a child who has been made anxious during meals by parental overurging and pushing. The tension makes it impossible for the child to eat. The answer is to try to make every mealtime an enjoyable experience.

Sleeping

Most twenty-one-month-olds will take a fairly long afternoon nap every day. If conditions are made right for them, toddlers generally will go right off to sleep after their luncheon. Sometimes toddlers decide that life is too exciting and they have too many things to explore so they will not nap. It is a good idea to put them in their bed anyway, perhaps with their favorite toy, and they can amuse themselves quietly even if they do not go to sleep. Many toddlers return to napping after several days of staying awake.

By twenty-one months, the toddler's sleep pattern begins to change. Total sleeping time is reduced and often the child has difficulty going to sleep. It is at this age that children seem to initiate the calling of a parent for drinks of water, another good-night kiss, and all the familiar requests that delay sleeping. Twenty-one-month-olds tend to wake early but, with a little consolation, may go back to sleep.

Toilet Learning

Today psychologists and pediatricians believe that too rigid or too early toilet learning might cause a child to be compulsive, fearful, negativistic, or aggressive in later childhood. Forced training may result in intense anxiety or hostility on the part of the child at the time of the training. Often a child who seems to have no difficulty mastering bowel control may manifest difficulties in previously non-problematic areas of behavior, such as disturbed sleep patterns, eating problems, and so on. Watchfulness for such anxieties and a reduction of pressures for toileting success by the parents usually will take care of such manifestations. A child may lose some self-confidence if expected to perform, on the command of the parent, a function that is necessarily related to his own body rhythm. Therefore, it is best to let your child indicate his readiness for bowel or urinary control.

Dressing

Twenty-one-month-olds can undress themselves completely and are so pleased with this accomplishment that often they will run around the house and backyard naked. They

actively help dress themselves now and want to choose the clothes they will wear. Many toddlers this age are able to put on their shoes, though without tying the laces. This skill will come later.

Play and Playthings

Much of the twenty-one-month-old's play is accompanied by words, becoming more expressive as new words are added to the child's speaking vocabulary. You will hear a toddler talk to a toy truck as she pushes it along the floor, or give a serious scolding to a doll or teddy bear.

Doll play is becoming a bit more involved now. The twenty-one-month-old makes the doll the "baby"—washing and drying its face and hands, feeding it ("More, baby—more toast?" for example), putting it to bed and covering it up. As a companion, the toddler will take the favorite doll to the store, out to the sandbox, talk to it, show the doll whatever delights him, read to it, and so forth. The child will also scold the doll, praise it, and explain to it in a way that suggests reinforcement of various parental admonitions and teachings. On rare occasions, a toddler may throw a doll in a show of anger, usually in an outburst against the mother. Toddlers often use a doll carriage as a conveyance for materials other than their dolls.

The pioneering early childhood educators —Maria Montessori, Caroline Pratt, and Patty Smith Hill—recognized the range of play activities that involve children's minds and muscles and set about designing and having produced appropriate equipment and play materials according to their strict standards. They knew that to help children realize their maturing gross-motor powers—running, skipping, hopping, climbing, balancing, and so on—adequate space also had to be provided.

Caroline Pratt understood that to allow children to use their hands to manipulate and playfully remake around them "lays the cornerstone of the child's feeling for himself in relation to the world."

It is the feeling today of many animal and early childhood researchers that this earliest play, starting when the brain is not yet "locked into place," has a powerful imprinting effect on the ego, self-esteem, creativeness, and self-confidence of children.

These pioneers did not just spout theories of play; they tried hard to get manufacturers to make the kinds of unstructured raw materials that would give children pleasure and satisfaction in their accomplishments. Unfortunately, few manufacturers took on the challenge of marketing them because these shapeless play materials did not sell off retail toy counters. Instead of investing money to educate parents about the value of such materials, today's toy manufacturers continue to choose the easiest way out, merchandising Mickey Mouse, Batman, Superman, and other like items. They now are using television to influence susceptible, immature child consumers.

Unstructured Playthings

Unstructured play materials continue to be paints, large-sized brushes, clay, community and family figures, thick crayons, large sheets of paper, building blocks (e.g., the Pratt unit blocks), and so forth. Using these promotes discoveries of the here-and-now of home and community living, of texture, color, pattern, design, and shape. As children begin to handle and explore such materials, they bring themselves and their ideas into play and create something uniquely their own. They learn the range of exploration the materials provide and discover their limitations.

Some materials invite multiple choices in their use; others do not. Inset puzzles have only one correct way to be completed. This type of self-corrective challenge is inherent in the Montessori method of learning. Her so-called "didactic materials" are designed to teach specific relationships of color, size, shape, number, texture, volume, and so on.

During the pioneering years of nursery education, few realistic toys were needed to stimulate dramatic play. The raw materials were used over and over again in creative ways every day.

The more a toy is designed to be played with in one way only, the more it restrains a child's imagination and creativity.

THE TWENTY-FIRST MONTH

Motor Development

Gross Motor

Walks up stairs, holding rail, with both feet on one step

Walks down stairs, one hand held

Gets onto and down from adult chair unaided

Kicks large ball in forward direction

Squats in play

Walks with one foot on walking board

Stands on either foot, holding on

Loves to jump, run, throw, and climb

Rhythmic response to music with whole body

Throws ball overhand

Jumps in place

Fine Motor

Makes tower of 5–6 cubes

Can fold a piece of paper once imitatively

Uses one hand more than the other

Language Acquisition

Speaking vocabulary of 20 or more words

Joins 2 words ("All gone," etc.)

Uses word combinations

Echoes 2 or more last words

Names 3 pictures of common objects

Listens to short rhymes with interesting sounds, especially when they are accompanied by actions or pictures

Likes to have lilting rhymes sung

Enjoys *Pat the Bunny* and other tactile books

Needs supervision while looking at books because often tears them at this age

Spontaneous humming or singing of syllables

Imitates 2- or 3-word sentence

Understands some personal pronouns; can distinguish "Give it to her," "Give it to him"

Tries to follow directions

Can point to 5 body parts

Sensory Powers/Learning

Points to parts of doll on request

Imitates simple actions on request

Imitates pushing a train he or she makes of a few cubes

Imitates crudely a circular scribble

Draws vertical line after demonstration

Can place triangle, circle, and square blocks correctly in formboard

Places 6 round pegs in holes of pegboard

Is interested in very tiny things, especially bugs

Will sit alone several minutes at a time thumbing one by one the pages in a picture book

Keenly aware of such sounds as clocks, whistles, and bells

Likes to make marks on paper with big crayon

Completes simple jigsaw puzzle of 2–3 large pieces

Identifies pictures in a book

Growth Chart

Social Development

In communicating, pulls person to show

Tries to tell experiences

Enjoys outdoor walks whenever offered

Will relinquish items that belong to others, upon request

Recognizes and can name familiar people and self in photos in family album

Responds less quickly to requests; is apt to do the opposite of what is asked

Dependable enough to go about home play yard with minimal supervision

May ask whether what he or she would like to do is acceptable to others

Personality/ Psychological

Sits on lap and hugs familiar adults

Is beginning to be able to sympathize with another person (can imagine to some extent the feelings of the other person)

Refers to self by name

Uses the personal pronoun "I"

Likes to claim "mine"

Can accept shared attention

Likes to help with housework, doing simple tasks

Self-Help Routines

Handles cup or glass well

Can zip and unzip large zipper

Takes off clothes with help on buttons

Puts shoes on part way (cannot do laces, etc.)

Asks for food, drink, and the toilet

Picks up and puts away toys, upon request

Squats, holds self, or verbalizes toilet needs

Likes to sweep, mop, dust, hammer, vacuum, shovel, scoop, or rake (household tasks he or she has seen performed)

Removes paper from candy, skin from banana, etc.

Participates in washing; makes washing motion toward mouth with washcloth

Uses spoon quite well

Play and Playthings

Plays contentedly alone if near adults

Will play near, but not with, other children

Throws small rubber ball

Pushes and pulls large toys and boxes

Maneuvers a Kiddie Kar well

Doll play involves very simple imitative actions

Plays a game of hide-and-seek with toys

Enjoys filling a toy dump truck with sand or pebbles and dumping same

Can imitate some of the play activity of older siblings

Likes to fit things together

Delights in using toy telephone

Uses a doll carriage as a conveyance for other materials

Enjoys playing tag with parent or older sibling

Dear Parents:

Do not regard this chart as a rigid timetable.

Babies are unpredictable individuals. Some perform an activity earlier or (as much as six months) later than the chart indicates, while others skip a behavior altogether (i.e., walking without crawling).

Just use this information to anticipate and appreciate normal child development and behavior. No norms are absolutes.

THE TWENTY-SECOND MONTH

Zigzagging Ahead

Child development researcher Burton L. White, Ph.D., of the Harvard University Graduate School of Education, believes that no job is more important than rearing a child in the first three years of life. This is how he puts it: "I have devoted my whole professional career to pursuing the question of how competent people get that way. On the basis of years of research I am totally convinced that the first priority with respect to helping each child to reach his maximum level of competence is to do the best possible job in structuring his experiences and opportunities during the first three years of life . . . any other kind of job . . . cannot really compete (in humanistic terms) with the job of helping a child make the most of his potential for a rich life."

Of course, parenting is hard work, but we believe that it is one of life's most precious offerings. Once you understand the growth patterns, requirements, and behaviors of children, you will find it easier to be unafraid and to be competent. Self-assured, loving, and optimistic mothers and fathers are better able to cope with the inevitable problems that arise during child rearing (and everyday living as well). Knowing how your own child functions and following your "educated intuitions" will permit you to enjoy your twenty-two-month-old as you continue to help her or him to become a self-reliant, capable individual.

Gross-Motor Development

Your twenty-two-month-old is a physical dynamo who is constantly on the go except when asleep. Just watching a toddler in action can be exhausting to an adult. There must be times when you wonder whether your child will ever slow down. Be assured that she will—at the time that is just right for her. If you try to slow your toddler down too much by restricting her freedom of movement now, you will not be doing her a favor. The quiet child is sometimes the one who has been squelched and kept from getting acquainted with the world. Conversely, there are toddlers who become increasingly restive when they are restrained unnecessarily.

Twenty-two-month-olds experiment with all kinds of large-muscle activities that also involve thrust and acceleration. They can throw a ball overhand with more sureness than last month and kick a ball quite well in a forward direction. They go easily from standing to running, but are still only fair at this particular form of physical coordination. They cannot slow down and are not yet able to turn sharp corners.

Twenty-two-month-olds continue to walk up and down stairs, holding the railing, and with both feet on each step. Sometimes they will still creep down stairs backward. They will

climb up to stand on a chair. This toddler eagerly and actively builds and knocks down, empties, pulls apart, feels, twists, and squeezes all available objects.

Fine-Motor Development

Twenty-two-month-olds still turn the pages of a book two or three at a time. Of course, they are able to turn the knobs of a radio and can turn on a television set. Since their wrist action is not yet developed enough, unscrewing the cap on a jar comes a bit later.

Toddlers this age begin to show hand preference when they scribble. They can build a firm tower of six or more cubes and are beginning to learn to put pop-it beads or blocks together.

Language Acquisition

For I was no longer a speechless infant. . . . It was not that my elders taught me words . . . in any set method; but I, longing by cries and broken accents and various motions of my limbs to express my thoughts . . . did myself . . . practice the sounds in my memory. When they named anything, and as they spoke turned towards it, I saw and remembered . . . by the name they uttered. . . . Thus I exchanged with those about me these current signs of our wills, and so launched deeper into the stormy intercourse of human life; yet depending on parental authority and the beck of elders.

Confessions of St. Augustine

As is true in all areas of child development, individuals acquire language differently and at varying rates of speed. Some toddlers seem to be bursting with words; others appear to be nonchalant; still others bide their time and listen, watch, and absorb the language around them until they are ready to speak. The growing variety of each toddler's experience is reflected in the number of words he uses.

Inasmuch as toddlers understand words before they use them, you should judge your child's vocabulary by how much she understands rather than by how many words she can say at this time. A child's vocabulary expands from hearing the same words used repeatedly to accompany such daily routines as eating, bathing, getting dressed, going to sleep, and so forth.

Twenty-two-month-olds adore nursery rhymes even when they do not understand all the words. They respond with vim and vigor to the rhyme and rhythm of these timeless jingles. You can have fun teaching your toddler simple rhyming games. We give you two below. At first you can place your toddler's hands on the appropriate part of himself. Before long, he will do it without your help.

Hands on hips, hands on knees,
Put them behind you, if you please.
Touch your shoulders, touch your toes,
Touch your knees and then your nose.
Raise your hands way up high
And let your fingers swiftly fly.
Then hold them out in front of you
While you clap them, one and two.

Two little eyes to look around,
Two little ears to hear each sound.
One little nose to smell what's sweet,
One little mouth that likes to eat.

Just as the ability of toddlers to make demands grows during this period, so does their ability to comment on objects and events that interest them. At an earlier age, the child typically commented on an interesting object by stating its name or by giving a simple description of the object's properties: *hot, wet, gone.* Now the toddler's list of adjectives is longer. However, the most striking thing about the comments is that they are used to communicate negative feelings. Instead of yelling when the puzzle pieces will not fit, the toddler says "Hard" or "Too big." Instead of crying when the diaper needs changing, the toddler says "Change" or "Baby wet."

How Words Help

Negative feelings need to be expressed, and until children are able to use words, they

have no alternative but to cry or strike out. Once words are available, however, it is fantastic how effective their use can be in releasing frustration, anger, disappointment, and other unpleasant feelings. You can help by using words such as *hurt, scared, mad, hard, tired,* and so on when you talk to your toddler about feelings.

Storybooks and Pictures

With increasing language acquisition, books and pictures become even more important. Twenty-two-month-olds can appreciate a short story. It may be necessary for you to paraphrase a story because some of the sentences in the book may be too complex or will refer to ideas your child cannot yet comprehend.

Reading a story works best if you first read the page silently and then tell your toddler in simple words what has happened, leaving out events that are too involved. Some parents think that because a young child's attention span is limited, they should read through a story as quickly as possible. Actually the reverse appears to be true: the faster the parent reads a book, the more likely the toddler is to lose interest. Reading slowly (but not too slowly) has many advantages. It allows the toddler enough time to grasp what has hap-

pened on one page before proceeding to the next. Even more important, it gives the toddler time to take an active part in the reading.

"At an earlier age, children use picture books for matching; i.e., they try to find like objects on different pages. Twenty-two-month-olds are still interested in this activity. While they listen to the story, they will be scanning the page looking for interesting objects to label or to match. Reading slowly permits your child to interrupt the story to point out these objects.

"Of course, the right pace for reading varies from toddler to toddler. The easiest way to set the pace is to let your child turn the pages. Sometimes toddlers will skip pages or turn the pages from back to front. Usually this signifies that they want to play a picture-matching game rather than listen to a story. There is nothing wrong with that; just as much can be learned by looking at the pictures as by listening to the story.

"Picture labeling takes place on a more advanced level when the toddler begins to talk about the past. Instead of simply labeling a picture of a bus, for instance, you and your toddler can talk about the bus you took to the zoo or the stalled bus you saw on the highway. Talking about past experiences is difficult for toddlers this age, but it does occur. You might encourage your toddler with such comments as 'Just like the bus at the zoo' or 'Remember the broken bus on the highway?' If your child seems to understand, this kind of comment is appropriate. If not, forget this for a while. In either case, do not bombard your toddler with all the associations you can recall regarding a particular picture. No one enjoys a lecture!

"Being able to appreciate a story is an act of the imagination. Your toddler is beginning to be able to use her imagination for pretending. This ability becomes increasingly apparent month by month. Again the child is using symbols (in this case, pretend behavior) to represent reality. Favorite pretend themes continue to revolve around eating, sleeping, cleaning, and other everyday activities. However, make-believe play is elaborated with more language. The eighteen- to twenty-

one-month old may have pretended to drink from an empty cup, but at twenty-two months likes to pretend that there is a particular liquid in the cup. Suppose you ask your toddler whether she wants lemonade or chocolate milk and the reply is 'Chocolate milk.' Then you can pretend to put some chocolate milk in the glass and to stir it around. Your toddler enjoys this elaboration and will respond if you ask other questions; for example, 'Do you need more chocolate?' or 'Is it too hot, need an ice cube?'

"Of course, at this age, most of the verbal elaboration of pretend play must come from the adult, but the toddler is an enthusiastic participant and listener. One popular form of imaginative play that stimulates the toddler to talk involves pretend telephone conversations. From an early age, children find the telephone a fascinating object to play with."

Toddlers this age use the names of all the familiar objects in their environment. They still express their desires mainly by utterances and gesturing. They can point to five body parts on themselves or on a doll—eyes, nose, mouth, ears, hair. In response to "Where is your mouth?" the twenty-two-month-old will correctly indicate either by pointing to or opening his mouth.

Your toddler can ask now for many things at the table by name (cookies, toast, milk, meat, juice, and so on). Twenty-two-month-olds begin to combine two words in their speech. Encourage this. How very thrilled you must have been when your child first referred to himself or herself by name; another linguistic and psychological forward stride.

Sensory Powers/Learning

In the process of responding to your toddler's commands and requests, you can also teach very elementary concepts of time and quantity. For example, most toddlers discover that they are not limited to the food on the table. They can request more cookies, ice cream, and other treats from the refrigerator. They can ask for gum or candy in almost every store they enter. If the refrigerator is empty, there always is more at the grocery store. For twenty-two-month-olds the possibilities are mind-boggling and parents are bombarded with requests for special treats. When a parent tries to compromise with a child over this issue, the concepts of time and quantity are introduced: "First eat your meat and then you can have a cookie," or "One animal cracker, but not two." Such comments make a significant contribution to a toddler's understanding of time and quantity.

Bright twenty-two-month-olds like to pretend to read. They will sit with an open book and recite familiar pages from memory. They are interested in all the pictures in a book. A toddler needs ample time to explore picture books, turning the pages, and searching for

particular pictures before he is ready to use the pictures to create an imaginative story. Once the toddler has accumulated enough experience to realize that every book represents a new story, this period of exploration will not be as important as it had been.

Toddlers this age are very curious about their animate and inanimate environment: people, small animals, birds, objects, and places. Suitable stories can spark interest.

Your toddler may be attempting to carry a tune—at least the notes will vary in pitch—and there is a hint of timing in her songs. Even if you think you cannot sing (everyone can sing if free enough), sing all kinds of songs and nursery rhymes for and with your child.

Social Development

These toddlers are always on the go, and because they cannot yet judge what is safe and what is dangerous, you will also be on the move most of the time. You have no doubt discovered that you possess supersonic hearing; that you wear a diadem of seeing eyes as a crown on your head; and that you have developed a canny instinct for what is going on in all parts of your house or apartment. Athina Aston writes in *How to Play with Your Baby,* "You are in the kitchen and the baby is in the living room. Suddenly you realize that it is *too* quiet—his conversational burble has stopped. You rush into the room, but back off on finding all is well: he's picking up the newspaper, magazines, and the junk mail that you have left on the coffee table for his special attention. He is studying a brochure from Pan Am. He holds it with one hand, pulls with the other and rrrrrip—now he has two pieces. Pleased with himself, he sits down to give more serious attention to this project. Remember: he's learning. Suppress your 'no, no,' and leave him alone. Pretty soon, the one-man safari will break camp again, but the campsite is clearly marked."

Twenty-two-month-olds have acquired a broader facility in using language and can communicate a great variety of requests and observations, at least to the parents who are familiar with their toddler's mode of verbal expression. They are able to use new phrases to order adults around and they experiment with all kinds of commands. When the mother sings a song, the toddler may yell "Stop it!" to see what will happen or may command the driver to "Go!" when the light turns green.

Parents often are surprised by this barrage of commands and sometimes are unsure about how to react. No one likes to be ordered

about, but it should be remembered that a toddler's commands are not threatening. After all, the commander is only a small child whose orders are a tentative attempt to control other people. Of course, a parent can stop a toddler at any time by telling her to be quiet, but this response seems worse than the problem.

The commands of twenty-two-month-olds are not of equal importance. Some are harmless and even amusing. Others represent a significant step forward by the toddler. When a toddler says "Open" or "Help me" instead of breaking a toy in frustration, progress most certainly has been made. Of course, it would be nicer for the parents if their child said "open, please" instead of shouting an order, but progress does not come all at once or smoothly—for children or their parents.

Another command that signals advancement is the word *look,* when a toddler asks the parents to admire his efforts. The child is seeking adult approval, which is good within limits. It would be unfortunate if the child felt everything had to be approved and praised by the parents, or if the parents felt that they had to make a big fuss over every little thing their child did. Extravagant praise is really a disservice to young children because it tends to make them overly dependent upon adult approval. It is important for children to develop confidence in their own judgment. Actually excessive praise is not even effective; children eventually detect the insincerity and become disillusioned.

At the worst, toddlers are using their parents as resources when they order them about. Of course, there are times when parents are unable to serve as resources. The child may ask a parent to play with her whenever the parent tries to read, watch television, write, or talk on the phone. Such activities seem senseless to toddlers because from their viewpoint the parent could spend her or his time better by playing. In general, very young children have difficulty understanding that there is a limit to the time a parent can devote to play.

If the parent reads a story to the toddler, the child wants it repeated. If the parent plays

hide-and-seek, the toddler does not want to stop. The child keeps commanding *more* and the parent tries to communicate, "Wait a minute, there is a limit." Of course, very young children cannot understand the responsibilities a mother and father face, but it is essential for parents to tell their child that a limit has been reached: "No more stories right now," "I'm tired of playing," or "I want to read the newspaper right now."

Compromising

Ideally, parents should be able to demonstrate the nature of compromise to their toddlers. When a story is read a second time, the parent and toddler are following the wishes of the child. When the parent reads the newspaper instead, they are following the parent's wishes. There are no formulas for compromise; it is a matter of negotiation. Each situation is different, of course.

Origins of Social Reactions

Caroline Pratt, founder of the City and Country School in New York City and creator of the unit building blocks, in her now out-of-print but lovely book *I Learn from Children,* wrote the following about the origins of social reactions: "One can almost predict, from the impact of a baby's first cry, whether his social relations are to be happy ones. How his mother receives his first vocal demand is a reasonably clear omen of his future. If he is unwanted, or wanted for the wrong reasons, he is already off to a bad start, and his way will be a hard one. If his mother loves him, if she offers him the simple respect which one human being owes to another human being however small and helpless, he is a lucky child. For him the world will have a friendly face, because the one on whom he first depended has tried to understand him. A good mother need not be gifted, or beautiful, or even very clever; she is a good mother if she offers her child understanding. But no child has gone far who has merely come to terms with his mother; there are many other relationships with which he must deal, and the good mother helps him by setting him gradually free among his equals."

Sibling Rivalry

The late Haim G. Ginott, Ph.D., author of *Between Parent and Child,* warned that parents are naive to believe that it is possible for children in a family to escape feelings of jealousy, no matter how loving the family.

"Jealousy, envy and rivalry will inevitably be there," Dr. Ginott wrote. "To fail to anticipate them, or to be shocked at their appearance, is an ignorance that is far from bliss."

Being loved completely by his or her parents is every child's dream and desire and the need to share that love is a difficult and fearful thing. Jealousy is bound to be present and it can assume many guises, from the toddler who smilingly loves the baby so fiercely that the mother has to caution, "Don't love the baby so hard, dear," to the child who develops eating or sleeping problems and thus wins some more of the attention for which she

is competing with the baby. What becomes important is to recognize the existence of jealousy in whatever form it takes and to work with the older sibling to bring it into the open and help the child deal with it there. It is interesting to note that jealousy and rivalry will be greatly increased if the children are born less than three years apart.

Of course, a twenty-two-month-old will be upset by the arrival of a new baby brother or sister. The toddler's jeálousy will be manifested by his reverting to more infantile behaviors (whining, crying easily, clinging to the parents, losing daytime bladder control, and so on). Sometimes the toddler's speech becomes more babyish, even "going under cover" for a while. All such behaviors signify that the toddler *feels* left out—unloved, unwanted, and no longer important to the parents—and may have decided that the only way to get attention is to act like a baby again.

The mother especially and the father need to show in acts and words that their toddler is loved by them as much as heretofore. Toddlers may also manifest their jealousy by trying to hurt the unwanted newcomer. When this happens, parents need to restrain their child from harming the baby.

Cooperation

Twenty-two-month-olds will come when called. They are affectionate and will reach for favorite people. They freely express their love for their parents. It is delightful to be hugged and kissed by an exuberant, responsive child.

Even though your toddler does not yet understand the principle of cooperation, she will try to cooperate a good part of the time. Upon your suggestion, your child will pick up and put away toys and other familiar objects. Your "mother's helper" will eagerly help you with some of your simpler household chores.

Twenty-two-month-olds are discovering that words can make the family pay attention to them, praise them, and do things for them. Their feelings are hurt easily by criticism or rejection.

The Push Toward Autonomy

The central theme of development during toddlerhood, as Dr. Erikson has vividly pointed out, is autonomy—becoming aware of oneself as a person among other people and wanting to do things for oneself. The toddler demonstrates his beginning autonomy and drive for more of it in the mastery of his own body (walking, climbing, jumping, and controlling the sphincter muscles); in the mastery of objects (typically the toddler wants to push the stroller instead of riding in it, wants to carry outsized things from place to place and back again, wants to put on and remove his own clothing even though he is not very adept at doing so); and in social relationships (the toddler learns language and begins to refuse parental commands and requests, as well as offers of help).

The twenty-two-month-old's push toward autonomy is by no means absolute and continuous. Throughout toddlerhood, the child vacillates between dependence and independence—a pattern that will persist in various guises well into adolescence.

The Importance of Self-Esteem

In *Childhood and Adolescence: A Psychology of the Growing Person,* Doctors Stone and Church point out that "it is only when the child esteems himself that he can esteem other people. . . . Lest it be feared that the child's self-esteem grow beyond all bounds or that he become too trustful of others . . . parental restraints and demands do exist . . . growing up always entails its share of frustrations . . . [and some] negative experiences will not damage him. It is only in a climate of constant criticism, reproach, and taboo that the child's experience of himself becomes fixed in a disagreeable self-consciousness . . . (that will be) quite damaging to his future development."

Nearing the Final Phase of Rapprochement

Male toddlers (if given a reasonable chance) show a tendency to separate themselves from the mother more easily than girls and to enjoy their role in their widening world. Girl toddlers appear to become more involved with mother in her presence. They demand greater closeness and seem more persistently entangled in the ambivalent aspects of the relationship. (Even at twenty-two-months, according to psychoanalytic thought, the narcissistic hurt experienced by girls because of not having a penis is almost without exception blamed on the mother.)

Many twenty-two-month-old girls become increasingly demanding and imperious. They demand whatever they want and become angry if they cannot get it. They go to the mother for help in any difficulty rather than attempting to find their own solutions. They may become more stubborn and negativistic at this time. Many girls this age may object to wearing the kind of clothes that the mother picks out for them and even have tantrums about having their hair combed. At the same time—maddeningly—they cling ever closer to the mother.

Short Attention Span

Twenty-two-month-olds still are highly distractible because of their brief attention spans and wide-ranging interests. For these reasons, it often is more expedient for parents to circumvent the *I want's* and *no's* by either offering a new diversion or changing the subject. Parents do not have to resolve *every* issue with their toddler. Diverting the child leaves his as yet unstable self intact, which would not be possible by yielding.

Possessiveness

The toddler's propensity to command is a kind of possessiveness. The toddler considers parents her own private property and the sense of ownership includes places and favorite objects. The twenty-two-month-old may regard the sofa or a particular chair as her private domain. People sitting in these places without the consent of the "owner" are trespassers.

During this age possessiveness often increases and toddlers become increasingly vocal in defending their property rights. This selfishness is upsetting to parents, but it does indicate that the child is developing a clearer picture of himself as a separate person with individual rights. Although possessiveness means that the toddler will not share, it does allow him to express feelings of love and concern, which is most evident in the child's attachment to favorite objects. During this time, a toddler can be observed taking care of things as if they were genuine friends. The toddler may place his stuffed dog in a wagon and give it a ride, may talk to the toy as it sits on the edge of the bathtub, or insist that it sit next to him at the table. Of course, toddlers express love for their parents and other favorite people, too, but right now one of their primary ways to extend their feelings of affection is through their attachment to possessions.

Dealing with Fears

The toddler who is afraid of a dog can play with a stuffed dog or listen to a story about dogs. When a feared object is also exciting, parents can help their child find experiences in which the excitement outweighs the fearfulness. Walking a dog on a leash may be exciting to the child who is, afraid of some dogs. Going down a slide may be an exciting substitute for the child who is afraid of swinging. The toddler who is afraid of having her hair washed may love to play in the spray from the outside sprinkler.

A parent's guidance in real and pretend experiences can help the toddler to overcome fears, and to distinguish between real and imagined danger.

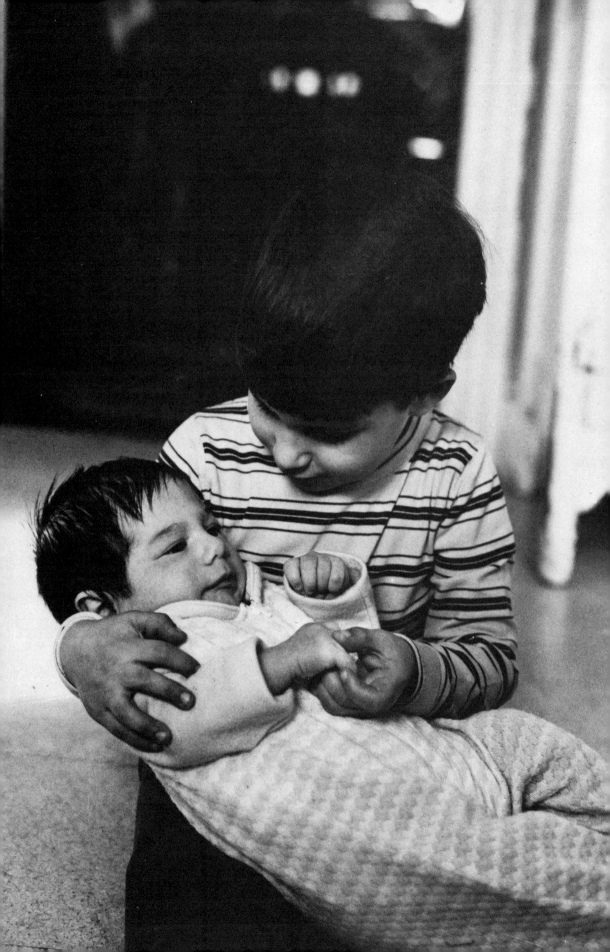

Love—Attention—Acceptance

Every child needs a healthy emotional unfolding, denial of which can lead to a troubled personality. Basic needs include love (interaction with affectionate human beings), attention (stability and trust), and acceptance (security). Unfortunately, many parents are not emotionally equipped to meet these requirements. Too often, middle-class parents substitute clean rooms, pretty clothes, toys, candy, birthday parties, and so on. Some children are tough and they survive poverty, cold, war, and deprivation. However, most infants and toddlers, if their needs are not met to some degree, may not survive, or if they do, may grow up twisted.

As Thomas C. McGinnis and John U. Ayres write in *Open Family Living: A New Approach for Enriching Your Life Together:* "Love is the child's emotional food fully as necessary for the development of his capacity to *feel* as physical food for development of the body. A child must not only be loved but must feel that he is being loved. Love must be physical as well as mental. Touching, hugging, roughhousing are some attributes that make love tangible. The attention he gets is the way the fact of love comes across to him. If attention is not freely given, he may feel more abandoned than loved."

Acceptance means that the parents not only love their child; they accept who and what he or she *is*. Many parents claim that they love their children, yet they do not fully accept them. They wish their girls were boys, for example. If parents wish their children different from what they are, the children sense this and get the feeling that they are not acceptable. All children require stability and a feeling of security if they are to build what Dr. Erikson calls a sense of "basic trust."

Self-Help Routines

They have made a little but not too much headway in their self-feeding abilities. There still is spilling of foods and sometimes spilling of liquids.

As twenty-two-month-olds gain skills with their hands, they want to do more things for themselves, especially those things that seem important to them. As every parent knows, it is hard for a child to learn to put on shoes (socks are easier). So much effort is spent on this activity that many children interpret it as an essential skill to be mastered as soon as possible. It is not unusual to see twenty-two- to twenty-four-month-olds struggling to buckle a left-footed sandal on a right foot. Another example is the seat belt in the car. Toddlers believe that fastening a seat belt is a very important adult skill because every time they go for a ride the mother buckles the belt and insists that it stay buckled. Even though unable to operate the mechanism, the child is likely to spend much effort trying to accomplish this skill.

Given sufficient time to practice particular skills, toddlers this age may surprise parents with their dexterity. For example, a toddler who considers Band-Aids important will learn to peel off the backing and put one on without help. A toddler who receives raisins as a treat will learn to open the lid of a small raisin box in order to treat herself. A twenty-two-month-old may become terribly frustrated trying to master a skill, but will be even angrier if the parent intervenes and completes a job the child has started. Probably the best way to help the toddler is to make the problem easier; i.e., the parent can put a sock on halfway and let the child pull it on the rest of the way, or loosen the faucet just enough for the toddler to turn it on when she wants to wash her hands.

Sleeping

If your toddler is sleepy, if the surroundings are conducive to sleep, and if there are no anxieties to disturb him (and if there are, you can see your child through them), he will sleep. (Your twenty-two-month-old may be ready to give up the crib in favor of a standard-height single bed.)

While we are on the question of sleeping, we want to warn you to watch out for *Tris.* The

Environmental Defense Fund has advised the Consumer Safety Product Commission that Tris—which is in 20 percent of all children's sleepwear—is a flame retardant that is a cancer-causing agent one hundred times more powerful than the carcinogens in cigarette smoke. The chemical can be absorbed through the wearer's skin, as well as through the mouth, when the nightwear is sucked by babies and toddlers.

Dressing

Twenty-two-month-olds will cooperate in dressing. They can totally undress themselves at this time, with a little help with still difficult laces (the laces need to be loosened so shoes can be pulled off, for example). Many toddlers can put on their shoes, but cannot fasten buckles or tie the laces.

Your lovable, loving twenty-two-month-old is eager to please you, but is strongly motivated to please himself or herself first. If you are able to accept your child's "rough" and "smooth" behaviors, life will be somewhat easier for the whole family. Enjoy!

Play and Playthings

Twenty-two-month-olds continue to engage in parallel play—i.e., they play independently, but the activities they choose naturally bring them among other agemates. They play with toys that are like those the children around them are using, but each plays as he or she sees fit—without trying to influence the activity of the nearby children. Thus, they play next to rather than with their peers.

These toddlers enjoy repetition and will latch onto a favorite toy, book, or puzzle. It is impossible for an adult to know the element of newness a child can find in the same object or the same situation. What appears to be plain repetition to parents can be a new aspect of familiarity to the child.

Everything a child does when she plays is done with her whole being. When something works, the toddler smiles or laughs, claps her hands, and feels good all over. When

frustrated, the twenty-two-month-old scowls, cries, or shrieks. Learning and emotion, thought and feeling, are linked in the child's play and fantasies.

The toddler's own pace, desire, and interest count in play. Parents who show disappointment or disapproval by their tone of voice or gesture dampen the fun and freeness of play because the child's reaction—self-doubt, anger, or frustration—intrudes and puts a crimp in his pleasure. The complete takeover by an adult can sour a child's play.

Parents need to be aware that make-believe play may not occur immediately with new toys. The toddler who receives a new toy telephone or a set of play dishes will investigate the physical properties of the objects before pretending. A twenty-two-month-old will push the buttons and twist the dial of the telephone and remove and replace the lids on the pans, and may even pour water from one cup to another. If an object has interesting possibilities as a manipulative toy, it may be quite a while before it is used for pretend play.

Twenty-two-month-olds concentrate intently as they play. They will put blocks together in rows and may begin stacking them. They are able to place rings correctly on a spindle toy.

Toddlers love to dig in the ground or sand. Your toddler may now be dependable enough to go about your fenced-in backyard with minimal supervision from you.

Although twenty-two-month-olds are not ready to play with their agemates, they should not be with their mothers all the time. To encourage your toddler to be self-reliant, teach her to play alone for at least an hour both in the morning and the afternoon. If possible, your child should have a room of her own where it is possible to play safely and freely. If your child cannot have a whole room, provide a corner somewhere that is her special domain. The end of the afternoon, when most toddlers begin to tire, is a good time for some quiet play with parents or older brothers and sisters.

THE TWENTY-SECOND MONTH

Motor Development

Gross Motor

Experiments with various kinds of large-muscle activities involving thrust or acceleration

Jumps with both feet off the bottom step of a staircase

Goes quite easily from standing to running

Walks up stairs and down stairs, holding on, both feet on each step

Pedals small tricycle

Pushes and pulls large toys, boxes, etc., around floor

Can quickly alternate between sitting and standing

Can kick a large ball without falling

Fine Motor

Builds tower of 6 or more cubes

Is beginning to learn to put pop-it beads together

Can string several large beads

Language Acquisition

Can point to 5 body parts of self or doll

Asks for things at table by name

Enjoys listening to simple stories

Uses simple 1- or 2-word questions to secure the names of objects or persons in his or her environment

Combines 2 words in speech

In response to "Where is your mouth?" correctly indicates either by pointing to or opening mouth

Is interested in sound and repetition (as in book, *Ask Mr. Bear*)

Calls all women and men *mommies* and *daddies*

Echoes adults' words and inflections

Sensory Powers/ Learning

After being shown, can make a crude perpendicular stroke with crayon or pencil

Builds and knocks down, empties, pulls apart, feels, twists, and squeezes all available objects

Actively curious about animate and inanimate environment: people, small animals, birds, objects, places, etc.

Spontaneous scribbling

Draws vertical line after demonstration

Takes interest in the pictures in a book and can turn pages one at a time

May show some evidence of a budding sense of humor

Makes a train of cubes

Likes listening to nursery rhymes and repeating them with adult

Recognizes when picture in book is upside down

Growth Chart

Social Development

Can accept shared attention

Discovers that words can make family pay attention, offer praise, and do things for her or him

Does not yet understand the principle of cooperation, but is able to cooperate a good part of the time

Likes to watch grown-ups

Comes when called

Is now more responsive to and more demanding of the adult

Likes to help with housework

Personality/ Psychological

Increased possessiveness

Expresses love for parents and other favorite people

Feelings are hurt easily by criticism

Uses own name in reference to self

Uses words *me* and *you*

Is continually testing limits, as well as ability and right to have own say

Realizes that he or she is a separate person with a distinct name; that other people are like yet different from him or her

Self-Help Routines

Likes to unwrap candy and packages

Puts things back in place when asked

Holds cup or glass with one hand and sets down after drinking

Totally undresses self

Helps in dressing

Helps pull underpants up or down

Uses spoon well

Puts shoes on, but cannot do buckles or tie laces

Washes and dries hands with some help

When hungry asks for food, when thirsty asks for drink

Asks to go to the toilet

Play and Playthings

Plays contentedly if near adults

Puts blocks together in rows; may begin stacking them

Loves to dig in the ground or sand

Places rings on a spindle toy

Concentrates intently when playing with toys

Eager for new toys

Enjoys water play

May exhibit capacity for pretend play

Enjoys tossing a ball at a target and throwing pebbles in a ditch

Can imitate much of play activity of older sibling

Wraps up doll or stuffed animal and puts it to bed

Dear Parents:
Do not regard this chart as a rigid timetable.
Babies are unpredictable individuals. Some perform an activity earlier or (as much as six months) later than the chart indicates, while others skip a behavior altogether (i.e., walking without crawling).
Just use this information to anticipate and appreciate normal child development and behavior. No norms are absolutes.

THE TWENTY-THIRD MONTH
Busy, Busy, Busy

The major preoccupation of the twenty-three-month-old is ongoing exploration and producing and using speech. However, there are other activities and skills that were initiated during the eighteenth- to twenty-third-month period that become full-blown now, all of which push the toddler closer to psychological separation from the mother and toward ultimate independence.

Psychological Separation

As toddlers approach their second birthdays, they are aware that they have a "self" and that they are separate from the world of people and things. They now want to act like separate social beings. Becoming a separate psychological being is the most complicated task a toddler has to face. During the two years starting from birth, the child establishes a very strong attachment to the mother. When dependence on her reaches a peak of satisfaction and begins to diminish, separation follows. The more enjoyable and secure the relationship with the mother has been, the easier the separation.

This is not the time for the mother to push independence by frustrating the toddler's continuing need for attachment. She would only create a yearning for far greater attachment that would extend the need beyond its normal duration. Dr. Akmakjian points out that children move to higher levels of needs only after earlier needs have been sufficiently met.

Any attempts at separation must come exclusively from the child and not the parents. Coming from you, they would be experienced as rejection; coming from the child, they are experienced as growth. The difference between the two is the difference between psychological health and illness.

Having convinced themselves that the mother would not disappear, twenty-three-month-olds show signs of being able to play alone and to feel secure enough to tolerate her absence for short periods. The secret is that the child is not really "alone," but feels the mother's emotional availability. Says Dr. Akmakjian, "The single most important feeling that a child can have at this time in a toddler's life is that the mother is emotionally available and that her availability can be counted on."

The Fear of Abandonment

As walking improves, the child begins to wander far away only to dash right back for emotional refueling. The toddler practices leaving you because he has a strong urge to increase the physical distance from you as part of separating psychologically from you. After this darting-away behavior eases off and the child no longer fears abandonment, a new phase begins—*rapprochement.* Your child

wants actively to be near you and have you share in his experiences.

Anxiety and Independence

The mixture of dependence anxiety—about being left by the mother—and independence—wanting to do everything her own way—can make the twenty-three-month-old hard to handle. The child adheres obsessively to routines and daily rituals. Before settling down to sleep, she will insist on a series of things in rigid order: a drink, a kissing routine, a book or story, a soft doll; then the door left open to a particular angle and a light outside. These rituals can be extended to an endless chain and become unmanageable.

Rituals spill over to other parts of the day. It has to be your toddler who brings in the paper from the door; it has to be a special bib tied in a special way before he will start to eat. However, these rituals can be redirected by you. Since your toddler enjoys helping you with household tasks, he can be recruited to put things away or help with setting the table.

Parting with a "Lovey"

As the toddler approaches her second birthday, most parents feel that the time has come for their growing up child to give up her security blanket, or some other "lovey." (Please note, nonetheless, that disaster can result if it is left behind on a family weekend outing!)

Some writers on child care suggest approaches to getting rid of a child's torn security blanket or worn stuffed toy. Actually, parents need not be concerned about this form of attachment unless their child shows any signs of excessive insecurity or uncertainty.

As toddlers extend their social horizons, they tend to let go of such props naturally and smoothly.

Gross-Motor Development

Twenty-three-month-olds set out to master activities associated with their maturing upright locomotion (a fancy word for walking). They walk sideways and backward. They run, but generally lack the ability to start efficiently and stop quickly. They go up and down stairs alone, but without alternating their feet. They can throw a ball into a basket. They try to imitate adults walking on their tiptoes. They can seat themselves at the dining table and lift and drink from a cup and then put the empty cup back on the table. Children this age can climb out of a crib. Therefore you may find it necessary to have your toddler give up the crib in favor of a standard-height single bed. Twenty-three-month-olds continue to like to lug, tug, push, pull, but with much greater coordination than at eighteen months.

Fine-Motor Development

With extra opportunities to explore and test gross- and fine-motor control through all kinds of activities, eye-hand motions become rapidly coordinated. Twenty-three-month-olds can pile up from three to six cubes, turn the pages of a book one at a time, fold a piece of paper, string large beads on laces that have extra-long tips, and so on. They can bend at the waist to pick something up from the floor without falling forward.

Muscle coordination is involved in all the explorations of twenty-three-month-olds. Whether scribbling with a crayon, balancing cubes, or zooming an airplane through the air, these toddlers are increasing their ability to coordinate a set of specific muscles to accomplish many different tasks. The motor skills that a toddler develops depend, of course, upon the nature of his interests and opportunities. Every new motor skill adds to the twenty-three-month-old's feeling of self-confidence and mastery.

Exercise for Toddlers

It seems inconceivable to parents that runabouts need any more exercise than that which comes naturally to them at this period. However, those of us who have adopted daily exercise, jogging, or swimming as part of our lives know that body control makes an enormous difference in the way we feel and in the conduct of our lives.

Starting early, when infants and toddlers regard daily exercise as a pleasurable part of their daily routines, makes great sense. Two physical therapists, Dr. Janine Levy of France and Suzy Prudden, daughter of Bonnie Prudden, America's foremost champion of physical fitness, have made it easy for parents to introduce exercise as an expansion of the daily routines of infants and toddlers. Their well-illustrated, clearly written books (which are included in our bibliography) show how building healthy and agile bodies can become an important part of a total learning experience, instilling self-confidence, stimulating imagination, and furthering pleasant interaction between parent and child. Dr. Levy points out "that the task of preparing and relaxing, correcting and reinforcing the child's control of movement can no longer be left to chance or instinct. . . . Nor can it be isolated from control of self (self-discipline) or exploration of all aspects of the environment. . . ." These physical therapists claim that education in movement (a fancy name for exercising) not only helps prevent deformities, but can correct posture and consolidate what has already been achieved. Very little equipment is needed. All the exercises are geared to different age levels from newborn to four years of age.

"If we had to select a single word to summarize the typical twenty-three-month-old, the word 'busy' would be a good choice. Whether practicing a new motor skill, investigating the potential of a box of crayons, constructing a block tower, or rearranging the shelves in the neighborhood supermarket, these toddlers are actively engaged in the task at hand. At times, the adults around them are delighted with this activity. They admire the scribbles, praise the block tower, and laugh at efforts to empty a grocery cart. At other times, these same adults disapprove of the explorations. Understandably, they scold their child when she crayons on the wall or knocks down the cans in the supermarket.

"Both the child and the parents are faced with a dilemma. The child wants to continue his explorations, but does not want to make the parents angry. The parents, on the other hand, want their child to be curious, but do not want him to be destructive or to make an unreasonable mess."

Marilyn Segal and Don Adcock, in *From One to Two Years,* write, "It is not an easy dilemma to solve. If parents allow their child to get into anything he wants, they will find it increasingly difficult to expose him to new experiences. If on the other hand they impose too many limits on their child's explorations he will be fearful of new experiences or else be defiant and reckless. Obviously, it is important for parents to strike a healthy balance, to find a way of imposing reasonable limits without destroying their child's most valuable asset—the spontaneous desire to learn."

Relations with Siblings

Twenty-three-month-olds try to establish a close relationship with their older siblings. They literally follow the older brother or sister around all day. They imitate many of his or her activities. When the older child decides to draw a picture, for instance, so does the toddler. Generally, however, both work independently.

If the age difference is more than three to six years, the mother often will turn the responsibility of supervising the toddler over to the older child. When the toddler fusses, the older child may try to amuse her by giving her a toy with which to play. But what the toddler wants is to play with the sibling's playthings. Inevitably conflicts ensue and take the form of teasing, yells for help, or tugs-of-war with shouts of "Mine" and "My paper." Despite such encounters, loyalty between siblings is strong. The toddler is willing to share cookies and even belongings to win the favor of the older one. These daily conflicts can develop into a pattern of aggression for the younger child, with attendant violence and even tantrums. Knowing how to handle this aggression is one of the more difficult child-rearing problems parents face.

The child of this age begins to play active social games with parents and siblings. He enjoys tickling games, making-silly-faces games, and touching and naming bodily parts.

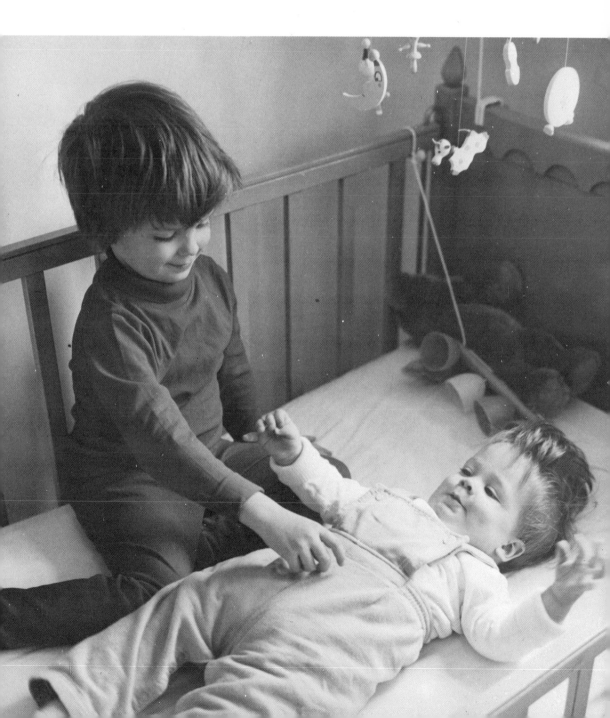

Self-Help Activities

Most twenty-three-month-olds like to help mother with the housework. They will sweep, mop the floor, and help make beds. They are not encouraged as yet to help with the cooking or washing dishes.

Twenty-three-month-olds anticipate routines and events. They are able to take off by themselves their shoes, stockings, coat, hat, mittens, and so on. They can turn on a water faucet, pick up toys and put them away (with adult encouragement), turn on the radio or television, turn a doorknob and open doors. They ask for food, drink, and the toilet. They especially like to unwrap and carry packages.

This age group fixates on a favorite object—a teddy bear, wool blanket, or a soft doll—and will initiate a number of "pretend" activities around such toys and objects. (The object can also be a live puppy.) The toddler will lay the object down for a nap and cover it with a blanket or seek a hat from mother for the doll's head. Twenty-three-month-olds love to dress up; they try on hats in front of a mirror and relish putting on mixed pairs of their parents' or brother's or sister's shoes.

To show their power of assertiveness, they develop the desire to choose their clothes and cereal at the supermarket. They are terribly frustrated by not being able to put on their socks or buckle their sandals. Parents learn to assuage these frustrations by putting socks on halfway and encouraging their child to pull up the balance.

Language Acquisition

Parents are astonished by how their twenty-three-month-old tries to put together a long sentence; for example, "Got Paul spoon me," which means that brother Paul had given the child a spoon. But most of their phrases are short; i.e., "I have baby," "Mommy, I can't," "Go outside," "Let's see eye."

Twenty-three-month-olds are still interested in picture books and request the names of objects with which they are not yet familiar. When they label an object, there is a slight questioning tone as if they expect confirmation of their label. They are most interested in people and animal names. They are as enamored of a toy telephone as the real instrument. They like to talk to relatives on the phone after mommy or daddy is through.

The Beginnings of Conscience

In a previous presentation of the building of conscience, we established that sixteen- to twenty-four-month-olds do not have a conscience in the proper sense of the word. They may know that certain behaviors are "right" or "wrong" because of parental approval or disapproval. When apprehended in some mischief, they may even feel ashamed. But they do not yet have the system of built-in controls that our culture calls a conscience. Whether the child feels ashamed of her "bad" behavior depends upon whether the mother is in the same room or not. At this age, the toddler feels ashamed only if the unacceptable behavior is discovered. The control, therefore, is external and dependent upon the parents.

Built-in control—self-control—shows up at the age of four or five and then becomes a part of a child's personality. At this later age, children are able to build their own inner controls into a conscience. If the parents have done a good job, they no longer need to prod their child. The child's conscience is now a schema, a moral code, which the child uses to evaluate all the social behaviors of himself and others.

Dr. Dodson points out that "the main function of a conscience is to prevent anti-social behavior—lying, stealing, etc.—not merely to make a child feel guilty after he has done something wrong." It will take all of the first five years for a child to internalize the requirements of social conformity. Do not rush your twenty-three-month-old!

Achievements of the Twenty-three-month-old

"Although the zest for exploration does not diminish as the toddler approaches two years of age, there is a change in focus. Kitchen cabinets, dresser drawers, the dog's dish, and the roll of toilet paper are beginning to lose their appeal. The toddler is ready to explore new horizons and is the first to agree to a walk to the store or an excursion in the car. On these outings, the child notices all kinds of things that escaped her attention earlier: things high up or far away, things that are tiny and intricate, things that are broken, or things that have changed a little. Your toddler may be the first to point out that the boy down the street is missing a tooth or the mailman has shaved off his moustache.

"Out-of-doors is a favorite place for the twenty-three-month-old. A backyard or corner lot is full of all kinds of interesting things: plants to tear up and taste, pebbles to toss, dirt to dig, a lawn mower to investigate, rocks to climb on, and puddles of water to splash in. The toddler who lives in a house or apartment with easy access to the out-of-doors may spend a great deal of time going in and out the door. Parents may feel that their child either cannot decide where he wants to be or else is just trying to be difficult. It is more likely that the child is contrasting the two environments and enjoys making a choice.

As Marilyn Segal and Don Adcock write, "A trip in the car that made him restless a few months ago is now a coveted activity. There are so many things to notice and point out. Things that he learned to identify at a standstill, he now identifies in motion. Some children point out everything that looks familiar: a snowman, a dog, a gas pump, a mail box. Other children select one thing that interests them and search for it everywhere. One youngster learned to identify McDonald's restaurants and would shout out excitedly whenever she spotted the sign. Another youngster learned to identify cement mixers, which he called *putty-putty.* He announced each *putty-putty* that went by and insisted that everyone else in the car take note of his find.

"The youngster's interest in pointing out faraway things as he goes on a drive is paralleled by a new interest in very tiny things. It is an age when a child is fascinated by bugs. Usually he learns the name of one particular bug and applies it to every bug he sees. Several children that we visited called every bug a fly. Other children may use the word *bee, ant, mosquito,* or *creepy* to designate the category of bugs. The child's reaction to this *ant, bee, fly,* or *creepy* may range from sheer delight to absolute terror, depending upon both his own first experiences and his parents' reactions to bugs. Once he has decided that a bug is either safe or dangerous, he is not apt to pay attention to his parents' attempts to discriminate between good bugs and bad bugs. If he has seen his father stamp disgustedly on a palmetto bug, he is not going to be soothed by his mother's assurances that the bug on his wagon is only a harmless dragonfly. On the other hand, if he and his mother have had fun chasing butterflies, he may not pay attention when his mother warns him that wasps aren't good things to chase.

"As the child points out cement mixers, ice-cream stands, McDonald's signs, or *creepies,* she is showing an ability to develop and extend a category. In other words, the child has developed a category of things in her mind and has determined the attributes that make something fall in that category. A large noisy truck with a back portion that spins is a *putty-putty;* a little thing that creeps or flies is a *creepy.* The more *putty-putties* or *creepies* the child finds, the more opportunities she has to solidify and extend her category. After a while she begins to subdivide her categories—perhaps she discovers that there are crawling bugs and flying bugs, or she develops broad categories that combine several smaller categories."

Exploring a New House

"One of the first broad categories that most youngsters form in their minds is the category *house.* They recognize that houses are different, but that there are certain things that belong in any house. Exploring a new house involves looking for all the things that belong in the category *house*. The child may search for a refrigerator, bathtub, wastepaper basket, television set, and doorbell. If he is told that there is no television set, he looks very confused. In the child's scheme, a television set goes with the house.

"As the child explores a new environment her interest may shift from taking a general inventory to checking out small details. She may hunt dials, keyholes, telephones or light switches. She may become particularly concerned about things that are broken or parts that are missing.

"A twenty-two-month-old boy we were observing was visiting his sister at nursery school. He picked up a set of earphones that plugged into a listening station. He was about to put them up to his ear when he noticed a disconnected wire. He turned to his mother and asked, 'Telephone broken?' A little later he picked up a balloon with some slight defects in the rubber. He put his finger on one of the spots and said, 'Measles, mommy?' "

Mental Schemata—Matching and Interpreting Pictures

"The visual inspection of detail that characterizes so many of the twenty-three-month-old's explorations makes books especially attractive. Now toddlers will sit by themselves for several minutes at a time thumbing through the pages of a book. When a particular picture appeals to them, they will point to it with one finger and may even give it a name. When they come to a picture that they do not recognize, they may try to translate it into something familiar. For instance, a city child reading a book about farm animals may come to a picture of a cow and call it dog, in a questioning voice. This gives the parent an opportunity to say, 'That is a cow—it goes *moo*. Let's find a picture of a dog.'

"The toddler's ability to interpret pictures and to recognize pictures of real objects is an example of her increasing ability to utilize symbols to extend her immediate experiences. As you watch your child thumb through a book, you see her associating pictures with past experiences while storing up images for future reference. In other words, pictures help a child extend herself in time as well as in space. For instance, the child may match the picture of a bridge with the bridge crossed on the way to grandma's house last week.

"It is not surprising that the child who is interested in pictures and in words is also interested in finding lost objects. A twenty-three-month-old may stuff a lollypop in the mother's purse. Several hours later the child will rummage through the purse until he finds it. Or the toddler might leave his teddy bear in an out-of-the-way spot before going to bed and hunt it up in the morning. In either case, the child has an image or representation of the object in mind; i.e., the toddler is able to remember this object without actually seeing it or holding it in his hands.

"Although the twenty-three-month-old is capable of this kind of mental imagery, the toddler has certainly not lost interest in manipulating real objects. Twenty-three-month-olds are seldom seen without something or other in their hands and they continue to search out ways of pulling things apart, rearranging things, and putting them back together. They are getting much better at aligning puzzle pieces and can probably fit several different shapes into a shape-sorting box or put together a simple inset puzzle."

"Messing Around"

"Although the child may enjoy playing with toys some of the time he is probably more interested in exploring some novel kinds of materials. He is fascinated by materials that stick to his fingers or adhere to other things. He enjoys activities like finger painting with shaving creme, dusting the furniture with talcum powder, buffing the floor with shoe polish, or painting himself with make-up. The greater the mess from the parent's point of view, the happier the child seems. This is an age when crayons and fountain pens are particularly intriguing. The child is delighted by the fact that the crayons make a mark. At first he may be satisfied with marking up a paper or a notebook but pretty soon he extends his explorations. He crayons the table, the kitchen floor, the wall paper, the back of his hand, or perhaps his mother's address book. He may turn his crayoning into a hidden object game and cover up a page in a book until the writing disappears."

Constructive Activities

"Twenty-three-month-olds are interested in stacking some things in high piles and arranging others in rows. They learn how to pack sand in a container and to make a row of mud pies. They experiment in their scribbling, adding crude circles to their linear markings. Parents can help their child turn mess-making into a creative activity by providing opportunities for 'controlled' experimentation. Teaching a child how to construct a simple tunnel or enclosure increases the fun of block play. A tub of soapy water and a washboard, a ball of dough and a rolling pin, a paintbrush and a bucket of water can provide the opportunity for making a mess within limits."

Body Movement

"Another kind of experimentation that plays a dominant role at this age involves body movement. Twenty-three-month-olds love to jump, run, throw, climb, wheel themselves

around on the playground or in the backyard. They experiment with various kinds of large-muscle activities involving thrust or acceleration. They jump with two feet off the bottom step of the staircase or go from standing to running. They ask for a push on the swing and delight at going up in the air. They get very involved in a variety of throwing games, such as tossing a ball at a target or throwing pebbles in a ditch. They make a toy airplane fly through the air or zoom a truck across the room. When just a little younger, the child held the airplane while she made it fly and pushed the truck across the room."

Toilet Learning

"One skill of concern to the parents of twenty-one- to twenty-four-month-olds is toilet learning. As we stated in prior chapters, this control requires muscle coordination. At this age, many toddlers acquire the muscle control needed to learn toileting skills. If your child goes long periods without wetting or soiling his diapers, or if he goes to the bathroom at regular intervals, it is a good sign that he is physically ready for learning to use the toilet."

Children have a sort of built-in "self-starter" for growing and thrive in an atmosphere that supports and facilitates that growth. They do not require a "trainer." Parents can trust their children's capacity to grow in the right direction without their pushing or pulling. In fact, parental intrusion on their children's natural course of growth, in order to teach or demand of them things the parents deem important at the time, can only interfere with children's optimal development.

Thus parents who are content to wait for toilet learning until their child essentially is ready to "train" herself generally will have no problem with this developmental step. The child needs a model of what to do, the physiological capacity to control the muscles responsible for holding in or letting go purposefully, the cognitive capacity to recognize when she has to go, and the motivation to assume control of her own body functions.

When all these elements are present, children will learn fairly quickly to assume control of their own body functions. Until such a time, the parents are merely *training themselves* to catch their child at the right time. At the same time, they might be creating emotional roadblocks to their child's learning on his own when he is ready.

Enough is known now about how children develop to state with confidence that they do not need to be "trained."

"There are many parents who choose to train their child before she is two years old and other parents who do not even consider training a child until later. Actually there is no set age at which children should be toilet trained. The right time for a particular child depends upon the expectations of the parents and the characteristics of the child. Just as some children continue to put objects in their mouths for a longer time than others, some children take longer to toilet train. A child may want to use the toilet because it makes her feel more grown-up and independent. Another child may feel more independent if she goes to the bathroom in her diapers whenever and wherever she pleases.

"The most important thing for parents is to be as relaxed as possible about toilet learning. As with other self-help skills, the child has mixed feelings about this. This child wants help in learning a new skill, but does not want to feel forced. When parents are very strict or overly concerned about toilet learning, conflict inevitably develops.

"With relaxed parents, children learn that they can use the toilet without giving up their autonomy. Parents choose different methods of toilet learning. Some try to establish habits by putting children on the toilet at regular intervals. Others try to anticipate and rush the child to the toilet at the 'right time.' Most parents rely to some extent on reward and punishment. Probably the oldest and most effective technique is modeling. The child learns by watching the other members of the family use the toilet."

Twenty-three-month-olds are usually totally involved in toilet learning. Many are "trained" on a small toilette and now the parents have to transfer the function of elimination to the adult bowl. This opens up a new area of exploration and it is common for toddlers to play with the water (and sometimes the feces) in the bowl and to pull the handle. Despite their encounters with a less than calm parent over this type of exploration, it is too hard for toddlers to resist and they will sneak back every chance they get. On trips to the supermarkets or the playground, they often will insist on going to the bathroom.

Fascination with Water

Preoccupation with water is typical of this age level. Streams, irrigation ditches, and pools, for instance, are areas to walk into, as well as to throw sticks, stones, and twigs into, and then watch which ones float and which ones sink. Because children this age have no fears, they will walk into a pool or ocean over their heads. They require careful supervision.

Bathing is a popular time. Now bath play becomes filling up and emptying cups, funneling, washing a doll, and so on. Toddlers also are involved with making value judgments about the cleanliness of sand versus mud and other materials. Mud on the hands or clothing sometimes upsets toddlers (probably because some adult called it dirty) and they will

already have mentioned that pretending represents one way to approach the problem. The frightening experience can become exciting through make believe. Although the 21- to 24-month-old child is not sophisticated enough to translate many fears into imaginative experience, he can make a start with adult help. The child who is afraid of sirens may enjoy a story record about firemen or he may make siren noises while playing with a toy fire truck. Even the drain can become part of pretend play. The parent and child can talk to the soapsuds that have gone down the drain, saying *good-bye* to them and then asking if they are hot or cold or hungry. More water can be sent down the drain to warm the soapsuds, to cool them or to feed them.

"Supporting the child in real experiences and encouraging pretend experiences are both valuable ways to deal with fears. Both are needed to help a child distinguish between fantasy and reality, to distinguish between imaginative fears and fears based on real danger. The two-year-old child is just beginning this process. His imagination will continue to bloom and it will become increasingly difficult for him to recognize the imaginative part of his fears. Encouraging the child during the next few years to extend his make-believe play will help him learn the power and limitations of his imagination."[*]

seek to have their hands washed immediately. However, spilling food on their hands does not bother them.

Exploring the Outdoors

Twenty-three-month-olds love to pick flowers and pretend to smell them. However, they cannot make a judgment about ownership of the flowers, and could care less even with the scoldings. On the trip to the supermarket, they like to push the stroller rather than ride in it. At the market, they like to help mother by pushing the shopping cart. When they return from shopping, the children enjoy putting cans away in the cupboard.

Fears

"As the imagination of the 21- to 24-month-old child increases, so do his fears. We

Roots of Intelligence

Most students in upper elementary school, high school, and even college are challenged by the competition for high marks in academic achievement. Once they leave the campus, they find that in the real world grade achievements mean little; that creativity, drive, and self-confidence are what count.

Jerome Bruner, Ph.D., states that much of the problem in leading a child to learning how to learn is "to free him from the immediate control of environmental rewards and punishments." Any learning that starts in re-

[*]Segal, Marilyn, and Adcock, Don. *From One to Two Years.* Ft. Lauderdale, FL: Nova University, n.d.

sponse to parental (or teacher) approval or avoidance of failure can too readily develop a pattern in which children seek cues as to how to conform to what is expected of them. Such children often are overachievers in school, but tend to be lower in analytic ability and creativity. They develop rote memory and rely on giving back what is expected. They tend not to respond creatively to a new situation.

In autonomous thinking, the child becomes able to use success and failure not as a reward or punishment, but as information. Dr. Bruner concludes "that when the task becomes the child's own, rather than meeting the environmental demand, he becomes his own 'paymaster.'" Seeking to gain control over the environment, children can treat success as indicating that they are on the right track. This has the effect of freeing learning from the rigid demands of academicians and permitting children to play with ideas without fear of not succeeding. Here again is where the home can be a powerful positive influence.

The Emotional Health of Children

By the end of a child's first year and a half of life, the style of the mother-child relationship has been established. It is this pattern of dealing with each other that reveals either a healthy or an unhealthy relationship. A mother will be responsive to her baby's signals and will have learned to read them accurately or she will misinterpret or be insensitive to the needs of her baby, thereby causing a communication gap. When the latter pattern emerges, it is important that the community step in to help the mother understand her developing infant and, if necessary, to help her with the actual care of the child.

The emotional health of children is one of the biggest public health problems today. If one waits until the trouble is discovered in nursery school, at the age of three or thereabouts, often it is too late to repair the damage. Preventive measures are essential and these must be taken in the earliest years of life.

One reason that these preventive measures often are not taken is that professionals have failed to spread to parents the knowledge that they have acquired and to disseminate it in a way that helps parents interpret their child's behavior in terms of its appropriateness. Parents need to learn why their child acts in the way he does in order to accept the child as an individual. Parents need to be told, for example, that endless running, climbing, and exploring are appropriate behaviors at age two, but not at age six.

One way to disseminate child-rearing information is to provide places for parents to go when their child is in trouble or when advice is needed on a developmental or educational problem. The Joint Commission on the Mental Health of Children has proposed that the country be covered with child development councils attached to such community centers as housing developments, day-care facilities, and well-baby clinics. If this is done, parents will always have a place to turn to for adequate diagnostic treatment and competent care and social services for children with behavioral, social, physical, and/or emotional problems.

Separation and Divorce

It is reported that one in every two marriages today results in divorce. If separation or divorce occurs in a family, it is only natural for the child to react adversely because home and parents are the center of a child's world. A drastic change occurs in every separation or divorce and children feel that their security and love are being threatened.

Mary Hoover, in the *Responsive Parent,* indicates that the greatest threat for children is that they will be abandoned with no one to love and take care of them. Proper parental guidance during and after a divorce is vital if the children are to develop into normal, healthy adults.

Newly divorced parents mention the negative reactions their children experience following their divorce. According to Dr. J. Louise Despert, in her book *Children of Divorce,* these children have been reacting negatively for a long time, unnoticed by their troubled parents. In many instances, separation or divorce results in a healthier climate for all concerned.

If separation or divorce occurs early in the baby's life, the mother may be so emotionally upset that she may not be able to care for her infant adequately. Since all infants need love and physical attention, especially from the mother, the result can be a nervous, irritable baby who has difficulties sleeping and eating. The opposite problem also can occur. As the child gets a little older, the mother may transfer the love and affection she previously gave her husband to her child. She can become overprotective and impede her child's development.

The father-child relationship develops most strongly as the child approaches the age of four. A child of this age, especially a girl, may find separation or divorce (with the father leaving home) a very traumatic experience.

Because of the separation or divorce of the parents, a young child may falter in the acquisition of new motor and emotional achievements, resulting in bedwetting, temper tantrums, or other regressions. Two questions are raised in parents' minds: (1) How can I help my child through this? (2) What do I do if the regression persists? Dr. Despert puts it this way: "If a parent can understand that such regression is a child's way of expressing anxiety and grief he feels but is not able to verbalize, it will help him not to compound the problem by punishing the child for his babyish behavior and thereby increase his sense of alienation from the parent with whom he is living. Since the child is responding not only to a loss, but to a break in routine, he will usually regain the controls he has temporarily lost."

Parental Guidelines to Help Children Adjust to Divorce

"The most important thing a child needs to understand is that neither his mother nor his father has abandoned him—that though marriage is broken by divorce, parenthood isn't,"

explains Jack Pollack in an article entitled "Seven Mistakes Divorced Parents Make." He outlines mistakes parents make that hurt and confuse children. These ideas have been corroborated by most authorities on the subject:

1. Parents try to hide the fact that they have decided to divorce. They delay in telling their children. Since the children involved learn this eventually, it is easier if they are told as early as possible so that they can accept it gradually.

2. One of the major problems that results from separation or divorce is a child's feelings of guilt. A small child may have wished in anger that one parent go away. Four- and five-year-olds develop a strong tie to the parent of the opposite sex and often feel that they are competing with one parent for the affection of the other. In all these cases, the children believe that they are the cause of the divorce. The problem arises because the parents have not adequately talked with their children about the divorce.

3. Constant arguing in front of children can be more detrimental than the divorce itself. A child's sense of security is threatened by constant tension. An "emotional divorce" often precedes the legal one. It involves the destructive emotional home situation in which there is perpetual bickering or total silence.

4. Parents should try not to belittle the other parent to the children. "To refrain from criticism of the other parent is one of the hardest, yet most essential things divorced parents should do. It is vital to a child's healthy development to feel free to love and respect both parents," explains Mr. Pollack.

5. Avoid making children take sides because this can only confuse them. When they become older, they may develop feelings of personal guilt and resentment against the parent who attempted to seek their agreement.

6. Try not to upset the child's routine. Children need to maintain the continuity of their daily lives in order to have some sense of security. The custody arrangement of six months with each parent is generally not good for children.

7. Finally, a warning about visitation rights. Parents should avoid feuding and using the child as a pawn when it comes to visiting the other parent.

The Parent Who Abandons

What if a mother or father suddenly leaves the family and does not return? The remaining parent should be honest and truthful, even though it may require telling the child that the parent may not return. Although the child may be initially upset, honesty will pay off as he or she gets older.

The entire family unit experiences a separation or divorce and undergoes radical, unhappy changes. Understanding is the first step in the process of adjustment. Firstly, the children must understand and accept the events as objective reality and then be helped to face attendant problems. Secondly, the parents must learn how to respond appropriately to their children's new needs and anxieties. Thirdly, professional help is available and should be sought when needed.

The Conquest of Language

"As twenty-three-month-olds drift off to sleep, they carry on a continuous monologue, experimenting with different arrangements of words and phrases, and playing back bits and pieces of their day's experiences. This conquest of language is the child's major accomplishment in the second year of life. It gives children the power to communicate feelings, interests, and desires to other people. At the same time, children use language to extend their immediate experiences. They ask questions about the future and talk about things that happened at a different time and in a different place. As they play with the phrase 'ride-a-horse, ride-a-horse,' they remember how they galloped on a grandparent's knee while he or she chanted the nursery rhyme.

"Learning language is an essential skill, but it is important for parents to remember that children develop according to individual timetables. There are early and late talkers. A child between twenty-one and twenty-four months of age may be bright, alert, and an excellent problem solver, and yet not be talking. It will do little good to try to force a child to talk. It is better to encourage language development by talking with your child and by avoiding the mistake of anticipating his every need. Instead of pouring a glass of milk when your toddler shows you an empty glass, ask what he would like and give him ample opportunity to respond.

"When we analyze a child's early vocabulary, we can appreciate how much learning must take place before children master language. Each word or word combination that a child uses represents an underlying concept or category of experience. Children need to be able to make sense of their experiences. They accomplish this by sorting these experiences into categories. Infants, for example, categorize the things that go into their mouths: things to eat, things to suck on, things to spit out. Or they categorize others into people they know and people they do not know. Over time, these categories become refined. Things to eat, for example, may be divided into stuff to chew and stuff to swallow. The category of familiar people is divided into mommy, daddy, and big sister or big brother.

"After a while, toddlers learn that things belonging in the same category share several characteristics and that one of the shared characteristics is their name. Dogs bark and sniff and have hair and are called *dogs.* Sometimes they associate a name with a big category, such as *food.* At other times, they associate a name with a small category, such as *cookie.* It takes a long time before a child can recognize that something can have two names or belong to two categories; i.e., that it can be both a cookie and food at the same time.

"By the time children are two years old, they have learned to associate names with most familiar objects. They have also learned through exploration that these objects have different attributes or properties; i.e., objects are heavy or light, rough or smooth, round or not round. The way they respond to an object is related to its attributes: balls are for throwing, rattles are to shake, Band-Aids are for sticking. Gradually they learn names for many attributes: *gooey, heavy, pretty, sticky, dirty.*

"As toddlers learn to name more objects and label their attributes, they become able to talk about things that are not within their reach or things that are not even present. The ability to talk about things that are not within reach makes the out-of-doors particularly appealing for twenty-one- to twenty-four-month-olds. They love to go for a ride in the car and to point out things they spot along the way. They also become interested in the way to get from one place to another and recognize landmarks on the way to a familiar place. They may recognize the turn to grandma's house or the place they stopped to buy ice cream on their last excursion."

Exploring Space

"In addition to this new interest in exploring the out-of-doors, these toddlers continue their explorations of immediate space. They are especially interested in what spaces they can get themselves into. They might try to squeeze under the coffee table, behind the sofa, or inside a suitcase or carton. Twenty-three-month-olds are interested in what it feels like to be way up high. They will want to climb on the highest table or to be lifted up to the ceiling by daddy.

"At the same time, explorations of objects are going apace. Twenty-three-month-olds build and knock down, empty, pull apart, feel, twist, and squeeze. In the course of these explorations, they begin to recognize that objects have quantitative attributes; i.e., that there is one object or many objects; that they are big or small, empty or full, heavy or light. When given a plate of cookies, they may begin to say numbers. They are not really counting the cookies, of course, but are associating number words with having more than one.

"Another attribute of objects that fascinates children at this age is movement. They dis-cover that things such as goldfish and cats and bugs *move by themselves;* that cars, television sets, and washing machines move by themselves *once they are started;* and that such items as wagons and baby carriages move *only when pushed.* The early experiences that children have watching things move and making things move help them understand the difference between animate and inanimate things.

"This ability to use language to elaborate imaginative play sometimes has its drawbacks. One little boy, Mark, was playing with a toy panda bear. As he fed his panda an imaginary biscuit, he began a long line of chatter. 'Eat panda—Eat, all gone—Don't bite—No, naughty—Don't bite—He bited—He bad panda.' At this point, Mark held one finger up in the air and ran crying to his mother. The two-year-old's tendency to elaborate his fantasies with words can cause him to imagine fearful experiences. Sometimes, he frightens himself with his own imaginings."

Encouraging Speech in Toddlers

Parents are the models for their child's speech. It is essential to keep this in mind in all interactions with one's child, especially during the period when language is developing at a rapid pace.

There are some basic rules when speaking to twenty-three-month-olds (also younger and older toddlers). Use simple, clear, slow speech. Talk about activities that you and your child do together, not only while actually engaged in them, but beforehand and afterward as well. This will help develop your child's concepts of time—past, present, and future. Give your toddler every chance to talk. Listen to what your child says and make her feel that it is truly important.

There are two types of talk that you can engage in when you are around your child: *self-talk* and *parallel talk.* Self-talk is that which you do by yourself. Talk out loud about what you are seeing, hearing, feeling, or doing even though it may seem commonplace to you. Children are excited by things that are

mundane to adults. Such an activity helps the child learn that there are words to describe all kinds of actions and feelings. Parallel talk differs from self-talk in that you speak about what is happening to your child rather than to yourself. Describe what your child is doing, seeing, or feeling. This will give your toddler a repertoire of words to use about himself.

Listening is a skill that is as important to language acquisition as talking. Give your child ample opportunity to practice it. There are several activities that may help. Call your child's attention to sounds both inside and outside the house and play games that require her to guess the sounds that she has heard. Let your child listen to people and talk on the telephone. Give her opportunities to show that she understands you by giving her simple directions to carry out. Listening games, such as ring-around-the-rosy or a verbal form of follow-the-leader can do much to develop listening skills, as do good children's records and special television programs for young children.

Enjoy this stage of your child's language development. Above all, do not demand perfection. This is a wonderful period for your toddler to have fun and to learn.

The ages from one to five are those in which the greatest intellectual, social, and emotional growth takes place. Most psychologists believe that the largest part of all character development is completed by the end of this stage. It is important for you to direct carefully the shaping experiences of your child throughout this vital period.

(The problems of delinquency and antisocial behavior in the adult often are linked with events that took place during the years of earliest childhood. Much research suggests that violence in our society has its roots in these early years. Most professionals feel that proper intervention at an early stage of development might prevent major troubles later on. Psychoanalysts are particularly concerned with the second year of life, in which the child is establishing verbal patterns that act as control elements in ordering an otherwise impulsive life.)

Character Formation

The relationship of early childhood experiences to cultural, social, and racial identity is another important factor in determining the direction that a child's character development will take. It is in the earliest years that the self-concept is first formed, and this is created by taking in both parental views and those of the immediate environment. Children respond not only to their parents' estimation of them, but also to the manner in which they are treated by the rest of society. Early in life children perceive group differences, and it is the way in which these are manifested that determines their view of themselves and their consequent emotional stability. Therefore, it behooves parents who wish to raise emotionally healthy children to teach them, through word and deed, self-respect and consideration for others.

Indoor Play

Indoor play takes the form of pushing along the floor, toy buses, trucks, and long floor trains. Twenty-three-month-olds enjoy piling up picture or solid nursery school blocks and then knocking them down. They can nest four or five round or square containers and fit several different shapes into a shape-sorting box. They will mess happily with clay or Play-Doh. They like to fill and empty, put in and pull out, tear apart and fit together; to taste, smell, touch, see, and rub all kinds of textured objects.

This age level likes putting together simple three-to five-piece puzzles. When they are unable to fit them into place the first time around, they resort to pushing them into the board. When they conquer this task, they rush to show their mother their success and enjoy deep satisfaction. Favorite toys are the replicas of what they see outdoors in the community—trucks, buses, garages, planes, fire engines, and so forth—anything that moves and makes noise. They play with dolls, but find a live puppy more responsive. Music and dancing are still favored, especially if

parents and siblings can be recruited for a rhythm band and dance program. Twenty-three-month-olds will climb up on a couch near a window to watch and point out the movement and flight of birds.

Ego and Self-Esteem

If you are like most parents, you have high hopes for your child's future. You want him to have inner confidence, a sense of purpose and involvement, meaningful relations with others, success at school and in his life's work. If your child has a high degree of self-esteem, a feeling of self-worth, he has it made. With this self-respect a child does not have to waste time and energy impressing others.

Says Dorothy Briggs, in her fine book *Your Child's Self-Esteem* (Garden City, NY: Doubleday, 1975): "Your child's judgment of himself influences the kinds of friends he chooses, how he gets along with others, the kind of person he marries, and how productive he will be. It affects his creativity, integrity, stability, and even whether he will be a leader or a follower."

Children who have a sense of personal worth feel free to explore, to test, and to attempt more than they have heretofore. The more children succeed, the more they build self-confidence. To put it another way, the better children feel about themselves, the people close to them, and their world, the more they build a healthy personality.

Social Acceptance Builds Self-Image

A child's ego power is initiated and encouraged by positive, responsive interpersonal relations between her parents and siblings in the first years of life. It continues to grow as the child is accepted and needed by members of the family and others. Infants respond with well-being and enthusiasm to their parents' approval of their various physical, play, and learning accomplishments. As infants enter toddlerdom, they increase the number of people they must relate to and from whom they require response.

In the beginning a child's sense of worth depends upon feeling loved and accepted by his parents and friends. He must know that he matters, that he feels competent to handle himself and his environment. He needs to feel that he has something to offer others.

Praise, an Important Ego-Builder

Praise is an important tool in building ego and self-confidence. A child receiving praise for her behavior will continue the behavior that brings parental love. Sometimes criticism is necessary, but it takes on greater impact if it is mixed with praise. "You can certainly throw a ball pretty well, but playing in the house may break a window." "Great! You are really learning how to dress yourself. Don't you think it might be more comfortable if you twisted your sock around so that the toes go into *this* part?"

Play and Ego

Play frees children to attain their potentialities at their own rate of progression. Children feel powerful each time they handle a situation well, whether at play or in a concrete life experience. They feel effective each time they come to apprehend the many forces acting upon them. They want to come to grips with the world, not merely exist in it.

The most uninhibited period in the lives of children during which they can build ego spans the years from one and a half to three. Play affords the greatest means of building self-image at this time. The child has to be the center of every play situation. At one-and-a-half years he wants to play the mother, father, or the baby. He is not yet ready to allow dolls or play people to be the characters. He has to embody each role himself. Sometime during the third year of life he begins to get a conception of himself as a person. Parents can be sure of this when their two-year-old calls himself by his name or says "me" or "I." The two-year-old is completely egotistic. He is unable to take the point of view of others. He

does everything in his play schemata to build his self-image and to prove and show off his own powers. One may well shudder to think what would happen if there were no time for this basic egocentric play. We are convinced that if children did not have this period of ego play, drive and will power would be adversely affected in their adulthood.

Jean Piaget points out that play allows a child to enjoy a "private reality of his own." It is the function of play to protect each child's egocentric world against forced accommodation to everyday reality. Parents who understand the ego needs of their children also know that their emotional health can be promoted through play. They provide their children with suitable and sufficient play materials, adequate play space, full opportunity for play, and the approbation and backing on which all human beings thrive. Some play materials are better for a child's ego building than others. Unstructured playthings lend themselves to the full expression of a child's imagination. Invariably they are more easily manipulated. They require no blueprints and little or no parent participation. Above all, they tend to strengthen a child's need to feel capable. ("I built a big house with my blocks." "This is my dollhouse. I made the curtains myself.")

Parent and Child Activities to Build Ego and Self-Esteem

Start a collection of your child's drawings, birthday cards, and so on.

Make a lifesized poster by laying your child down on a roll of wrapping paper and tracing the outline of her body. Then have your child draw in hair, clothes, eyes, ears, nose, mouth, and fingernails. When the portrait is done, help her cut it out, and hang it up for everyone to see.

Make paper-bag masks. Help him cut out eyes. Color in details.

Make a picture map of the neighborhood or block. Show where your child lives, the supermarket she goes to, her play group headquarters, and so on.

Receiving mail—work it out for grandma to send mail and your toddler to receive it.

Make a family tree with old photographs.

Make a special vest. Decorate it with the family dog, goldfish, house, initials, street sign.

Have a favorite picture blown up to lifesize.

Make a time line. Find old photographs and hang them on a clothesline. Include the day your child was born, when he moved to this house, when he learned to pedal a bicycle.

Record her voice and play it back to your child.

Put a full-length mirror in his bedroom.

THE TWENTY-THIRD MONTH

Motor Development

Gross Motor

Can seat self at table

Can throw a ball into a basket

Walks up and down stairs alone, both feet on one step at a time, holding onto railing

Bends at waist to pick up something off floor without falling

Tries to stand on tiptoe imitatively

Runs fairly well

Throws object overhand instead of tossing

Usually runs when moving from one place to another; runs rather than walks

Squats on floor

Jumps in place

Pedals small tricycle

Climbs out of crib

Stands on walking board with both feet

Fine Motor

Can make a train of 3 or more cubes

Strings large beads together

A little more adept at joining pop-it beads together

Builds tower of 6 or more cubes

Language Acquisition

Speaking vocabulary of 20 clear words

Asks for food when hungry and water when thirsty

Uses 2-word sentences (subject and verb)

Enjoys hearing rhymes in *Mother Goose* book, etc.

Is substituting words for some physical acts

Knows 3 to 5 body parts

Understands more words than able to use

Has learned to form some sentences of 2 words, but still relies on gestures, facial expression, and total body movement, as well as grunts, squeals, and shrieks for communication

Answers "What is your name?" "What does the doggy say?" "What does the kitty say?"

Can name familiar objects: ball, car, chair, bed, baby, etc.

Increase in communicative behavior and interest in language

Discards jargon

Sensory Powers/ Learning

Correctly nests 4 or more small square boxes

Imitates simple actions

Likes to fill and empty, put in and pull out, tear apart and fit together; to taste, smell, touch, see, and rub all available objects

Draws crude pictures

Much better now at aligning jigsaw puzzle pieces

After demonstration, can make circular scribbles on a piece of paper with crayon or pencil

May sit and "read" picture books, turning pages for self

Imitates horizontal, vertical, and circular strokes crudely

Attention span is still short; will flit from one activity to another

Follows simple directions

Growth Chart

Social Development

Can accept shared attention

Likes to participate in household tasks; tries to dust, sweep, or mop; attempts a kitchen job that a parent or older sibling is doing

Has genuine interest in the mother-baby relationship

Likes to please others

Is still dependent on adult for all major needs

Personality/ Psychological

Is afraid of disapproval and rejection

Has established own characteristic ways of coping with separateness

Uses own name in reference to self

Is beginning to learn command "No" even when not accompanied by physical restraint

May fear the noise of trains, trucks, thunder, flushing of toilet, vacuum cleaner; also rain, wind, wild animals

Becomes frustrated easily

Recognizes own power to be effective and successful

Self-Help Routines

Likes to unwrap packages

Puts things back in place when asked

Inconsistently indicates need to go to the bathroom

Uses spoon and cup adroitly

Puts shoes on, but cannot tie laces or do buckles

Removes all simple garments

Washes and dries hands with some help

Eats table food, including chewy meat

Turns doorknobs and opens doors

Play and Playthings

Plays contentedly alone if near adults

Can build very simple structures with blocks

Can fit several different shapes into a shape-sorting box

Asks for a push on the swing and delights at going up in the air

Enjoys piling picture blocks and knocking them down

Messes happily with soft modeling clay or Play-Doh

Teddy bear or soft doll still a favored toy

Likes to take things apart and put them together; also to fit one object inside another

Stacks 5 rings on a peg toy in correct order

Dear Parents:
   Do not regard this chart as a rigid timetable.
   Babies are unpredictable individuals. Some perform an activity earlier or (as much as six months) later than the chart indicates, while others skip a behavior altogether (i.e., walking without crawling).
   Just use this information to anticipate and appreciate normal child development and behavior. No norms are absolutes.

THE TWENTY-FOURTH MONTH

"Walkee-Talkee"

Twenty-four-month-olds have many of the more obvious skills of adults. No longer are they helpless babes. In fact, they are independent, assertive individuals. Although they climb and run actively, there still are some gross-motor movements they cannot carry out—hopping, for one. Their eyes are as sharp as they ever will be. They can pick out small objects at a distance and can distinguish between small-print letters. Their hearing is remarkably keen—as adults discover when their toddlers repeat things they were not supposed to hear.

The speech of twenty-four-month-olds improves rapidly; new words appear almost day by day. They have a lot of difficulty controlling their feelings so they cry easily and frequently lose their tempers. Of course, there are great variations among toddlers in the ages at which they talk, become dry at night, give up having naps, manage to go to the toilet without parental assistance, and so forth.

Toddlerhood reaches a climax at the end of the twenty-fourth month of life. In her *Life and Ways of the Two-Year-Old,* Louise Woodcock has this to say about the twenty-four-month-old's style of action: "His impulses are to move and explore; to react to experience that he meets by some direct, overt behavior; to affect his environment by such changes as he can bring about in it. His attention span is short, his threshold of distractibility is low. His inhibitory apparatus is only slightly developed; he readily takes impulse to action from sights and sounds around him. His tempo is normally slow, and time as a measure, means nothing to him. His information is scanty and unorganized. His language is unelaborated and often inadequate to his earnest efforts at communication. He is immature in social awareness and his techniques are primitive to an extreme."

Generally speaking, by the time toddlers reach their second birthday, they have a good grasp of their immediate world. They have organized their experiences in a time frame as well as a space frame. They have developed a good idea of where things are located in and around the house and can anticipate routine events. These toddlers now have some ideas relating to the properties of things and have learned to use language to represent and extend these concepts. It is to be hoped they have learned to communicate with others to pretend in simple ways, to love and to receive love, and to recognize their own power to be effective and successful.

Gross-Motor Development

Twenty-four-month-olds are still highly geared to gross-motor activity. They run and romp, lug, tug, push, and pull, but with greater coordination than heretofore. They are able to climb out of their cribs. If you have not yet

done so, now is the time to get a standard-height single bed for your climber par excellence. Your child will also climb out of a bed, but will have less of a distance to fall. Every piece of furniture in your home remains a climbing challenge.

Toddlers this age can quickly alternate between sitting and standing. Since they are sturdy on their feet, twenty-four-month-olds are less likely to fall. They visually monitor their walking, watching the placement of their feet in order to be able to deal with obstacles in their paths by avoiding them. If you observe closely, you will find that your child's walking rhythm has stabilized and become even. These toddlers can walk approximately on line, another indication of increased locomotor control. They can walk sideward and backward about ten feet, and stand on a walking board with both feet. Twenty-four-month-olds enjoy walking on walls with one hand held. They even can walk a few steps on tiptoe.

Twenty-four-month-olds run, but generally lack the ability to start efficiently or to stop quickly. They can jump in place, but not for too long. They also can jump crudely with a two-foot takeoff. They go up and down stairs alone, holding onto the handrail, but still without alternating their feet. Now they can be trusted alone on stairs. They are much surer of their motor capabilities than they were just a few months ago. They try to balance themselves on either foot, but not yet with success. (They will not be able to balance on one foot for five seconds until they are about two and a half years old; for ten seconds in the beginning of their third year of life. From their third through fourth years they will be able to hop on one foot.)

Fine-Motor Development

Twenty-four-month-olds can turn the pages of a book one page at a time. Only last month they turned several pages at once. They manipulate more freely with one hand at this time and alternate from one hand to the other, although now they have fully developed right- or left-handedness. (Do not try to change your child's hand preference.) These toddlers have increased smoothness of coordination in their fine-motor movements. With more wrist action, many twenty-four-month-olds can unscrew lids. They are able to build a firm tower of six to eight cubes and can fold a piece of paper. They are adept at stringing large wood or plastic beads.

Language Acquisition

"The speech of toddlers is not a 'mechanical playback' of adult speech. From the beginning, they bring something of themselves to their language expression. To call their speech wholly imitative is incorrect because their articulation differs from that of adults. Also, very young children combine words in fresh and unique ways and they make up words. For example, they use 'foots' as the plural of 'foot' or use 'gooder' as the comparative of 'good.' Toddlers indicate that they fit their own language system into the one they were born into. Instead of criticizing early errors, parents should accept with joy evidences that their toddlers have been clever enough to figure out some of the principles that govern the language system they hear around them.

"Twenty-four-month-olds usually telescope their pronunciation. You will hear a beginning consonant, and often a final consonant is present, but medial consonants tend to be omitted. A squeaky-sounding voice is common. Bear in mind that these toddlers constantly repeat words or phrases they hear or say. Try never to grow impatient or bored with them or their utterances."

Two-Word Sentences

When toddlers start to use two words together, it indicates that underlying their ability to link two words is an understanding of some of the rules governing language. Of course, their beginning word combinations are completely different from those used by adults.

Martin Bax and Judy Bernal in *Your Child's First Five Years,* write "Of course, some of his earliest two- and three-word phrases are picked up parrot-fashion from the people around him: he may say 'Here you are' long before he is able to build up his own three-word sentences. . . . Here are some of the most common ways that children start using two words together: pointing and naming things may become extended—where he said 'car' he now says 'see car,' 'there car,' 'this car.' . . . Repetition or absence of things are often commented on: 'more biscuit,' 'all gone car.' He doesn't use 'and' yet, but may link two things by simply saying 'car truck.' He does not use subject/verb/object at this stage, but may use two of these: 'Mommy write.' "

Bilingualism

A child who succeeds in adapting to a bilingual environment performs the extraordinary feat of developing two entirely different language rule systems at the same time. Learning to speak two languages is not simply a quantitatively extreme form of input-categorizing diversity, it also is qualitatively different. An environment in which objects, events, and the symbolic rule systems for representing them have two entirely different codes that are not parallel is much more complex than a monolingual environment that has a multitude of elements within it.

It is one thing to say that there are many kinds of garments for covering the head; i.e., a cap, hat, hood, and so on. It is an altogether different proposition to confront a toddler with the reality that the same hat can be called a *hat* or *chapeau* (in French)—and that everything in the environment is subject to the same duality of labeling.

Of course, not all toddlers flourish equally well in a bilingual environment. However, enough of them can and do succeed in bilingual settings and learn their two languages with equal fluency to suggest that many babies in monolingual settings possess untapped language-learning resources.

Nursery Rhymes

Twenty-four-month-olds are fascinated by words and word play and continue to love nursery rhymes with their rhythm and repetition of sounds. They will repeat something until they feel they have mastered it. They enjoy the repetition in familiar nursery tales, such as "The Three Little Pigs" or "Chicken Little." *Ask Mr. Bear* is a delightful little book that pleases almost every toddler. They like to recognize what is coming next in a story and chant it with the parent. They also love sounds of all sorts, especially unusual or funny sounds. When you read books of sounds to your child, emphasize all the sounds and give your toddler a chance to repeat them with you and alone.

Reading Books

As in previous months, twenty-four-month-olds relish stories about the here-and-now of their everyday world: going to the market with mother, riding in a car or bus, playing in the park, going to a zoo, and so on. Animal stories are particularly popular at this age.

Reading to twenty-four-month-olds should be a two-way activity. They like to look at the pictures and touch them. They like to be asked to find things in the illustrations. Often they have favorite books that they will want read to them day after day. Parents know what happens if they try to change a phrase in a familiar story; their child will not let them get away with it, insisting upon all the proper words.

Check at your local public library for suitable books for your child. A book that appeals to one twenty-four-month-old may be too advanced or babyish for another toddler this age. It also is a good idea for your child to look through a picture book before you borrow or buy it.

Words That Express the Sense of Space

The expanding sense of space of twenty-four-month-olds is manifested by their use of

such words and phrases as *there, where, other side, outdoors,* and *up high.* The more complex notion of container and contained is reflected in the use of the words *in* and *out. In* is the most used space word at this age. *All gone* also is prominently used.

Language acquisition continues to gain momentum and dynamic interest in words is evident. As was the case heretofore, twenty-four-month-olds understand more words than they can yet speak. They have discarded jargon speech and now ask for things by a combination of words and gestures. They can name almost everything they have daily contact with in their homes or on walks (for example, ball, dolly, chair, bed, baby, teddy, car, and so on). They continue their exciting discovery that everything has a name. These toddlers tend to call all women *mommies* and all men *daddies.* Most have an expressive vocabulary of fifty or more words. Although they have learned to form some two- and even three-word phrases, twenty-four-month-olds still rely on facial expressions, gestures, and total body movement—as well as grunts, squeals, and shrieks—for communication.

Very young children echo the words and inflections of the adults around them. They like to talk to themselves and repeat words, name things, and try to suit words to actions. They understand and ask for *another* or *more* and can distinguish between *one* and *many.* They expertly point to and imitate the names for the hair, hands, feet, nose, eyes, mouth. They use the pronouns *me, you,* and sometimes *I,* but not always correctly.

Some twenty-four-month-olds are able to give their first and last names upon request. Most can answer such questions as "What does the doggy say?" "What does the kitty say?" "What does the birdie say?" They will respond, by pointing to the proper picture in a familiar book, to such requests as "Show me a dog." "Show me a man." "Show me a hat." "Show me the ball." They have come a long way linguistically.

Sensory Powers/Learning

Your toddler will benefit at this time from spending a short period with you each day on structured learning; i.e., education that is aimed at a specific result. Although this should be treated as a relaxed playtime and be wholly enjoyable, your child will benefit from activities that are planned to strengthen her sensory skills. Games should be stopped the moment your toddler appears tired or bored.

Teach Your Child to Listen

Being able to listen well and to hear accurately are essential to learning at all ages. There are several games that can help to sharpen listening ability. The materials you will need are a water glass with ice cubes in it, a book, and a hand bell.

1. Shake the glass with the ice and ask your toddler to listen to the sound the ice makes against the glass.
2. Open the book, then shut it with a bang, pointing out the distinctive sound it made.
3. Ring the bell while your child is paying close attention.

Then ask your toddler to close his eyes and have his back to you while you slowly repeat the three operations listed above. Ask your child to identify the source of each sound, one at a time. If your child guesses incorrectly, repeat the game, again showing what made each sound. If your child guesses correctly, praise him and repeat the sounds to reinforce the fact that your child was right. You can change places with your child and have him make the sounds while you take a turn "guessing." Your child will enjoy this.

After your toddler is able to correctly identify the three sounds, you can add other sounds, one at a time. Set up a screen by draping a blanket over a chair. Behind the screen and onto a hardwood or linoleum floor drop a ball, a safety pin, some wired aluminum measuring spoons, a rubber band, and so on. Identify each item and have your child listen as each one hits the floor. Then see if your child is able to guess the one you drop.

Tactile Discrimination

You can show your toddler the difference between hard and soft (a wooden cooking spoon and a soft stuffed animal, for example), rough and smooth (a piece of sandpaper and a mirror), and other materials of various textures (fur, velvet, silk, cotton, wool, and so on). Name each item as you distinguish among them all for your child. Then place from two to four of the items in a paper bag and have your child feel inside and describe the object; i.e., hard spoon, soft dog, and so forth.

Phonograph Records

Records are an excellent aid in strengthening listening skills. Play fast- and slow-tempo records and tell your child that one is a running rhythm and the other is a walking one. Have your toddler clap the tempo with you. Then you both can run or walk as the tempo of the record suggests. Play a march and suggest that your child march with the music until it stops, at which time she is to stop and plop to the floor. Later on, you can stop the music at different places to see how quickly she can respond.

The Concept of Time

"When toddlers anticipate a frightening event, they are operating within a framework of time. Of course, the twenty-four-month-old's concept of time is quite limited. He has no real notion of clock or calendar time. Time for toddlers is defined by routines. For example, they understand time for breakfast and ask for juice. They recognize that the sun is setting and look out the window for their dad-

dies. They are told that it is time for bed and bring their parent a handful of diapers. However, even this very limited concept of time is an important development. After all, the world is less chaotic when one can anticipate to some degree what will happen next. Twenty-four-month-olds understand the meaning of *soon* and are beginning to learn to wait, albeit impatiently."

Cognitive Accomplishments

"Although the attention span of twenty-four-month-olds is still short and they will flit from one activity to another, at this plateau of their cognitive development they are able to identify objects, differentiate the elements in their environment, including their body parts, and recognize and remember known people, things, actions, and routine happenings. For example, they have a good idea of where things are located, are able to match familiar objects, and recognize when a picture in a book is upside down."

They can complete a three-piece form-board comprised of a circle, triangle, and square and stack five rings on a peg toy in proper order. If television is available, they may spontaneously identify familiar objects they see on the screen.

Twenty-four-month-olds will scribble spontaneously with a crayon or pencil on paper. They make single-line and multiple-line markings. They are able to distinguish vertical from horizontal lines. Upon demonstration, they can imitate a circular as well as a V stroke crudely. Now they are on the way to drawing as opposed to mere scribbling.

Twenty-four-month-olds have been aware for several months of such parts of their body as the eyes, nose, ears, mouth, and hair. Now they can sometimes verbally identify such gross body parts as the feet, as well as the thumbs, hands, and eyebrows. When asked to do so, they can touch the tummy, back, arms, and legs. However, they cannot distinguish yet between the two sides of the body.

Social Development

Despite their growing sense of identity and ongoing push toward independence, twenty-four-month-olds remain very much bound up with the mother and other family members. If they are separated from the mother—for whatever reason—they may become anxious and unhappy and cling to her when she returns. At the same time, their dependent feelings are no longer centered completely on the mother. For the most part, she can leave for part of the day if there is another loved adult at home; i.e., daddy, grandma, or a familiar, agreeable babysitter.

Quality Parenting

Dr. Helen De Rosis, in her helpful book *Parent Power/Child Power,* writes the following about parenting: "In case you are thinking that this parent business is too much for you, you must understand that you cannot be expected to be busy parenting twenty-four hours a day and seven days a week. Less is fine, too, as long as it's *quality parenting.* The quality is the important thing, rather than the quantity. . . . Read everything you can; play, study, work, socialize, love your spouse and accept all those limitations that you know by heart. . . . Arrange your time so that the children are not 'all'—because if they are, you'll find, paradoxically, that they won't be nearly enough for you."

Social Skills

"In the area of social development, a child's social style seems to become well established by the time she is twenty-four months old. Along with the many shades of emotional mood that they exhibit in their interactions with adults and children, twenty-four-month-olds are far less abrupt than the younger child in their mood shifts.

"They now possess a variety of social abilities and patterns of behavior, and under the

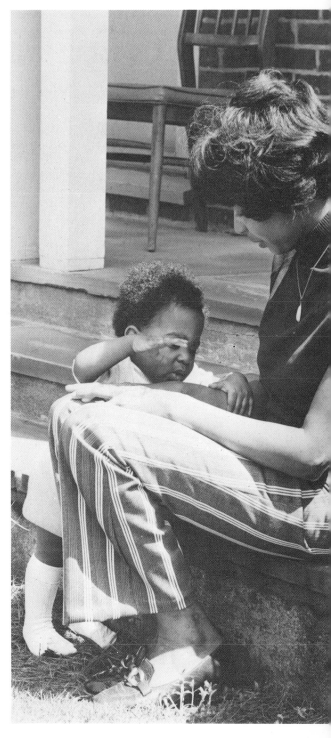

best of circumstances, they have acquired most of the social skills they will manifest at the age of six. These skills include getting the attention of adults and holding it, sometimes in very subtle ways, and using an adult as a resource to help them deal with problems. They also are able to express aggression and hostility toward adults in a variety of ways. They exhibit a budding capacity to direct the adult in many different activities. All in all, the twenty-four-month-old has become a far more complicated social being. Part of this is due to this toddler's ability to communicate feelings, desires, and interests to others, using words and gestures."

The Sense of Trust

Healthy, happy twenty-four-month-olds indicate a sense of trust in adults and prefer a relationship with one adult at a time. One indication of their continued ambivalence is that although they like to control others and order them about, they also like to please others. They can judge better than heretofore what others expect of them and what they intend for them to do or not to do. On rare occasions, these toddlers are able to put another person's wishes above their own. But do not expect miracles!

Negativism

If all has gone well, you will find a general decline in negativism sometime around your toddler's second birthday. Not only will your child become less contentious, but you can look forward to an increase in his sociability. Child rearing has many welcome "lights in the clearing."

Sibling Rivalry and Fighting

According to many child psychologists, sibling rivalry emanates essentially from the older child's sense of loss of love and prestige. The child feels that the mother's love and attention have been diminished or lost to her. Such a feeling can arise from reality or from complete fantasy. Children with such feelings are inclined to regard their loss as a total one.

The most characteristic responses are regression to infantile behaviors; i.e., the surrender of some developmental progress, and physical aggression toward the younger brother or sister who appears to them to have captured ascendancy in the family—especially in the eyes of its most important member, the mother. A sympathetically voiced refusal to accept either regressive or aggressive behavior (both of which are defensive extremes) appears to be the pattern chosen by most parents.

"As we mentioned earlier, two-year-olds are able to assert themselves and to express their aggressiveness. They may even be able to do it in a devious manner. Many parents state that their two-year-old child knows how to get older siblings in trouble by yelling for help when the older siblings actually are not bothering him."

Marilyn Segal and Don Adcock write: "Sooner or later the classic dilemma of parents arises. Should they intervene when children are fighting or let the children fight it out by themselves? There seems to be broad agreement among parents that no single response is appropriate all the time. If a child is being hurt seriously, parents should intervene. On the other hand, parents should not interfere in every little squabble. Within these broad guidelines there remains plenty of room for individual differences between parents. Clearly there is no perfect response for every situation. Within reason, one parent's judgment is as valid as another's.

"In determining the extent to which you should intervene in fights between your children, there are numerous considerations. For instance, if you are present when your children are fighting, the situation is different from when you are absent. When you are present, you can see whether one of the children is teasing, hitting, or bullying. Perhaps the fight is being resolved by the children themselves in a way that you consider healthy; i.e., one child is standing up to the bully or the children are arguing in a 'constructive' manner. In such a case, your silence communicates to your children that you approve of their behavior. However, if you disapprove of their actions but say nothing, you are sending your children the wrong signal. You are condoning behavior that is unacceptable to you.

"If you are in another room, your children can interpret your lack of response as indicating that you did not hear the fight or were too busy to find out what the trouble was all about. Often children arrive at their own solution to a conflict. However, you are forced to intervene if the fight intensifies. Actually what you decide to do is determined by your attitude and the kind of discipline you feel comfortable using."

Above all, whatever child-rearing advice you read must be used in conjunction with your common sense, intuitive feelings, and learned interacting behavior. Parents who are informed about child development certainly are more aware of problems that appear and also may be able to act before a situation gets out of control. The important consideration is not to adhere too rigidly to any one child-rearing approach.

Personality/Psychological Development

Most twenty-four-month-olds are upset when parents scold them. Although they may be defiant from time to time, their feelings are hurt easily by criticism. They struggle to accept and obey their parents' rules. For the most part, they want to do the accepted thing and are afraid of disapproval. Language helps them deal with this concern. Frequently a toddler will recite the rules that the parents have been trying to teach her. For example, whenever anyone in the house yells, the toddler may say "shh," or every time the child sees someone step in a puddle on the sidewalk, she may say "Shoes wet."

Expressing Feelings via Language

"Why does a toddler keep reciting the rules that he finds difficult to follow? Partly because the child is learning through practice and repeating a rule out loud seems to imprint it better in his mind. Also, the toddler is using language to check his perception; that is, to find out if a rule really applies to a particular situation. The toddler wants an adult to respond, to say, 'Yes, that's right, I was talking too loudly,' or 'No, it doesn't matter if the man steps in the puddle; see, he has boots on.'

"Responding to toddlers in this way is important. It helps them learn the exceptions to a rule (and there always are plenty) and shows them that adults, as well as children, break the rules. Toddlers can accept their own mistakes more easily when they see that grownups also can talk too loudly and walk through puddles."

Dependence/Independence

"At best, twenty-four-month-olds are a long way from being truly independent. Although they have learned new skills, new concepts, and new ways of controlling the people and things in their world, they remain dependent on an adult for all their important needs. Their next several years will be spent mastering and perfecting the skills they already have and acquiring competencies that will enable them to function in many new ways. If they have lived in a physical environment and social and psychological milieu that have fostered their curiosity and provided them with feelings of competence and well-being, they will be ready to take advantage of the learning opportunities that their ongoing years will provide."

Fears

There is no way to raise a child, even under the best of circumstances, without her experiencing some anxieties and fears at one time or another in the course of growing up. It is natural for twenty-four-month-olds to react with anxiety to being separated from their mothers because now they have come to associate their mothers with every situation and experience in their lives. When a toddler becomes upset over being separated from her mother, it is not cause for alarm; rather, it is an indication of a normal, close mother-child relationship.

Toddlers this age frequently become fearful of doctors, dentists, and barbers because they have learned that the doctor "means shots" and subsequently transfer this fear to the dentist and barber because they, too, wear white coats.

They also are anxious now over potential physical behaviors, as expressed by fear of high places or large or ferocious animals. Later on such imaginary creatures as ogres, bogeymen, giants, and monsters creep into the sometimes frightening world of the two-year-old.

Child psychologists indicate that children this age are also apt to develop fears about their "intactness." Some toddlers are afraid of or refuse to have anything to do with broken toys or broken cookies because they have an empathetic reaction to such brokenness; i.e., "If it happened to the cookie, it might happen to me!"

Studies indicate that twenty-four-month-olds often experience fear and anxiety when they are treated inconsistently by their parents; by unrealistic parental expectations; by overly negative parental reactions to their accomplishments; and most certainly, by overly harsh punishment.

Toddlers also learn fears from their parents, especially fear of thunderstorms, snakes, mice, airplanes, and so forth. Many twenty-four-month-olds fear rain and wind and animals (especially large or wild creatures). They may fear the noise of trains, trucks, a vacuum cleaner, and the flushing of the toilet (of course, most twenty-four-month-olds have become adjusted to both the vacuum and toilet flushing by now).

Sharing

Possession—*all mine!*—is one device twenty-four-month-olds appear to use to "hammer out their autonomy." Therefore, the right of ownership takes on special significance to them. To these toddlers, being separate is equated with the right to possess.

Just as the ability to stand comes before walking, owning comes before sharing—and small children need ample time (a few years, in fact) in which to get the feel of ownership embedded in their experience before they can let go of things. According to Dorothy Corkille Briggs, writer of *Your Child's Self-Esteem,* "Only fifty percent of 'three's' can share and then only briefly; yet, unthinkingly, in our conscientious efforts to teach social graces, we push against the toddler's need to own." Respecting your child's emotional need in this regard and being tolerant until your child is able to share—and behaving with generosity of spirit yourself—is the wisest course to follow.

Brief Sketch of the Twenty-four-month-old

The sense of self-importance of twenty-four-month-olds is intense at this time. Although they recognize their power to be effective and successful, they are painfully aware of their dependence and their inadequacies. Nonetheless, this is a stage of rather marked equilibrium. At the same time, twenty-four-month-olds continually test the limits of their parents and themselves and their ability and right to have a say of their own. Their dependence/independence conflict results in their becoming frustrated easily.

On the positive side, the twenty-four-month-old realizes that he is a separate person with a distinct name and that other people are like him, yet different. These toddlers are able to love and to receive love. Usually, however, they are more reserved with strangers than the one-year-old.

They want their own way in everything and have strong positive or negative reactions. Now such phrases as "I don't like it," "Go away," "It's mine!" and "I don't want to" replace or accompany temper tantrums. They manifest some of their aggressive tendencies by slapping, hitting, biting, and challenging their parents' wishes.

Self-Help Routines

There are such individual variations between what twenty-four-month-olds need and between family routines that giving average figures for naptime and bedtime requirements is not useful. As far as bedtime goes, it is a help to be quite clear when *you* think it should be and to keep it a peaceful, happy time. (Dreams, nightmares, and night-walking appear to be more common around three years of age.)

There also is much variation in a child's dryness at night. Most toddlers become dry between two and three years of age and some are dry at night well before they have stopped wetting during the day. Other children do not become dry until they are over three years of age—and boys often are later than girls in this. There is no need to "train" toddlers for this control; it comes with the natural maturing of the urinary system.

Usually it is at around two and a half that toddlers reach the stage of going to the toilet for bowel movements all by themselves. Although they usually need help with wiping, parents can help their toddlers learn how to do this by themselves.

Parents need to remember to praise their toddler's successes and to accept the failures. Years from now it will make little difference when complete control was attained, but a great deal of difference whether it was accomplished agreeably or otherwise.

Eating

Some twenty-four-month-olds are able to feed themselves entirely and will accept no

help. They seem to know that they do better alone and dismiss the parent with "Mommy way!" If the mother remains in the room, she may have to be careful not even to look at her toddler. There are some, however, who eat better when partially fed. With still others who are really poor eaters, the distraction of a song or story may be needed, especially when they are eating foods they do not enjoy.

The muscles of the jaws of twenty-four-month-olds are coming under complete voluntary control, resulting in improved mastication. They will eat all table foods, including chewy meat, celery, and so on. They now inhibit the turning of a spoon in self-feeding and are able to lift and drink from a cup by themselves, replacing it properly on the table. For the most part, twenty-four-month-olds can do a quite efficient self-feeding job.

"Do it myself!"

The most consistent stance of the twenty-four-month-old is "Do it myself!" Your toddler enjoys washing and drying her face and hands, with a little help from you. You can encourage washing in the bathtub by providing a washcloth or sponge your child can easily handle; i.e., one that is not too unwieldy. Your toddler likes to brush her teeth (of course, you have to do the real cleaning).

Your toddler will cooperate in dressing and undressing and is able to take off his shoes (if you loosen the laces), socks, coat, hat, mittens, and so on. He can pull on simple garments, but does not differentiate front and back or right and left. He can now unzip *and* zip up zippers.

Twenty-four-month-olds remain interested in unwrapping packages and candy wrapped in paper. They are adept at turning doorknobs and opening doors and now can turn on a water faucet (further proof of greatly improved fine-motor coordination). Take advantage of your toddler's ongoing desire to help you with your housework. This proclivity will disappear before too long. With encouragement from you, your child will pick up toys and other objects and put them away where they belong.

Play and Playthings

Much of twenty-four-month-olds' pattern of play follows their style of movement and consists of the exploration and exploitation of their capacities for action. They do things less with the intention of objective accomplishment than to see how they feel. Joseph L. Stone and Joseph Church write, "They love the spring of a jumping board under their feet, the swooping movement of a swing, the tug and jounce of riding in a wagon, the unwieldy weight of big objects that they can lift and push and haul."

They love vehicles of all kinds and will work hard to master the pedals of a small tricycle. They love doll carriages and dolls and will push them endlessly through the house or about the neighborhood. They care for, hug, carry, and discipline their dolls and favorite stuffed animal.

Twenty-four-month-olds sometimes will play briefly together, handing a toy back and forth, but most characteristic at this age is parallel play with peers (the toddlers go about their individual play activities side by side or back to back, but not together). Although there is no apparent interplay, the toddlers seem to derive pleasure from this nearness. Often toddlers will spend long periods watching other children at play and sometimes imitate their actions. Interlaced with this emerging sociality are intervals of solitary play. Although twenty-four-month-olds are not ready for cooperative play with their peers, they can play well with older children.

Toddlers confine themselves to simple themes for their dramatic play: telephoning, ringing the doorbell, going for a walk, shaving, drinking tea, shining shoes, fixing the car, bathing the baby. The emphasis is on common, everyday, domestic activities.

Twenty-four-month-olds love to drape themselves in odd garments, scarves, and blankets. They love to wear hats and shoes and like nothing better than clomping about the house in the parents' shoes.

They like to watch mother at her work and will imitate the gestures of mixing batter, breaking eggs, dusting, sweeping, and sewing. Frequently they will insist that the mother interrupt her housework to "play"—which means only that the parent keep the toddler company for a while. Twenty-four-month-olds shift rapidly from one activity to another in keeping with their brief attention spans. Sometimes they give the impression of trying to do half a dozen things at once.

Creative Activities

Toddlers this age like to sit and watch others make things. Even though they cannot participate yet, they can learn a great deal by hearing you talk about what you are doing. Moist clay and Play-Doh provide enjoyable activities for twenty-four-month-olds and give them sensory and release experiences. They like to feel, examine, roll, squeeze, and pound the clay (watch out—some even taste it!).

You can, if you wish, introduce finger paints to your child at this time. It is a bit less messy activity if you supervise it. It is best to use only one color at a sitting. Your child will appreciate your hanging up one of her "creations." Try finger painting yourself—it's great fun.

You also can introduce painting with poster paints. Your twenty-four-month-old will paint with whole-arm movements and will make very few strokes on a sheet of paper. Toddlers this age are satisfied with only one color. Often they paint with a brush in each hand. Since they are easily distracted, they do not always watch their hand movements and may just as likely paint themselves, the table, and so on. Your supervision is required, but the reward for your child is great.

Play Activities

Twenty-four-month-olds continue to enjoy their toys and play activities of past months, but they are now beginning to play with their toys in more sophisticated ways. During this period, much of their play is accompanied by words; i.e., they will talk to a teddy bear as they take it for a ride in a wagon or tuck a doll in for a nap. They have become increasingly adroit with manipulative toys. Just watch your toddler put together a familiar puzzle or pound on a peg bench. Twenty-four-month-olds still like to take things apart and put them together and are better able to fit rings on a Color Cone or pile blocks on top of one another.

Action toys are preferred—anything the toddler can do something interesting with: a toy telephone, interlocking wooden train, all kinds of sturdy cars and trucks, airplanes, a Kiddie Kar or small tricycle. A hobby horse and rocking chair are put to happy use by these toddlers.

You can now introduce block play. Unit building blocks are available in good toy shops everywhere, and even in the toy sections of department stores. Introduce a few pieces and a shape or two in the beginning and show your toddler how to make a train out of blocks, a roadway for cars, a little building,

and so on. Almost all children enjoy playing with building blocks during the years of their childhood. Frank Lloyd Wright, the world-famous architect, used them as a professional to design and lay out his buildings. Natural hardwood unit building blocks will be your best toy investment. (Blocks are hard to make at home because of the need for heavy-duty cutting and sanding tools and very precise measuring.)

Equipping the Playroom

Certain basic pieces of equipment belong in every playroom during the early childhood years. The items listed below will be used for many years for art expression, quiet play, dramatic play, and so on. You may want to consider some of them for your toddler's second birthday:

Double Easel. A double, adjustable painting easel permits two children to paint at the same time without their getting in each other's way. Good ones are made by Community Playthings (Rifkin, NY 12471) and Childcraft Education Corp. (Edison, NJ 08817). These companies issue mail-order catalogues, which are sent without charge upon customer request.

The easel boards of the double easel need to be large enough (twenty-five by thirty-seven inches) to hold eighteen-by-twenty-four-inch sheets of unprinted newsprint paper. Each board is attached to two frames by wingnuts. Holes on the two leg members make the easel adjustable to the size of a growing child. The easel paint trays have open holes for six to ten bottles of two-ounce (or half-pint) jars of poster paints.

For drying your child's pictures, a collapsible clothes dryer can be used.

Bulletin Board. Every playroom should have a large bulletin board (four by eight feet is a good size) to display the child's art work: paintings, drawings, finger paintings (and later, collages and constructions). Right now you could display colorful posters to add visual interest to your child's room. A burlap-covered soft Cellutex board makes an excellent bulletin board. Burlap can be purchased by the yard in most fabric shops. An advantage is that tack holes do not show.

Another popular approach is the use of "do-it-yourself" cork board squares. These permit great flexibility since they can be cut to fit any available wall space and things can be tacked and retacked without making holes in the cork.

Table, Chairs, and Rocker. Every twenty-four-month-old (and older) child needs a washable work and play table. A Formica top is impervious to water and is fine for finger painting, playing with clay, drawing, and so on. Most playroom tables come as twenty-four-by forty-eight-inch rectangles or thirty- to thirty-six-inch rounds. Preferred are those with legs that can be removed so the table will "grow" with the child (for example, your child can now use a table that is from eighteen to twenty inches high). Chairs come in various heights also. Allow an eight- to ten-inch height difference from the top of the table to the top of the seat for your toddler.

We believe that every playroom should be equipped with a sturdy rocker. Community Playthings carries a slatted wood rocker made in Appalachia that is well built and attractive. Most school supply houses are good centers for tables, chairs, and rockers. (Consult the yellow pages of your telephone directory for their locations.)

Homemaking Equipment for Social Play. Sooner or later, loving grandparents or very good friends will want to give your child a child-sized play stove, cupboard, or sink—also a wooden ironing board, toy iron, pots, pans, and cutlery, a housecleaning set, and so on. Parents who like woodworking will find that making a child-sized wooden doll bed and doll buggy is fun—and money saving. (Dollhouses come later.) There are excellent books available that provide blueprints for making such equipment. One of the better ones is *How to Make Children's Furniture and Play Equipment* by Mario Del Fabbro (published by McGraw-Hill). Look for a copy in your local public library or book store.

You may question the repetition in the home of the equipment that usually is found in the better child-care centers and nursery schools, but remember—the hours toddlers spend at home are longer than those spent in any preschool center.

Happy Second Birthday!

THE TWENTY-FOURTH MONTH

Motor Development

Gross Motor

Visually monitors walking, watching placement of feet in order to be able to deal with obstacles in path by avoiding them

Runs, but generally lacks ability to start efficiently or stop quickly

Jumps crudely with 2-foot takeoff

Walking rhythm stabilizes and becomes even

Goes up and down stairs alone without alternating feet

Can walk approximately on line

Likes to walk on low walls with one hand held

Can walk a few steps on tiptoe

Can be trusted alone on stairs

Can walk backwards 10 feet

Can quickly alternate between sitting and standing

Tries to balance self on either foot, not yet successfully

Is sturdy on feet; less likely to fall

Still geared to gross-motor activity

Fine Motor

Turns pages of a book, one at a time

Manipulates more freely with one hand; alternates from one hand to the other

Has fully developed right- or left-handedness

Increased smoothness of coordination in fine-motor movements

Language Acquisition

Can name almost everything she or he has daily contact with at home or on walks

Can associate names with most familiar objects

Understands and asks for "another," "more"

Shows and imitates names for hair, hands, feet, nose, eyes, mouth, shoes

Actively imitates words

Expressive vocabulary of 50 or more words

Listens to and enjoys simple stories

Responds to: "Show me a dog," "Show me a man," "Show me a hat," etc.

Names 3 or more pictures in book

Echoes adult's words and inflections

Is beginning to discover that everything has a name

May be able to give first and last names

Sensory Powers/ Learning

Can match familiar objects

If television is available, may spontaneously identify familiar objects seen on the screen

Spontaneously scribbles with a pencil; makes multiple and single-line crossings

Is capable of judgments that indicate the acquisition of size and distance constancy

Distinguishes vertical from horizontal lines

Engages in long periods of looking

Can imitate crudely a V stroke in drawing

Cannot distinguish yet between the 2 sides of the body

Completes 3-piece formboard

Understanding of time quite limited; has no real notion of clock or calendar time

Has a good idea of where things are located in and around the house

Has learned through exploration that objects have different attributes

Can sometimes verbally identify gross body parts; can touch tummy, back, arms, legs, and eyebrows and thumbs when asked to do so

Can distinguish between "one" and "many"

Comprehends meaning of "soon" (is learning to wait)

Identifies, differentiates, recognizes, remembers

Growth Chart

Social Development

Demands are not quite as strong as they were earlier

Likes to control others and order them around

Often tells immediate experiences

Able to communicate feelings, desires, and interests to other people, using words and gestures

Prefers a relationship with one adult at a time

Cannot share possessions as yet

Can judge better than before what others expect and what they intend for him or her to do or not to do

Indicates a sense of trust in adults

Behavior is much better organized than heretofore

Can *occasionally* put another person's wishes above own

Personality/ Psychological

Is at an age of rather marked equilibrium

Uses own name in reference to self

Shows some aggressive tendencies; slaps, bites, hits

Uses pronouns "I," "me," and "you," but not always correctly

Is assuming an increasingly more self-sufficient attitude

Challenges parents' desires

Sense of self-importance is intense

Has strong positive or negative reactions

Such words as, "It's mine," "I don't like it," "Go away," "I don't want to," etc. replace or accompany temper tantrums

Wants own way in everything

Is able to love and receive love

Has rudimentary sense of ownership; holds onto possessions, even hides them

Seems to be testing powers of self-assertion

Is especially obstinate or "negativistic"

Has a positive self-concept

Self-Help Routines

Can turn on a water faucet

Wants to "do it myself!"

Anticipates routine events

Does not turn spoon in self-feeding

Picks up toys and then puts them away, with some encouragement

Lifts and drinks from cup

Verbalizes toilet needs fairly consistently

Rebels against bedtime

Daytime bowel and bladder control may be fairly well established

Zips and unzips zippers

Brushes teeth with supervision

Puts on simple garments, not differentiating front and back or right and left

Play and Playthings

Parallel play predominates, not yet ready for cooperative play

Prefers action toys: train, telephone, cars, Kiddie Kar, etc.

Loves to fill and dump containers with sand

Pushes and pulls large wheel toys

Enjoys a rocking boat, swing, rocking chair, hobby horse, etc.

Plays well with older children

Likes play that mimics parents' behaviors

Not yet able to share or let another child play with toys

Dancing to music includes running, turning in circles, and the beginnings of bouncing up and down

Can open screw-type toy and reassemble same

Much play is accompanied by words; talks to teddy bear when tucking it in for bedtime, etc.

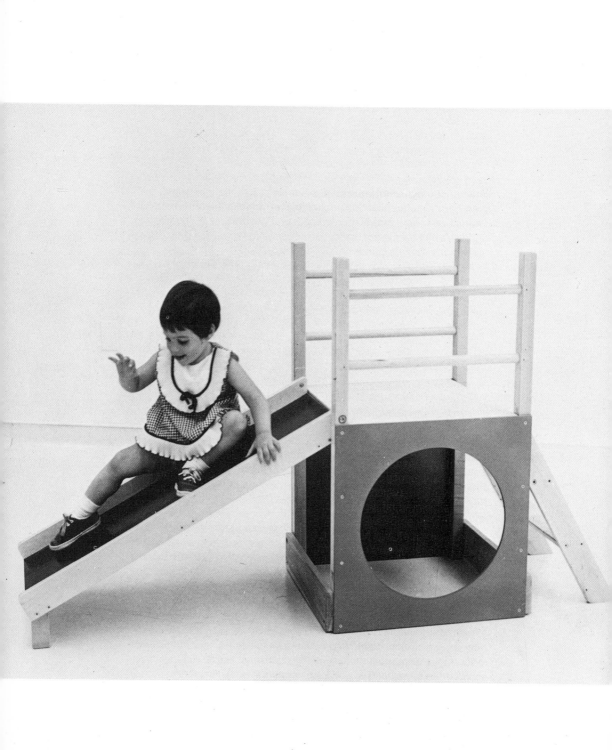

Epilogue

We have sought to describe the new abilities that children in the second twelve months of life acquire at various stages of their growth and development; how the desire to practice each maturing skill brings about readjustment in family life (and often conflicts); how the need for survival during infancy forces the establishment of a strong attachment with parents and other consistent caregivers; how the new achievement of walking and talking sets into motion the toddler's drive for independence, assertiveness, and self-help; how the curiosity of toddlers (propelled by their locomotive power) permits them to discover, interact with, and control their immediate environment of "people and things"; and how the acquisition of language forwards their functioning as social members of society.

When we speak of relationships between adults and infants that involve give and take we do not mean to suggest that such relationships are "coequal" in quite the same sense as those between adults. Clearly adults must ultimately determine what is safe or dangerous for their children and what within some limits constitutes appropriate behavior. Infants are dependent upon the adults around them to sustain life itself, and adults who take on child-rearing roles assume this responsibility with all of its ramifications. Infants are not mere vessels to be filled with food, knowledge, and direction; rather they are persons in their own right with their own requirements and interests.

A facilitating relationship between a parent and toddler is one that takes the needs of both persons into account. Such a relationship cannot develop, however, unless a mother is able to take her child's point of view, to infer his or her needs and interests, and to figure out some way of balancing them against her own and those of other family members. Some mothers are able to do this naturally. In our present-day society, however, many parents seem to have difficulty achieving and maintaining such relationships with their children.

Any useful child-rearing book should embody a systematic view of child development that "makes sense" of infant and toddler behaviors. We hope we have provided a framework for inferring and anticipating the developmental needs of infants and toddlers and for interacting with them in ways that might facilitate their optimal development.

Infants do not have to be *induced* to develop—they are motivated from the moment of birth to actively engage and experience their proximate environments. Infants are innately curious and this gives rise to exploration. Later experimentation provides opportunities for discovery and gradual mastery of their physical, social, and symbolic environments (nonverbal gestures, language, play, imitation).

Of course, infants are completely dependent upon adults to provide a range of opportunities for such experiences. Parents need to be able to accurately perceive their toddler's requirements and to provide adequate emotional support and suitable opportunities for mastering themselves and their world. Toddlers need to try out new concepts and activities in a variety of situations. Realizing this, parents will be better able to recognize and support each developmental behavior when it occurs.

The ability of children to symbolically represent external reality develops gradually over a lifetime, beginning with their earliest attempts at imitation. Between one and two years of age, deferred imitation (in which imitation occurs apart from the stimulus) appears in the child's play as *pretending*. Imitation is an important factor in both the socialization of the child and the development of representational abilities. It is important that parents understand the role of imitative behavior in the learning-to-learn development of their children. During early childhood, pretend or make-believe play is an important part of learning. However, just because toddlers imitate an activity does not mean that they have acquired the underlying conceptual structure.

Although early learning does not depend upon language development, during toddlerhood, the ability to use language effectively is fundamental to human communication and success as a social being. During the first twelve months of life, language acquisition is mainly receptive. Infants learn to discriminate between speech sounds and patterns of intonation in the speech of others. Very gradually they begin to imitate speech sounds and simple words. Most nine-month-olds begin to show some understanding of what others say. During the second twelve months of life, the expressive dimension of language development spurts forward. Toddlers begin to use simple words and then groups of words in more adult ways with the clear intention of expressing themselves.

Parents need to be aware that language abilities are developing long before their children begin to use conventional speech. Mothers and fathers can facilitate language acquisition by engaging in early verbal "fun and games" with their babies. Later they can focus directly on particular activities in which their child is engaged.

The period from twelve through twenty-four months is particularly striking in child development. Infatuated with novelty, infants want to get into everything and do everything. They have gained new mobility through crawling, then walking, climbing, and so on that gives them increasing access to things in the environment. They are developing effective eye-hand coordination that permits them to manipulate the elements in the environment in new and often novel ways. All along the way, they are developing a sense of self and of autonomy (i.e., they have their own ideas about what they want to do and not do and what belongs to them).

The growing ability of infants to interact with their environment is healthy and normal. Parents need to realize that this behavior, albeit irritating and tiresome at times, is not mean. Rather than suppress the curiosity of young children, parents need to provide sufficient and varied opportunities for its expression in ways that will keep to a minimum conflicts with others in the household. Positive alternatives are found in parents who recognize the developmental needs of their children and who attempt to engage them in agreeable relationships; i.e., their verbal interactions rely more on questioning, expansion, and praise to direct their toddler's activities. These parents are able to structure the environment in ways that usually avoid confrontations over *no-no's* and do not severely limit their child's experience. In short, while the parents set firm limits to their child's activity, their objective is to involve him or her in allowable and agreeable pursuits.

As children develop a sense of autonomy, it is possible to avoid some conflicts by providing them with access to interesting materials and experiences and by really allowing them opportunities to participate in deciding what they want to do. Of course, a balance between the needs and desires of young children and those of others is difficult to maintain, but it is important that toddlers experience a sense of potency and worth in their social milieu.

The necessity of infants for strong affective ties needs to be recognized and accommodated by parents. Although attempts to force toddlers to be independent and the refusal to intervene appropriately have negative effects, so does the encouragement of clinging dependency. Parents who facilitate their young children's exploratory play and mastery and who respond in supportive ways (whenever feasible, at their child's initiative) seem to be able to achieve a healthy balance.

We all know that parenting is not a science. One problem with child-rearing advice is that parents have different ideas about the sort of person they would like their child to become and their aspirations determine the way in which they expect their child to behave. Another difficulty is that we do not yet understand the relationship between the ways of bringing up children and how each child develops at adulthood. At the same time, there are great differences in the personalities of children at birth and the ways they relate to their parents and other adults—and vice versa.

We hope that this presentation of the month-by-month development of thirteen- to twenty-four-month-olds will help you to watch your own toddler's fascinating unfolding. We have tried to make it clear that the way you bring up your child is your decision and for this reason we have provided you with the most up-to-date information and available research data to help you choose the proper course to take.

Before we conclude *The Second Twelve Months of Life,* we should like to reiterate that there are as yet no absolute data on how best to rear children and that the information we have presented and our interpretations thereof need to be regarded as nondefinitive. However, some child-rearing practices do appear to help children develop optimally. It is our hope that you will employ your "educated intuitions" to enjoy your children as you are forwarding their maturation.

If you have enjoyed using our books as baby-watching guides, please write and tell us how you used them and how we can improve upon them. Write to Frank and Theresa Caplan at the Princeton Center for Infancy, 306 Alexander Street, Princeton, NJ 08540.

Bibliography

Akmakjian, Hiag. *The Natural Way to Raise a Healthy Child.* New York: Praeger, 1975.

Aston, Athina. *How to Play with Your Baby.* New York: Learning Child, Inc., 1971.

Bax, Martin, and Bernal, Judy. *Your Child's First Five Years.* New York: St. Martin's Press, 1974.

Beyer, Evelyn. *Teaching Young Children.* New York: Pegasus, 1968.

Bloom, Benjamin S. *Stability and Chance in Human Characteristics.* New York: Wiley, 1964.

Braga, Joseph, and Braga, Laurie. *Children and Adults.* Englewood Cliffs, N.J.: Prentice-Hall, 1976.

Brazelton, T. Berry, M.D. *Doctor and Child.* New York: Delacorte Press, 1976.

Briggs, Dorothy Corkille. *Your Child's Self-Esteem.* Garden City, N.Y.: Doubleday, 1970.

Broadribb, Violet, R.N., M.S., and Lee, Henry F., M.D. *The Modern Parents' Guide to Baby and Child Care.* Philadelphia: Lippincott, 1973.

Caplan, Frank, General Editor. *The Parenting Advisor.* Garden City, N.Y.: Anchor Press/Doubleday, 1977.

————, and Caplan, Theresa. *The Power of Play.* Garden City, N.Y.: Doubleday, 1973.

Church, Joseph. *Understanding Your Child from Birth to Three.* New York: Random House, 1973.

Cratty, Bryant J., Ed.D. *Perceptual and Motor Development in Infants and Children.* New York: Macmillan, 1970.

De Rosis, Helen, M.D. *Parent Power/Child Power.* Indianapolis: Bobbs-Merrill, 1974.

Despert, J. Louise. *Children of Divorce.* Garden City, N.Y.: Doubleday/Dolphin Books, 1962.

Dodson, Fitzhugh, Ph.D. *How to Parent.* Los Angeles: Nash Publishing, 1970.

Dreikurs, Rudolf. *Coping with Children's Misbehavior.* New York: Hawthorn Books, 1972.

Eden, Alvin N., M.D. *Growing Up Thin.* New York: Berkeley Publishing, 1975.

Erikson, Erik H. "Identity and the Life Cycle," *Psychological Issues,* Monograph No. 1, 1959.

Fraiberg, Selma. *The Magic Years.* New York: Scribner, 1959.

Furfey, Paul Hanly, ed. *Education of Children Aged One to Three.* Washington, D.C.: Catholic University of America, 1972.

Gesell, Arnold L. *The First Five Years of Life.* New York: Harper & Row, 1940.

———— and Ilg, Frances L. *Infant and Child in the Culture of Today.* New York: Harper, 1943.

Gilbert, Sara D. *Three Years to Grow.* New York: Parents' Magazine Press, 1972.

Ginott, Haim G. *Between Parent and Child.* New York: Macmillan, 1965.

Guillaume, Paul. *Imitation in Children.* Chicago: University of Chicago Press, 1968.

Hartley, Ruth E., and Goldenson, Robert M. *The Complete Book of Children's Play*. New York: Crowell, 1963.

Hoover, Mary. *The Responsive Parent*. New York: Parents' Magazine Press, 1972.

Hunter, Marvin H., Schucman, Helen, and Friedlander, George. *The Retarded Child from Birth to Five*. New York: John Day, 1972.

Hymes, James L., Jr. *Teaching the Child Under Six*. Columbus, Ohio: Merrill, 1968.

——— *Enjoy Your Child—Ages 1, 2, and 3*. New York: Public Affairs Committee, 1950.

Kelly, Marguerite, and Parsons, Elia. *The Mother's Almanac*. Garden City, N.Y.: Doubleday, 1975.

Lehane, Stephen. *Help Your Baby Learn*. Englewood Cliffs, N.J.: Prentice-Hall, 1976.

Levy, Janine. *The Baby Exercise Book*. New York: Random House, 1973.

Lewis, Morris M. *Language, Thought and Personality in Infancy and Childhood*. London: Harrap & Co., 1963.

Lichtenberg, Philip, and Norton, Dolores. *Cognitive and Mental Development in the First Five Years of Life*. Rockville, Md.: National Institute of Mental Health, 1970.

Ligon, Ernest M., *et al*. *Let Me Introduce Myself*. Schenectady, N.Y.: Character Research Press, 1976.

Mackenzie, Catherine. *Parent and Child*. New York: Sloane Associates, 1949.

Mahler, Margaret S., Pine, Fred, and Bergman, Anni. *The Psychological Birth of the Human Infant*. New York: Basic Books, 1975.

Marzollo, Jean, and Lloyd, Janice. *Learning Through Play*. New York: Harper & Row, 1972.

Maynard, Fredelle. *Guiding Your Child to a More Creative Life*. Garden City, N.Y.: Doubleday, 1973.

McGinnis, Thomas C., and Ayres, John U. *Open Family Living: A New Approach for Enriching Your Life Together*. Garden City, N.Y.: Doubleday, 1976.

Piaget, Jean. *Play, Dreams, and Reality*. New York: Basic Books, 1969.

Pomeranz, Virginia, M.D., and Schultz, Dodi. *The First Five Years*. Garden City, N.Y.: Doubleday, 1973.

Princeton Center for Infancy and Early Childhood. *The First Twelve Months of Life*. New York: Grosset & Dunlap, 1973.

Prudden, Suzy, and Sussman, Jeffrey. *Creative Fitness for Baby and Child*. New York: William Morrow, 1972.

Segal, Marilyn, and Adcock, Don. *From One to Two Years*. Ft. Lauderdale, FL.: Nova University, n.d.

Stone, L. Joseph, and Church, Joseph. *Childhood and Adolescence: A Psychology of the Growing Person*. New York: Random House, 1957.

Vernon, M. D. *The Psychology of Perception*. London: University of London Press, 1965.

Warner, Silas L., M.D., and Rosenberg, Edward B. *Your Child Learns Naturally*. Garden City, N.Y.: Doubleday, 1976.

White, Burton L. *The First Three Years of Life*. Englewood Cliffs, N.J.: Prentice-Hall, 1973.

———, Carew, Jean, *et al*. *Experience and Environment*. Englewood Cliffs, N.J.: Prentice-Hall, 1973.

Wiener, Joan, and Glick, Joyce. *A Motherhood Book*. New York: Collier Books, 1974.

Wolf, Katherine M. *As Your Child Grows: The First 18 Months*. New York: Child Study Assn., 1955.

Index

The Thirteenth Month

The Fourteenth Month

The Fifteenth Month

The Nineteenth Month

The Twentieth Month

The Twenty-First Month

The Sixteenth Month

The Seventeenth Month

The Eighteenth Month

The Twenty-Second Month

The Twenty-Third Month

The Twenty-Fourth Month

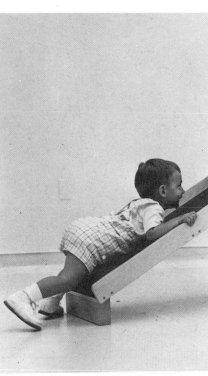